Cisco Networking Academy Program

CCNP 1: Advanced Routing
Companion Guide

Second Edition

Cisco Systems, Inc.

Cisco Networking Academy Program

Cisco Press

800 East 96th Street

Indianapolis, Indiana 46240 USA

Cisco Networking Academy Program
CCNP 1: Advanced Routing
Companion Guide
Second Edition

Cisco Systems, Inc.

Cisco Networking Academy Program

Copyright© 2004 Cisco Systems, Inc.

Published by:
Cisco Press
800 East 96th Street, 3rd Floor
Indianapolis, Indiana 46240 USA

Printed in the United States of America 2 3 4 5 6 7 8 9 0

Second Printing September 2004

Library of Congress Cataloging-in-Publication Number: 2003114387

ISBN: 1-58713-135-8

Trademark Acknowledgments

Warning and Disclaimer

CISCO SYSTEMS

Corporate and Government Sales

Cisco Press offers excellent discounts on this book when ordered in quantity for bulk purchases or special sales. For more information, please contact:

U.S. Corporate and Government Sales 1-800-382-3419 corpsales@pearsontechgroup.com

For sales outside of the U.S. please contact: **International Sales** international@pearsontechgroup.com

Feedback Information

At Cisco Press, our goal is to create in-depth technical books of the highest quality and value. Each book is crafted with care and precision, undergoing rigorous development that involves the unique expertise of members of the professional technical community.

Reader feedback is a natural continuation of this process. If you have any comments on how we could improve the quality of this book, or otherwise alter it to better suit your needs, you can contact us through e-mail at feedback@cisco-press.com. Please be sure to include the book title and ISBN in your message.

We greatly appreciate your assistance.

Publisher	*John Wait*
Editor-in-Chief	*John Kane*
Executive Editor	*Mary Beth Ray*
Cisco Representative	*Anthony Wolfenden*
Cisco Press Program Manager	*Nannette M. Noble*
Production Manager	*Patrick Kanouse*
Development Editor	*Andrew Cupp*
Project Editor	*Marc Fowler*
Copy Editor	*Gayle Johnson*
Technical Editors	*Randy Ivener, Jim Lorenz*
Cover Designer	*Louisa Adair*
Compositor	*Mark Shirar*
Indexer	*Larry Sweazy*

Corporate Headquarters
Cisco Systems, Inc.
170 West Tasman Drive
San Jose, CA 95134-1706
USA
www.cisco.com
Tel: 408 526-4000
800 553-NETS (6387)
Fax: 408 526-4100

European Headquarters
Cisco Systems International BV
Haarlerbergpark
Haarlerbergweg 13-19
1101 CH Amsterdam
The Netherlands
www-europe.cisco.com
Tel: 31 0 20 357 1000
Fax: 31 0 20 357 1100

Americas Headquarters
Cisco Systems, Inc.
170 West Tasman Drive
San Jose, CA 95134-1706
USA
www.cisco.com
Tel: 408 526-7660
Fax: 408 527-0883

Asia Pacific Headquarters
Cisco Systems, Inc.
Capital Tower
168 Robinson Road
#22-01 to #29-01
Singapore 068912
www.cisco.com
Tel: +65 6317 7777
Fax: +65 6317 7799

Cisco Systems has more than 200 offices in the following countries and regions. Addresses, phone numbers, and fax numbers are listed on the
Cisco.com Web site at www.cisco.com/go/offices.

Argentina • Australia • Austria • Belgium • Brazil • Bulgaria • Canada • Chile • China PRC • Colombia • Costa Rica • Croatia • Czech Republic
Denmark • Dubai, UAE • Finland • France • Germany • Greece • Hong Kong SAR • Hungary • India • Indonesia • Ireland • Israel • Italy
Japan • Korea • Luxembourg • Malaysia • Mexico • The Netherlands • New Zealand • Norway • Peru • Philippines • Poland • Portugal
Puerto Rico • Romania • Russia • Saudi Arabia • Scotland • Singapore • Slovakia • Slovenia • South Africa • Spain • Sweden
Switzerland • Taiwan • Thailand • Turkey • Ukraine • United Kingdom • United States • Venezuela • Vietnam • Zimbabwe

About the Technical Reviewers

Randy Ivener, CCIE No. 10722, is a security specialist with Cisco Systems Advanced Services. He is a Certified Information Systems Security Professional and ASQ Certified Software Quality Engineer. He has spent several years as a network security consultant, helping companies understand and secure their networks. He has worked with many security products and technologies, including firewalls, VPNs, intrusion detection, and authentication systems. Before becoming immersed in security, he spent time in software development and as a training instructor. He graduated from the U.S. Naval Academy and holds a master's degree in business administration.

Jim Lorenz is an instructor and curriculum developer for the Cisco Networking Academy Program. He has more than 20 years of experience in information systems and has held various IT positions in Fortune 500 companies, including Honeywell and Motorola. He has developed and taught computer and networking courses for both public and private institutions for more than 15 years. He is coauthor of the course Cisco Networking Academy Program Fundamentals of UNIX, he is a contributing author for the CCNA Lab Companion manuals, and he is a technical editor for the CCNA Companion Guides. He is a Cisco Certified Academy Instructor (CCAI) for CCNA and CCNP courses. He has a bachelor's degree in computer information systems and is working on his master's in information networking and telecommunications. He and his wife, Mary, have two daughters, Jessica and Natasha.

Contents at a Glance

Contents

Cisco Systems Networking Icon Legend

Cisco Systems, Inc. uses a standardized set of icons to represent devices in network topology illustrations. The following icon legend shows the most commonly used icons you will encounter throughout this book.

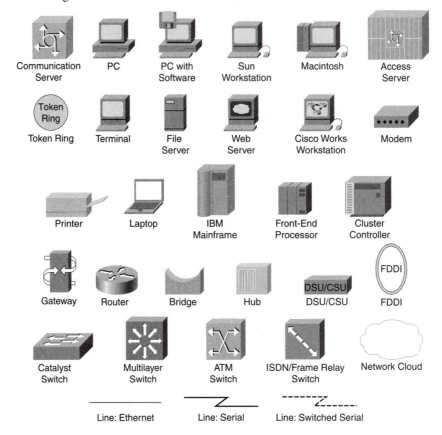

Command Syntax Conventions

The conventions used to present command syntax in this book are the same conventions used in the Cisco IOS software Command Reference. The Command Reference describes these conventions as follows:

- Vertical bars (|) separate alternative, mutually exclusive elements.
- Square brackets ([ ]) indicate an optional element.
- Braces ({ }) indicate a required choice.
- Braces within brackets ([{ }]) indicate a required choice within an optional element.
- **Bold** indicates commands and keywords that are entered exactly as shown.
- *Italic* indicates arguments for which you supply values.

Foreword

Throughout the world, the Internet has brought tremendous new opportunities for individuals and their employers. Companies and other organizations are seeing dramatic increases in productivity by investing in robust networking capabilities. Some studies have shown measurable productivity improvements in entire economies. The promise of enhanced efficiency, profitability, and standard of living is real and growing.

Such productivity gains aren't achieved by simply purchasing networking equipment. Skilled professionals are needed to plan, design, install, deploy, configure, operate, maintain, and troubleshoot today's networks. Network managers must ensure that they have planned for network security and continued operation. They need to design for the required performance level in their organization. They must implement new capabilities as the demands of their organization, and its reliance on the network, expand.

To meet the many educational needs of the internetworking community, Cisco Systems established the Cisco Networking Academy Program. The Networking Academy is a comprehensive learning program that provides students with the Internet technology skills that are essential in a global economy. The Networking Academy integrates face-to-face teaching, web-based content, online assessment, student performance tracking, hands-on labs, instructor training and support, and preparation for industry-standard certifications.

The Networking Academy continually raises the bar on blended learning and educational processes. The Internet-based assessment and instructor support systems are some of the most extensive and validated ever developed, including a 24/7 customer service system for Networking Academy instructors. Through community feedback and electronic assessment, the Networking Academy adapts the curriculum to improve outcomes and student achievement. The Cisco Global Learning Network infrastructure designed for the Networking Academy delivers a rich, interactive, personalized curriculum to students worldwide. The Internet has the power to change the way people work, live, play, and learn, and the Cisco Networking Academy Program is at the forefront of this transformation.

This Cisco Press book is one in a series of best-selling companion titles for the Cisco Networking Academy Program. Designed by Cisco Worldwide Education and Cisco Press, these books provide integrated support for the online learning content that is made available to Academies all over the world. These Cisco Press books are the only books authorized for the Networking Academy by Cisco Systems. They provide print and CD-ROM materials that ensure the greatest possible learning experience for Networking Academy students.

I hope you are successful as you embark on your learning path with Cisco Systems and the Internet. I also hope that you will choose to continue your learning after you complete the Networking Academy curriculum. In addition to its Cisco Networking Academy Program titles, Cisco Press publishes an extensive list of networking technology and certification publications that provide a wide range of resources. Cisco Systems has also established a network of professional training companies—the Cisco Learning Partners—that provide a full range of Cisco training courses. They offer training in many formats, including e-learning, self-paced, and instructor-led classes. Their instructors are Cisco-certified, and Cisco creates their materials. When you are ready, please visit the Learning & Events area at Cisco.com to learn about all the educational support that Cisco and its partners have to offer.

Thank you for choosing this book and the Cisco Networking Academy Program.

Kevin Warner
Senior Director, Marketing
Worldwide Education
Cisco Systems, Inc.

Introduction

This companion guide is designed as a desk reference to supplement your classroom and laboratory experience with version 3 of the CCNP 1 course in the Cisco Networking Academy Program.

CCNP 1: Advanced Routing is one of four courses leading to the Cisco Certified Network Professional certification. CCNP 1 teaches you how to design, configure, maintain, and scale routed networks. You will learn to use VLSMs, private addressing, and NAT to enable more efficient use of IP addresses. This book also teaches you how to implement routing protocols such as RIPv2, EIGRP, OSPF, IS-IS, and BGP. In addition, it details the important techniques used for route filtering and redistribution. While taking the course, use this companion guide to help you prepare for the Building Scalable Cisco Internetworks 642-801 BSCI exam, which is one of the four required exams to obtain the CCNP certification.

This Book's Goal

The goal of this book is to build on the routing concepts you learned while studying for the CCNA exam and to teach you the foundations of advanced routing concepts. The topics are designed to prepare you to pass the Building Scalable Cisco Internetworks exam (642-801 BSCI).

The Building Scalable Cisco Internetworks exam is a qualifying exam for the CCNP, CCDP, and CCIP certifications. The 642-801 BSCI exam tests materials covered under the new Building Scalable Cisco Internetworks course and exam objectives. The exam certifies that the successful candidate has the knowledge and skills necessary to use advanced IP addressing and routing to implement scalability for Cisco routers connected to LANs and WANs. The exam covers advanced IP addressing; routing principles; configuring EIGRP, OSPF, and IS-IS; manipulating routing updates; and configuring basic BGP.

One key methodology used in this book is to help you discover the exam topics you need to review in more depth, to help you fully understand and remember those details, and to help you prove to yourself that you have retained your knowledge of those topics. This book does not try to help you pass by memorization; it helps you truly learn and understand the topics. This book focuses on introducing techniques and technology for enabling WAN solutions. To fully benefit from this book, you should be familiar with general networking terms and concepts, and you should have basic knowledge of the following:

- Basic Cisco router operation and configuration
- TCP/IP operation and configuration
- Routing protocols such as RIP, OSPF, IGRP, and EIGRP
- Routed protocols

This Book's Audience

This book has a few different audiences. First, this book is intended for students interested in advanced routing technologies. In particular, it is targeted toward students in the Cisco Networking Academy Program CCNP 1: Advanced Routing course. In the classroom, this book serves as a supplement to the online curriculum. This book is also appropriate for corporate training faculty and staff members, as well as general users.

This book is also useful for network administrators who are responsible for implementing and troubleshooting enterprise Cisco routers and router configuration. It is also valuable for anyone who is interested in learning advanced routing concepts and passing the Building Scalable Cisco Internetworks exam (BSCI 642-801).

This Book's Features

Many of this book's features help facilitate a full understanding of the topics covered in this book:

- **Objectives**—Each chapter starts with a list of objectives that you should have mastered by the end of the chapter. The objectives reference the key concepts covered in the chapter.
- **Figures, examples, tables, and scenarios**—This book contains figures, examples, and tables that help explain theories, concepts, commands, and setup sequences that reinforce concepts and help you visualize the content covered in the chapter. In addition, the specific scenarios provide real-life situations that detail the problem and the solution.
- **Chapter summaries**—At the end of each chapter is a summary of the concepts covered in the chapter. It provides a synopsis of the chapter and serves as a study aid.
- **Key terms**—Each chapter includes a list of defined key terms that are covered in the chapter. The key terms appear in color throughout the chapter where they are used in context. The definitions of these terms serve as a study aid. In addition, the key terms reinforce the concepts introduced in the chapter and help you understand the chapter material before you move on to new concepts.
- **Check Your Understanding questions and answers**—Review questions, presented at the end of each chapter, serve as a self-assessment tool. They reinforce the concepts introduced in the chapter and help test your understanding before you move on to a new chapter. An answer key to all the questions is provided in Appendix B, "Answers to the Check Your Understanding Questions."
- **Study guides and certification exam practice questions**—To further assess your understanding, you will find on the companion CD-ROM additional in-depth questions in study guides created for each chapter. You will also find a test bank of questions included in a test engine that simulates the exam environment for the CCNP certification's 642-801 BSCI exam.

■ **Skill-building activities**—Throughout the book are references to additional skill-building activities to connect theory with practice. You can easily spot these activities by the following icons:

 Interactive Media Activities included on the companion CD-ROM are hands-on drag-and-drop, fill-in-the-blank, and matching exercises that help you master basic networking concepts.

 The collection of lab activities developed for the course can be found in the *Cisco Networking Academy Program CCNP 1: Advanced Routing Lab Companion,* Second Edition.

How This Book Is Organized

Although you could read this book cover-to-cover, it is designed to be flexible and to allow you to easily move between chapters and sections of chapters to cover just the material you need to work with more. If you do intend to read all of the chapters, the order in which they are presented is the ideal sequence. This book also contains three appendixes. The following list summarizes the topics of this book's elements:

■ **Chapter 1, "Overview of Scalable Internetworks"**—Good design is the key to a network's ability to scale. Poor design, not just an outdated protocol or router, prevents a network from scaling properly. A network design should follow a hierarchical model to be scalable. This chapter discusses the components of the hierarchical network design model and the key characteristics of scalable internetworks.

■ **Chapter 2, "Advanced IP Addressing Management"**—Unfortunately, the architects of TCP/IP could not have predicted that their protocol would eventually sustain a global network of information, commerce, and entertainment. Twenty years ago, IP version 4 (IPv4) offered an addressing strategy that, although scalable for a time, resulted in an inefficient allocation of addresses. Over the past two decades, engineers have successfully modified IPv4 so that it can survive the Internet's exponential growth. Meanwhile, an even more extensible and scalable version of IP, IP version 6 (IPv6), has been defined and developed. Today, IPv6 is slowly being implemented in select networks. Eventually, IPv6 might replace IPv4 as the dominant Internet protocol. This chapter explores the evolution and extension of IPv4, including the key scalability features that engineers have added to it over the years, such as subnetting, classless interdomain routing (CIDR), variable-length subnet masking (VLSM), and route summarization. Finally, this chapter examines advanced IP implementation techniques such as IP unnumbered, Dynamic Host Configuration Protocol (DHCP), and helper addresses.

- **Chapter 3, "Routing Overview"**—Many of the scalable design features explored in the first two chapters, such as load balancing and route summarization, work very differently depending on the routing protocol used. Routing protocols are the rules that govern the exchange of routing information between routers. TCP/IP's open architecture and global popularity have encouraged the development of more than a half-dozen prominent IP routing protocols. Each protocol has a unique combination of strengths and weaknesses. Because routing protocols are key to network performance, you must have a clear understanding of the attributes of each protocol, including convergence times, overhead, and scalability features. This chapter explores various routing processes, including default routing, floating static routes, convergence, and route calculation.

- **Chapter 4, "Routing Information Protocol Version 2"**—RIPv2 is defined in RFC 1723 and is supported in Cisco IOS software Releases 11.1 and later. RIPv2 is similar to RIPv1 but is not a new protocol. RIPv2 features extensions to bring it up-to-date with modern routing environments. RIPv2 is the first of the classless routing protocols discussed in this book. This chapter introduces classless routing and RIPv2.

- **Chapter 5, "EIGRP"**—Enhanced Interior Gateway Routing Protocol (EIGRP) is a Cisco-proprietary routing protocol based on IGRP. Unlike IGRP, which is a classful routing protocol, EIGRP supports CIDR, allowing network designers to maximize address space by using CIDR and VLSM. Compared to IGRP, EIGRP boasts faster convergence times, improved scalability, and superior handling of routing loops.

  This chapter surveys EIGRP's key concepts, technologies, and data structures. This conceptual overview is followed by a study of EIGRP convergence and basic operation. Finally, this chapter shows you how to configure and verify EIGRP and the use of route summarization.

- **Chapter 6, "OSPF"**—This chapter describes how to create and configure OSPF. Specifically, it examines the different OSPF area types, including stubby, totally stubby, and not-so-stubby areas (NSSAs). Each of these different area types uses a special advertisement to exchange routing information with the rest of the OSPF network. Therefore, link-state advertisements (LSAs) are covered in detail. The Area 0 backbone rule and how virtual links can work around backbone connectivity problems are also reviewed. Finally, this chapter surveys important **show** commands that can be used to verify multiarea OSPF operation.

- **Chapter 7, "IS-IS"**—In recent years, the Intermediate System-to-Intermediate System (IS-IS) routing protocol has become increasingly popular, with widespread usage among service providers. IS-IS enables very fast convergence and is very scalable. It is also a very flexible protocol and has been extended to incorporate leading-edge features such as Multiprotocol Label Switching Traffic Engineering (MPLS/TE). IS-IS features include hierarchical routing, classless behavior, rapid flooding of new information, fast convergence, good scalability, and flexible timer tuning. The Cisco IOS software implementation of IS-IS also supports multiarea routing, route leaking, and overload bit. All of these concepts are discussed in this chapter, beginning with an introduction to OSI protocols.

- **Chapter 8, "Route Optimization"**—Dynamic routing, even in small internetworks, can involve much more than just enabling a routing protocol's default behavior. A few simple commands might be enough to get dynamic routing started. However, more advanced configuration must be done to enable such features as routing update control and exchanges among multiple routing protocols. You can optimize routing in a network by controlling when a router exchanges routing updates and what those updates contain. This chapter examines the key IOS route optimization features, including routing update control, policy-based routing, and route redistribution.

- **Chapter 9, "BGP"**—This chapter provides an overview of the different types of autonomous systems and then focuses on basic BGP operation, including BGP neighbor negotiation. It also looks at how to use the Cisco IOS software to configure BGP and verify its operation. Finally, it examines BGP peering and the BGP routing process.

- **Appendix A, "Glossary of Key Terms"**—This appendix provides a complied list of all the key terms that appear throughout the book.

- **Appendix B, "Answers to the Check Your Understanding Questions"**—This appendix provides the answers to the quizzes that appear at the end of each chapter.

- **Appendix C, "Case Studies"**—This appendix provides case studies that let you apply the concepts you learn throughout this book to real-life routing scenarios. The case studies cover EIGRP, OSPF, and BGP/OSPF.

About the CD-ROM

The CD-ROM included with this book provides Interactive Media Activities, a test engine, and Study Guides to enhance your learning experience. You will see these referred to throughout the book.

Objectives

Upon completing this chapter, you will be able to

- Describe the hierarchical network design model
- State the key characteristics of scalable networks

You can reinforce your understanding of the objectives covered in this chapter by opening the interactive media activities on the CD accompanying this book and performing the lab activities collected in the *Cisco Networking Academy Program CCNP 1: Advanced Routing Lab Companion*. Throughout this chapter, you will see references to these activities by title and by icon. They look like this:

 Interactive Media Activity

 Lab Activity

Chapter 1

Overview of Scalable Internetworks

Initially, Transmission Control Protocol/Internet Protocol (TCP/IP) networks relied on simple distance vector routing protocols and classful 32-bit IP addressing. These technologies offered a limited capacity for growth. Network designers must now modify, redesign, or abandon these early technologies to build modern networks that can scale to handle fast growth and constant change. This chapter explores networking technologies that have evolved to meet this demand for scalability.

Scalability is a network's capability to grow and adapt without major redesign or reinstallation. It seems obvious to allow for growth in a network, but growth can be difficult to achieve without redesign. This redesign might be significant and costly. For example, a network might give a small company access to e-mail, the Internet, and shared files. If the company tripled in size and demanded streaming video or e-commerce services, could the original networking media and devices adequately serve these new applications? Most organizations cannot afford to recable or redesign their networks when users are relocated, new nodes are added, or new applications are introduced.

Good design is the key to a network's ability to scale. Poor design, not an outdated protocol or router, prevents a network from scaling properly. A network design should follow a hierarchical model to be scalable. This chapter discusses the components of the hierarchical network design model and the key characteristics of scalable internetworks.

The Hierarchical Network Design Model

If allowed to grow helter-skelter, strictly as needs demanded, most networks would quickly become unrecognizable and unmanageable. Worse, someday you might reach the point where no more growth can be accommodated. Following a standardized design model allows your network to grow in an established pattern that will not limit future growth.

The Three-Layer Hierarchical Design Model

A hierarchical network design model breaks the complex problem of network design into smaller, more manageable problems. Each level or tier in the hierarchy addresses a different set of problems. This helps the designer optimize network hardware and software to perform specific roles. For example, devices at the lowest tier are optimized to accept traffic into a network and pass that traffic to the higher layers. Cisco offers a three-tiered hierarchy as the preferred approach to network design, as illustrated in Figure 1-1.

Figure 1-1 Scalable Network Design

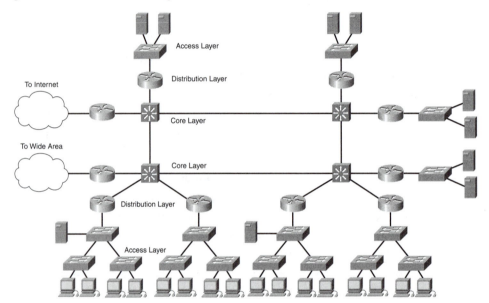

In the three-layer network design model, shown in Figure 1-2, network devices and links are grouped according to the following three layers:

- Core
- Distribution
- Access

Figure 1-2 Three-Layer Network Design Model

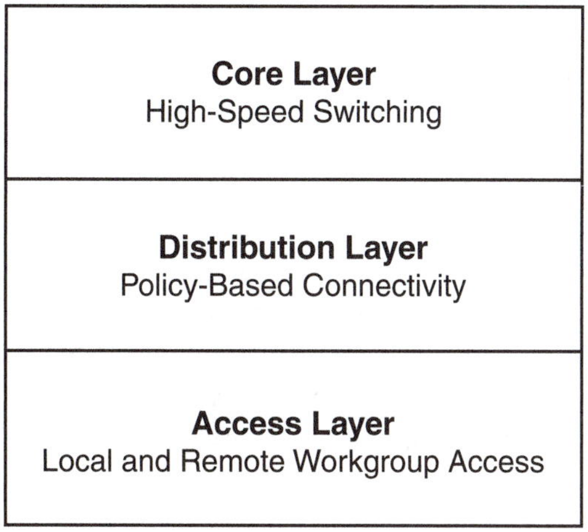

Core Layer
High-Speed Switching
Distribution Layer
Policy-Based Connectivity
Access Layer
Local and Remote Workgroup Access

The three-layer model is a conceptual framework. It is an abstract picture of a network similar to the concept of the Open System Interconnection (OSI) reference model.

Layered models are useful because they facilitate modularity. Devices at each layer have similar and well-defined functions. This allows administrators to easily add, replace, and remove individual pieces of the network. This kind of flexibility and adaptability makes a hierarchical network design highly scalable.

At the same time, layered models can be difficult to comprehend, because the exact composition of each layer varies from network to network. Each layer of the three-tiered design model may include the following:

- A router
- A switch
- A link
- A combination of these

Some networks might combine the function of two layers into a single device or omit a layer entirely.

The following sections discuss each of the three layers in detail.

The Core Layer

The *core layer* provides an optimized and reliable transport structure by forwarding traffic at very high speeds. In other words, the core layer switches packets as fast as possible. Devices at the core layer should not be burdened with any processes that stand in the way of switching

NOTE

Although a modern Layer 3 fast switch with Policy Feature Cards can process access lists in hardware, this function normally is not activated at the core layer so that traffic can proceed as quickly as possible.

packets at top speed. Examples of processes that are best performed outside the core include the following:

- Access list checking
- Data encryption
- Address translation

The Distribution Layer

The *distribution layer* is located between the access and core layers. It helps differentiate the core from the rest of the network. The purpose of this layer is to provide boundary definition using access lists and other filters to limit what gets into the core. Therefore, this layer defines policy for the network. A policy is an approach to handling certain kinds of traffic, including the following:

- Routing updates
- Route summaries
- Virtual LAN (VLAN) traffic
- Address aggregation

Use these policies to secure networks and to preserve resources by preventing unnecessary traffic.

If a network has two or more routing protocols, such as Routing Information Protocol (RIP) and Interior Gateway Routing Protocol (IGRP), information between the different routing domains is shared, or redistributed, at the distribution layer.

The Access Layer

The *access layer* supplies traffic to the network and performs network entry control. End users access network resources by way of the access layer. Acting as the front door to a network, the access layer employs access lists designed to prevent unauthorized users from gaining entry. The access layer can also give remote sites access to the network by way of a wide-area technology, such as Frame Relay, ISDN, leased lines, DSL, cable modem, or one of several wireless and satellite technologies.

 Interactive Media Activity   Point and Click: Layered Design Model

In this media activity, you learn characteristics of the layered design model. This is a point-and-click activity where you click the correct choice.

Router Function in the Hierarchy

The core, distribution, and access layers each have clearly defined functions. For this reason, each layer demands a different set of features than routers, switches, and links. Routers that operate in the same layer can be configured in a consistent way, because they all must perform similar tasks. The router is the primary device that maintains logical and physical hierarchy in a network. Therefore, proper and consistent configurations are imperative. Cisco offers several router product lines. Each product line has a particular set of features for one of the three layers:

- **Core layer**—12000, 7500, 7200, and 7000 series routers, shown in Figures 1-3 and 1-4.

Figure 1-3 Cisco 12000 Series Core-Layer Router

Figure 1-4 Cisco 7000 Series Core-Layer Routers

■ **Distribution layer**—4500, 4000, and 3600 series routers, shown in Figures 1-5 and 1-6.

Figure 1-5 Cisco 4000 Series Distribution-Layer Router

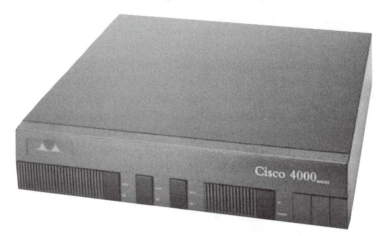

Figure 1-6 Cisco 3600 Series Distribution-Layer Routers

■ **Access layer**—2600, 2500, 1700, and 1600 series routers, shown in Figures 1-7 and 1-8.

Figure 1-7 Cisco 2600 Series Access-Layer Routers

Figure 1-8 Cisco 1700 Series Access-Layer Routers

The following sections revisit each layer and examine the specific routers and other devices used.

 Interactive Media Activity   Drag and Drop: Defining the Role of the Router in the Hierarchy

In this media activity, you identify the functions of each hierarchy layer.

Core Layer Example

The core layer is the center of the network and is designed to be fast and reliable. Access lists should be avoided in the core layer. Access lists add latency, and end users should not have direct access to the core. In a hierarchical network, end-user traffic should reach *core routers* only after those packets have passed through the distribution and access layers. Access lists may exist in those two lower layers.

Core routing is done without access lists, address translation, or other packet manipulation. Because of this, it might seem as though the least powerful routers would work well for so simple a task. However, the opposite is true. The most powerful Cisco routers serve the core, because they have the fastest switching technologies and the largest capacity for physical interfaces.

The 7000, 7200, and 7500 series routers feature the fastest switching modes available. These are the Cisco enterprise core routers. The 12000 series router is also a core router designed to meet the core routing needs of Internet service providers (ISPs). Unless the company is in the business of providing Internet access to other companies, it is unlikely that a 12000 series router will be found in the telecommunications closet.

The 7000, 7200, and 7500 series routers are modular. This provides scalability, because administrators can add interface modules when needed. The large chassis of this series can accommodate dozens of interfaces on multiple modules for virtually any media type. This makes these routers scalable and reliable core solutions.

Core routers achieve reliability through the use of redundant links, usually to all other core routers. When possible, these redundant links should be symmetrical, having equal through-put, so that equal-cost load balancing may be used. Core routers need a relatively large number of interfaces to enable this configuration. Core routers achieve reliability through redundant power supplies. They usually feature two or more hot-swappable power supplies, which may be removed and replaced individually without shutting down the router.

Figure 1-9 shows a simple core topology using 7507 router routers at three key sites in an enterprise. Each Cisco 7507 router is directly connected to every other router. This type of configuration is a full mesh. There are also two links between each router to provide redundancy. Core links should be the fastest and most reliable leased lines in the WAN and can include

- T1
- T3
- OC3
- Anything better

Figure 1-9 Core Layer Example

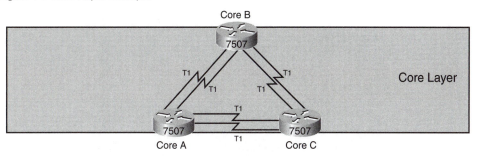

If redundant T1s are used for this WAN core, each router needs four serial interfaces for two point-to-point connections to each site. Ultimately, the design requires even more than this, because other routers at the distribution layer also need to connect to the core routers. Fortunately, interfaces can be added to the 7507 router because of modularity.

With the high-end routers and WAN links involved, the core can become a huge expense, even in a simple example such as this. Some designers choose not to use symmetrical links in the core to reduce cost. In place of redundant lines, packet-switched and dial-on-demand technologies such as Frame Relay and ISDN may be used as backup links. The trade-off for saving money by using such technologies is performance. Using ISDN BRIs as backup links can eliminate the capability of equal-cost load balancing.

The core of a network does not have to exist in the WAN. A LAN *backbone* also may be considered part of the core layer. Campus networks, or large networks that span an office complex or adjacent buildings, might have a LAN-based core. Switched Fast Ethernet and Gigabit Ethernet are the most common core technologies, usually run over fiber. Enterprise switches, such as the Catalyst 3550, 4500, and 6500 series, shoulder the load in LAN cores, as shown in Figures 1-10, 1-11, and 1-12. This is because they switch frames at Layer 2 much faster than routers can switch packets at Layer 3. The 4500 and 6500 switches are modular devices and can be equipped with route switch modules (RSMs) adding Layer 3 routing functionality to the switch chassis. The 3550 series is an enterprise-class stackable switch with Layer 3 capabilities built in. It can serve as a core or distribution layer switch, depending on the port configuration.

Figure 1-10 Catalyst 3550 Series Core Layer Switches

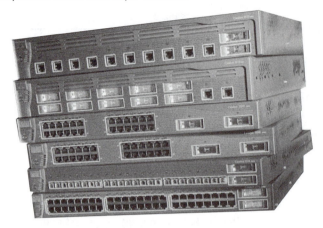

Figure 1-11 Catalyst 4500 Series Core Layer Switches

Figure 1-12 Catalyst 6500 Series Core Layer Switches

Distribution Layer Example

The distribution layer, shown in Figure 1-13, enforces policies to limit traffic to and from the core. Distribution layer routers handle less traffic than core-layer routers, so they need fewer interfaces and less switching speed. However, a fast core is useless if a slowdown of data transfer at the distribution layer prevents user traffic from accessing core links. For this reason, Cisco offers robust, powerful distribution routers, such as the 4000, 4500, and 3600 series routers. These routers are modular, allowing interfaces to be added and removed, depending on what is needed. However, the smaller chassis of these series are much more limiting than those of the 7000, 7200, and 7500 series.

Figure 1-13 Distribution Layer Example

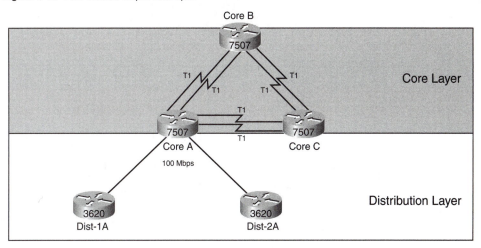

Distribution layer routers bring policy to the network by using a combination of the following:

- Access lists
- Route summarization
- Distribution lists
- Route maps
- Other rules to define how a router should deal with traffic and routing updates

Many of these techniques are covered later in the book.

Figure 1-13 shows that two 3620 routers have been added at Core A, in the same wiring closet as the 7507 router. In this example, high-speed LAN links connect the distribution routers to the core router. Depending on the network's size, these links may be part of the campus backbone and will most likely be fiber running 100 or 1000 Mbps Ethernet. In this example, Dist-1A and Dist-2A are part of the Core A campus backbone. Dist-1A serves remote sites, and Dist-2A serves access routers at Site A. If Site A uses VLANs, Dist-2A may be responsible for routing between the VLANs.

Both Dist-1A and Dist-2A use access lists to prevent unwanted traffic from reaching the core. In addition, these routers summarize their routing tables in updates to Core A. This keeps the Core A routing table small and efficient.

Access Layer Example

Routers at the access layer, as shown in Figure 1-14, give users at Site A access to the network. Routers at remote sites Y and Z also give users access to the network.

Figure 1-14 Access Layer Example

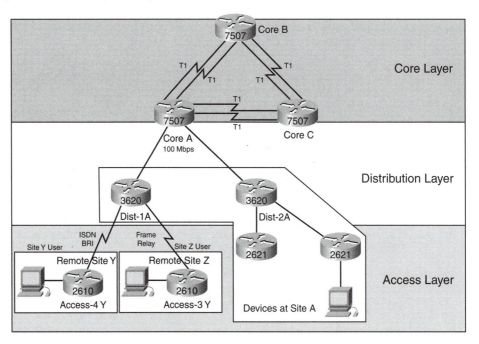

Access routers generally offer fewer physical interfaces than distribution and core routers. For this reason, Cisco access routers feature a small, streamlined chassis that might or might not support modular interfaces. This includes the 1600, 1700, 2500, and 2600 series routers.

Two 2621s have been added to the network's access layer at Site A. These 2621 routers have two FastEthernet interfaces. User-end stations connect through a workgroup switch or hub to one FastEthernet interface. The other FastEthernet interface connects to the high-speed campus backbone of Site A.

Each remote site in the example requires only one Ethernet interface for the LAN side and one serial interface for the WAN side. The WAN interface connects by way of Frame Relay or ISDN to the distribution router in Site A's wiring closet. For this application, the 2610 router provides a single 10/100-Mbps FastEthernet port and works well at these locations. These remote sites, Y and Z, are small branch offices that must access the core through Site A. Therefore, Dist-1A is a WAN hub for the organization. As the network scales, more remote sites may access the core with a connection to the distribution routers at the WAN hub. Switches such as the 2950, shown in Figure 1-15, provide edge-access connections for individual workstations and servers at the access layer.

Figure 1-15 Catalyst 2950 Series Access Layer Switches

Key Characteristics of Scalable Internetworks

This section outlines several attributes of a good network. A well-constructed network is reliable, serviceable, and scalable. This section helps you recognize good network design when you see it.

Five Characteristics of a Scalable Network

Although every large internetwork has unique features, all scalable networks have essential attributes in common. A scalable network has five key characteristics:

- **Reliable and available**—A reliable network should be built with quality components, including cabling and networking devices. Redundant links and backup devices may be employed to increase reliability. In a highly reliable and available network, fault tolerance and redundancy can reduce the impact of outages and failures on end users.

- **Responsive**—A responsive network should provide quality of service (QoS) for various applications and protocols without making responses at the desktop worse. The internetwork must be capable of responding to latency issues common for time-sensitive traffic, such as Systems Network Architecture (SNA) traffic and streaming video and audio communications. However, the internetwork must still route desktop traffic without compromising QoS.

- **Efficient**—Large internetworks must optimize the use of resources, especially bandwidth. It is possible to increase data throughput without adding hardware or buying more WAN services. To do this, reduce unnecessary broadcasts, service location requests, and routing updates.

- **Adaptable**—An adaptable network can accommodate different protocols, applications, and hardware technologies.

- **Accessible but secure**—An accessible network allows for connections using dedicated, dialup, and switched services while maintaining network integrity.

The Cisco IOS software offers a rich set of features that support network scalability. The remainder of this chapter discusses IOS features that support these five characteristics of a scalable network.

Making the Network Reliable and Available

A reliable and available network provides users with 24-hour-a-day, seven-day-a-week access. In a highly reliable and available network, fault tolerance and redundancy make outages and failures invisible to the end user, as shown in Figure 1-16. The high-end devices and telecommunication links that ensure this kind of performance come with a high price tag. Network designers constantly have to balance the needs of users with the resources at hand.

Figure 1-16 Reliable and Available Network

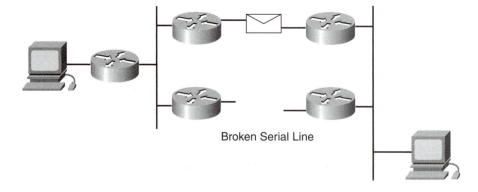

Broken Serial Line

When choosing between high performance and low cost at the core layer, the network administrator should choose the best available routers and dedicated WAN links. The core must be designed to be the most reliable and available layer. If a core router fails or a core link becomes unstable, routing for the entire internetwork might be adversely affected.

Core routers maintain reliability and availability by rerouting traffic in the event of a failure. Robust networks can adapt to failures quickly and effectively. To build robust networks, the Cisco IOS software offers several features that enhance reliability and availability:

- Support for scalable routing protocols
- Alternative paths
- Load balancing
- Protocol tunnels
- Dial backup

The following sections describe these features.

Scalable Routing Protocols

Routers in the core of a network should converge rapidly and maintain reachability to all networks and subnetworks within an autonomous system (AS). Simple distance vector routing protocols such as RIP take too long to update and adapt to topology changes to be viable core solutions. Compatibility issues might require that some areas of a network run simple distance vector protocols such as RIP and Routing Table Maintenance Protocol (RTMP), an Apple-proprietary routing protocol. It is best to use a scalable routing protocol in the core layer. Good choices include Open Shortest Path First (OSPF), Intermediate System-to-Intermediate System (IS-IS), and Enhanced Interior Gateway Routing Protocol (EIGRP).

Alternative Paths

Redundant links maximize network reliability and availability, but they are expensive to deploy throughout a large internetwork. Core links should always be redundant. Other areas of a network also might need redundant telecommunication links. If a remote site exchanges mission-critical information with the rest of the internetwork, that site is a candidate for redundant links. To provide another dimension of reliability, an organization might even invest in redundant routers to connect to these links. A network that consists of multiple links and redundant routers contains several paths to a given destination. If a network uses a scalable routing protocol, each router maintains a map of the entire network topology. This map helps routers select an alternative path quickly if a primary path fails. EIGRP actually maintains a database of all alternative paths if the primary route is lost.

Load Balancing

Redundant links do not necessarily remain idle until a link fails. Routers can distribute the traffic load across multiple links to the same destination. This process is called *load balancing*. Load balancing can be implemented using alternative paths with the same cost or metric. This is called *equal-cost load balancing*. They can also be implemented over alternative paths with different metrics. This is called *unequal-cost load balancing*. When routing IP, the Cisco IOS software offers two methods of load balancing—per-packet and per-destination. If fast switching is enabled, only one of the alternative routes is cached for the destination address. All packets in the packet stream bound for a specific host take the same path. Packets bound for a different host on the same network may use an alternative route. This way, traffic is load-balanced on a per-destination basis.

Per-packet load balancing requires more CPU time than per-destination load balancing. However, per-packet load balancing allows load balancing that is proportional to the metrics of unequal paths, which can help use bandwidth efficiently. The proportional distribution makes per-packet load balancing better than per-destination load balancing in these cases.

Protocol Tunnels

An IP network with Novell NetWare running Internetwork Packet Exchange (IPX) at a handful of remote sites may provide IPX connectivity between the remote sites by routing IPX in the core. Even if only two or three offices use NetWare IPX sparingly, this creates additional overhead associated with routing a second routed protocol, or IPX, in the core. It also requires that all routers in the data path have the appropriate IOS and hardware to support IPX. For this reason, many organizations have adopted "IP only" policies at the network core, because IP has become the dominant routed protocol and is essential for access to the Internet.

Tunneling gives an administrator a second, and more agreeable, option. The administrator can configure a point-to-point link through the core between the two routers using IP. When this link is configured, IPX packets can be encapsulated inside IP packets. IPX can then traverse the core over IP links, and the core can be spared the additional burden of routing IPX. Using tunnels, the administrator increases the availability of network services.

Dial Backup

Sometimes two redundant WAN links are not enough, or a single link needs to be fault-tolerant. However, the possibility of purchasing a full-time redundant link is too expensive. In these cases, a backup link can be configured over a dialup technology, such as ISDN, or even an ordinary analog phone line. These relatively low-bandwidth links remain idle until the primary link fails.

Dial backup can be a cost-effective insurance policy, but it is not a substitute for redundant links that can effectively double throughput by using equal-cost load balancing.

Making the Network Responsive

End users notice network responsiveness as they use the network to perform routine tasks. Users expect network resources to respond quickly, as if network applications were running from a local hard drive. Networks must be configured to meet the needs of all applications, especially time-delay-sensitive applications such as voice and video. The IOS offers traffic prioritization features to tune responsiveness in a congested network. Routers may be configured to prioritize certain kinds of traffic based on protocol information, such as TCP port numbers. Traffic prioritization ensures that packets carrying mission-critical data take precedence over less-important traffic. Figure 1-17 illustrates this concept by showing how the FTP traffic waits while higher-priority voice and video traffic enters through the router interface.

If the router schedules these packets for transmission on a first-come, first-served basis, users could experience an unacceptable lack of responsiveness. For example, an end user sending delay-sensitive voice traffic might be forced to wait too long while the router empties its buffer of queued packets.

Figure 1-17 Traffic Prioritization

The IOS addresses priority and responsiveness issues through queuing. Routers that maintain a slow WAN connection often experience congestion. These routers need a method to give certain traffic priority. Queuing is the process that the router uses to schedule packets for transmission during periods of congestion. By using the queuing feature, a congested router can be configured to reorder packets so that mission-critical and delay-sensitive traffic is processed first. These higher-priority packets are sent first even if other low-priority packets arrive ahead of them. The IOS supports four methods of queuing:

- First-in, first-out (FIFO) queuing
- *Priority queuing*
- Custom queuing
- Weighted Fair Queuing (WFQ)

Only one of these queuing methods can be applied per interface, because each method handles traffic in a unique way.

Making the Network Efficient

An efficient network should not waste bandwidth, especially over costly WAN links. To be efficient, routers should prevent unnecessary traffic from traversing the WAN and minimize the size and frequency of routing updates. The IOS includes several features designed to optimize a WAN connection:

- Access lists
- Snapshot routing
- Compression over WANs

The following sections describe each of these features.

Access Lists

Access lists, illustrated in Figure 1-18, also called Access Control Lists (ACLs), can be used to do all of the following:

- Prevent traffic that the administrator defines as unnecessary, undesirable, or unauthorized
- Control routing updates
- Apply route maps
- Implement other network policies that improve efficiency by curtailing traffic

Figure 1-18 Access Lists

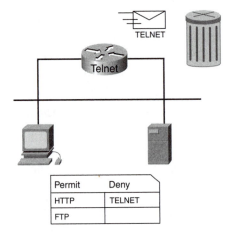

One access list may be applied on an interface for each protocol, per direction, in or out. Different filtering policies can be defined for different protocols, such as IP, IPX, and AppleTalk.

Snapshot Routing

Distance vector routing protocols typically update neighbor routers with their complete routing table at regular intervals. These timed updates occur even when there have been no changes in the network topology since the last update. If a remote site relies on a dialup technology, such as ISDN, it would be cost-prohibitive to maintain the WAN link in an active state 24 hours a day. RIP routers expect updates every 30 seconds by default. This would cause the ISDN link to reestablish twice a minute to maintain the routing tables. It is possible to adjust the RIP timers, but snapshot routing provides a better solution to maximize network efficiency.

Snapshot routing allows routers using distance vector protocols to exchange their complete tables during an initial connection. Snapshot routing then waits until the next active period on the line before exchanging routing information again. The router takes a snapshot of the routing table. The router then uses this picture for routing table entries while the dialup link is down. The result is that the routing table is kept unchanged so that routes are not lost because a routing update was not received. When the link is reestablished, usually because the router has identified interesting traffic that needs to be routed over the WAN, the router again updates its neighbors.

Compression over WANs

The IOS supports several compression techniques that can maximize bandwidth by reducing the number of bits in all or part of a frame. Compression is accomplished through mathematical formulas or compression algorithms. Unfortunately, routers must dedicate a significant amount of processor time to compress and decompress traffic, increasing latency. Therefore, compression tends to be an efficient measure only on links with extremely limited bandwidth.

The IOS also supports the following bandwidth optimization features:

- Dial-on-demand routing (DDR)
- Route summarization
- Incremental updates

Dial-on-Demand Routing

Dedicated WAN circuits, even Frame Relay, might be cost-prohibitive for every remote site. DDR offers an efficient, economic alternative for sites that require only occasional WAN connectivity. A router configured for DDR listens for interesting traffic and waits to establish the WAN link. The administrator defines what interesting traffic is. When the router receives traffic that meets the criteria, the link is activated. DDR is most commonly used with ISDN circuits.

Route Summarization

The number of entries in a routing table can be reduced if the router uses one network address and mask to represent multiple networks or subnetworks. This technique is called *route aggregation or route summarization*. Some routing protocols automatically summarize subnet routes based on the major network number. Other routing protocols, such as OSPF and EIGRP, allow manual summarization. Route summarization is discussed in Chapter 2, "Advanced IP Addressing Management."

Incremental Updates

Routing protocols such as OSPF, IS-IS, and EIGRP send routing updates that contain information only about routes that have changed. These incremental routing updates use the bandwidth more efficiently than simple distance vector protocols that transmit their complete routing table at fixed intervals, whether or not a change has occurred.

Making the Network Adaptable

An adaptable network handles the addition and coexistence of multiple routed and routing protocols. EIGRP is an exceptionally adaptable protocol because it supports routing information for three routed protocols:

- IP
- IPX
- AppleTalk

The IOS also supports route redistribution, which is described in Chapter 8, "Route Optimization." Route redistribution allows routing information to be shared among two or more different routing protocols. For example, RIP routes can be redistributed, or injected, into an OSPF area.

Mixing Routable and Nonroutable Protocols

A network delivering both routable and nonroutable traffic has some unique problems. Routable protocols, such as IP, can be forwarded from one network to another based on a network-layer address. Nonroutable protocols, such as SNA, do not contain a network layer address and cannot be forwarded by routers. Most nonroutable protocols also lack a mechanism to provide flow control and are sensitive to delays in delivery. Any delays in delivery causing packets to arrive out of order can result in the session's being dropped. An adaptable network must accommodate both routable and nonroutable protocols.

Making the Network Accessible but Secure

Accessible networks let users connect easily over a variety of technologies, as shown in Figure 1-19. Campus LAN users typically connect to routers at the access layer through Ethernet or Token Ring. Remote users and sites might have access to several types of WAN services. Cost and geography play a significant role in determining what type of WAN services an organization can deploy. Therefore, Cisco routers support all major WAN connection types. As shown in Figure 1-19, these services include all of the following:

- Dialup or circuit-switched networks
- Dedicated or leased lines
- Packet-switched networks

Figure 1-19 Accessible Networks

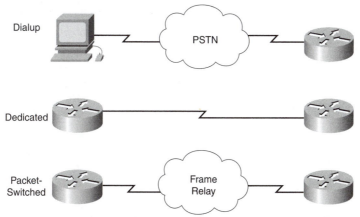

Dialup connections are circuit-switched, and leased lines are dedicated. Packet-switched networks, on the other hand, provide connectivity on a packet-by-packet basis:

- **Dialup and dedicated access**—Cisco routers can be directly connected to basic telephone service or digital services such as T1/E1. Dialup links can be used for backup or remote sites that need occasional WAN access, and dedicated leased lines provide a high-speed, high-capacity WAN core between key sites.
- **Packet-switched**—Cisco routers support Frame Relay, X.25, Switched Multimegabit Data Service (SMDS), and ATM. With this variety of support, the WAN service, or combination of WAN services, to deploy can be determined based on cost, location, and need.

Often, the easier it is for legitimate remote users to access the network, the easier it is for unauthorized users to break in. An access strategy must be carefully planned so that resources, such as remote-access routers and servers, are secure. If a company lets users telecommute through a dialup modem or via the Internet, the network administrator must secure access. The routers can be secured with access lists. Routers can also be secured with an authentication protocol, such as Password Authentication Protocol (PAP) or Challenge Handshake Authentication Protocol (CHAP). These protocols require the user to provide a valid name and password before the router permits access to other network resources.

Basic Router Configuration Lab Exercises

You can find the following introductory labs in the *Cisco Networking Academy Program CCNP 1: Advanced Routing Lab Companion*, Second Edition.

Lab 1.4.1   Introductory Lab 1: Getting Started and Building start.txt

This lab introduces the CCNP lab equipment and some IOS features that might be new. This introductory activity also describes how to use a simple text editor to create all or part of a router configuration and apply that configuration to a router.

Lab 1.4.2   Introductory Lab 2: Capturing HyperTerminal and Telnet Sessions

This activity describes how to capture HyperTerminal and Telnet sessions.

Lab 1.4.3   Introductory Lab 3: Access Control List Basics and Extended Ping

This lab activity reviews the basics of standard and extended access lists, which are used extensively in the CCNP curriculum.

Lab 1.4.4   Implementing Quality of Service with Priority Queuing

This lab activity shows you how to implement quality of service by replacing the default queuing method with priority queuing based on protocol type.

Load Balancing Lab Exercises

You can find the following introductory labs in the *Cisco Networking Academy Program CCNP 1: Advanced Routing Lab Companion*, Second Edition

Lab 1.5.1   Equal-Cost Load Balancing with RIP

In this lab, you observe equal-cost load balancing on a per-packet and per-destination basis by using advanced **debug** commands.

Lab 1.5.2   Unequal-Cost Load Balancing with IGRP

In this lab, you observe unequal-cost load balancing on an IGRP network by using advanced **debug** commands.

Summary

This chapter defined scalability and provided examples of Cisco IOS software features that enable successful network expansion. It also explained the three-layer design model. This conceptual model helps administrators configure routers to meet a layer's specific needs. Recall that scalable networks also have the following characteristics:

- Reliable and available
- Responsive
- Efficient
- Adaptable
- Accessible but secure

These concepts apply throughout the entire CCNP 1 curriculum.

Key Terms

access layer   Supplies traffic to the network and performs network-entry control.

access list   A list kept by Cisco routers to control access to or from the router for a number of services (for example, to prevent packets with a certain IP address from leaving a particular interface on the router).

backbone   The part of a network that acts as the primary path for traffic that is most often sourced from, and destined for, other networks.

core layer   Provides an optimized and reliable transport structure by forwarding traffic at very high speeds.

core router   In a packet-switched star topology, a router that is part of the backbone and that serves as the single pipe through which all traffic from peripheral networks must pass on its way to other peripheral networks.

distribution layer   Located between the access and core layers. Helps differentiate the core from the rest of the network.

priority queuing   A method of queuing that is used to guarantee bandwidth for traffic by assigning queue space to each protocol according to the defined rules.

Check Your Understanding

Complete all of the review questions to test your understanding of the topics and concepts in this chapter. The answers appear in Appendix B, "Answers to the Check Your Understanding Questions."

For additional, more in-depth questions, refer to the chapter-specific study guides on the companion CD-ROM.

1. The core and access layers are two of the three layers in the hierarchical design model. What is the third layer?

    A. Internetwork layer

    B. Distribution layer

    C. Workgroup layer

    D. Backbone layer

2. What is a recommended practice for the core layer?

    A. Data compression for efficient link usage

    B. Avoiding redundant links

    C. Direct access by end users

    D. Avoiding access lists because of latency

3. What is an important function of the access layer?

    A. It connects the campus backbone network devices

    B. It provides direct connections to the Internet

    C. It provides workgroup access to corporate resources

    D. It performs high-speed LAN switching

4. What method should be used to prevent regular routing updates from constantly activating a dialup WAN link?

    A. Dialer access list

    B. Distance vector

    C. Incremental updates

    D. Snapshot routing

5. What feature characterizes a network that is reliable and available?

    A. Load balancing

    B. Securable

    C. Queuing

    D. Protocol integration

6. What is the primary purpose of dial backup?

    A. Tunneling

    B. Load balancing

    C. Fault tolerance

    D. Traffic prioritization

7. Which Cisco IOS software feature supports responsiveness on slow WAN links?

    A. DDR

    B. Tunnels

    C. Queuing

    D. Route summarization

8. Which three features are offered in the Cisco IOS software to optimize the efficiency of a WAN connection?

   A. Access lists

   B. Protocol tunnels

   C. Snapshot routing

   D. Compression

   E. Dynamic data aggregation

9. What is a characteristic of a scalable routing protocol?

   A. Fast convergence

   B. Slow convergence

   C. Reachability limitations

   D. Simple configuration

10. What is a characteristic of nonroutable protocols?

    A. No frame header

    B. No network-layer addressing

    C. Appropriate for WAN links

    D. Best-route determination by broadcast

Objectives

Upon completing this chapter, you will be able to

- Create and configure IPv4 addresses
- Understand and resolve IP addressing crises
- Assign a VLSM addressing scheme
- Configure route summarization
- Configure private addressing and NAT
- Use IP unnumbered
- Understand and configure DHCP and Easy IP
- Know when to use helper addresses
- Understand the concepts of IPv6

You can reinforce your understanding of the objectives covered in this chapter by opening the interactive media activities on the CD accompanying this book and performing the lab activities collected in the *Cisco Networking Academy Program CCNP 1: Advanced Routing Lab Companion*. Throughout this chapter, you will see references to these activities by title and by icon. They look like this:

   Interactive Media Activity

   Lab Activity

Chapter 2

Advanced IP Addressing Management

A scalable network requires an addressing scheme that allows for growth. However, several unanticipated consequences can result from unmanaged network growth. As new nodes and networks are added to the enterprise, existing addresses might need to be reassigned. Excessively large routing tables might slow down older routers, and the supply of available addresses might simply run out. You can avoid these unpleasant consequences with careful planning and deployment of a scalable network addressing system.

Network designers can choose from among many different network protocols and addressing schemes. However, with the emergence of the Internet and its nonproprietary protocol, Transmission Control Protocol/Internet Protocol (TCP/IP), this has meant that virtually every enterprise must implement an IP addressing scheme. In addition to TCP/IP, several proprietary network protocols and addressing schemes have been used. Companies such as Apple and Novell have recently migrated their network software to TCP/IP and away from their proprietary protocols. Presently, many organizations choose to run TCP/IP as the only routed protocol on the network. The bottom line is that administrators must find ways to scale their networks by using IP addressing.

Unfortunately, the architects of TCP/IP could not have predicted that their protocol would eventually sustain a global network of information, commerce, and entertainment. Twenty years ago, IP version 4 (IPv4) offered an addressing strategy that, although scalable for a time, resulted in an inefficient allocation of addresses. Over the past two decades, engineers have successfully modified IPv4 so that it can survive the Internet's exponential growth. Meanwhile, an even more extensible and scalable version of IP, IP version 6 (IPv6), has been defined and developed. Today, IPv6 is slowly being implemented in select networks. Eventually, IPv6 might replace IPv4 as the dominant Internet protocol.

This chapter explores the evolution and extension of IPv4, including the key scalability features that engineers have added to it over the years:

- Subnetting
- *Classless interdomain routing (CIDR)*
- *Variable-length subnet masking (VLSM)*
- Route summarization

Finally, this chapter examines advanced IP implementation techniques such as the following:

- IP unnumbered
- Dynamic Host Configuration Protocol
- Helper addresses

IPv4 Addressing

This section covers some of the basic concepts of IPv4 addressing, such as how the Internet's address architecture uses the binary and dotted-decimal versions of IPv4 addressing. This section also reviews the structure of IPv4 addresses, such as the various classes of IPv4 addresses. Finally, this section reviews how IPv4 addresses use subnet masks to help divide and manage the size and growth of the Internet and computer networks.

Address Architecture of the Internet

When TCP/IP was introduced in the 1980s, it relied on a two-level addressing scheme. At the time, this scheme offered adequate scalability. The 32-bit-long IPv4 address identifies a network number and a host number, as shown in Figure 2-1.

Figure 2-1 IP Address Structure

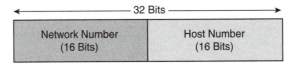

Together, the network number and the host number uniquely identify all hosts connected by way of the Internet. It is possible that the needs of a small networked community, such as a LAN, could be satisfied with just host addresses. However, network addresses are necessary for end systems on different networks to communicate with each other. Routers use the network portion of the address to make routing decisions and to facilitate communication between hosts that belong to different networks.

Unlike routers, humans find working with strings of 32 1s and 0s tedious and clumsy. Therefore, 32-bit IP addresses are written using dotted-decimal notation. Each 32-bit address is divided into four groups of eight, called octets. Each octet is converted to decimal and then separated by decimal points, or dots. This is illustrated as follows:

- A 32-bit IP address is a binary number:

  10101100000111101000000000010001

- This binary number can be divided into four octets:

  10101100 00011110 10000000 00010001

- Each octet (or byte) can be converted to decimal:

  172 30 128 17

- Finally, the address can be written in dotted-decimal notation:

  172.30.128.17

In the dotted-decimal address 172.30.128.17, which of these four numbers represents the network portion of the address? Which numbers are the host numbers? Finding the answers to these questions is complicated by the fact that IP addresses are not really four numbers. They actually consist of 32 different numbers, or 32 bits.

In the early days of TCP/IP, a class system was used to define the network and host portions of the address. IPv4 addresses were grouped into five distinct classes. This was done according to the value of the first few bits in the first octet of the address. Although the class system can still be applied to IP addresses, networks today often ignore the rules of class in favor of a classless IP scheme.

The next few sections cover all of the following topics related to IP addressing:

- The limitations of the IP address classes
- The subsequent addition of the subnet mask
- The addressing crisis that led to the adoption of a classless system

Class A and B IP Addresses

In a class system, IP addresses can be grouped into one of five different classes:

- A
- B
- C
- D
- E

Each of the four octets of an IP address represents either the network portion or the host portion of the address, depending on the address class. The network and host portions of the respective Class A, B, C, and D addresses are shown in Figure 2-2.

Figure 2-2 Address Structure

Class A	Network	Host		
Octet	1	2	3	4

Class B	Network		Host	
Octet	1	2	3	4

Class C	Network			Host
Octet	1	2	3	4

Class D	Host			
Octet	1	2	3	4

Only the first three classes—A, B, and C—are used to address actual hosts on IP networks. Class D addresses are used for multicasting. Class E addresses are reserved for experimentation and are not shown in Figure 2-2. The following sections explore each of the five classes of addresses.

Class A Addresses

If the first bit of the first octet of an IP address is a binary 0, the address is a Class A address. With that first bit being a 0, the lowest number that can be represented is 00000000, decimal 0. The highest number that can be represented is 01111111, decimal 127. Any address that starts with a value between 0 and 127 in the first octet is a Class A address. These two numbers, 0 and 127, are reserved and cannot be used as a network address.

Class A addresses were intended to accommodate very large networks, so only the first octet is used to represent the network number. This leaves three octets, or 24 bits, to represent the host portion of the address. With 24 bits total, 2^{24} combinations are possible, yielding 16,777,216 possible addresses. Two of those possibilities, the lowest and highest values, are reserved for special purposes. The low value is 24 0s, and the high value is 24 1s. Therefore, each Class A address can support up to 16,777,214 unique host addresses.

Why are two host addresses reserved for special purposes? Every network requires a network number. A network number is an ID number that is used to refer to the entire range of hosts when building routing tables. The address that contains all 0s in the host portion is used as the network number and cannot be used to address an individual node. 46.0.0.0 is a Class A network number. Similarly, every network requires a broadcast address that can be used to address a message to every host on a network. It is created when the host portion of the address has all 1s. For example, a broadcast address for network 46.0.0.0 would be 46.255.255.255.

With almost 17 million host addresses available, a Class A network actually provides too many possibilities for one company or campus. Although it is easy to imagine an enormous global network with that many nodes, the hosts in such a network could not function as members of the same logical group. Administrators require much smaller logical groupings to control broadcasts, apply policies, and troubleshoot problems. Fortunately, the subnet mask allows subnetting, which breaks a large block of addresses into smaller groups called subnetworks. All Class A networks are subnetted. If they were not, Class A networks would represent huge waste and inefficiency.

How many Class A addresses are there? Because only the first octet is used as a network number, and it contains a value between 0 and 126, 126 Class A networks exist. Each of the 126 Class A addresses has almost 17 million possible host addresses that make up about half of the entire IPv4 address space. Recall that the network address 127.0.0.1 is reserved for the local loopback address, which is why Class A addresses stop at 126.0.0.0 and Class B addresses start at 128.0.0.0. Under this system, a mere handful of organizations control half of the available Internet addresses.

Class B Addresses

Class B addresses start with a binary 10 in the first 2 bits of the first octet. Therefore, the lowest number that can be represented with a Class B address is 10000000, decimal 128. The highest number that can be represented is 10111111, decimal 191. Any address that starts with a value in the range of 128 to 191 in the first octet is a Class B address.

Class B addresses were intended to accommodate medium-size networks. Therefore, the first two octets are used to represent the network number, which leaves two octets or 16 bits to represent the host portion of the address. With 16 bits total, 2^{16} combinations are possible, yielding 65,536 Class B addresses. Recall that two of those numbers, the lowest and highest values, are reserved for special purposes. Therefore, each Class B address can support up to 65,534 hosts. Although it is significantly smaller than the networks created by Class A addresses, a logical group of more than 65,000 hosts is still unmanageable and impractical. Therefore, like Class A networks, Class B addresses are subnetted to improve efficiency.

Because the first 2 bits of a Class B address are always 10, 14 bits are left in the network portion of the address, resulting in 2^{14} or 16,384 Class B networks. The first octet of a Class B address offers 64 possibilities, 128 to 191. The second octet has 256 possibilities, 0 to 255.

That yields 16,384 addresses, or 25 percent of the total IP space. Nevertheless, given the popularity and importance of the Internet, these addresses have run out quickly. This essentially leaves only Class C addresses available for new growth.

Classes of IP Addresses: C, D, and E

This section covers Class C, D, and E IP addresses.

Class C Addresses

A Class C address begins with binary 110. Therefore, the lowest number that can be represented is 11000000, decimal 192. The highest number that can be represented is 11011111, decimal 223. If an IPv4 address contains a number in the range of 192 to 223 in the first octet, it is a Class C address.

Class C addresses were originally intended to support small networks. The first three octets of a Class C address represent the network number. The last octet may be used for hosts. One host octet yields 256 (2^8) possibilities. After the all-0s network number and the all-1s broadcast address are subtracted, only 254 hosts may be addressed on a Class C network. Whereas Class A and Class B networks prove impossibly large without subnetting, Class C networks can impose an overly restrictive limit on hosts.

Because the first 3 bits of a Class C address are always 110, 21 bits are left in the network portion of the address, resulting in 2^{21} or 2,097,152 Class C networks. With 2,097,152 total network addresses containing a mere 254 hosts each, Class C addresses account for 12.5 percent of the Internet address space. Because Class A and B addresses are nearly exhausted, the remaining Class C addresses are all that is left to be assigned to new organizations that need IP networks. Table 2-1 summarizes the ranges and availability of the three address classes used to address Internet hosts.

Table 2-1 IP Addresses Available to Internet Hosts

Address Class	First Octet Range	Number of Possible Networks	Number of Hosts Per Network
Class A	0 to 126	127 (2 are reserved)	16,777,214
Class B	128 to 191	16,384	65,534
Class C	192 to 223	2,097,152	254

Class D Addresses

A Class D address begins with binary 1110 in the first octet. Therefore, the first octet range for a Class D address is 11100000 to 11101111, or 224 to 239. Class D addresses are not used to address individual hosts. Instead, each Class D address can be used to represent a group of hosts called a host group, or multicast group.

For example, a router configured to run Enhanced Interior Gateway Routing Protocol (EIGRP) joins a group that includes other nodes that are also running EIGRP. Members of this group still have unique IP addresses from the Class A, B, or C range, but they also listen for messages addressed to 224.0.0.10. The 224 octet designates the address as a Class D address. Therefore, a single routing update message can be sent to 224.0.0.10, and all EIGRP routers will receive it. A single message sent to several select recipients is called a multicast. Class D addresses are also called multicast addresses.

A multicast is different from a broadcast. Every device on a logical network must process a broadcast, whereas only devices configured to listen for a Class D address receive a multicast.

Class E Addresses

If the first octet of an IP address begins with 1111, the address is a Class E address. Therefore, the first octet range for Class E addresses is 11110000 to 1111111, or 240 to 255. Class E addresses are reserved for experimental purposes and should not be used to address hosts or multicast groups.

Subnet Masking

Subnet masking, or subnetting, is used to break one large group into several smaller subnetworks, as shown in Figure 2-3. These subnets can then be distributed throughout an enterprise. This results in less IP address waste and better logical organization. Formalized with RFC 950 in 1985, subnetting introduced a third level of hierarchy to the IPv4 addressing structure. The number of bits available to the network, subnet, and host portions of a given address varies depending on the size of the subnet mask.

Figure 2-3 IP Address Structure After Subnetting

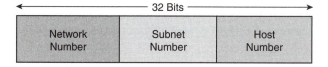

A subnet mask is a 32-bit number that acts as a counterpart to the IP address. Each bit in the mask corresponds to its counterpart bit in the IP address. Logical ANDing is applied to the address and mask. If a bit in the IP address corresponds to a 1 bit in the subnet mask, the IP address bit represents a network number. If a bit in the IP address corresponds to a 0 bit in the subnet mask, the IP address bit represents a host number.

When the subnet mask is known, it overrides the address class to determine whether a bit is either a network or a host. This allows routers to recognize addresses differently than the format dictated by class. The mask can be used to tell hosts that although their addresses are Class B, the first three octets, instead of the first two, are the network number. In this case, the additional octet acts like part of the network number, but only inside the organization where the mask is configured.

The subnet mask applied to an address ultimately determines the network and host portions of an IP address. The network and host portions change when the subnet mask changes. If a 16-bit mask, 255.255.0.0, is applied to an IP address, only the first 16 bits, or two octets, of the IP address 172.24.100.45 represent the network number. Therefore, the network number for this host address is 172.24.0.0. The colored portion of the address shown in Figure 2-4 indicates the network number.

Figure 2-4 Class B Address Without Subnetting

IP Address 172.24.100.45

Dotted Decimal	172	24	100	45
Binary	10101100	00011000	01100100	00101101

Subnet Mask 255.255.0.0

Binary	11111111	11111111	00000000	00000000
Dotted Decimal	255	255	0	0

Because the rules of class dictate that the first two octets of a Class B address are the network number, this 16-bit mask does not create subnets within the 172.24.0.0 network.

To create subnets with this Class B address, a mask must be used that identifies bits in the third or fourth octet as part of the network number.

If a 24-bit mask such as 255.255.255.0 is applied, the first 24 bits of the IP address are specified as the network number. The network number for the host in this example is 172.24.100.0. The gray portion of the address shown in Figure 2-5 indicates this.

Routers and hosts configured with this mask see all 8 bits in the third octet as part of the network number. These 8 bits are considered to be the subnet field because they represent network bits beyond the two octets prescribed by classful addressing.

Inside this network, devices configured with a 24-bit mask use the 8 bits of the third octet to determine to what subnet a host belongs. Because 8 bits remain in the host field, 254 hosts may populate each network. Just as hosts must have identical network addresses, they also must match subnet fields to communicate with each other directly. Otherwise, the services of a router must be used so that a host on one network or subnet can talk to a host on another.

Figure 2-5 Class B Address with Subnetting

IP Address 172.24.100.45			Subnet Field	
Dotted Decimal	172	24	100	45
Binary	10101100	00011000	01100100	00101101

Subnet Mask 255.255.255.0			Subnet Field	
Binary	11111111	11111111	11111111	00000000
Dotted Decimal	255	255	255	0

A Class B network with an 8-bit subnet field creates 2^8, or 256, potential subnets, each one equivalent to one Class C network. Because 8 bits remain in the host field, 254 hosts may populate each network. Two host addresses are reserved as the network number and broadcast address, respectively. By dividing a Class B network into smaller logical groups, the internetwork can be made more manageable, more efficient, and more scalable.

Notice that subnet masks are not sent as part of an IP packet header. This means that routers outside this network will not know what subnet mask is configured inside the network. An outside router, therefore, treats 172.24.100.45 as just one of 65,000 hosts that belong to the 172.24.0.0 network. In effect, subnetting classful IP addresses provides a logical structure that is hidden from the outside world.

 Interactive Media Activity   Fill in the Blank: Subnet Tool

After completing this activity, you will have a better understanding of the concept of subnetting.

IP Addressing Crisis and Solutions

This section discusses some of the restraints involved in using IPv4 addressing. It also discusses some of the various methods and solutions that can be used to help get the most out of the depleted IPv4 address pool, such as CIDR, VLSM, route aggregation, and supernetting.

IP Addressing Crisis

Class A and B addresses make up 75 percent of the IPv4 address space. However, a relative handful of organizations, fewer than 17,000, can be assigned a Class A or B network number. Class C network addresses are far more numerous than Class A and B addresses, although they account for only 12.5 percent of the possible 4 billion, or 2^{32}, IP hosts, as illustrated in Figure 2-6.

Figure 2-6 IP Address Allocation

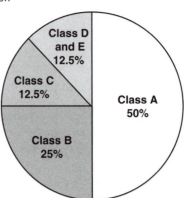

Unfortunately, Class C addresses are limited to 254 hosts, which will not meet the needs of larger organizations that cannot acquire a Class A or B address. Even if there were more Class A, B, and C addresses, too many network addresses would cause Internet routers to grind to a halt under the weight of enormous routing tables.

Ultimately, the classful system of IP addressing, even with subnetting, could not scale to effectively handle global demand for Internet connectivity. As early as 1992, the Internet Engineering Task Force (IETF) identified two specific concerns:

NOTE

CIDR is pronounced "cider." In a classful system, a router determines the class of an address and then identifies the network and host octets based on that class. With CIDR, a router uses a bit mask to determine the network and host portions of an address, which are no longer restricted to using an entire octet.

- Exhaustion of the remaining, unassigned IPv4 network addresses. At the time, the Class B space was on the verge of depletion.

- The rapid and substantial increase in the size of the Internet routing tables is because of the Internet's growth. As more Class C addresses came online, the resulting flood of new network information threatened the capability of Internet routers to cope effectively.

In the short term, the IETF decided that a retooled IPv4 would have to hold out long enough for engineers to design and deploy a completely new Internet Protocol. That new protocol, IPv6, solves the address crisis by using a 128-bit address space. After years of planning and development, IPv6 promises to be ready for wide-scale implementation. However, IPv6 continues, for the most part, to wait for that implementation.

One reason that IPv6 has not been rushed into service is that the short-term extensions to IPv4 have been so effective. By eliminating the rules of class, IPv4 now enjoys renewed viability.

Classless Interdomain Routing

Routers use a form of IPv4 addressing called Classless Interdomain Routing (CIDR) that ignores class.

CIDR was introduced in 1993 by RFCs 1517, 1518, 1519, and 1520. It was deployed in 1994. CIDR dramatically improves the scalability and efficiency of IPv4 by providing the following:

- Replacement of classful addressing with a more flexible and less wasteful classless scheme

- Enhanced route aggregation, also known as supernetting or summarization

- Supernetting, which is the combination of contiguous network addresses into a new address defined by the subnet mask

The following sections describe route aggregation, supernetting, and address allocation in more detail.

Route Aggregation and Supernetting

CIDR allows routers to aggregate, or summarize, routing information. It does this by using a bit mask instead of an address class to determine the network portion of an address. This shrinks the size of the routing tables used by the router. In other words, just one address and mask combination can represent the routes to multiple networks.

Without CIDR and route aggregation, a router must maintain many individual entries for the routes within the same network, as opposed to one route for that particular network when using CIDR addressing.

The shaded entries in Table 2-2 identify the 16 bits that, based on the rules of class, represent the network number. Classful routers are forced to handle Class B networks using these 16 bits. Because the first 16 bits of each of these eight network numbers are unique, a classful router sees eight unique networks and must create a routing table entry for each. However, these eight networks do have common bits.

Table 2-2 Route Aggregation and Supernetting

Network Number	First Octet	Second Octet	Third Octet	Fourth Octet
172.24.0.0/16	10101100	00011000	00000000	00000000
172.25.0.0/16	10101100	00011001	00000000	00000000
172.26.0.0/16	10101100	00011010	00000000	00000000
172.27.0.0/16	10101100	00011011	00000000	00000000
172.28.0.0/16	10101100	00011100	00000000	00000000
172.29.0.0/16	10101100	00011101	00000000	00000000
172.30.0.0/16	10101100	00011110	00000000	00000000
172.31.0.0/16	10101100	00011111	00000000	00000000

Table 2-3 shows that the eight network addresses have the first 13 bits in common. A CIDR-compliant router can summarize routes to these eight networks by using a 13-bit prefix. Only these eight networks share these bits:

10101100 00011

Table 2-3 Dotted-Decimal Notation

Network Number	First Octet	Second Octet	Third Octet	Fourth Octet
172.24.0.0/16	10101100	00011000	00000000	00000000
172.25.0.0/16	10101100	00011001	00000000	00000000
172.26.0.0/16	10101100	00011010	00000000	00000000
172.27.0.0/16	10101100	00011011	00000000	00000000
172.28.0.0/16	10101100	00011100	00000000	00000000
172.29.0.0/16	10101100	00011101	00000000	00000000
172.30.0.0/16	10101100	00011110	00000000	00000000
172.31.0.0/16	10101100	00011111	00000000	00000000

To represent this prefix in decimal terms, the rest of the address is padded with 0s and then paired with a 13-bit subnet mask:

10101100 00011000 00000000 00000000 = 172.24.0.0

11111111 11111000 00000000 00000000 = 255.248.0.0

Therefore, a single address and mask define a classless prefix that summarizes routes to the eight networks, 172.24.0.0/13.

By using a prefix address to summarize routes, routing table entries can be kept more manageable. The following benefits are a result of the summarized routes:

- More efficient routing
- Reduced number of CPU cycles when recalculating a routing table or when sorting through the routing table entries to find a match
- Reduced router memory requirements

Supernetting is the practice of using a bit mask to group multiple classful networks as a single network address. Supernetting and route aggregation are different names for the same process. However, the term supernetting is most often applied when the aggregated networks are under common administrative control. Supernetting takes bits from the network portion of the network mask, whereas subnetting takes bits from the host portion of the subnet mask. Supernetting and route aggregation are essentially the inverse of subnetting.

Recall that the Class A and Class B address space is almost exhausted, leaving large organizations little choice but to request multiple Class C network addresses from providers. If a company can acquire a block of contiguous Class C network addresses, supernetting can be used so that the addresses appear as a single large network, or supernet.

Supernetting and Address Allocation

Consider Company XYZ, which requires addresses for 400 hosts. Under the classful addressing system, XYZ could apply to a central Internet address authority for a Class B address. If the company got the Class B address and then used it to address one logical group of 400 hosts, tens of thousands of addresses would be wasted. A second option for XYZ would be to request two Class C network numbers, yielding 508, or 2 * 254, host addresses. The drawback of this approach is that XYZ would have to route between its own logical networks. Also, Internet routers would still need to maintain two routing table entries for the XYZ network, rather than just one.

Under a classless addressing system, supernetting allows XYZ to get the address space it needs without wasting addresses or increasing the size of routing tables unnecessarily. Using CIDR, XYZ asks for an address block from its Internet service provider (ISP), not a central authority, such as the Internet Assigned Numbers Authority (IANA). The ISP assesses XYZ's needs and allocates address space from its own large CIDR block of addresses. Providers assume the burden of managing address space in a classless system. With this system, Internet routers keep only one summary route, or supernet route, to the provider network. The provider keeps routes that are more specific to its customer networks. This method drastically reduces the size of Internet routing tables.

In the following example, XYZ receives two contiguous Class C addresses, 207.21.54.0 and 207.21.55.0. If you examine the shaded portions of Table 2-4, you will see that these network addresses have this common 23-bit prefix:

11001111 00010101 0011011

Table 2-4 Supernetting and Address Allocation

Network Number	First Octet	Second Octet	Third Octet	Fourth Octet
207.21.54.0	11001111	00010101	00110110	00000000
207.21.55.0	11001111	00010101	00110111	00000000

When the sample topology shown in Figure 2-7 is supernetted with a 23-bit mask, 207.21.54.0/23, the address space provides well over 400, or 2^9, host addresses without the tremendous waste of a Class B address. With the ISP acting as the addressing authority for a

CIDR block of addresses, the ISP's customer networks, which include XYZ, can be advertised among Internet routers as a single supernet. The ISP manages a block of 256 Class C network addresses and advertises them to the world using a 16-bit prefix:

207.21.0.0/16

Figure 2-7 Addressing with CIDR

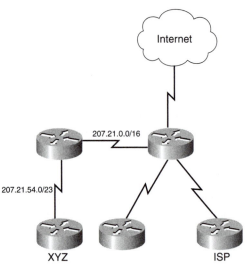

When CIDR enabled ISPs to hierarchically distribute and manage blocks of contiguous addresses, IPv4 address space enjoyed the following benefits:

- Efficient allocation of addresses
- Reduced number of routing table entries

VLSM

This section discusses VLSMs and how they can be used to further maximize IPv4 addressing efficiency.

Variable-Length Subnet Masks

VLSM allows an organization to use more than one subnet mask within the same network address space. Implementing VLSM is often called subnetting a subnet. It can be used to maximize addressing efficiency.

Consider Table 2-5, in which the subnets are created by borrowing 3 bits from the host portion of the Class C address, 207.21.24.0.

Table 2-5 Subnetting with One Mask

Subnet Number	Subnet Address
Subnet 0	207.21.24.0/27
Subnet 1	207.21.24.32/27
Subnet 2	207.21.24.64/27
Subnet 3	207.21.24.96/27
Subnet 4	207.21.24.128/27
Subnet 5	207.21.24.160/27
Subnet 6	207.21.24.192/27
Subnet 7	207.21.24.224/27

If the **ip subnet-zero** command is used, this mask creates seven usable subnets of 30 hosts each. Four of these subnets can be used to address remote offices at Sites A, B, C, and D, as shown in Figure 2-8.

Figure 2-8 Using Subnets to Address a WAN

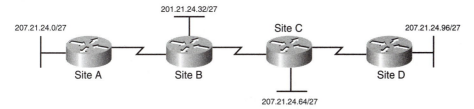

Unfortunately, only three subnets are left for future growth, and three point-to-point WAN links between the four sites remain to be addressed. If the three remaining subnets were assigned to the WAN links, the supply of IP addresses would be completely exhausted. This addressing scheme would also waste more than a third of the available address space.

There are ways to avoid this kind of waste. Over the past 20 years, network engineers have developed three critical strategies for efficiently addressing point-to-point WAN links:

- Use VLSM
- Use private addressing (RFC 1918)
- Use IP unnumbered

Private addresses and IP unnumbered are discussed in detail later in this chapter. This section focuses on VLSM. When VLSM is applied to an addressing problem, it breaks the address into groups or subnets of various sizes. Large subnets are created for addressing LANs, and very small subnets are created for WAN links and other special cases.

A 30-bit mask is used to create subnets with two valid host addresses. This is the exact number needed for a point-to-point connection. Figure 2-9 shows what happens if one of the three remaining subnets is subnetted again, using a 30-bit mask.

Figure 2-9 Subnetting with VLSMs

Subnet 0	207.21.24.0/27
Subnet 1	207.21.24.32/27
Subnet 2	207.21.24.64/27
Subnet 3	207.21.24.96/27
Subnet 4	207.21.24.128/27
Subnet 5	207.21.24.160/27
Subnet 6	207.21.24.192/27
Subnet 7	207.21.24.224/27

Sub-Subnet 0	207.21.24.192/30
Sub-Subnet 1	207.21.24.196/30
Sub-Subnet 2	207.21.24.200/30
Sub-Subnet 3	207.21.24.204/30
Sub-Subnet 4	207.21.24.208/30
Sub-Subnet 5	207.21.24.212/30
Sub-Subnet 6	207.21.24.216/30
Sub-Subnet 7	207.21.24.220/30

Subnetting the 207.21.24.192/27 subnet in this way supplies another eight ranges of addresses to be used for point-to-point networks. For example, in Figure 2-10, the network 207.21.24.192/30 can be used to address the point-to-point serial link between the Site A router and the Site B router.

Figure 2-10 Using VLSM to Address Point-to-Point Links

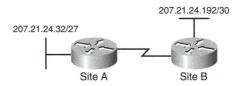

Example 2-1 shows the commands needed to configure the Site A router, labeled RTA, with a 27-bit mask on its Ethernet port and a 30-bit mask on its serial port.

Example 2-1 *Configuring VLSM*

```
RTA(config)#interface e0
RTA(config-if)#ip address 207.21.24.33 255.255.255.224
RTA(config-if)#interface s0
RTA(config-if)#ip address 207.21.24.193 255.255.255.252
```

Interactive Media Activity   Drag and Drop: VLSM Calculation

After completing this activity, you will have a better understanding of VLSM.

Lab 2.10.1   Configuring VLSM and IP Unnumbered

In this lab, you will configure VLSM and test its functionality with two different routing protocols, RIPv1 and RIPv2. Finally, you will use IP unnumbered in place of VLSM to further conserve addresses.

Classless and Classful Routing Protocols

For routers in a variably subnetted network to properly update each other, they must send masks in their routing updates. Without subnet information in the routing updates, routers would have nothing but the address class and their own subnet mask to go on. Only routing protocols that ignore the rules of address class and use classless prefixes work properly with VLSM. Table 2-6 lists common classful and classless routing protocols.

Table 2-6 Classful and Classless Routing Protocols

Classful Routing Protocols	Classless Routing Protocols
RIP Version 1	RIP Version 2
IGRP	EIGRP
EGP	OSPF
BGP3	IS-IS
	BGP4

Routing Information Protocol version 1 (RIPv1) and Interior Gateway Routing Protocol (IGRP), common interior gateway protocols, cannot support VLSM because they do not send subnet information in their updates. Upon receiving an update packet, these classful routing protocols use one of the following methods to determine an address's network prefix:

- If the router receives information about a network, and if the receiving interface belongs to that same network, but on a different subnet, the router applies the subnet mask that is configured on the receiving interface.
- If the router receives information about a network address that is not the same as the one configured on the receiving interface, it applies the default, subnet mask (by class).

Despite its limitations, RIP is a very popular routing protocol and is supported by virtually all IP routers. RIP's popularity stems from its simplicity and universal compatibility. However, the first version of RIP, RIPv1, suffers from several critical deficiencies:

- RIPv1 does not send subnet mask information in its updates. Without subnet information, VLSM and CIDR cannot be supported.
- RIPv1 broadcasts its updates, increasing network traffic.
- RIPv1 does not support authentication.

In 1988, RFC 1058 prescribed the new and improved *Routing Information Protocol version 2 (RIPv2)* to address these deficiencies. RIPv2 has the following features:

- RIPv2 sends subnet information and, therefore, supports VLSM and CIDR.
- RIPv2 multicasts routing updates using the Class D address 224.0.0.9, providing better efficiency.
- RIPv2 provides for authentication in its updates.

Because of these key features, RIPv2 should always be preferred over RIPv1, unless some legacy device on the network does not support it.

When RIP is first enabled on a Cisco router, the router listens for version 1 and 2 updates but sends only version 1. To take advantage of the RIPv2 features, turn off version 1 support, and enable version 2 updates with the following commands:

```
Router(config)#router rip
Router(config-router)#version 2
```

The straightforward RIP design ensures that it will continue to survive. A new version has already been designed to support future IPv6 networks.

Lab 2.10.2a   VLSM 1

In this lab, you create an addressing scheme using VLSM.

Lab 2.10.2b   VLSM 2

In this lab, you create an addressing scheme using VLSM.

Lab 2.10.2c   VLSM 3

In this lab, you create an addressing scheme using VLSM.

Lab 2.10.2d   VLSM 4

In this lab, you create an addressing scheme using VLSM.

Route Summarization

This section discusses some of the details of route summarization and how CIDR and VLSMs use it to deal with the size of routing tables.

An Overview of Route Summarization

The use of CIDR and VLSM not only reduces address waste, but it also promotes route aggregation, or *route summarization*. Without route summarization, Internet backbone routing would likely have collapsed sometime before 1997.

Figure 2-11 shows how route summarization reduces the burden on upstream routers. This complex hierarchy of variable-sized networks and subnetworks is summarized at various points using a prefix address until the entire network is advertised as a single aggregate route of 192.168.48.0/20.

Figure 2-11 Route Summarization

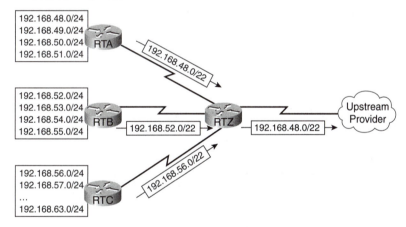

Recall that this kind of route summarization, or supernetting, is possible only if the network routers run a classless routing protocol, such as OSPF or EIGRP. Classless routing protocols carry the prefix length and subnet mask with the 32-bit address in routing updates. In Figure 2-11, the summary route that eventually reaches the provider contains a 20-bit prefix common to all the addresses in the organization. This prefix is 192.168.48.0/20, or 11000000.10101000.00110000.00000000, with a subnet mask of 11111111.11111111. 11110000.00000000. For summarization to work properly, addresses must be carefully assigned in a hierarchical fashion so that summarized addresses share the same high-order bits.

Route Flapping

Route flapping occurs when a router interface alternates rapidly between the up and down states. This can be caused by a number of factors, including a faulty interface or poorly terminated media.

Summarization can effectively insulate upstream routers from route-flapping problems. Consider RTC in Figure 2-12. If the RTC interface connected to the 200.199.56.0 network goes down, RTC removes that route from its table. If the routers were not configured to summarize, RTC would then send a triggered update to RTZ about the removal of the specific network, 200.199.56.0. In turn, RTZ would update the next router upstream, and so on. Every time these routers are updated with new information, their processors must go to work. It is possible, especially in the case of OSPF routing, that the processors can work hard enough to noticeably affect performance. Now, consider the impact on performance if the RTC interface to network 200.199.56.0 comes back up after only a few seconds. The routers update each other and recalculate. In addition, what happens when the RTC link goes back down seconds later? And then back up? This is called route flapping, and it can cripple a router with excessive updates and recalculations.

Figure 2-12 Routes Summarized to 200.199.48.0/20

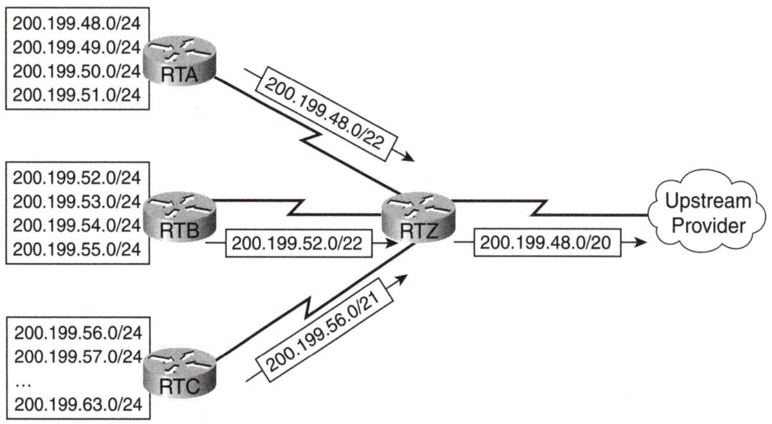

However, the summarization configuration prevents the RTC route flapping from affecting any other routers. RTC updates RTZ about a supernet, 200.199.56.0/21, which includes eight networks, 200.199.56.0 through 200.199.63.0. The loss of one network does not invalidate the route to the supernet. While RTC might be kept busy dealing with its own route flap, RTZ, all upstream routers are unaware of any downstream problem. Summarization effectively insulates the other routers from the problem of route flapping.

Private Addressing and NAT

This section explains Network Address Translation (NAT) and how it can limit the waste of IP addresses by using the private addressing scheme.

Private IP Addresses (RFC 1918)

Because TCP/IP is the dominant routed protocol in the world, most network applications and operating systems offer extensive support for it. Therefore, many designers build their networks around TCP/IP, even if they do not require Internet connectivity. Internet hosts require globally unique IP addresses. However, private hosts that are not connected to the Internet can use any valid address, as long as it is unique within the private network.

Because many private networks exist alongside public networks, just grabbing any address is strongly discouraged. RFC 1918 sets aside three blocks of IP addresses for private or internal use:

- A Class A range
- A Class B range
- A Class C range

Addresses in one of these ranges, shown in Table 2-7, are not routed on the Internet backbone. Internet routers immediately discard private addresses.

Table 2-7 Private Addresses in the WAN

Class	RFC 1918 Internal Address Range	CIDR Prefix
A	10.0.0.0 to 10.255.255.255	10.0.0.0/8
B	172.16.0.0 to 172.31.255.255	172.16.0.0/12
C	192.168.0.0 to 192.168.255.255	192.168.0.0/16

If any of the following are being addressed, these private addresses can be used instead of globally unique addresses:

- A nonpublic intranet
- A test lab
- A home network

Global addresses must be obtained from a provider or a registry at some expense.

RFC 1918 addresses have found a home in production networks as well. Earlier in this chapter, the advantages of using VLSM to address the point-to-point WAN links in an internetwork were discussed. Recall that with VLSM, you can further subnet one of the subnets left in the address space of a Class C network. Although this solution is better than wasting an entire 30-host subnet on each two-host WAN link, it still costs one subnet that could have been used for future growth. A less-wasteful solution is to address the WAN links using private network numbers. The WAN links shown in Figure 2-13 are addressed using subnets from the private address space, 10.0.0.0/8.

Figure 2-13 Using Subnets to Address the WAN

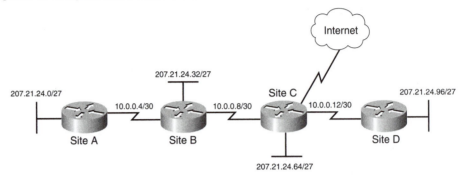

How can these routers use private addresses if LAN users at Sites A, B, C, and D expect to access the Internet? End users at these sites should have no problem, because they use globally unique addresses from the 207.21.24.0 network. The routers use their serial interfaces with private addresses merely to forward traffic and exchange routing information. Upstream providers and Internet routers see only the source and destination IP addresses in the packet. Upstream providers do not care if the packet traveled through links with private addresses at some point. In fact, many providers use RFC 1918 network numbers in the core of their network to avoid depleting their supply of globally unique addresses.

There is one trade-off when using private numbers on WAN links. The serial interfaces cannot be the original source of traffic bound for the Internet or the final destination of traffic from the Internet. Routers normally do not spend time surfing the web. Therefore, this limitation typically becomes an issue only when you're troubleshooting with Internet Control Message Protocol (ICMP), using Simple Network Management Protocol (SNMP), or connecting remotely with Telnet over the Internet. In those cases, the router can be addressed only by its globally unique LAN interfaces.

The following sections discuss implementing a private address scheme, including the pitfalls of discontiguous subnets and the advantages of NAT.

Discontiguous Subnets

Mixing private addresses with globally unique addresses can create discontiguous subnets. Discontiguous subnets are subnets from the same major network that are separated by a completely different major network or subnet.

In Figure 2-14, Site A and Site B both have LANs that are addressed using subnets from the same major network, 207.21.24.0. They are discontiguous because the 10.0.0.4/30 network separates them. Classful routing protocols—notably, RIPv1 and IGRP—cannot support discontiguous subnets because the subnet mask is not included in routing updates. If Site A and Site B are running RIPv1, Site A receives updates about network 207.21.24.0/24 but not about 207.21.24.32/27. This is because the subnet mask is not included in the update. Because Site A has an interface directly connected to that network—in this case, e0—Site A rejects the Site B route.

Figure 2-14 Discontiguous Subnets

Even some classless routing protocols require additional configuration to solve the problem of discontiguous subnets. RIPv2 and EIGRP automatically summarize on classful boundaries, unless explicitly told not to. Usually, this type of summarization is desirable. However, in the case of discontiguous subnets, you must enter the following command for both RIPv2 and EIGRP to disable automatic summarization:

```
Router(config-router)#no auto-summary
```

Finally, when using private addresses on a network that is connected to the Internet, packets and routing updates should be filtered. This is done to avoid leaking any RFC 1918 addresses between autonomous systems. If both the LAN and the provider use addresses from the 192.168.0.0/16 block, the routers could get confused if confronted with updates from both systems.

Network Address Translation (NAT)

NAT, as defined by RFC 1631, is the process of swapping one address for another in the IP packet header. In practice, NAT is used to allow hosts that are privately addressed using RFC 1918 addresses to access the Internet.

A NAT-enabled device, such as a UNIX computer or a Cisco router, operates at the border of a stub domain. An example is an internetwork that has a single connection to the outside world. When a host inside the stub domain wants to transmit to a host on the outside, it forwards the packet to the NAT-enabled device. The NAT process then looks inside the IP header and, if appropriate, replaces the inside IP address with a globally unique IP address. When an outside host sends a response, as shown in Figure 2-15, the NAT does the following:

1. Receives it.

2. Checks the current table of network address translations.

3. Replaces the destination address with the original inside source.

Figure 2-15 NAT Router

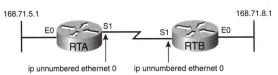

168.71.5.1   168.71.8.1

ip unnumbered ethernet 0   ip unnumbered ethernet 0

NAT translations can occur dynamically or statically and can be used for a variety of purposes.

The most powerful feature of NAT routers is their capability to use Port Address Translation (PAT), which allows multiple inside addresses to map to the same global address. This is sometimes called a many-to-one NAT. With PAT, or address overloading, literally hundreds of privately addressed nodes can access the Internet using only one global address. The NAT router keeps track of the different conversations by mapping TCP and UDP port numbers.

 Lab 2.10.4a   Network Address Translation: Static NAT and Dynamic NAT

In this lab, you learn how to configure static and dynamic NAT.

 Lab 2.10.4b   Network Address Translation: Port Address Translation and Port Forwarding

In this lab, you learn how to configure PAT and port forwarding.

IP Unnumbered

This chapter has presented several ways to maximize the use of IP addresses in an organization. In previous sections, you learned that you can avoid wasting an entire subnet on point-to-point serial links by using VLSM, or use private addresses instead. Neither technique can be supported by classful routing protocols, such as the popular RIPv1 and IGRP. Fortunately, the Cisco IOS software offers a third option for efficiently addressing serial links—IP unnumbered.

Using IP Unnumbered

When a serial interface is configured for IP unnumbered, it does not need its own address. This is because it borrows the IP address of another interface, usually a LAN interface or loopback interface. Example 2-2 shows how to configure an unnumbered interface. Not only does IP unnumbered avoid wasting addresses on point-to-point WAN links, but it also can be used with classful routing protocols, whereas VLSM and discontiguous subnets cannot. If the network runs RIPv1 or IGRP, IP unnumbered might be the only solution to maximize the addresses.

Example 2-2 *Configuring an IP Unnumbered Interface*

```
RTA(config)#interface e0
RTA(config-if)#ip address 168.71.5.1 255.255.255.0
RTA(config-if)#interface s1
RTA(config-if)#ip unnumbered e0
RTB(config)#interface e0
RTB(config-if)#ip address 168.71.8.1 255.255.255.0
RTB(config-if)#interface s1
RTB(config-if)#ip unnumbered e0
```

RTA e0, 168.71.5.1, and RTB e0, 168.71.8.1, can communicate using TCP/IP over this serial link, even though they do not belong to the same IP network, as shown in Figure 2-16. This is possible because the serial link is a point-to-point link, so there is no confusion about which device a packet is originating from or destined for. In this case, the command **ip unnumbered e0** is entered in serial 1 interface configuration mode on both RTA and RTB. Configuring IP unnumbered on an interface has two ground rules:

- The interface is both serial and connected by way of a point-to-point link.
- The same major network with the same mask is used to address the LAN interfaces that lend their IP address on both sides of the WAN link.

       or

   Different major networks with no subnetting are used to address the LAN interfaces on both sides of the WAN link.

Figure 2-16 IP Unnumbered Interfaces

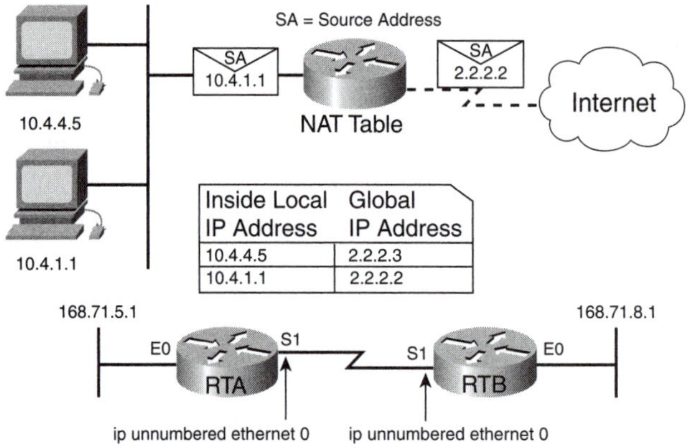

Certain drawbacks come with using IP unnumbered:

- The use of ping cannot determine whether the interface is up, because the interface has no IP address.
- A network IOS image cannot boot over an unnumbered serial interface.
- IP security options cannot be supported on an unnumbered interface.

DHCP and Easy IP

This section discusses DHCP and its operation. It covers how to configure DHCP, and use Easy IP as well.

DHCP Overview

After designing a scalable IP addressing scheme for the enterprise, the next step is implementation. Routers, servers, and other key nodes usually require special attention from administrators. However, desktop clients are often automatically assigned IP configurations using Dynamic Host Configuration Protocol (DHCP). Because desktop clients typically make up the bulk of network nodes, DHCP is good news for systems administrators. Small offices and home offices can also take advantage of DHCP by using Easy IP, a Cisco IOS software feature set that combines DHCP with NAT functions.

DHCP works by configuring servers to give out IP configuration information to clients. Clients lease the information from the server for an administratively defined period. When the lease is up, the host must ask for another address, although it is typically reassigned the same one. Figures 2-17 and 2-18 illustrate this process. In Figure 2-17, Host A issues a DHCP request for an IP address. In Figure 2-18, the DHCP server replies to the DHCP request by leasing an IP address from the configured IP address pool.

Figure 2-17 Simple DHCP Operation: Client/Server

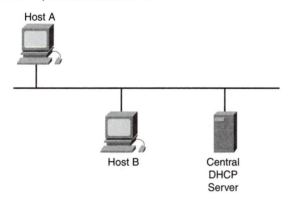

Figure 2-18 Simple DHCP Operation: Reply

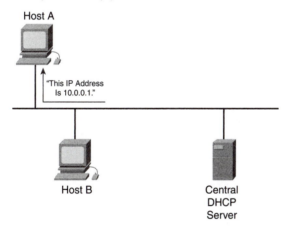

Administrators typically prefer to use a Microsoft 2000 server or a UNIX computer to offer DHCP services because these solutions are highly scalable and relatively easy to manage. Even so, the Cisco IOS software offers an optional, fully featured DHCP server, which leases configurations for 24 hours by default.

Administrators set up DHCP servers to assign addresses from predefined pools. DHCP servers can also provide other information:

- Default gateway address
- DNS server addresses
- WINS server addresses
- Domain names

NOTE

BOOTP was originally defined in RFC 951 in 1985. It is the predecessor of DHCP, and it shares some operational characteristics. Both protocols use UDP ports 67 and 68, which are well-known as BOOTP ports, because BOOTP came before DHCP.

Most DHCP servers also let you specifically define what client MAC addresses can be serviced and automatically assign the same number to a particular host each time.

DHCP Operation

The DHCP client configuration process is shown in Figure 2-19.

Figure 2-19 DHCP Operation

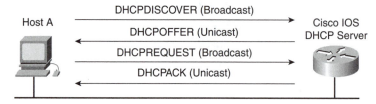

The DHCP client configuration process follows these steps:

1. When a client is set up for DHCP and needs an IP configuration, typically at boot time, it tries to locate a DHCP server by sending a broadcast called a DHCPDISCOVER.

2. The server sends a DHCPOFFER unicast to the client. When the server receives the broadcast, it determines whether it can service the request from its own database. If it cannot, the server might forward the request to another DHCP server or servers, depending on its configuration. If it can service the request, the DHCP server offers the client IP configuration information in the form of a unicast DHCPOFFER. The DHCPOFFER is a proposed configuration that may include IP address, DNS server address, and lease time.

3. The client sends a DHCPREQUEST broadcast to all nodes. If the client finds the offer agreeable, it sends another broadcast. This broadcast is a DHCPREQUEST, specifically requesting those particular IP parameters. Why does the client broadcast the request instead of unicasting it to the server? A broadcast is used because the very first message, the DHCPDISCOVER, might have reached more than one DHCP server. After all, it was a broadcast. If more than one server makes an offer, the broadcasted DHCPREQUEST lets the servers know which offer was accepted, which is usually the first offer received.

4. The server sends a DHCPACK unicast to the client. The server that receives the DHCPREQUEST makes the configuration official by sending a unicast acknowledgment, the DHCPACK. Note that it is possible but highly unlikely that the server will not send the DHCPACK, because it might have leased that information to another client in the interim. Receipt of the DHCPACK message lets the client begin using the assigned address immediately.

Depending on an organization's policies, it might be possible for an end user or administrator to statically assign a host an IP address that belongs in the DHCP server address pool. Just in case, the Cisco IOS software DHCP server always checks to make sure that an address is not in use before the server offers it to a client. The server issues ICMP echo requests (pings) to a pool address before sending the DHCPOFFER to a client. Although it can be configured, the default number of pings used to check for potential IP address conflict is two. The more pings, the longer the configuration process takes.

Configuring the IOS DHCP Server

The DHCP server process is enabled by default on versions of the Cisco IOS software that support it. If for some reason the DHCP server process becomes disabled, you can reenable it by using the **service dhcp** global configuration command. The **no service dhcp** command disables the server.

Like NAT, DHCP servers require that the administrator define a pool of addresses. In Example 2-3, the **ip dhcp pool** command defines which addresses are assigned to hosts.

Example 2-3 *Configuring a DHCP Address Pool*

```
RTA(config)#ip dhcp pool room12
RTA(dhcp-config)#network 172.16.1.0 255.255.255.0
RTA(dhcp-config)#exit
RTA(config-if)#ip dhcp excluded-address 172.16.1.1 172.16.1.10
```

The first command, **ip dhcp pool room12**, creates a pool named room12 and puts the router in a specialized DHCP configuration mode. In this mode, you use the **network** statement to define the range of addresses to be leased. If specific addresses are to be excluded on this network, return to global configuration mode and enter the **ip dhcp excluded-address** command.

The **ip dhcp excluded-address** command configures the router to exclude 172.16.1.1 through 172.16.1.10 when assigning addresses to clients. The **ip dhcp excluded-address** command may be used to reserve addresses that are statically assigned to key hosts.

A DHCP server can configure much more than an IP address. Other IP configuration values can be set from DHCP configuration mode, as shown in Example 2-4.

Example 2-4 *Assigning Key DHCP Information*

```
RTA(config)#ip dhcp pool room12
RTA(dhcp-config)#dns-server 172.16.1.2
RTA(dhcp-config)#netbios-name-server 172.16.1.2
RTA(config-if)#default-router 172.16.1.1
```

IP clients will not get very far without a default gateway, which can be set by using the **default-router** command. The address of the DNS server, **dns-server**, and WINS server, **netbios-name-server**, can be configured here as well. The IOS DHCP server can configure clients with virtually any TCP/IP information.

Table 2-8 lists the key IOS DHCP server commands. These commands are entered in DHCP pool configuration mode, identified by the router(dhcp-config)# prompt.

Table 2-8 Key DHCP Server Commands

Command	Description
network *network-number* [*mask* | */prefix-length*]	Specifies the subnet network number and mask of the DHCP address pool. The *prefix-length* portion specifies the number of bits that comprise the address prefix. The prefix is the alternative way of specifying the client's network mask. The *prefix-length* must be preceded by a slash (/).
default-router address [*address2...address8*]	Specifies the IP address of the default router or default gateway for a DHCP client. One IP address is required, although up to eight addresses can be specified in one command line.
dns-server address [*address2...address8*]	Specifies the IP address of a DNS server that is available to a DHCP client. One IP address is required, although up to eight addresses can be specified in one command line.
netbios-name-server address [*address2...address8*]	Specifies the IP address of the NetBIOS WINS server that is available to a Microsoft DHCP client. One IP address is required, although up to eight addresses can be specified in one command line.
domain-name *domain*	Specifies the client's domain name.
lease {*days* [*hours*] [*minutes*] | *infinite*}	Specifies the duration of the DHCP lease. The default is a one-day lease.

Use the EXEC mode commands, shown in Table 2-9, to monitor DHCP server operation.

Table 2-9 Key Commands for Monitoring DHCP Operation

Command	Definition
show ip dhcp binding [*address*]	Displays a list of all bindings (MAC to IP address) created on a specific DHCP server.
show ip dhcp conflict [*address*]	Displays a list of all address conflicts recorded by a specific DHCP server.
show ip dhcp database [*url*]	Displays recent activity on the DHCP database. (Use this command in privileged EXEC mode.)
show ip dhcp server statistics	Displays count information about server statistics and messages sent and received.

Easy IP

Easy IP is a combination suite of Cisco IOS software features that allows a router to negotiate its own IP address, as a DHCP client, and to do NAT through that negotiated address. Easy IP is typically deployed on a small office, home office (SOHO) router. It is useful in cases where a small LAN connects to the Internet by way of a provider that dynamically assigns only one IP address for the entire remote site, as shown in Figure 2-20.

Figure 2-20 Cisco IOS Easy IP

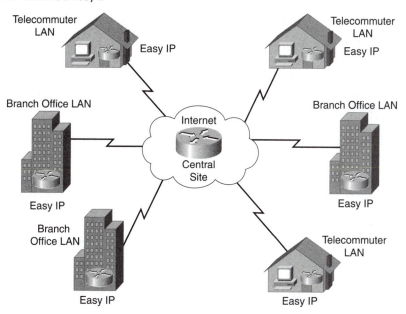

A SOHO router with the Easy IP feature set uses DHCP, as a server, to automatically address local LAN clients with RFC 1918 addresses. When the router dynamically receives its WAN interface address by way of PPP, it uses NAT overload to translate between local inside addresses and its single global address. Therefore, both the LAN side and the WAN side are dynamically configured with little or no administrative intervention. In effect, Easy IP offers plug-and-play routing.

Helper Addresses

This section describes how networks and routers use helper addresses to forward broadcasts to another server or router on another network. This section describes some of the purposes of and scenarios in which to use helper addresses.

Using Helper Addresses

DHCP is not the only critical service that uses broadcasts. Cisco routers and other devices might use broadcasts to locate TFTP servers. Some clients might need to broadcast to locate a TACACS security server. In a complex hierarchical network, clients might not reside on the same subnet as key servers. Such remote clients broadcast to locate these servers, but routers, by default, do not forward client broadcasts beyond their subnet. Some clients are unable to make a connection without services such as DHCP. For this reason, the administrator must provide DHCP and DNS servers on all subnets or use the Cisco IOS software helper address feature. Running services such as DHCP or DNS on several computers creates overhead and administrative problems, so the first option is not very appealing. When possible, administrators use the **ip helper-address** command to relay broadcast requests for these key User Datagram Protocol (UDP) services.

By using the **ip helper-address** command, a router can be configured to accept a broadcast request for a UDP service and then forward it as a unicast to a specific IP address, as shown in Figure 2-21. Alternatively, the router can forward these requests as directed broadcasts to a specific network or subnetwork.

Figure 2-21 Helper Addresses

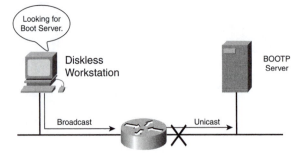

Configuring IP Helper Addresses

To configure the helper address, identify the router interface that will receive the broadcasts for UDP services. In interface configuration mode, use the **ip helper-address** command to define the address to which UDP broadcasts for services should be forwarded.

By default, the **ip helper-address** command forwards the eight UDP services listed in Table 2-10.

Table 2-10 Default Forward UDP Services

Service	Port
Time	37
TACACS	49
DNS	53
BOOTP/DHCP Server	67
BOOTP/DHCP Client	68
TFTP	69
NetBIOS name service	137
NetBIOS datagram service	138

What if Company XYZ needs to forward requests for a service not on this list? The Cisco IOS software provides the global configuration command **ip forward-protocol** to allow an administrator to forward any UDP port in addition to the default eight. To forward UDP on port 517, use the global configuration command **ip forward-protocol udp 517**. This command is used not only to add a UDP port to the default eight, but also to subtract an unwanted service from the default group. When forwarding DHCP, TFTP, and DNS without forwarding Time, TACACS, and NetBIOS, the Cisco IOS software requires that the router be configured according to the syntax shown in Example 2-5.

Example 2-5 *Forwarding UDP Services*

```
RTA(config-if)#ip helper-address 192.168.1.254
RTA(config-if)#exit
RTA(config)#ip forward-protocol udp 517
RTA(config)#no ip forward-protocol udp 37
RTA(config)#no ip forward-protocol udp 49
RTA(config)#no ip forward-protocol udp 137
RTA(config)#no ip forward-protocol udp 138
```

IP Helper Address Example

Consider the complex sample helper address configuration shown in Figure 2-22. You want Host A to automatically obtain its IP configuration from the DHCP server at 172.24.1.9. Because RTA will not forward the Host A DHCPDISCOVER broadcast, RTA must be configured to help Host A.

Figure 2-22 IP Helper Address Example

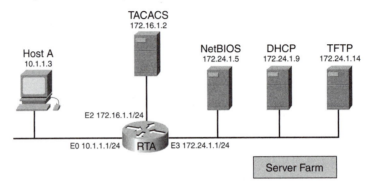

To configure RTA e0, the interface that receives the Host A broadcasts, to relay DHCP broadcasts as a unicast to the DHCP server, use the following commands:

```
RTA(config)#interface e0
RTA(config-if)#ip helper-address 172.24.1.9
```

With this simple configuration, Host A broadcasts using any of the eight default UDP ports that are relayed to the DHCP server's IP address. However, what if Host A also needs to use the services of the NetBIOS server at 172.24.1.5? As configured, RTA forwards NetBIOS broadcasts from Host A to the DHCP server. Moreover, if Host A sends a broadcast TFTP packet, RTA also forwards this to the DHCP server at 172.24.1.9. What is needed in this example is a helper address configuration that relays broadcasts to all servers on the segment. The following commands configure a directed broadcast to the IP subnet that is being used as a server farm:

```
RTA(config)#interface e0
RTA(config-if)#ip helper-address 172.24.1.255
```

Configuring a directed broadcast to the server segment, 172.24.1.255, is more efficient than entering the IP address of every server that could potentially respond to the Host A UDP broadcasts.

Finally, some devices on the Host A segment need to broadcast to the TACACS server, which does not reside in the server farm. Configure the RTA e0 to make it work by adding the command **ip helper-address 172.16.1.2**.

Verify the correct helper configuration with the **show ip interface** command, as shown in Example 2-6.

Example 2-6 *Verifying IP Helper Address Configuration*

```
RTA#show ip interface e0
Ethernet0 is up, line protocol is up
    Internet address is 10.1.1.1/24
    Broadcast address is 255.255.255.255
    Address determined by setup command
    MTU is 1500 bytes
    Helper addresses are 172.24.1.255
                         172.16.1.2
    Directed broadcast forwarding is disabled
    <output omitted>
```

NOTE

Because directed broadcasts—particularly Internet Control Message Protocol (ICMP) directed broadcasts—have been abused by malicious persons, it is recommended that security-conscious users disable the **ip directed-broadcast** command on any interface where directed broadcasts are unneeded and that they use access lists to limit the number of exploded packets.

Notice that the RTA interface e3 in Example 2-7, which connects to the server farm, is not configured with helper addresses. However, the output shows that for this interface, directed broadcast forwarding is disabled. This means that the router does not convert the logical broadcast 172.24.1.255 into a physical broadcast with a Layer 2 address of FF-FF-FF-FF-FF-FF.

Example 2-7 *Verifying Directed Broadcast Forwarding*

```
RTA#show ip interface e3
Ethernet3 is up, line protocol is up
    Internet address is 172.24.1.1/24
    Broadcast address is 255.255.255.255
    Address determined by setup command
    MTU is 1500 bytes
    Helper addresses is not set
    Directed broadcast forwarding is disabled
    <output omitted>
```

To allow all the nodes in the server farm to receive the broadcasts at Layer 2, configure e3 to forward directed broadcasts with the following commands:

```
RTA(config)#interface e3
RTA(config-if)#ip directed-broadcast
```

Lab 2.10.3   Using DHCP and IP Helper Addresses

In this lab, configure a Cisco router to act as a DHCP server for clients on two separate subnets and the IP helper address feature to forward DHCP requests from a remote subnet.

IPv6

IPv6 is an alternative and a solution to the IPv4 address crisis. This section explains what IPv6 is and describes its address structure.

IP Address Issues Solutions

This chapter has shown that IPv4 addressing faces two major issues:

- The depletion of addresses, particularly the key medium-sized space
- The pervasive growth of Internet routing tables, which is illustrated in Figure 2-23

Figure 2-23 Growth of Routing Tables

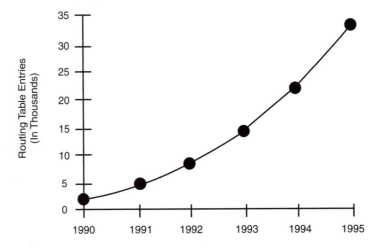

In the early 1990s, CIDR ingeniously built on the concept of the address mask and stepped forward to temporarily alleviate these overwhelming problems. CIDR's hierarchical nature dramatically improved IPv4's scalability. Once again, a hierarchical design has proven to be a scalable one.

Yet even with subnetting in 1985, variable-length subnetting in 1987, and CIDR in 1993, a hierarchical structure could not save IPv4 from one simple problem: not enough addresses exist to meet future needs. At roughly four billion possibilities, the IPv4 address space is formidable. However, it will not suffice in a future world of mobile Internet-enabled devices and IP-addressable household appliances.

Recent short-term IPv4 solutions to the address crunch have been developed. These include RFC 1918, which sets aside private addresses for unlimited internal use, and NAT, which allows thousands of hosts to access the Internet with only a handful of valid addresses.

However, the ultimate solution to the address shortage is the introduction of IPv6 and its 128-bit address. Developed to create a supply of addresses that would outlive demand, IPv6 is on course to eventually replace IPv4. IPv6's large address space will provide not only far more addresses than IPv4, but additional levels of hierarchy as well.

In 1994, the IETF proposed IPv6 in RFC 1752, and a number of working groups were formed in response. IPv6 covers issues such as the following:

- Address depletion
- Quality of service
- Address autoconfiguration
- Authentication
- Security

It will not be easy for organizations deeply invested in the IPv4 scheme to migrate to a totally new architecture. As long as IPv4, with its recent extensions and CIDR-enabled hierarchy, remains viable, administrators will shy away from adopting IPv6. A new IP protocol requires new software, new hardware, and new methods of administration. It is likely that IPv4 and IPv6 will coexist, even within an autonomous system, for years.

IPv6 Address Format

As defined in RFC 1884 and later revised in RFC 2373, IPv6 addresses are 128-bit identifiers for interfaces and sets of interfaces, not nodes. Three general types of addresses exist:

- *Unicast*—An identifier for a single interface. A packet sent to a unicast address is delivered to the interface identified by that address.
- *Anycast*—An identifier for a set of interfaces that typically belong to different nodes. A packet sent to an anycast address is delivered to the nearest interface in the anycast group.
- *Multicast*—An identifier for a set of interfaces that typically belong to different nodes. A packet sent to a multicast address is delivered to all interfaces in the multicast group.

To write 128-bit addresses so that they are more readable to human eyes, the IPv6 architects abandoned dotted-decimal notation in favor of a hexadecimal format. Therefore, IPv6 is written as 32-hex digits, with colons separating the values of the eight 16-bit pieces of the address.

NOTE

128 bits allows for 340,282,366,920,938,463, 463,374,607,431,768,211, 456 possibilities.

IPv6 addresses are written in hexadecimal:

1080:0000:0000:0000:0008:0800:200C:417A

Leading 0s in each 16-bit value can be omitted, so this address can be expressed as follows:

1080:0:0:0:8:800:200C:417A

Because IPv6 addresses, especially in the early implementation phase, might contain consecutive 16-bit values of 0, one such string of 0s per address can be omitted and replaced by a double colon. As a result, this address can be shortened as follows:

1080::8:800:200C:417A

Under current plans, IPv6 nodes that connect to the Internet will use what is called an aggregatable global unicast address. This is the familiar counterpart to the IPv4 global addresses. Like CIDR-enhanced IPv4, aggregatable global unicast addresses rely on hierarchy to keep Internet routing tables manageable. IPv6 global unicast addresses feature three levels of hierarchy:

- *Public topology* —The collection of providers that offer Internet connectivity.
- *Site topology* —The level local to an organization that does not provide connectivity to nodes outside itself.
- *Interface identifier* —The level specific to a node's individual interface.

This three-level hierarchy is reflected by the structure of the aggregatable global unicast address (see Figure 2-24), which includes the following fields:

- *Format Prefix (FP) field, 3 bits* —The 3-bit FP is used to identify the type of address—unicast, multicast, and so on. The bits 001 identify aggregatable global unicasts.
- *Top-Level Aggregation Identifier (TLA ID) field, 13 bits* —The TLA ID field is used to identify the authority responsible for the address at the highest level of the routing hierarchy. Internet routers necessarily maintain routes to all TLA IDs. With 13 bits set aside, this field can represent up to 8192 TLAs.
- *Reserved (Res) field, 8 bits* —IPv6 architecture defined the Res field so that the TLA or NLA IDs could be expanded as future growth warrants. Currently, this field must be set to 0.
- *Next-Level Aggregation Identifier (NLA ID) field, 24 bits* —The NLA ID field is used by organizations assigned a TLA ID to create an addressing hierarchy and to identify sites.
- *Site-Level Aggregation Identifier (SLA ID) field, 16 bits* —The SLA ID is used by an individual organization to create its own local addressing hierarchy and to identify subnets.
- *Interface ID field, 64 bits* —The Interface ID field is used to identify individual interfaces on a link. This field is analogous to the host portion of an IPv4 address, but it is

derived using the IEEE EUI-64 format. When this field is on LAN interfaces, the Interface ID adds a 16-bit field to the interface MAC address.

Figure 2-24 IPv6 Address Format

Number of Bits

3	13	8	24	16	64
FP	TLA ID	Res	NLA ID	SLA ID	Interface ID
Public Topology				Site Topology	Interface Identifier

In addition to the global unicast address space, IPv6 offers internal network numbers, or site local use addresses. These are analogous to RFC 1918 addresses. If a node is not normally addressed with a global unicast address or an internal site local use address, it can be addressed using a link local use address, which is specific to a network segment.

Summary

This chapter described how all of the following can enable more efficient use of IP addresses:

- Subnet masks
- VLSMs
- Private addressing
- NAT

This chapter also showed that hierarchical addressing allows for efficient allocation of addresses and a reduced number of routing table entries. VLSMs, specifically, provide the capability to include more than one subnet mask within a network and the capability to subnet an already subnetted network address. Proper IP addressing is required to ensure the most efficient network operations. Finally, the IPv6 addressing format was presented.

Key Terms

anycast   An identifier for a set of interfaces that typically belong to different nodes. A packet sent to an anycast address is delivered to the nearest, or first, interface in the anycast group.

CIDR (classless interdomain routing)   An IP addressing scheme that replaces the older system based on Classes A, B, and C. With CIDR, a single IP address can be used to designate many unique IP addresses.

Format Prefix (FP) field   The 3-bit FP identifies the type of address—unicast, multicast, and so on. The bits 001 identify aggregatable global unicasts.

interface identifier   The level specific to a node's individual interface.

Interface ID field   The 64-bit Interface ID field identifies individual interfaces on a link. This field is analogous to the host portion of an IPv4 address, but it is derived using the IEEE EUI-64 format. When this field is on LAN interfaces, the Interface ID adds a 16-bit field to the interface MAC address.

multicast   An identifier for a set of interfaces that typically belong to different nodes. A packet sent to a multicast address is delivered to all interfaces in the multicast group.

Next-Level Aggregation Identifier (NLA ID) field   The 24-bit NLA ID field is used to identify ISPs. The field itself can be organized to reflect a hierarchy or a multitiered relationship among providers.

public topology   The collection of providers that offer Internet connectivity.

Reserved (Res) field   The IPv6 architecture defines the 8-bit Res field so that the TLA or NLA IDs can be expanded as future growth warrants. Currently, this field must be set to 0.

RIP (Routing Information Protocol)   An Interior Gateway Protocol (IGP) supplied with the FreeBSD version of UNIX. The most common IGP in the Internet. RIP uses hop count as a routing metric.

RIPv2 (Routing Information Protocol version 2)   Defined in RFC 1723 and supported in Cisco IOS software versions 11.1 and later. RIPv2 is not a new protocol; it is just RIPv1 with some extensions to bring it up-to-date with modern routing environments. RIPv2 has been updated to support VLSM, authentication, and multicast updates.

route summarization   The consolidation of advertised addresses in OSPF and IS-IS. In OSPF, this causes a single summary route to be advertised to other areas by an area border router.

Site-Level Aggregation Identifier (SLA ID) field   The 16-bit SLA ID is used by an individual organization to create its own local addressing hierarchy and to identify subnets.

site topology   The level local to an organization that does not provide connectivity to nodes outside itself.

Top-Level Aggregation Identifier (TLA ID) field   The 13-bit TLA ID field is used to identify the authority responsible for the address at the highest level of the routing hierarchy. Internet routers necessarily maintain routes to all TLA IDs. With 13 bits set aside, this field can represent up to 8192 TLAs.

unicast   An identifier for a single interface. A packet sent to a unicast address is delivered to the interface identified by that address.

VLSM (variable-length subnet masking)   The ability to specify a different subnet mask for the same network number on different subnets. VLSM can help optimize available address space.

Check Your Understanding

Complete all of the review questions to test your understanding of the topics and concepts in this chapter. The answers appear in Appendix B, "Answers to the Check Your Understanding Questions."

For additional, more in-depth questions, refer to the chapter-specific study guides on the companion CD-ROM.

1. What feature lets a Cisco router act as a DHCP client?

   A. NAT

   B. DHCP

   C. DNS

   D. Easy IP

2. What is a summarization address for the networks 172.21.136.0/24 and 172.21.143.0/24?

   A. 172.21.136.0/21

   B. 172.21.136.0/20

   C. 172.21.136.0/22

   D. 172.21.128.0/21

3. The subnet 172.6.32.0/20 is again subnetted to 172.6.32.0/26. What is the result?

   A. 1024 subnets

   B. 64 hosts per subnet

   C. 62 hosts per subnet

   D. 2044 subnets

4. What routing protocol does not contain subnet mask information in its routing updates?

   A. EIGRP

   B. OSPF

   C. RIP

   D. RIPv2

5. What method is used to represent a collection of IP network addresses with a single IP network address?

   A. Classful routing

   B. Subnetting

   C. Address translation

   D. Route summarization

6. According to RFC 1918, which of the following is a private Internet address?

   A. 10.215.34.124

   B. 192.32.146.23

   C. 172.34.221.18

   D. 119.12.73.215

7. Which of the following is a characteristic of IP unnumbered?

   A. Avoids wasted addresses on multiaccess links

   B. Efficient addressing on Ethernet links

   C. Uses another router interface address

   D. May be used with classful and classless routing protocols

8. How many bits make up an IPv6 address?

   A. 32

   B. 48

   C. 64

   D. 128

9. What is the purpose of IP helper addresses?

   A. To relay key UDP broadcast requests to hosts on the same subnet

   B. To relay key UDP broadcast requests to hosts on the other subnets

   C. To relay key TCP broadcast requests to hosts on other subnets

   D. To relay key TCP broadcast requests to hosts on the same subnet

10. What are the three general types of IPv6 addresses?

   A. Class 1, Class 2, Class 3

   B. Class A, Class B, Class C

   C. Unicast, anycast, multicast

   D. Public, site, interface

Objectives

Upon completing this chapter, you will be able to

- Understand the fundamentals of routing
- Configure default routing
- Configure floating static routes
- Understand how convergence issues affect routing
- Determine route calculation

You can reinforce your understanding of the objectives covered in this chapter by opening the interactive media activities on the CD accompanying this book and performing the lab activities collected in the *Cisco Networking Academy Program CCNP 1: Advanced Routing Lab Companion*. Throughout this chapter, you will see references to these activities by title and by icon. They look like this:

 Interactive Media Activity

 Lab Activity

Chapter 3

Routing Overview

Many of the scalable design features explored in the first two chapters, such as load balancing and route summarization, work very differently depending on the routing protocol used. Routing protocols are the rules that govern the exchange of routing information between routers. The Transmission Control Protocol/Internet Protocol (TCP/IP) open architecture and global popularity have encouraged the development of more than a half-dozen prominent IP routing protocols. Each protocol has a unique combination of strengths and weaknesses. Because routing protocols are key to network performance, you need to understand the following attributes of each protocol:

- Convergence times
- Overhead
- Scalability features

This chapter explores various routing processes, including default routing, floating static routes, convergence, and route calculation.

Routing

One of a router's primary jobs is to determine the best path to a given destination. A router learns paths, or routes, from the static configuration entered by an administrator or dynamically from other routers, through routing protocols. Routers keep a routing table in RAM. A routing table is a list of the best-known available routes. Routers use this table to make decisions about how to forward a packet.

Routing Fundamentals

To view the TCP/IP routing table, issue the **show ip route** command. A routing table maps network prefixes to an outbound interface, as shown in Example 3-1. When RTA receives a packet destined for 192.168.4.46, it looks for the prefix 192.168.4.0/24 in the routing table. RTA then forwards the packet out an interface, such as Ethernet0, based on the routing table entry. If RTA receives a packet destined for 10.3.21.5/16, it sends that packet out Serial0 (S0).

Example 3-1 show ip route *Command*

```
RTA#show ip route
Codes: C - connected, S - static, I - IGRP, R - RIP, M - mobile
       B - BGP, D - EIGRP, EX - EIGRP external, O - OSPF
IA - OSPF inter area, N1 - OSPF NSSA external type 1
N2 - OSPF NSSA external type 2, E1 - OSPF external type 1
E2 - OSPF external type 2, E - EGP, i - IS-IS
L1 - IS-IS level-1, L2 - IS-IS level-2, ia - IS-IS inter area
          * - candidate default, U - per-user static route, o - ODR
          P - periodic downloaded static route


Gateway of last resort is not set


C    192.168.4.0/24 is directly connected, Ethernet0
     10.0.0.0/16 is subnetted, 3 subnets
C    10.3.0.0 is directly connected, Serial0
C    10.4.0.0 is directly connected, Serial1
C    10.5.0.0 is directly connected, Ethernet1
```

The first few lines in Example 3-1 list the possible codes that designate how the router learned the route. This table shows four routes for directly connected networks. They are labeled with a C in the routing table. RTA drops any packet destined for a network that is not listed in the routing table. To forward to other destinations, the routing table for RTA needs to include more routes. You can add new routes by using one of the following methods:

- *Static routing*—An administrator manually defines routes to one or more destination networks.
- *Dynamic routing*—Routers follow rules defined by routing protocols to exchange routing information and independently select the best path.

Administratively defined routes are called static routes, because they do not change until a network administrator manually programs the changes. Table 3-1 compares the advantages and disadvantages of static routing. Routes learned from other routers are dynamic, because they change automatically as neighboring routers update each other with new information. Table 3-2 compares the advantages and disadvantages of dynamic routing. Each method has fundamental advantages and disadvantages.

Table 3-1 Advantages and Disadvantages of Static Routing

Static Routing Advantages	Static Routing Disadvantages
Low processor overhead. Routers do not spend valuable CPU cycles calculating the best path. This requires less memory, less processing power, and therefore a less-expensive router.	High maintenance configuration. Administrators must configure all static routes manually. Complex networks might require constant reconfiguration, which is impractical.
No bandwidth utilization. Routers do not take up bandwidth updating each other about static routes.	No adaptability. Statically configured routes cannot adapt to changes in link status.
Secure operation. Routers that do not send updates do not inadvertently advertise network information to an untrusted source. Routers that do not accept routing updates are less vulnerable to attacks.	
Predictability. Static routes let an administrator precisely control the router path selection. Dynamic routing sometimes yields unexpected results, even in small networks.	

Table 3-2 Advantages and Disadvantages of Dynamic Routing

Dynamic Routing Advantages	Dynamic Routing Disadvantages
High degree of adaptability. Routers automatically learn a network's topology and select optimum paths.	Increased processor overhead and memory utilization. Dynamic routing processes can require a significant amount of CPU time and system memory.
Low maintenance configuration. After the basic parameters for a routing protocol are set correctly, administrative intervention is not required.	High bandwidth utilization. Routers use bandwidth to send and receive routing updates, which can detrimentally affect performance on slow WAN links.
Routers can alert each other about links that have gone down or about newly discovered paths.	

The following sections describe how to configure both static and dynamic routing on a Cisco router.

Static Routing

Static routing is useful in networks that do not have multiple paths to any destination network. Static routing reduces the memory and processing burdens on a router. Even on large internetworks, administrators often configure static routes on access routers that connect stub

networks. Stub networks have only one way in and one way out. In Figure 3-1, RTZ is configured with a static route to 172.24.4.0/24.

Figure 3-1 Static Route Example

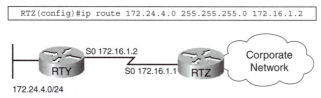

To configure static routing on a Cisco router, use the **ip route** command. This command has
the following syntax:

```
Router(config)#ip route destination-prefix destination-prefix-mask
    {address | interface} [distance] [tag tag] [permanent]
```

Table 3-3 describes the parameters that are used with this command.

Table 3-3 ip route Command Syntax

Parameter	Description
destination-prefix	The IP network or subnetwork address for the destination.
destination-prefix-mask	Subnet mask for the destination IP network address.
address	IP address of the next hop that can be used to reach the network.
interface	Network interface to use.
distance	Optional. An administrative distance.
tag *tag*	Optional. A tag value that can be used as a match value for controlling redistribution using route maps.
permanent	Optional. A specification that the route will not be removed, even if the interface shuts down.

You can manually add an entry to a routing table by using one of the following versions of the
ip route command:

```
RTA(config)#ip route 10.6.0.0 255.255.0.0 s1
```

or

```
RTA(config)#ip route 10.7.0.0 255.255.0.0 10.4.0.2
```

Both of these global configuration commands add a static route to the routing table. The first
command maps a network prefix, 10.6.0.0/16, to a local physical interface, S1, on the router.
A directly connected network is also mapped to an interface, as shown in Example 3-1. If the
static route is created using the local interface, the administrative distance is 0 because it is
treated like a directly connected interface. The second command maps the network prefix,

10.7.0.0/16, to the next-hop address, 10.4.0.2. When the next-hop address is used, the administrative distance is 1.

In Example 3-2, the route to 10.6.0.0 is identified as a static route by the S at the beginning of the line. However, it is formatted similarly to a directly connected route. This is because the router has been configured to forward packets for 10.6.0.0 out S1. The entry in the routing table for the static route to 10.7.0.0 is configured with a next-hop address. This entry in the routing table is similar to dynamic routes. The next-hop address is included in the routing table because the packets destined for 10.7.0.0 should be forwarded to an interface at 10.4.0.2 on another router. What is the difference between these two kinds of static routes?

Example 3-2 *Routing Table with Static Routes Configured*

```
RTA#show ip route
Codes: C - connected, S - static, I - IGRP, R - RIP, M - mobile
       B - BGP, D - EIGRP, EX - EIGRP external, O - OSPF
IA - OSPF inter area, N1 - OSPF NSSA external type 1
N2 - OSPF NSSA external type 2, E1 - OSPF external type 1
E2 - OSPF external type 2, E - EGP, i - IS-IS
L1 - IS-IS level-1, L2 - IS-IS level-2, ia - IS-IS inter area
          * - candidate default, U - per-user static route, o - ODR
          P - periodic downloaded static route

Gateway of last resort is not set

C    192.168.4.0/24 is directly connected, Ethernet0
     10.0.0.0/16 is subnetted, 3 subnets
C    10.3.0.0 is directly connected, Serial0
C    10.4.0.0 is directly connected, Serial1
C    10.5.0.0 is directly connected, Ethernet1
S    10.6.0.0 is directly connected, Serial1
S    10.7.0.0 [1/0] via 10.4.0.2
```

When a routing protocol such as RIP or Interior Gateway Routing Protocol (IGRP) is used, static routes that are shown as directly connected are automatically advertised to other routers, if the appropriate **network** command has been issued. The next-hop static route is not advertised without additional configuration. These static routes can be included in updates if they are injected, or redistributed, into the dynamic routing protocol.

NOTE

As a rule, the next-hop address should always be used when defining a static route on a multiaccess network, such as Ethernet. A router interface on a multiaccess network can have several link partners, so the next-hop address must be used to specify which neighbor should receive traffic for a given network.

When an interface goes down, all static routes mapped to that interface are removed from the IP routing table. If the router can no longer find a valid next hop for the address specified in a static route, the static route is removed from the table. An alternative method is to map a static IP address to a loopback interface, because a loopback interface is a virtual interface. Therefore, it is always active and cannot go down like a real interface.

Static routing is unsuitable for large, complex networks that include redundant links, multiple protocols, and meshed topologies. Routers in complex networks must adapt to topology changes quickly and select the best route from multiple candidates. Therefore, dynamic routing is the better choice.

Configuring Dynamic Routing

Dynamic routing of TCP/IP can be implemented using one or more protocols. These protocols are often grouped according to where they are used. Routing protocols designed to work inside an autonomous system are categorized as Interior Gateway Protocols (IGPs), and protocols that work between autonomous systems are classified as Exterior Gateway Protocols (EGPs). Table 3-4 lists widely supported EGPs and IGPs for TCP/IP routing.

Table 3-4 Common EGPs and IGPs

EGPs	IGPs
EGP3	RIPv1 and RIPv2
BGP4	IGRP
	EIGRP
	OSPF
	IS-IS

This chapter focuses on IGPs. A comprehensive discussion of EGPs, particularly BGP4, appears in Chapter 8, "Route Optimization." These protocols can be further categorized as either distance vector or link-state routing protocols, depending on their method of operation, as shown in Table 3-5.

Table 3-5 Common Distance Vector and Link-State Routing Protocols

Distance Vector Protocols	Link-State Protocols
RIPv1 and RIPv2	OSPF
IGRP	IS-IS
EIGRP	

Routing Protocols for IPX and AppleTalk

Despite the dominance of IP, a significant number of organizations continue to support legacy protocols, such as Novell IPX and AppleTalk. A *legacy technology* is one that is supported because of a significant past investment or deployment. Many organizations continue to support IPX and AppleTalk because of a past investment in protocol-specific printers, software, and servers. Although Cisco Enhanced Interior Gateway Routing Protocol (EIGRP) offers comprehensive support for both IPX and AppleTalk, it is important to be familiar with three proprietary routing protocols—IPX or Novell RIP, NetWare Link Services Protocol (NLSP), and AppleTalk Routing Table Maintenance Protocol (RTMP), as illustrated in Table 3-6. Implementing AppleTalk and Novell proprietary routing protocols is beyond the scope of this book.

Table 3-6 Common Proprietary Routing Protocols for Non-IP Networks

Distance Vector Protocols	Link-State Protocols
IPX or Novell RIP	NetWare Link Services Protocol (NLSP)
AppleTalk Routing Maintenance Protocol (RTMP)	

IP Routing Protocols and the Routing Table

Cisco IOS software commands enable dynamic routing based on the routing protocol used. Example 3-3 displays the routing table of a router configured to use two IP routing protocols—RIP and EIGRP. Note that most organizations normally do not use more than one or two routing protocols.

Example 3-3 *Sample Routing Table with Multiple Dynamic Routing Protocols*

```
RTA#show ip route
Codes: C - connected, S - static, I - IGRP, R - RIP, M - mobile
       B - BGP, D - EIGRP, EX - EIGRP external, O - OSPF
IA - OSPF inter area, N1 - OSPF NSSA external type 1
N2 - OSPF NSSA external type 2, E1 - OSPF external type 1
E2 - OSPF external type 2, E - EGP, i - IS-IS
L1 - IS-IS level-1, L2 - IS-IS level-2, ia - IS-IS inter area
          * - candidate default, U - per-user static route, o - ODR
          P - periodic downloaded static route


Gateway of last resort is not set

C    192.168.4.0/24 is directly connected, Ethernet0
R    192.168.1.0/24 [120/3] via 10.3.0.1, 00:00:06, Serial0
     10.0.0.0/16 is subnetted, 6 subnets
D    10.2.0.0 [90/2681856] via 10.3.0.1, 00:26:12, Serial0
C    10.3.0.0 is directly connected, Serial1
```

Figure 3-2 examines the specific table entry for 192.168.1.0/24. Routes in the routing table that are not directly connected include two numbers in brackets—[*administrative distance/ metric*]. For example, [120/3] means that the administrative distance is 120 and the metric is 3. Routers base their evaluations of routes on these two numbers. Because this is a RIP route, the metric represents hop count.

Figure 3-2 Anatomy of a Sample Routing Table Entry

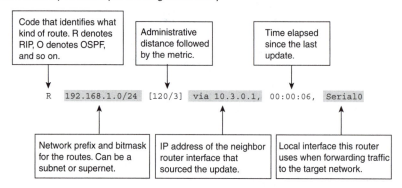

Routers use metrics to evaluate, or measure, routes. When multiple routes to the same network exist and they are from the same routing protocol, the route with the lowest metric is considered the best. Hop count is the only factor that IP RIP uses to determine the metric. In the sample entry shown in Figure 3-2, the number 3 indicates that the destination network is three hops away.

Each routing protocol calculates its metrics differently. EIGRP uses a complex combination of factors that include bandwidth and reliability to calculate its metric. Using the default settings, the EIGRP metric for the same route to 192.168.1.0 is 3,219,456. If RTA receives a RIP update and an EIGRP update for this same network, it uses the administrative distance metric to compare the two. If this administrative distance metric were used, it would be similar to comparing three apples to more than three million oranges.

When a router receives updates from different routing protocols about the same network, it cannot use dissimilar metrics to evaluate a route. The router uses administrative distance as the deciding metric for route validation. The Cisco IOS software assigns a default administrative distance to every routing protocol. A lower value signifies a more trustworthy routing protocol. In the case of RTA, the EIGRP route is installed in the routing table because its administrative distance of 90 is lower than RIP, which is 120. A complete list of administrative distances can be found in Chapter 8.

 Interactive Media Activity   Drag and Drop: Routing Table Entry

In this media activity, you identify the different fields in a routing table entry.

Distance Vector Routing Protocols

Routing protocols can be classified as either distance vector or link-state. These classifications describe the algorithm, or formula, that routers use to calculate and exchange routing information. Distance vector routing protocols are based on the Bellman-Ford algorithm.

Routers configured to use a *distance vector routing* protocol typically send their complete routing table at regular intervals to neighbor routers, as shown in Figure 3-3. Simple distance vector protocols, such as RIP and IGRP, broadcast or multicast their routing tables on all configured interfaces. Routers that use these protocols do not actually identify their neighbors for direct communication.

Figure 3-3 Distance Vector Routing Protocols Send Routing Tables

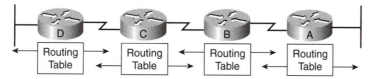

A neighbor router receiving the broadcast update examines it and compares the information to its current routing table. Routes to new networks, or routes to known networks with better metrics, are inserted in the table. The neighbor then broadcasts its routing table, which includes any updated routes.

Distance vector routing protocols are concerned with the distance and vector, or direction, of destination networks. Before sending an update, each router adds its own distance value to the route metric. When a router receives an update, it maps the learned network to the receiving interface, as shown in Figure 3-4. The router then uses that interface to reach those destinations.

Figure 3-4 Distance Vector Network Discovery

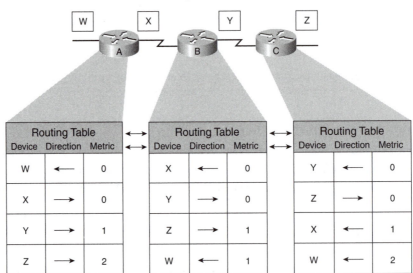

Simple distance vector routing protocols offer two primary advantages over link-state protocols. They are relatively easy to configure, and they generally use less memory and processing power. RIPv1 has the added advantage of almost universal support among all routing software. It is often used as a common denominator in mixed-vendor or legacy routing environments.

Simple distance vector routing protocols do not scale as well as their link-state counterparts. RIPv1 and IGRP are classful routing protocols, which means that they do not send subnet information in updates. They are unable to support scalability features, such as variable-length subnet masking (VLSM) or supernetting. In general, simple distance vector routing protocols converge more slowly than link-state protocols. Most complex and scalable internetworks require routing protocols that achieve convergence quickly when all routers agree on the state of the network topology. Therefore, distance vector protocols usually are inappropriate. RIP restricts networks from growing beyond 15 hops between any two destinations, which is too limiting for large networks. IGRP overcomes this limitation by supporting a 255-hop maximum. IGRP is a proprietary protocol developed by Cisco that does not support a multivendor routing environment.

Because of the limitations of simple distance vector routing protocols, network administrators often use link-state routing in complex internetworks.

 Interactive Media Activity   Interactivity: Distance Vector Routing

In this activity, you learn about distance vector routing and route metrics.

Link-State Routing Protocols

Link-state routing protocols offer greater scalability and faster convergence than distance vector protocols, such as RIP and IGRP. Link-state routing protocols require more memory and processing power from the router and more knowledge and expertise from the administrator than distance vector routing protocols.

Link-state protocols are based on *Dijkstra's algorithm*, sometimes called the shortest path first (SPF) algorithm. The most common link-state routing protocol, Open Shortest Path First (OSPF), is examined in Chapter 6, "OSPF."

Routers running a link-state protocol are concerned with the state of link interfaces on other routers in the network. A link-state router builds a complete database of all the link states of every router in its area. In other words, a link-state router gathers enough information to create its own map of the network. Each router then individually runs the SPF algorithm on its own map, or link-state database, to identify the best paths to be installed in the routing table. These paths to other networks form a tree with the local router as its root, as shown in Figure 3-5.

Figure 3-5 Link-State Algorithm Creates the SPF Tree

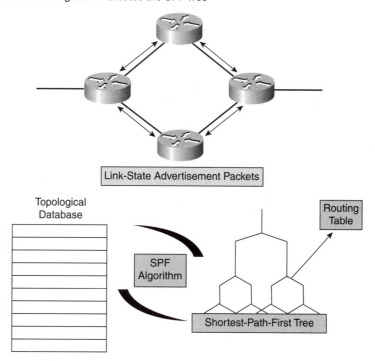

Instead of learning routes and then broadcasting them with incremented distances to neighbors, link-state routers advertise the states of their own links to all other routers in the area so that each router can build a complete link-state database, as shown in Figure 3-6. These advertisements are called link-state advertisements (LSAs). Unlike distance vector routers, link-state routers can form special relationships with their neighbors and other link-state routers to ensure that the LSA information is properly and efficiently exchanged.

Figure 3-6 Link-State Advertisements Establish Neighbors

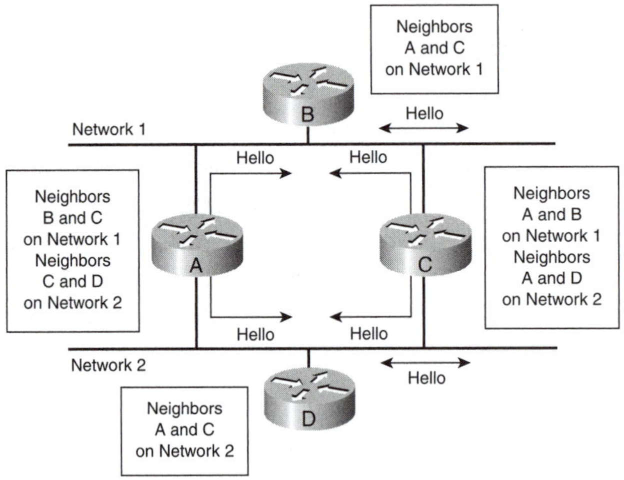

There is an initial flood of LSAs to provide routers with the information they need to build a link-state database. Routing updates occur only when a link state changes or if no changes have occurred after a specific interval. If a link state changes, a partial update is sent immediately. The partial update contains only link states that have changed, not a complete routing table. An administrator concerned about WAN link utilization will find these partial and infrequent updates an efficient alternative to distance vector routing, which sends out a complete routing table at each update interval. When a change occurs, link-state routers are all notified immediately by the partial update. Distance vector routers have to wait for neighbors to note the change, increment the change, and then pass it on to the next neighbor down the line.

The benefits of link-state routing include faster convergence and improved bandwidth utilization over distance vector protocols. Link-state protocols support classless interdomain routing (CIDR), VLSM, and supernetting. This makes them a good choice for complex, scalable networks. In fact, link-state protocols generally outperform distance vector protocols on any size network. Link-state protocols do have two major disadvantages:

- Link-state routing can overtax low-end hardware. Link-state routers require more memory and processing power than distance vector routers, potentially making link-state routing cost-prohibitive for organizations with tight budgets and legacy hardware.

- Link-state routing protocols require complex administration. Configuring link-state routing can be a daunting task, and many administrators prefer to avoid its complexity and implement distance vector routing. Even capable administrators might choose a distance vector protocol on a small network.

Hybrid Routing Protocol: EIGRP

The proprietary EIGRP offered by Cisco is an advanced distance vector protocol that employs the best features of link-state routing. For the most part, EIGRP configuration is similar to configuring a simple distance vector protocol, such as IGRP. However, like their link-state counterparts, EIGRP routers use partial updates, special neighbor relationships, and topological databases to provide optimal convergence. EIGRP, which is sometimes referred to as a hybrid protocol, is discussed in Chapter 5, "EIGRP."

 Lab 3.6.1   Migrating from RIP to EIGRP

In this lab, you configure RIPv2 and EIGRP to compare their metrics.

Default Routing

It is not feasible, or even desirable, for every router to maintain routes to every possible destination. Instead, routers keep a default route or a gateway of last resort.

Default Routing Overview

Default routes are used when the router cannot match a destination network with a specific entry in the routing table. For example, in Figure 3-7, the use of a default route is helpful if the next hop is not explicitly listed in the routing table. In Figure 3-7, if no entry exists for the destination network, the packet is sent to the default route (Router B) instead. The router must use the default route, or the gateway of last resort, to send the packet to another router. The next router has a route to that destination or its own default route to a third router. If it is a default route to a third router, that router must have the route to the destination or another default route, and so on. Eventually, the packet should be routed to a router that has a route to the destination.

Figure 3-7 Default Routing Example

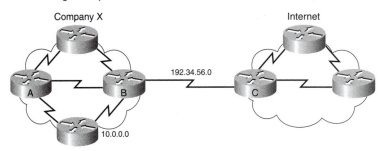

Routing Table A

No entry for destination network.
Send packet to the default route
(Router B) instead.

Using default routes to keep routing tables small is a key scalability feature. They make it possible for routers to forward packets destined for any Internet host without having to maintain a table entry for every destination network. Default routes can be statically entered by an administrator or dynamically learned through a routing protocol.

Before routers can dynamically exchange default information, an administrator must configure at least one router with a default route. An administrator can use two different commands to statically configure default routes—**ip route 0.0.0.0 0.0.0.0** and **ip default-network**.

The following sections explore these two methods in detail.

Configuring Static Default Routes

Creating an **ip route** to 0.0.0.0/0 is the simplest way to configure a default route. This is done using the following syntax:

```
Router(config)#ip route 0.0.0.0 0.0.0.0 [next-hop-ip-address | exit-interface]
```

To the Cisco IOS software, network 0.0.0.0/0 has special meaning as the gateway of last resort. All destination addresses match this route because a mask of all 0s requires none of the 32 bits in an address to be an exact match.

A route to 0.0.0.0/0 is often called a quad-zero route. Manually configuring 0.0.0.0/0 routes on every router might suffice in a simple network. Routers might need to dynamically exchange default routes in more complex situations. The exchange of default information works differently, depending on the routing protocol being used. It can create severe problems when improperly configured. Default routes typically point outside the network. Therefore, default routes are noticeable when they fail.

Static routes to 0.0.0.0/0 are automatically propagated to other routers in RIP updates. The only way to stop this automatic update is to use a route filter. A route filter configuration option is discussed in Chapter 8.

In Cisco IOS Releases 12.0T and later, RIP does not propagate a static default route automatically. When you're using RIP and Cisco IOS Release 12.0T or later, you must manually configure the RIP process to advertise the static default route by issuing the **network 0.0.0.0** command.

Alternatively, the **default-information originate** or the **redistribute static** command may be used to configure static default route propagation. Regardless of the Cisco IOS release, OSPF requires the **default-information originate** command to propagate the static default routes. The following configuration output shows this configuration for RIP, which is illustrated in Figure 3-8:

```
RTY(config)#ip route 0.0.0.0 0.0.0.0 172.16.1.2
RTY(config)#router rip
RTY(config-router)#default-information originate
```

Figure 3-8 Static Default Route

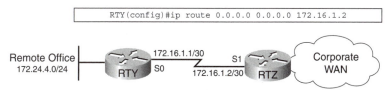

Using the **default-information originate** command, an administrator can statically configure a single RIP router with a 0.0.0.0/0 route, and that default route will be propagated to other routers. The **default-information originate** command can also be used with OSPF to achieve the same effect.

Default Routing with IGRP

IGRP treats 0.0.0.0/0 routes differently. In fact, IGRP does not recognize the network 0.0.0.0/0 and does not include it in updates. To configure a dynamic exchange of default information in an IGRP network, you must use the **ip default-network** command. The **ip default-network** command can flag a route to any IP network, not just 0.0.0.0/0, as a candidate default route. Use the following command syntax:

```
Router(config)#ip default-network ip-network-address
```

The internetwork shown in Figure 3-9 is an example of where this command is used. An asterisk (*) in the routing table denotes a candidate default route. The candidate default route is considered, along with any other candidates for the role of gateway of last resort.

Figure 3-9 *Default Routing with IGRP*

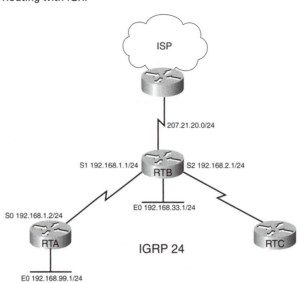

As a boundary router, RTB must be manually configured to send default traffic to its link partner, the ISP router. A 0.0.0.0/0 route can be configured on RTB, but IGRP does not propagate this route to the other routers. To avoid manually configuring 0.0.0.0/0 routes on all routers, configure RTB to flag its route to 207.21.20.0/24 as a candidate default route:

```
RTB(config)#ip default-network 207.21.20.0
```

The network 207.21.20.0/24 now has special properties as an exterior network. The exterior network is the outside network that serves as a gateway of last resort. RTB sends this information in IGRP routing updates to RTA and RTC. These routers can now dynamically learn that network 207.21.20.0/24 is an exterior network, making RTB the gateway of last resort for both of these routers. Both RTA and RTC propagate this route, flagged as a candidate default, to other IGRP neighbors if they are present.

Unlike a static 0.0.0.0/0 route configuration, the **ip default-network** command gives an administrator a great deal of flexibility. In complex topologies, several networks can be flagged as candidate defaults. Routers can then choose from among the available candidates to pick the lowest-cost route.

Running IGRP, the **ip default-network** command must be used to enable the exchange of default information. Using RIP, a 0.0.0.0/0 route usually suffices. The **ip default-network** command can be used on a RIP router, but RIP routers propagate IP default networks as 0.0.0.0/0 routes. In other words, a RIP router configured with the **ip default-network 192.168.1.0** command sends neighbors a route to 0.0.0.0/0, not a flagged route to 192.168.1.0.

Lab 3.6.2   Configuring IGRP

In this lab you configure IGRP for unequal-cost load balancing and tune the IGRP timers to improve performance.

Lab 3.6.3   Configuring Default Routing with RIP and IGRP

In this lab you configure a default route and use RIP to propagate this default information to other routers. The network must then be migrated from RIP to IGRP and the default routing configured.

Default Route Caveats

A router does not use a gateway of last resort for addresses that are part of its local domain. A local domain is a major network to which the router is connected. In Figure 3-10, RTX has two interfaces configured with IP addresses that belong to the major network, 172.16.0.0.

Figure 3-10 RTX Has Two Interfaces Connected to the Major Network

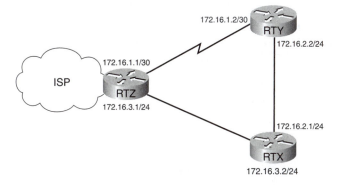

If all three routers are running IGRP, RTX does not learn about the subnet 172.16.1.1/30 because a variable-length subnet mask is used. IGRP does not support VLSM.

A ping issued to 172.16.1.1 from RTX would be expected to use its default route to send the ping to RTZ. RTX has interfaces connected to the major net 172.16.0.0. Therefore, RTX considers 172.16.0.0 a local domain and does not use a default route to reach 172.16.1.0 or any other local domain address. Without additional configuration, the ping will fail.

This problem may be solved in a number of ways. One approach is to configure the router with the **ip classless** global configuration command. With **ip classless** enabled (this is the default in Cisco IOS Releases 11.3 and later), the router uses the best prefix match available, including a supernet route, such as 172.0.0.0/8 or 0.0.0.0/0. By enabling **ip classless**, RTX uses the 0.0.0.0/0 route to reach unknown subnets in its local domain, 172.16.0.0.

A second approach is to configure RTX with an explicit route for the major network 172.16.0.0:

```
RTX(config)#ip route 172.16.0.0 255.255.0.0 172.16.3.1
```

Without a more specific route available for 172.16.1.1, RTX uses the static route to the major network number 172.16.0.0/16 and successfully routes packets destined for 172.16.1.1.

Floating Static Routes

One of the disadvantages of static routing is that it cannot adapt to topology changes. However, you can configure static routing to have limited adaptability by creating *floating static routes*.

Floating static routes are static routes configured with an administrative distance value that is greater than that of the primary route or routes. Floating static routes are fallback routes, or backup routes, that do not appear in the routing table until another route to the same destination fails. Assume that RTB is connected to network 10.0.0.0/8 through two different links, as shown in Figure 3-11, and that the RTB preferred route to network 10.0.0.0/8 is through RTC because that link has a higher bandwidth. This route is learned by RIP. RTB should use the slower link to 10.0.0.0/8 through RTA only if the primary route fails. The route to RTA is statically configured.

Figure 3-11 Sample Topology for Configuring Floating Static Routes

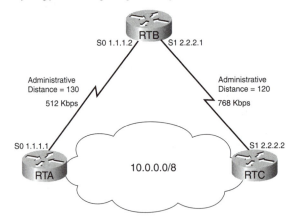

Configuring Floating Static Routes

A floating static route must be used to statically configure RTB so that it will use the slower link to reach 10.0.0.0/8 after the RIP route fails:

```
RTB(config)#ip route 10.0.0.0 255.0.0.0 1.1.1.1 130
```

This **ip route** command includes an administrative distance of 130. Recall that static routes have a default administrative distance of 1 unless the local interface is used, in which case it is 0. To create a floating static route, the administrative distance value must be manually configured. This value must be greater than the primary route administrative distance value. In this example, the primary route is learned by RIP and has an administrative distance of 120. By configuring the static route with an administrative distance of 130, the static route is less desirable than the primary route. The RIP route through RTC is preferred. However, if the RIP route is lost, the floating static route takes its place in the routing table.

Floating static routes can be used in conjunction with other static routes to create a semi-adaptable static routing scheme, as shown in Example 3-4.

Example 3-4 *Configuring Floating Static Routes*

```
RTZ(config)#ip route 0.0.0.0 0.0.0.0 serial0
RTZ(config)#ip route 0.0.0.0 0.0.0.0 serial1 5
RTZ(config)#ip route 4.0.0.0 255.0.0.0 serial2
RTZ(config)#ip route 4.0.0.0 255.0.0.0 serial3 5
RTZ(config)#ip route 4.0.0.0 255.0.0.0 serial4 10
```

If RTZ is configured with these commands, it installs one route to 0.0.0.0/0 using S0 and one route to 4.0.0.0/8 using S2. If S0 becomes unavailable, RTZ installs the floating static route to 0.0.0.0/0, using S1, into its routing table. If S2 fails, RTZ goes back to using S3 to reach 4.0.0.0/8. Finally, if both S2 and S3 go down, RTZ uses the least-desirable static route to 4.0.0.0/8, with an administrative distance of 10.

Lab 3.6.4   Configuring Floating Static Routes

In this lab, you learn how to configure a floating static route.

Convergence

This process is both collaborative and independent. The routers share information with each other, but they must individually recalculate their own routing tables. For individual routing tables to be accurate, all routers must have a common view of the network topology. When all routers in a network agree on the topology, they are considered to have *converged*. Rapid convergence means rapid recovery from link failure or other network changes. Routing protocols and network designs are ultimately judged by how rapidly they converge.

Convergence Issues

When routers are in the process of converging, the network is susceptible to routing problems. Some routers learn that a link is down while others incorrectly believe it is still up. If this happens, the individual tables are contradictory. This can lead to dropped packets or devastating routing loops.

It is virtually impossible for all routers in a network to simultaneously detect a topology change. Depending on the routing protocol in use, a significant amount of time might pass before all of the routers in a network converge. Factors affecting the convergence time include the following:

- The routing protocol used
- The distance of the router, or the number of hops from the point of change
- How many routers in the network use dynamic routing protocols
- The bandwidth and traffic load on communications links
- The load on the router
- The traffic patterns in relation to the topology change

The effects of some of these factors can be minimized through careful network design. A network can be designed to minimize the load on any given router or communications link. Other factors, such as the number of routers in the network, must be accepted as risks inherent in network design. Large internetworks can reduce the number of routers that must converge by using static default routes for stub networks.

Although proper network design can significantly reduce convergence time, the routing protocol's ability to update and calculate routes efficiently also might improve convergence.

Route Calculation

This section covers the following:

- Route calculation fundamentals
- The initiation of routing updates
- Routing metrics

Route Calculation Fundamentals

The capability of a routing protocol to update and calculate routes efficiently is based on several factors:

- Whether the protocol calculates and stores multiple routes to each destination
- The manner in which routing updates are initiated
- The metrics used to calculate distances or costs

The following sections discuss these three factors in detail.

Multiple Routes to a Single Destination

Some routing protocols allow the router to install only a single route to a destination network in its routing table. Other routing protocols permit the router to store multiple routes to each destination, at the cost of additional overhead, as illustrated in Figure 3-12. One advantage of multiple routes is that equal-cost load balancing or unequal-cost load balancing may be used. Another advantage is that maintaining multiple routes to a single destination reduces the network's vulnerability to routing loops and dropped packets when a link fails. If a router maintains two different routes to 10.0.0.0 and one route fails, the router can continue to route to 10.0.0.0 using the second route, without waiting for an alternative route to propagate. Maintaining multiple routes does not reduce convergence time, but it can insulate a router from instabilities during the convergence process.

Figure 3-12 Using Multiple Routes

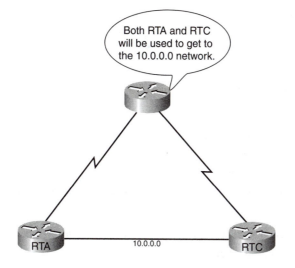

The Initiation of Routing Updates

Routing protocols can instruct a router to update neighbors after a specific amount of time has passed, after a certain event has occurred, or both. Time-driven routing protocols wait for the update timer to expire and then send an update. RIP sends a complete update every 30 seconds by default even if its routing table is unchanged since the last update, as shown in Figure 3-13. In contrast, protocols that are event-driven do not require the router to update neighbors until it detects a change in the network topology, as shown in Figure 3-14. Link-state protocols and EIGRP send a partial update that includes only the changed information. Other protocols might send their entire table when triggered by an event.

Figure 3-13 Timed Updates

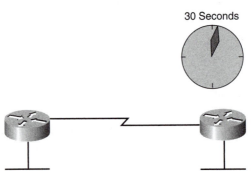

Figure 3-14 Event-Driven Updates

Routing protocols that are exclusively time-driven react poorly to topology changes. If a router detects a change but has to wait 30 seconds before alerting neighbors, routing in that network could break down, and several minutes could pass before convergence. In the meantime, routers unaware of the change might send packets the wrong way, leading to routing loops or loss of connectivity.

Routing protocols that are exclusively event-driven could go for extended periods of time without sending updates. If there is no other mechanism to ensure that routers regularly communicate, such as a Hello Timer, routers could base their routing decisions on outdated information.

For these reasons, most routing protocols use a combination of time-driven and event-driven updates. RIP is time-driven, but the Cisco implementation of RIP sends triggered updates whenever a change is detected. Topology changes also trigger immediate updates in IGRP routers, regardless of the update timer. Without triggered updates, RIP and IGRP do not perform.

Protocols that are primarily event-driven typically use timers as well. OSPF routers assign a MaxAge to the routing information. As soon as the information reaches its MaxAge, it can no longer be used in the routing table, and a new update must be requested.

Routing Metrics

A *routing metric* is a value that measures desirability. Some routing protocols use only one factor to calculate a metric. IP RIP uses hop count as the only factor to determine a route's metric. Other protocols base their metric on two or more factors, including hop count, bandwidth, delay, load, and reliability.

Bandwidth and delay are static. They remain the same for each interface until the router is reconfigured or the network is redesigned. Load and reliability are dynamic and are calculated for each interface in real time by the router.

The more factors that make up a metric, the greater the ability to adapt network operation to meet specific needs. IGRP, by default, uses two static factors to calculate the metric—bandwidth and delay. These can be configured manually, allowing precise control over what routes a router chooses. IGRP can also be configured to include two dynamic factors in the metric calculation—load and reliability. By using dynamic factors, IGRP routers can make decisions based on changing conditions. Therefore, if a link becomes heavily loaded or unreliable, IGRP increases the metric of routes using that link, and alternative routes presenting a lower metric are used.

Summary

One of the most important decisions in a network design is the selection of an appropriate routing protocol or protocols. Such selection should be done carefully and with an appreciation of the decision's long-term implications. This chapter provided an overview of the various ways in which routing can be performed, as well as the benefits and limitations of each.

Key Terms

convergence   The speed and ability of a group of internetworking devices running a specific routing protocol to agree on the topology of an internetwork after a change in that topology.

Dijkstra's algorithm   Also known as the shortest path first algorithm. A routing algorithm that iterates on path length to determine a shortest-path spanning tree. Commonly used in link-state routing algorithms.

distance vector routing   A class of routing algorithms that iterate on the number of hops in a route to find a shortest-path spanning tree. Distance vector routing algorithms call for each router to send its entire routing table in each update, but only to its neighbors. Distance vector routing algorithms can be prone to routing loops but are computationally simpler than link-state routing algorithms.

dynamic routing   Routers follow rules defined by routing protocols to exchange routing information and independently select the best path.

floating static route   A static route that is configured with an administrative distance value that is greater than that of the primary route or routes. Used for fallback routes or backup routes; they do not appear in the routing table until another route to the same destination fails.

legacy technology   A technology that is supported because of a significant past investment or deployment.

link-state routing   A routing algorithm in which each router broadcasts or multicasts information on the cost of reaching each of its neighbors to all nodes in the internetwork. Link-state algorithms create a consistent view of the network and, therefore, are not prone to routing loops. However, they achieve this at the cost of relatively greater computational difficulty and more widespread traffic (compared with distance vector routing algorithms).

routing metric   A method by which a routing algorithm determines that one route is better than another. This information is stored in routing tables. Metrics include bandwidth, communication cost, delay, hop count, load, path cost, and reliability. Sometimes it is simply called a *metric*.

static routing   An administrator manually defines routes to one or more destination networks.

Check Your Understanding

Complete all of the review questions to test your understanding of the topics and concepts in this chapter. The answers appear in Appendix B, "Answers to the Check Your Understanding Questions."

For additional, more in-depth questions, refer to the chapter-specific study guides on the companion CD-ROM.

1. What is an advantage of static routing compared to dynamic routing?

   A. Static routing sometimes yields unexpected results, even in small networks

   B. Routers that don't accept updates are less vulnerable to attack

   C. The routing table contains only directly connected routes to router interfaces

   D. Static routes remain in routing tables regardless of the mapped router interface status

2. What routing protocol would be used in a mixed-vender or legacy routing environment within an autonomous system?

   A. RIPv1

   B. RIPv2

   C. IGRP

   D. EIGRP

   E. IS-IS

3. Which of the following commands would statically configure IGRP to use and propagate a default route?

   A. **ip route 0.0.0.0 255.255.255.255**

   B. **ip default-network**

   C. **ip route default-network**

   D. **ip default network 0.0.0.0**

4. What command must you use to automatically propagate a candidate default route to IGRP neighbors?

   A. **ip default-network** *ip-address*

   B. **ip default-gateway** *ip-address*

   C. **default-information originate**

   D. **redistribute static neighbors**

5. What is a disadvantage of static routing?

    A. It can cause unpredictable routing behavior

    B. There is no mechanism to recover from a failed link

    C. All route information is transmitted in each update

    D. It produces high processor overhead

6. What is the primary purpose of configuring floating static routes?

    A. To provide unlimited adaptability to network topology changes

    B. To create a semiadaptable static routing scheme to activate backup routes

    C. To create static routes with an administrative distance of 1

    D. To create a static route that is more desirable than a dynamic route with equal administrative distance

7. What would be a logical routing protocol configuration approach to significantly reduce the convergence time in a large internetwork?

    A. Configure static default routes for stub networks

    B. Increase the router processor and memory capacity

    C. Configure static routes between all routers in the network

    D. Decrease the number of hops between all routes in the network

8. How are stub networks defined?

    A. Networks with only one router

    B. Networks with multiple ways into and out of a network

    C. Networks with only one ingress and egress point

    D. Networks with routing policies that are controlled by a single organization

9. What mechanism ensures that a router configured with an event-driven routing protocol regularly communicates with its neighbors?

    A. Hello timer

    B. MaxAge timer

    C. Triggered update

    D. Update timer

10. What routing protocol measures route desirability based on bandwidth and delay and maintains a topological database?

A. RIPv2

B. RTMP

C. EIGRP

D. OSPF

E. IS-IS

F. NLSP

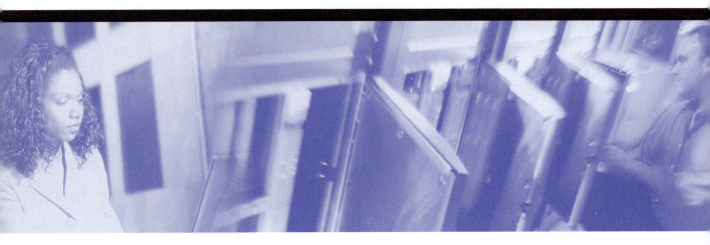

Objectives

Upon completing this chapter, you will be able to

- Understand the operation of RIPv2
- Configure RIPv2
- Verify RIPv2 operation

You can reinforce your understanding of the objectives covered in this chapter by opening the interactive media activities on the CD accompanying this book and performing the lab activities collected in the *Cisco Networking Academy Program CCNP 1: Advanced Routing Lab Companion*. Throughout this chapter, you will see references to these activities by title and by icon. They look like this:

 Interactive Media Activity

 Lab Activity

Chapter 4

Routing Information Protocol Version 2

Routing Information Protocol version 2 (RIPv2) is defined in RFC 1723 and is supported in Cisco IOS Release 11.1 and later. RIPv2 is similar to RIPv1 but is not a new protocol. RIPv2 features extensions to bring it up-to-date with modern routing environments. The RIPv2 extensions are as follows:

- Subnet masks carried with each route entry
- Authentication for *routing updates*
- Next-hop addressing carried with each route entry
- Route tags for external use
- Queries in response to RIPv1 requests

The most important extension listed is the subnet mask field for routing-update entries. The subnet mask field enables the use of variable-length subnet masks (VLSMs) and qualifies RIPv2 as a classless routing protocol.

RIPv2 is the first of the classless routing protocols discussed in this book. The following section introduces classless routing and RIPv2.

RIPv2 Overview

All of the operational procedures, timers, and stability functions of RIPv1 remain the same in RIPv2, with the exception of the broadcast updates. RIPv2 sends updates to other RIPv2 internetwork routers by *multicasting*. This occurs by using the reserved Class D address 224.0.0.9. The advantage of multicasting is that devices on the local network that are not concerned with

RIP routing do not have to spend time unwrapping broadcast packets from the router. Multi-cast updates are examined further in the section "Compatibility with RIPv1."

After looking at how the RIP message format accommodates the version 2 extensions, this section focuses on the operation and benefits of these additional features.

RIPv2 Operation

RIPv2 is a distance vector routing protocol. It supports VLSM, authentication, and multicast updates. RIPv2 supports VLSM by including the subnet mask in the route information. Neighbor routers are authenticated before the routes are exchanged. Because RIPv2 uses the multicast address of 224.0.0.9, only devices that are part of the 224.0.0.9 multicast group receive the RIPv2 updates.

Figures 4-1 through 4-5 illustrate how routers configured to run RIPv2 update their routing tables. Router A in Figure 4-1 adds its directly connected network to its routing table. When RIPv2 is enabled, it multicasts using 224.0.0.9 as the destination address to other RIP routers. Router A uses "cisco" as the authentication password. Router A directly connected networks have a *metric* of 0.

Figure 4-1 RIPv2 Network Operation

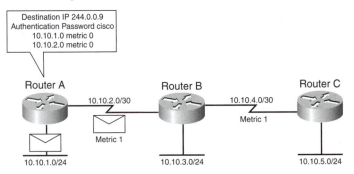

When Router B receives the routes from Router A, Router B updates its routing table, as shown in Figure 4-2. The updates are sent through all connected interfaces at the next routing update time interval. Notice that a metric of 1 was added to the 10.10.1.0 network. That is the metric for the link between Router A and Router B. RIPv2 adds 1 to the metric value for every hop the route passes.

Figure 4-2 RIPv2 Updates on Router B

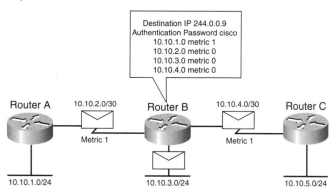

When Router C receives the routes from Router B, Router C updates its routing table, as shown in Figure 4-3. The updates are sent through all connected interfaces at the next routing update time interval. The metric for network 10.10.1.0 changes to 2. This metric of 2 represents the sum of the two hops between Router A and Router C.

Figure 4-3 RIPv2 Updates on Router C

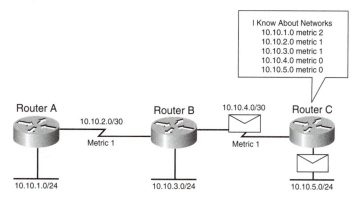

When Router B receives the routes from Router C, Router B updates its routing table, as shown in Figure 4-4. The updates are sent through all connected interfaces at the next routing update time interval. The metric for network 10.10.5.0 is 1. This represents the hop between Router B and Router C.

Figure 4-4 RIPv2 Updates on Router B

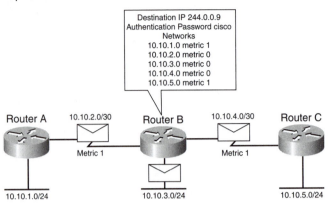

When Router A receives the routes from Router B, Router A updates its routing table, as shown in Figure 4-5. The updates are sent through all connected interfaces at the next routing update time interval. The metric for network 10.10.5.0 is 2. This metric of 2 represents the sum of the two hops between Router A and Router C.

Figure 4-5 RIPv2 Operation

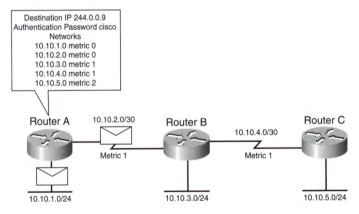

Now all of the routers have learned about all of the routes in the entire network and have reached *convergence*.

Issues Addressed by RIPv2

The following four features are the most significant new features added to RIPv2:

- **Authentication of the transmitting RIPv2 node to other RIPv2 nodes**—RIPv2 added support for the authentication of the node that is transmitting response messages. Response messages are used to propagate routing information throughout a network. Authenticating the originator of a response message was intended to prevent routing tables from being corrupted with illegitimate routes from a fraudulent source.

- **Subnet masks**—RIPv2 allocates a four-octet field to associate a subnet mask to a destination IP address. When used in tandem, the IP address and its subnet mask allow RIPv2 to specifically identify the type of destination to which the route leads. This allows RIPv2 to route to specific subnets, regardless of whether the subnet mask is fixed or of variable length.

- **Next-hop IP addresses**—The inclusion of a Next Hop identification field helps make RIPv2 more efficient than RIPv1 by preventing unnecessary hops. This feature is particularly effective for network environments using multiple routing protocols simultaneously. Some routes go undiscovered when multiple or dissimilar routing protocols exist.

- **Multicasting RIPv2 messages**—Multicasting is a technique for simultaneously advertising routing information to multiple RIPv2 devices. Multicasting is beneficial whenever multiple destinations must receive identical information.

 Interactive Media Activity   Drag and Drop: RIPv1 and RIPv2 Comparison Table

In this activity, you identify the differences between RIPv1 and RIPv2.

RIPv2 Message Format

RIPv2 uses a special message format, or packet, to collect and share information about distances to known internetworked destinations, as shown in Figure 4-6. The basic structure is the same as for RIPv1. All of the extensions to the original protocol are carried in the unused fields. RIPv2 updates can contain entries for up to 25 routes, as in RIPv1. Like RIPv1, RIPv2 operates from UDP port 520, has an 8-byte header, and has a maximum datagram size of 512 bytes.

Figure 4-6 RIPv2 Message Format

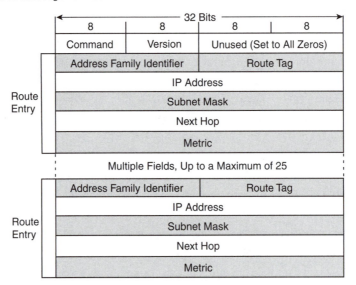

The Command field remains unchanged from RIPv1. It indicates whether the RIPv2 route was generated as a request or as a response to a request.

The Version field is set to 2 for RIPv2. If it is set to 0 or 1 and the message is not a valid RIPv1 format, the message is discarded. RIPv2 processes valid RIPv1 messages.

The Address Family Identifier (AFI) field is set to 2 for IP. The only exception is a request for a full routing table of a router or host, in which case it is set to 0.

The Route Tag field provides a way to differentiate between internal and external routes. An internal route is one that was learned by the RIPv2 protocols within the network or autonomous system. External routes are those that were learned from other routing protocols that have been redistributed into the RIPv2 process. One suggested use of this 16-bit field is to carry the autonomous system number of routes that have been imported from an external routing protocol.

The IP Address field contains the destination address. It may be a major network address, a subnet, or a host route.

The Subnet Mask field contains a 32-bit mask that identifies the network and subnet portion of the IP address. The addition of this field is the single most important change made to the RIPv2 message structure.

The Next Hop field contains the IP address of the next hop listed in the IP Address field.

The Metric field indicates how many internetwork hops or routers have been traversed in the trip to the destination. This value is between 1 and 15 for a valid route or 16 for an unreachable route.

 Interactive Media Activity   Drag and Drop: RIPv2 Packet

After completing this activity, you will be able to identify the different fields in a RIPv2 packet.

Compatibility with RIPv1

RIPv2 handles updates in a flexible manner. If the Version Number field in the RIPv2 Message field indicates version 1, and if any bits in the unused field are set to 1, the update is discarded. If the RIP version is greater than 1, the fields defined as unused are ignored, and the message is processed. Therefore, newer versions of the RIP protocol are backward-compatible with previous RIP versions.

RFC 1723 defines a compatibility switch with the following four settings, which allows versions 1 and 2 to interoperate:

1. RIPv1, in which only RIPv1 messages are transmitted

2. RIPv1 Compatibility, which causes RIPv2 to broadcast its messages instead of multicasting them so that RIPv1 may receive them

3. RIPv2, in which RIPv2 messages are multicast to destination address 224.0.0.9

4. None, in which no updates are sent

RFC 1723 recommends that switches be configurable on a per-interface basis. The Cisco commands for settings 1 through 3 are presented in the section "Configuring RIPv2." The Cisco command for setting 4 is accomplished by using the **passive-interface** command.

Additionally, RFC 1723 defines a receive control switch to regulate the reception of updates. The four recommended settings of this switch are

1. RIPv1 only

2. RIPv2 only

3. Both

4. None

This switch should also be configurable on a per-interface basis. The Cisco commands for settings 1 through 3 are also presented in the section "Configuring RIPv2." Setting 4 can be accomplished by using an access list to filter UDP source port 520, by not including a **network** statement for the interface, or by configuring a route filter.

Classless Route Lookups

Chapter 2, "Advanced IP Addressing Management," explains classful route lookups, in which a destination address is first matched to its major network address in the routing table and then is matched to a subnet of the major network. If no match is found at either of these steps, the packet is dropped.

This default behavior can be changed, even for classful routing protocols such as RIPv1 and Interior Gateway Routing Protocol (IGRP). You change the default behavior by entering the **ip classless** global command. When a router performs classless route lookups, it does not pay attention to the class of the destination address. Instead, it performs a bit-by-bit best match between the destination address and all its known routes. This capability can be very useful when you're working with default routes, as demonstrated in Chapter 3, "Routing Overview." Classless route lookups can be very powerful when coupled with the other features of classless routing protocols. According to rules of class, a router must keep eight separate table entries for these Class B networks, as shown in Table 4-1. A CIDR-compliant router can summarize these eight Class B networks based on their common bits of 10101100 00011, as shown in Table 4-2.

Table 4-1 Route Aggregation and Supernetting

NetworkNumber	First Octet	Second Octet	Third Octet	Fourth Octet
172.24.0.0/16	10101100	00011000	00000000	00000000
172.25.0.0/16	10101100	00011001	00000000	00000000
172.26.0.0/16	10101100	00011010	00000000	00000000
172.27.0.0/16	10101100	00011011	00000000	00000000
172.28.0.0/16	10101100	00011100	00000000	00000000
172.29.0.0/16	10101100	00011101	00000000	00000000
172.30.0.0/16	10101100	00011110	00000000	00000000
172.31.0.0/16	10101100	00011111	00000000	00000000

Table 4-2 Classless Route Summarization

Network Number	First Octet	Second Octet	Third Octet	Fourth Octet
172.24.0.0/16	10101100	00011000	00000000	00000000
172.25.0.0/16	10101100	00011001	00000000	00000000
172.26.0.0/16	10101100	00011010	00000000	00000000
172.27.0.0/16	10101100	00011011	00000000	00000000
172.28.0.0/16	10101100	00011100	00000000	00000000

Table 4-2 Classless Route Summarization (Continued)

Network Number	First Octet	Second Octet	Third Octet	Fourth Octet
172.29.0.0/16	10101100	00011101	00000000	00000000
172.30.0.0/16	10101100	00011110	00000000	00000000
172.31.0.0/16	10101100	00011111	00000000	00000000

Classless Routing Protocols

The true defining characteristic of classless routing protocols is their capability to carry subnet masks in their route advertisements. One benefit of having a mask associated with each route is that the all-0s and all-1s subnets are now available for use. Classful routing protocols cannot distinguish between an all-0s subnet, such as 172.16.0.0, and the major network number 172.16.0.0. Likewise, they cannot distinguish between a broadcast on the all-1s subnet 172.16.255.255 and an all-subnets broadcast 172.16.255.255.

If the subnet masks are included, this difficulty disappears. In this example, 172.16.0.0/16 is the major network number, and 172.16.0.0/24 is an all-0s subnet. 172.16.255.255/16 and 172.16.255.255/24 are just as distinguishable.

By default, the Cisco IOS software rejects any attempt to configure an all-0s subnet as an invalid address/mask combination, even if a classless routing protocol is running. To override this default behavior, enter the global command **ip subnet-zero**. This command is the default behavior in Cisco IOS Release 12.0 and later.

A much greater benefit of having a subnet mask associated with each route is being able to use VLSM and being able to summarize a group of major network addresses with a single aggregate address. Variable-length subnet masks and address aggregation or supernetting, are examined in greater detail in Chapter 5, "EIGRP."

The major classful routing protocols are

- RIPv1
- IGRP
- BGP3

The major classless routing protocols are

- RIPv2
- EIGRP
- OSPF
- IS-IS
- BGP4

Interactive Media Activity   Checkbox: Classless Routing Protocols

After completing this activity, you will be able to identify the difference between classful and classless routing protocols.

Authentication

A security concern with any routing protocol is the possibility of a router's accepting invalid routing updates. The source of invalid updates might be an attacker trying to maliciously disrupt the internetwork or something as simple as misconfiguration of the router. The attacker might be trying to capture packets by tricking the router into sending them to the wrong destination. A more mundane source of invalid updates might be a malfunctioning router. RIPv2 includes the capability to authenticate the source of a routing update by including a password.

Authentication is supported by modifying what would normally be the first route entry of the RIP message, as shown in Figure 4-7. Note that with authentication, the maximum number of entries a single update can carry is reduced to 24. The presence of authentication is indicated by setting the Address Family Identifier field to all 1s, 0xFFFF. The Authentication Type for simple password authentication is 2, 0x0002, and the remaining 16 octets carry an alphanumeric password of up to 16 characters. The password is left-justified in the field. If the password is less than 16 octets, the unused bits of the field are set to 0.

Figure 4-7 RIPv2 Authentication

← 32 Bits →			
8	8	8	8
Command	Version	Unused (Set to All Zeros)	
0xFFFF		Authentication Type	
Password (Bytes 0-3)			
Password (Bytes 4-7)			
Password (Bytes 8-11)			
Password (Bytes 12-15)			
Address Family Identifier		Route Tag	
IP Address			
Subnet Mask			
Next Hop			
Metric			
Multiple Fields, Up to Maximum of 25			

Authentication

Example 4-1 shows an analyzer capture of a RIPv2 message with authentication. The output reveals a security concern with default RIPv2 authentication. The password is transmitted in plain text. Anyone who can capture a packet containing a RIPv2 update message can read the authentication password.

Example 4-1 *Message Capture*

```
RIP (TCP/IP) - Routing Information Protocol
   Decode Status: -
   Command: 2 (Response)
   Version: 2
   Unused: 0x00


   Entry 1
   Address Family ID: 0xFFFFF Authentication
   Authentication Type: 0x02 (Type 2)
   Authentication: SunDevils


   Entry 2
   Address Family ID: 0x02 (IP)
   Route Tag: 0x00
   IP Address: 172.25.16.0
   Subnet Mask: 255.255.255.0
   Next Hop: 0.0.0.0
   Metric: 0x1


   Entry 3
   Address Family ID: 0x02 (IP)
   Route Tag: 0x00
   IP Address: 172.25.16.0
   Subnet Mask: 255.255.255.0
   Next Hop: 0.0.0.0
   Metric: 0x1
```

Although RFC 1723 describes only simple password authentication, foresight is shown by including the Authentication Type field. Cisco IOS software takes advantage of this feature and provides the option of using Message Digest 5 (MD5) authentication instead of simple password authentication. Cisco uses the first and last route entry spaces for MD5 authentication purposes.

MD5 is a one-way message digest or secure hash function produced by RSA Data Security, Inc. It is also called a cryptographic checksum because it works in somewhat the same way as an arithmetic checksum. MD5 computes a 128-bit hash value from a plain-text message of arbitrary length and a password. An example is a RIPv2 update. This fingerprint is transmitted along with the message. The receiver, knowing the same password, calculates its own hash value. If nothing in the message has changed, the receiver hash value should match the sender value transmitted with the message.

Limitations of RIPv2

Despite its overhaul, RIPv2 could not compensate for all of its predecessor's limitations. In fairness to the creators of RIPv2, they did not seek to make it anything but a modernized RIP. This included maintaining its original purpose as an Interior Gateway Protocol (IGP) for use in small networks or autonomous systems. Therefore, all of the original functional limitations designed into RIP also apply to RIPv2. A critical difference is that RIPv2 can be used in networks that require either support for authentication or variable-length subnet masks.

Some of the more significant limitations that were inherited by RIPv2 include the following:

■ **Lack of alternative routes**—RIPv2 continues to maintain a single route to any given destination in its routing tables. If a route becomes invalid, like the route to Network 1 in Figure 4-8, the RIPv2 node does not know any other routes to the destination of the failed route. Consequently, it must wait for a routing update before it can begin assessing potential alternative routes to that destination. This approach to routing minimizes the size of routing tables but can result in the temporary unreachability of destinations during a link or router failure, as shown in Figure 4-8.

Figure 4-8 Lack of Alternative Routes Slows Convergence

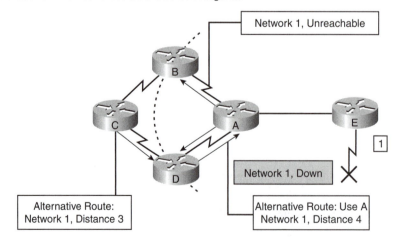

- **Counting to infinity**—RIPv2 continues to rely on counting to infinity as a means of resolving certain error conditions within the network. One such error condition is a routing loop. RIPv2 remains dependent on timers to generate updates. Therefore, it is also relatively slow to converge on a consensus of the network topology following any change to that topology. The more time it takes to converge, the greater the opportunity for obsolete information to be mistakenly propagated as current information. The result could be a routing loop, as shown in Figure 4-9.

Figure 4-9 Routing Loop

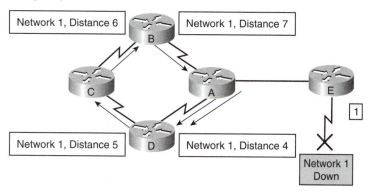

- **15-hop maximum**—Perhaps the single greatest limitation that RIPv2 inherited from RIP is that its interpretation of infinity remains at 16. After a route cost is incremented to 16, that route becomes invalid, and the destination is considered unreachable, as shown in Figure 4-10. This limits the use of RIPv2 to networks with a maximum diameter of 15 or fewer hops.

Figure 4-10 Counting to Infinity

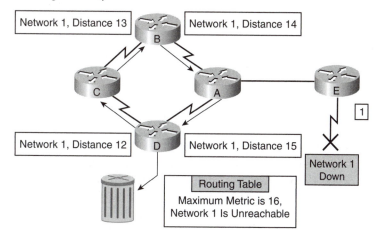

■ **Static distance vector metrics**—Another inherited limitation is found in the RIPv2 static cost metrics. The default value of 1 is just like RIP. However, the network administrator can manually adjust the default value. This metric remains constant; only the administrator can change it. Therefore, RIPv2 remains unsuitable for network environments that require routes to be selected in real time based on either delay, traffic loads, or any other dynamic network performance metric.

Configuring RIPv2

RIPv2 is merely an enhancement of RIPv1; it is not a separate protocol. The commands for manipulating timers, metrics, and updates are exactly the same in both versions. After a brief look at configuring a RIPv2 process, the rest of this section concentrates on configuring the new extensions.

Basic RIPv2 Configuration

When RIP is first enabled on a Cisco router, the router listens for version 1 and 2 updates but sends only version 1. To take advantage of version 2 features, you must turn off version 1 support and enable version 2 updates with the following commands:

■ Enable RIPv2 on the router using the following commands:

```
Router(config)#router rip
Router(config-router)#version 2
Router(config-router)#network network-number
```

By default, a RIP process configured on a Cisco router sends only RIPv1 messages but listens to both RIPv1 and RIPv2. This default is changed with the **version** command. In this mode, the router sends and receives only RIPv2 messages.

■ The router can also be configured to send and receive only RIPv1 messages:

```
Router(config)#router rip
Router(config-router)#version 1
Router(config-router)#network network-number
```

You can restore the default behavior by entering the command **no version** in the config-router mode.

Compatibility with RIPv1

The interface-level compatibility switches recommended by RFC 1723 are implemented in Cisco IOS software with the commands **ip rip send version** and **ip rip receive version**. The New York router shown in Figure 4-11 is built with the configuration shown in Example 4-2.

Figure 4-11 RIPv2 Compatibility with RIPv1

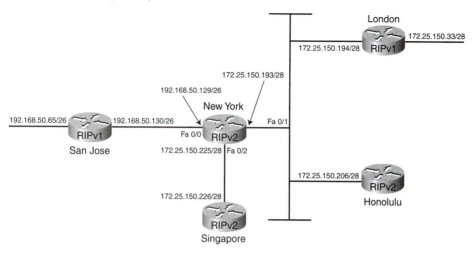

Example 4-2 *Configuration for the New York Router*

```
NewYork(config)#interface fastethernet0/0
NewYork(config-if)#ip address 192.168.50.129 255.255.255.192
NewYork(config-if)#ip rip send version 1
NewYork(config-if)#ip rip receive version 1
NewYork(config)#interface fastethernet0/1
NewYork(config-if)#ip address 172.25.150.193 255.255.255.240
NewYork(config-if)#ip rip send version 1 2
NewYork(config)#interface fastethernet0/2
NewYork(config-if)#ip address 172.25.150.225 225.255.255.240
NewYork(config)#router rip
NewYork(config-router)#version 2
NewYork(config-router)#network 172.25.0.0
NewYork(config-router)#network 192.168.50.0
```

Interface FastEthernet0/0 is configured to send and receive RIPv1 updates, and
FastEthernet0/1 is configured to send both version 1 and 2 updates. FastEthernet0/2 has no
special configuration and, therefore, sends and receives version 2 by default.

 Interactive Media Activity   Drag and Drop: RIPv2 Compatibility

After completing this activity, you will be able to identify the differences between
IGRP and EIGRP.

Lab 4.4.1 Routing Between RIPv1 and RIPv2

In this lab, you examine a networking scenario in which the RIPv1 and RIPv2 routing protocols are running. You also configure RIPv1 and RIPv2 routing protocols. RIPv2 is configured to accept RIPv1 updates.

Discontiguous Subnets and Classless Routing

Route summarization reduces the amount of routing information in the routing tables. RIPv1 always uses automatic summarization. The default behavior of RIPv2 is to summarize at network boundaries, the same as RIPv1. Use the **no auto-summary** command with the RIP process to turn off summarization and allow subnets to be advertised across network boundaries. This allows RIPv2 to perform routing between discontiguous subnets by advertising subnet information, as shown in Figure 4-12. Example 4-3 shows an example of using the **no auto-summary** command.

Figure 4-12 Discontiguous Subnets

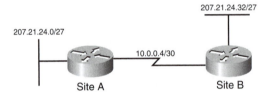

Example 4-3 **no auto-summary** *Command*

```
Router(config)#router rip
Router(config-router)#version 2
Router(config-router)#no auto-summary
```

Configuring Authentication

The implementation of RIPv2 message authentication by Cisco includes the choice of a simple password or MD5 authentication and the option of defining multiple keys, or passwords, on a key chain. The router then may be configured to use different keys at different times. Plain-text authentication is the default setting in every RIPv2 packet.

The steps for setting up RIPv2 authentication are as follows:

Step 1   Define a key chain with a name.

Step 2   Define the key or keys on the key chain.

Step 3   Enable authentication on an interface, and specify the key chain to be used.

Step 4   Specify whether the interface will use clear text or MD5 authentication.

Step 5   Optionally configure key management.

In Example 4-4, a key chain named Romeo is configured. Key 1, the only key on the chain, has a password of Juliet. FastEthernet0/0 then uses the key with MD5 authentication to validate updates from neighboring RIPv2 routers.

Example 4-4 *Key Chain Configuration Example*

```
Router(config)#key chain Romeo
Router(config-keychain)#key 1
Router(config-keychain-key)#key-string Juliet
Router(config-keychain-key)#interface fastethernet 0/0
Router(config-if)#ip rip authentication key-chain Romeo
Router(config-if)#ip rip authentication mode md5
```

If the command **ip rip authentication mode md5** is not added, the interface uses the default clear-text authentication. Although clear-text authentication might be necessary to communicate with some RIPv2 implementations, for security concerns, use the more secure MD5 authentication whenever possible.

A key chain must be configured even if it has only one key. Although any routers that will exchange authenticated updates must have the same password, the name of the key chain has significance only on the local router.

 Interactive Media Activity   Drag and Drop: RIPv2 Authentication

In this Media Activity, you learn the steps required for setting up RIPv2 authentication.

 Lab 4.4.2   RIPv2 MD5 Authentication

In this lab, you examine a networking scenario with RIPv2. You learn how to configure RIPv2 MD5 authentication.

Verifying RIPv2 Operation

This section covers RIP **show** and **debug** commands.

show Commands

Use the **show ip protocols** command to verify which routes are summarized. Example 4-5 shows an interface with this command carried on a router.

Example 4-5 **show ip protocols** *Command Output*

```
Router#show ip protocols
Routing Protocol is "rip"
Sending updates every 30 seconds, next due in 10 seconds
  Invalid after 180 seconds, hold down 180, flushed after 240
  Outgoing update filter list for all interfaces is not set
  Incoming update filter list for all interfaces is not set
  Redistributing: rip
  Default version control: send version 2, receive version 2
    Interface          Send  Recv  Triggered RIP  Key-chain
    Ethernet2           2     2
    Ethernet3           2     2
    Ethernet4           2     2
    Ethernet5           2     2
  Automatic network summarization is in effect
  Maximum path: 4
  Routing for Networks:
    172.25.0.0
    192.168.50.0
  Routing Information Sources:
    Gateway         Distance      Last Update
  Distance: (default is 120)
```

Use the **show ip rip database** command to check summary address entries in the RIP database, as shown in Example 4-6. These entries appear in the database if only relevant child or specific routes are being summarized. When the last child route for a summary address becomes invalid, the summary address is also removed from the routing table.

Example 4-6 **show ip rip database** *Command Output*

```
Router#show ip rip database
172.19.0.0/16 auto-summary
172.19.64.0/24 directly connected, Ethernet0
172.19.65.0/24
```

Example 4-6 show ip rip database *Command Output (Continued)*

```
[1] via 172.19.70.36, 00:00:17, Serial1
[2] via 172.19.67.38, 00:00:25, Serial0
172.19.67.0/24 directly connected, Serial0
172.19.67.38/32 directly connected, Serial0
172.19.70.0/24 directly connected, Serial1
172.19.86.0/24
[1] via 172.19.67.38, 00:00:25, Serial0
[1] via 172.19.70.36, 00:00:17, Serial1
```

Use the **show ip route** EXEC command to display the current state of the routing table, as
shown in Example 4-7.

Example 4-7 show ip route *Command*

```
Router#show ip route
Codes: C - connected, S - static, I - IGRP, R - RIP, M - mobile, B - BGP
D - EIGRP, EX - EIGRP external, O - OSPF, IA - OSPF inter area
       N1 - OSPF NSSA external type 1, N2 - OSPF NSSA external type 2
       E1 - OSPF external type 1, E2 - OSPF external type 2, E - EGP
i - IS-IS, L1 - IS-IS level-1, L2 - IS-IS level-2, ia - IS-IS inter area
* - candidate default, U - per-user static route, o - ODR, P - periodic
    downloaded static route


Gateway of last resort is not set


       144.253.0.0/24 is subnetted, 1 subnets
C      144.253.100.0 is directly connected. FastEthernet0/1
R      133.3.0.0  [120/1] via 183.8.64.130, 00:00:17, Serial0/1


R      153.50.0.0 [120/1] via 183.8.128.12, 00:00:09, FastEthernet0/0
183.8.0.0/25 is subnetted, 4 subnets
R      183.8.0.128 [120/1] via 183.8.128.130, 00:00:17, Serial0/0
C      183.8.128.0 is directly connected, FastEthernet0/0
C      183.8.64.128 is directly connected, Serial0/1
C      183.8.128.128 is directly connected, FastEthernet0/0
```

debug Commands

Two configuration problems common to RIPv2 are mismatched versions and misconfigured authentication. Both difficulties are easy to discover with the following debugging commands.

Use the **debug ip rip** EXEC command to display information on RIP routing transactions. The **no** form of this command disables debugging output. Using the **debug ip rip** command helps identify problems, such as a malformed packet from the sender. This is usually the case when the following output is returned when this command is entered:

```
Router#debug ip rip
RIP: bad version 128 from 160.89.80.43
```

Use the **debug ip routing** EXEC command to display information on RIP routing table updates and route-cache updates. The **no** form of this command disables debugging output. Using the **debug ip routing** command can help identify misconfiguration problems by monitoring the output, as shown in Example 4-8. Example 4-8 shows the "holddown" and "cache invalidation" lines. Most of the distance vector routing protocols use "holddown" to avoid typical problems, such as counting to infinity and routing loops. If you look at the output of the **show ip protocols** command, you will see the timer values for "holddown" and "cache invalidation." "cache invalidation" corresponds to "came out of holddown." "delete route" is triggered when a better path comes along. It removes the old inferior path.

Example 4-8 debug ip routing *Output*

```
Router#debug ip routing
RT: delete route to 172.26.219.0 via 172.24.76.30, igrp metric [100/10816]
RT: no routes to 172.26.219.0, entering holddown
IP: cache invalidation from 0x115248 0x1378A, new version 5737
RT: 172.26.219.0 came out of holddown
```

Summary

RIP is still used despite the emergence of more sophisticated routing protocols. RIP is mature, stable, widely supported, and easy to configure. Although RIPv2 offers some decided improvements over RIPv1, it is still limited to a maximum of 15 hops and small internetworks. Design strategies such as VLSM have become very powerful tools for controlling protocols. One of the major improvements in and benefits of using RIPv2 compared to RIPv1 is that RIPv2 provides authentication.

Key Terms

convergence   The speed and ability of a group of internetworking devices running a specific routing protocol to agree on an internetwork's topology after a change in that topology.

metric   A method by which a routing algorithm determines that one route is better than another. This information is stored in routing tables. Metrics include bandwidth, communication cost, delay, hop count, load, path cost, and reliability.

multicasting   A technique for simultaneously advertising routing information to multiple RIPv2 devices.

RIPv2 (Routing Information Protocol version 2)   Defined in RFC 1723 and supported in Cisco IOS Release 11.1 and later. RIPv2 is not a new protocol; it is just RIPv1 with some extensions to bring it up-to-date with modern routing environments. RIPv2 has been updated to support VLSM, authentication, and multicast updates.

route summarization   Consolidation of advertised addresses. This causes a single summary route to be advertised to other routers.

routing update   A message sent from a router to indicate network reachability and associated cost information. Routing updates are typically sent at regular intervals and after a change in network topology.

Check Your Understanding

Complete all of the review questions to test your understanding of the topics and concepts in this chapter. The answers appear in Appendix B, "Answers to the Check Your Understanding Questions."

For additional, more in-depth questions, refer to the chapter-specific study guides on the companion CD-ROM.

1. What command disables the default network summarization in RIPv2?

   A. **no ip rip-summary**

   B. **no rip auto-summarization**

   C. **no auto-summary**

   D. **no route-summarization**

2. What command displays summary address entries in the RIP database?

   A. **show ip protocols**

   B. **show ip route database**

   C. **show ip rip database**

   D. **show ip route**

   E. **show ip rip**

3. What command allows the use of the first subnet of any network?

   A. **ip subnet-zero**

   B. **no ip subnet-zero**

   C. **all-zero network**

   D. **ip network-zero**

4. What multicast address does RIPv2 use?

   A. 224.0.0.4

   B. 224.0.0.5

   C. 224.0.0.8

   D. 224.0.0.9

5. What is an advantage of multicasting RIPv2 updates instead of broadcasting them?

   A. Ethernet interfaces ignore the multicast messages

   B. It makes RIPv2 compatible with EIGRP and OSPF

   C. Hosts and non-RIPv2 routers ignore the multicast messages

   D. It enables faster convergence than RIPv1

6. Which statement describes the characteristics of RIPv1 and RIPv2?

  A. RIPv1 imposes a maximum hop count of 16, and RIPv2 allows for a maximum of 32 hops

  B. RIPv1 is classful, and RIPv2 is classless

  C. RIPv1 uses only hop count, and RIPv2 uses hop count and bandwidth

  D. RIPv1 sends periodical updates, and RIPv2 sends updates only as changes occur

7. Which three fields are now populated in the RIPv2 message format?

  A. Route Tag

  B. Subnet Mask

  C. Autonomous System

  D. Next Hop

  E. Protocol

Objectives

Upon completing this chapter, you will be able to

- Understand the fundamentals of EIGRP
- Explain the features of EIGRP
- Identify the components of EIGRP
- Explain the principles of EIGRP operation
- Configure EIGRP
- Monitor EIGRP

You can reinforce your understanding of the objectives covered in this chapter by opening the interactive media activities on the CD accompanying this book and performing the lab activities collected in the *Cisco Networking Academy Program CCNP 1: Advanced Routing Lab Companion*. Throughout this chapter, you will see references to these activities by title and by icon. They look like this:

 Interactive Media Activity

 Lab Activity

Chapter 5

EIGRP

Enhanced Interior Gateway Routing Protocol (EIGRP) is a Cisco-proprietary routing protocol based on Interior Gateway Routing Protocol (IGRP). Unlike IGRP, which is a classful routing protocol, EIGRP supports classless interdomain routing (CIDR), allowing network designers to maximize address space by using CIDR and variable-length subnet masking (VLSM). Compared to IGRP, EIGRP boasts faster convergence times, improved scalability, and superior handling of routing loops.

EIGRP has been described as a hybrid routing protocol offering the best of distance vector and link-state algorithms. Technically, EIGRP is an advanced distance vector routing protocol that relies on features commonly associated with link-state protocols. The best traits of Open Shortest Path First (OSPF), such as partial updates and neighbor discovery, are similarly used by EIGRP. However, some benefits of OSPF, especially its hierarchical design, come at the price of administrative complexity. Multiarea implementation of OSPF requires mastery of a complex terminology and command set. Yet, EIGRP's advanced features can be easily implemented and maintained. Although it does not mirror the classic hierarchical design of OSPF, EIGRP is an ideal choice for large, multiprotocol networks built primarily on Cisco routers.

This chapter surveys the key concepts, technologies, and data structures of EIGRP. This conceptual overview is followed by a study of EIGRP convergence and basic operation. Finally, this chapter shows you how to configure and verify EIGRP and use route summarization.

EIGRP Fundamentals

Cisco released EIGRP in 1994 as a scalable, improved version of its proprietary distance vector routing protocol, IGRP. IGRP and EIGRP are compatible with each other, although EIGRP offers multiprotocol support and IGRP does not.

EIGRP and IGRP Compatibility

Despite being compatible with IGRP, EIGRP uses a different metric calculation and hop-count limitation. EIGRP scales the IGRP metric by a factor of 256. This is because EIGRP uses a metric that is 32 bits long, and IGRP uses a 24-bit metric. By multiplying or dividing by 256, EIGRP can easily exchange information with IGRP. Both EIGRP and IGRP use the following metric calculation:

metric = [K1 * bandwidth + (K2 * bandwidth)/(256 – load) + (K3 * delay)] * [K5/(reliability + K4)]

The following are the default constant values:

K1 = 1, K2 = 0, K3 = 1, K4 = 0, K5 = 0

When K4 and K5 are 0, the [K5/(reliability + K4)] portion of the equation is not factored into the metric. Constants K1 and K3 are the only ones set to 1 by default. Therefore, with the default constant values, the metric equation is as follows:

metric = bandwidth + delay

IGRP and EIGRP, which scale the value by 256, use the following equations to determine the values used in the metric calculation:

bandwidth for IGRP = (10000000/bandwidth)

bandwidth for EIGRP = (10000000/bandwidth) * 256

delay for IGRP = delay/10

delay for EIGRP = (delay/10) * 256

EIGRP also imposes a maximum hop limit of 224, which is slightly less than IGRP's 255-hop limit. However, this is more than enough to support most of the largest internetworks.

Getting dissimilar routing protocols, such as OSPF and Routing Information Protocol (RIP), to share information requires advanced configuration. However, sharing or redistribution is automatic between IGRP and EIGRP, as long as both processes use the same autonomous system (AS) number. In Figure 5-1, RTB automatically redistributes routes learned by EIGRP to the IGRP AS, and vice versa. To do this, the configuration shown in Example 5-1 is entered on RTB.

Figure 5-1 Using EIGRP with IGRP

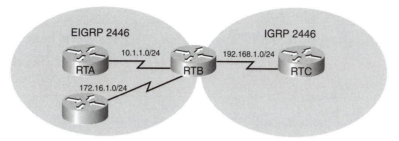

Example 5-1 *Using EIGRP with IGRP Configuration*

```
RTB(config)#router igrp 2446
RTB(config-router)#network 192.168.1.0
RTB(config)#router eigrp 2446
RTB(config-router)#network 10.1.1.0
RTB(config-router)#network 172.16.1.0
```

EIGRP tags routes learned from IGRP, or any outside source, as external because they do not originate from EIGRP routers. On the other hand, IGRP cannot differentiate between internal and external routes. Notice that in the **show ip route** command output for RTA and RTC, shown in Example 5-2, EIGRP routes are flagged with D, and external routes are denoted by EX. RTA differentiates between the network learned via EIGRP (172.16.0.0) and the network redistributed from IGRP (192.168.1.0). The table on RTC shows that IGRP makes no such distinction.

Example 5-2 *Routing Tables Using EIGRP with IGRP*

```
RTA#show ip route
<output omitted>
C    10.1.1.0 is directly connected, Serial0
D    172.16.1.0 [90/2681856] via 10.1.1.1, Serial0
D EX 192.168.1.0 [170/2681859] via 10.1.1.1, 00:00:04, Serial0


RTC#show ip route
<output omitted>
C    192.168.1.0 is directly connected, Serial0
I    10.0.0.0 [100/10476] via 192.168.1.0, 00:00:04, Serial0
I    172.16.1.0 [100/10476] via 192.168.1.0, 00:00:04, Serial0
```

RTC, which is running IGRP only, sees only IGRP routes, despite the fact that both 10.1.1.0 and 172.16.0.0 were redistributed from EIGRP.

Interactive Media Activity   Drag and Drop: IGRP and EIGRP Comparison

After completing this activity, you will be able to identify the differences between IGRP and EIGRP.

Interactive Media Activity   Drag and Drop: EIGRP Metric Calculation

After completing this activity, you will be able to identify the equation for calculating EIGRP and IGRP metrics.

EIGRP Design

Even though EIGRP is compatible with IGRP, it operates quite differently from its predecessor. As an advanced distance vector routing protocol, EIGRP acts like a link-state protocol when updating neighbors and maintaining routing information. The advantages of EIGRP over simple distance vector protocols include the following:

- **Rapid convergence**—EIGRP routers converge quickly because they rely on a state-of-the-art routing algorithm called the Diffusing Update Algorithm (DUAL). DUAL guarantees loop-free operation at every instant during route computation and allows all routers involved in a topology change to synchronize more quickly.

- **Efficient use of bandwidth**—EIGRP makes efficient use of bandwidth by sending partial, bounded updates. It also consumes minimal bandwidth when the network is stable:
  - **Partial, bounded updates**—EIGRP routers make partial, incremental updates rather than sending their complete tables. This is similar to OSPF operation. However, unlike OSPF routers, EIGRP routers send these partial updates only to the routers that need the information. They do not send to all routers in an area. For this reason, they are called bounded updates.
  - **Minimal consumption of bandwidth when the network is stable**—EIGRP does not use timed routing updates. Instead, EIGRP routers keep in touch with each other using small *hello packets*. Although they are exchanged regularly, hello packets do not use a significant amount of bandwidth.

- **Support for VLSM and CIDR**—Unlike IGRP, EIGRP offers full support for classless IP addressing by exchanging subnet masks in routing updates.

- **Multiple network layer support**—EIGRP supports IP, Internetwork Packet Exchange (IPX), and AppleTalk through protocol-dependent modules (PDMs).

- **Independence from routed protocols**—PDMs protect EIGRP from painstaking revision. Evolution of a routed protocol, such as IP, might require a new protocol module but not necessarily a reworking of EIGRP itself.

EIGRP Terminology

EIGRP routers keep route and topology information readily available in Random Access Memory so that they can react quickly to changes. Like OSPF, EIGRP keeps this information in several tables, or databases. The following terms are related to EIGRP and its tables and are used throughout this chapter:

- *Neighbor table*—Each EIGRP router maintains a neighbor table that lists adjacent routers. This table is comparable to the adjacency database used by OSPF. There is a neighbor table for each protocol EIGRP supports.

- *Topology table*—Every EIGRP router maintains a topology table for each configured network protocol. This table includes route entries for all destinations that the router has learned. All learned routes to a destination are maintained in the topology table.

- *Routing table*—EIGRP chooses the best routes to a destination from the topology table and places these routes in the routing table. Each EIGRP router maintains a routing table for each network protocol.

- *Successor*—A successor is a route selected as the primary route to use to reach a destination. Successors are the entries kept in the routing table. Multiple successors for a destination can be retained in the routing table.

- *Feasible successor*—A feasible successor is a backup route. These routes are selected at the same time the successors are identified, but they are kept in the topology table. Multiple feasible successors for a destination can be retained in the topology table.

 Interactive Media Activity   Matching: EIGRP Terminology

After completing this activity, you will be able to identify EIGRP terminology.

EIGRP Features

The following sections describe some of the main features that make up EIGRP. These technologies fall into one of the following four categories:

- Neighbor discovery and recovery
- Reliable Transport Protocol
- DUAL finite-state machine
- Protocol-specific modules

The following sections examine these technologies in detail.

EIGRP Technologies

EIGRP includes many new technologies. Each of these represents an improvement in operating efficiency, rapidity of convergence, or functionality relative to IGRP and other routing protocols.

Neighbor Discovery and Recovery

Remember that simple distance vector routers do not establish any relationship with their neighbors. RIP and IGRP routers merely broadcast or multicast updates on configured interfaces. In contrast, EIGRP routers actively establish relationships with their neighbors, much the same way OSPF routers do.

EIGRP routers establish adjacencies with neighbor routers by using small hello packets, as shown in Figure 5-2. Hellos are sent by default every 5 seconds. An EIGRP router assumes that as long as it is receiving hello packets from known neighbors, those neighbors (and their routes) remain viable. By forming adjacencies, EIGRP routers do the following:

- Dynamically learn of new routes that join their network
- Identify routers that become either unreachable or inoperable
- Rediscover routers that previously were unreachable

Figure 5-2 EIGRP Routers Establish Adjacencies

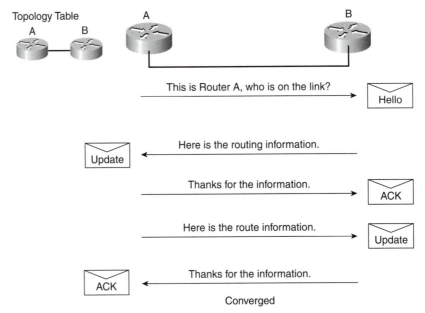

Interactive Media Activity   Drag and Drop: EIGRP Operation

After completing this activity, you will be able to identify the four key steps of EIGRP operation.

Reliable Transport Protocol

Reliable Transport Protocol (RTP) is a proprietary transport-layer protocol that can guarantee ordered delivery of EIGRP packets to all neighbors. On an IP network, hosts use TCP to sequence packets and ensure their timely delivery. However, EIGRP is protocol-independent. Therefore, EIGRP does not rely on TCP/IP to exchange routing information the way RIP does. To stay independent of IP, EIGRP uses its own proprietary transport-layer protocol, RTP, to guarantee delivery of routing information.

EIGRP can call on RTP to provide reliable or unreliable service as the situation warrants. For example, hello packets do not require the overhead of reliable delivery because they are frequent and should be kept small. The reliable delivery of other routing information can actually speed convergence because EIGRP routers are not waiting for a timer to expire before they retransmit.

With RTP, EIGRP can multicast and unicast to different peers simultaneously, allowing for maximum efficiency.

Interactive Media Activity   Checkbox: Reliable Transport Protocol

After completing this activity, you will be able to identify the operation of RTP.

DUAL Finite-State Machine

The focal point of EIGRP is DUAL. This is EIGRP's route-calculation engine. The full name of this technology is DUAL finite-state machine (FSM). An FSM is an abstract machine, not a mechanical device with moving parts. It defines a set of possible states that something can go through, what events cause those states, and what events result from those states. Designers use FSMs to describe how a device, computer program, or routing algorithm will react to a set of input events. The DUAL FSM contains all of the logic used to calculate and compare routes in an EIGRP network.

DUAL tracks all of the routes advertised by neighbors in addition to using the composite metric of each route to compare them. DUAL also guarantees that each path is loop-free. DUAL then inserts the lowest-cost paths into the routing table.

As noted earlier, EIGRP keeps important route and topology information readily available. This information is stored in a neighbor table and a topology table. These tables supply DUAL with comprehensive route information in case of network disruption. DUAL quickly selects alternative routes by using the information in these tables. If a link goes down, DUAL looks for a feasible successor in its neighbor and topology tables.

A successor is a neighboring router that is currently being used for packet forwarding. A successor also provides the least-cost route to the destination and is not part of a routing loop. Feasible successors provide the next lowest-cost path without introducing routing loops. Feasible successor routes can be used if the existing route fails. Packets to the destination network are immediately forwarded to the feasible successor. The router is then promoted to the status of successor. This process is shown in Figures 5-3 through 5-9.

Figure 5-3 D Has a Route via B and C

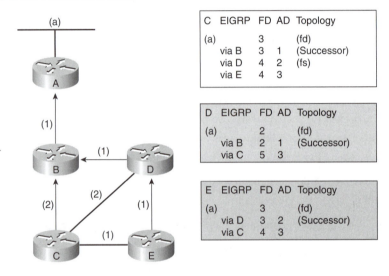

Figure 5-4 Successor Route for D Goes Down

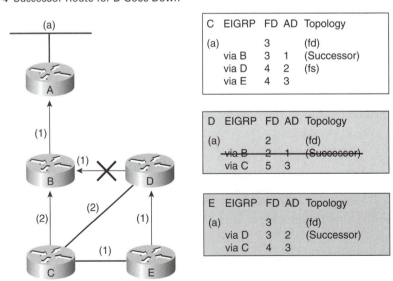

Figure 5-5 D Sends Queries to Begin Looking for a Feasible Successor

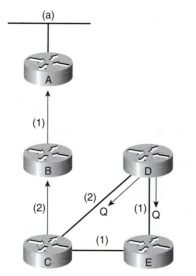

C	EIGRP	FD	AD	Topology
(a)		3		(fd)
	via B	3	1	(Successor)
	via D			
	via E	4	3	

D	EIGRP	FD ·	AD	Topology
(a)**ACTIVE**–1				(fd)
	via B			(q)
	via C	5	3	

E	EIGRP	FD	AD	Topology
(a)		3		(fd)
	~~via D~~	~~3~~	~~2~~	~~(Successor)~~
	via C	4	3	

Figure 5-6 E Queries C to Find a New Route

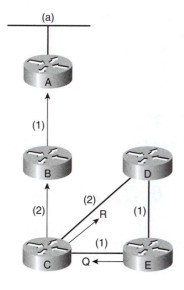

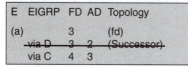

C	EIGRP	FD	AD	Topology
(a)		3		(fd)
	via B	3	1	(Successor)
	via D	4	2	(fs)
	via E	4	3	

D	EIGRP		FD	AD	Topology
(a)	**ACTIVE**		–1		(fd)
	via B				(q)
	via C		5	3	(q)

E	EIGRP		FD	AD	Topology
(a)	**ACTIVE**		–1		(fd)
	via D				
	via C		4	3	(q)

Figure 5-7 C Sends a Reply to E Stating That a Feasible Successor Already Exists

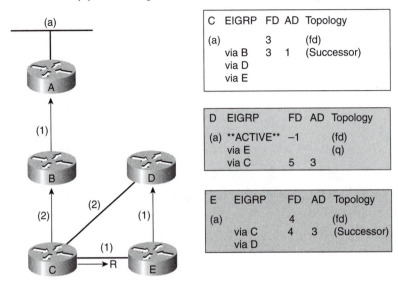

Figure 5-8 E Sends the Reply to D to Inform D of the Existing Feasible Successor

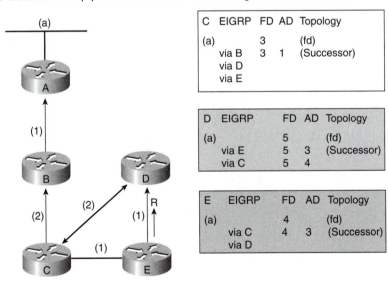

Figure 5-9 D Has a New Successor and Route via C and E

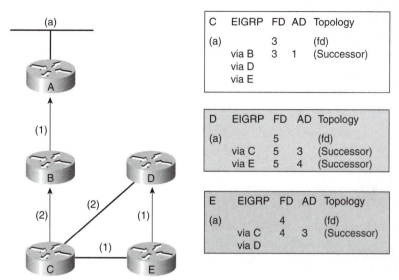

Notice that in Figure 5-3, Router D does not identify a feasible successor. The *feasible distance (FD)* for Router D to Router A is 2, and the advertised distance (AD) by way of Router C is 3. Because the AD is smaller than the best-route metric but larger than the FD, no feasible successor is placed in the topology table. Router C has a feasible successor identified as well as Router E because the router is loop-free and because the AD for the next-hop router is less than the FD for the successor.

Protocol-Dependent Modules

The modular design is one of the most attractive features of EIGRP. Modular designs are the most scalable and adaptable. Support for routed protocols such as IP, IPX, and AppleTalk is included in EIGRP through protocol-dependent modules (PDMs). In theory, EIGRP can easily adapt to new or revised routed protocols by adding PDMs.

Each PDM is responsible for all functions related to its specific routed protocol, as shown in Figure 5-10. The IP-EIGRP module is responsible for the following:

- Sending and receiving EIGRP packets that bear IP data
- Notifying DUAL of new IP routing information that is received
- Maintaining the results of DUAL routing decisions in the IP routing table
- Redistributing routing information that was learned by other IP-capable routing protocols

Figure 5-10 EIGRP PDMs

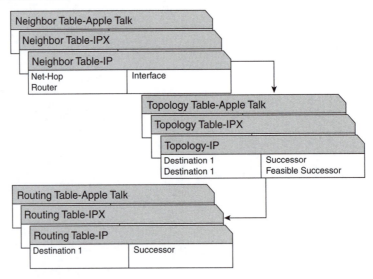

EIGRP Components

As with any routing protocol, several components contribute to the proper functionality of EIGRP. The following sections cover these components—EIGRP packet types, EIGRP tables, and route tagging.

EIGRP Packet Types

Like OSPF, EIGRP relies on several kinds of packets to maintain its various tables and establish complex relationships with neighbor routers:

- Hello
- Acknowledgment
- Update
- Query
- Reply

The following sections describe these packet types in detail.

Hello Packets

EIGRP relies on hello packets to discover, verify, and rediscover neighbor routers. Rediscovery occurs if EIGRP routers do not receive each other's hellos for a *hold time* interval but then reestablish communication.

EIGRP routers send hellos at a fixed and configurable interval, called the hello interval. The default hello interval depends on the interface's bandwidth, as outlined in Table 5-1.

Table 5-1 Default Hello Intervals and Hold Times for EIGRP

Bandwidth	Sample Link	Default Hello Interval	Default Hold Time
1.544 Mbps or less	T1, multipoint Frame Relay	60 seconds	180 seconds
Greater than 1.544 Mbps	Ethernet	5 seconds	15 seconds

EIGRP hello packets are multicast. On IP networks, EIGRP routers send hellos to the multicast IP address 224.0.0.10.

An EIGRP router stores information about neighbors in the neighbor table, including the last time each neighbor responded. The information is stored only if any of its EIGRP packets, hello or otherwise, are received. If a neighbor is not heard from for the duration of the hold time, EIGRP considers that neighbor down, and DUAL must step in to reevaluate the routing table. By default, the hold time is 3 times the hello interval, but an administrator can configure both timers as desired.

OSPF (which is covered in Chapter 6, "OSPF") requires neighbor routers to have the same hello and dead intervals to communicate. EIGRP has no such restriction. Neighbor routers learn about each other's respective timers through the exchange of hello packets. They use that information to forge a stable relationship, even with unlike timers.

Acknowledgment Packets

An EIGRP router uses *acknowledgment packets* to indicate receipt of any EIGRP packet during a reliable exchange. Recall that RTP can provide reliable communication between EIGRP hosts. To be reliable, a sender's message must be acknowledged by the recipient. Acknowledgment packets, which are dataless hello packets, are used for this purpose. Unlike multicast hellos, acknowledgment packets are unicast. Acknowledgments can also be made by piggybacking on other kinds of EIGRP packets, such as reply packets. Hello packets are always sent unreliably and, therefore, do not require acknowledgment.

Update Packets

Update packets are used when a router discovers a new neighbor. An EIGRP router sends unicast update packets to that new neighbor so that the new router can add to its topology table. More than one update packet might be needed to convey all the topology information to the newly discovered neighbor.

Update packets are also used when a router detects a topology change. In this case, the EIGRP router sends a multicast update packet to all neighbors, alerting them to the change. All update packets are sent reliably.

Query and Reply Packets

An EIGRP router uses *query packets* whenever it needs specific information from one or all of its neighbors. A reply packet is used to respond to a query.

If an EIGRP router loses its successor and cannot find a feasible successor for a route, DUAL places the route in the active state. At this point, the router multicasts a query to all neighbors, searching for a successor to the destination network. Neighbors must send replies that either provide information on successors or indicate that no successor information is available. Queries can be multicast or unicast, whereas replies are always unicast. Both packet types are sent reliably.

Interactive Media Activity   Drag and Drop: EIGRP Timer Basics

After completing this activity, you will be able to identify the default hello intervals and hold times for EIGRP.

Interactive Media Activity   Drag and Drop: EIGRP Packet Types

After completing this activity, you will be able to identify the different EIGRP packet types.

EIGRP Tables

DUAL can select alternative routes based on the tables kept by EIGRP. By building these tables, every EIGRP router can track all of the routing information in an AS, not just the best routes.

The following sections examine the EIGRP neighbor table and the EIGRP topology table in detail and provide an example of each. In addition, the various packet types used by EIGRP to build and maintain these tables are investigated.

The Neighbor Table

The most important table in EIGRP is the neighbor table, shown in Example 5-3. The neighbor relationships tracked in the neighbor table are the basis of all the EIGRP routing update and convergence activity.

Example 5-3 *EIGRP Neighbor Tables*

```
Router#show ip eigrp neighbors
IP-EIGRP neighbors for process 100
H   Address         Interface  Hold Uptime    SRTT   RTO   Q    Seq Num
                               (sec)          (ms)         (Cnt)
2   200.10.10.10  Se1        13 00:19:09    26     200   0    10
1   200.10.10.5   Se0        12 03:31:36    50     300   0    39
0   199.55.32.10  Et0        11 03:31:40    10     400   0    40
```

The neighbor table contains information about adjacent neighboring EIGRP routers. Whenever a new neighbor is discovered, its address and the interface used to reach it are recorded in a new neighbor table entry.

A neighbor table is used to support reliable, sequenced delivery of packets. One field in each row of the table includes the sequence number of the last packet received from that neighbor. EIGRP uses this field to acknowledge a neighbor's transmission and to identify packets that are out of sequence.

An EIGRP neighbor table includes the following key elements:

- *Neighbor address (address)*—The network layer address of the neighbor router.
- **Hold time (hold uptime)**—The interval to wait without receiving anything from a neighbor before considering the link unavailable. Originally, the expected packet was a hello packet. However, in current Cisco IOS software releases, any EIGRP packets received after the first hello reset the timer.
- *Smooth Round-Trip Timer (SRTT)*—The average amount of time it takes to send and receive packets to and from a neighbor. This timer is used to determine the retransmit interval.
- *Queue count (Q Cnt)*—The number of packets waiting in queue to be sent. If this value is constantly higher than 0, there might be a congestion problem at the router. A 0 means that no EIGRP packets are in the queue.

Note that an EIGRP router can maintain multiple neighbor tables, one for each PDM running, such as IP, IPX, and AppleTalk. A router must run a unique EIGRP process for each routed protocol, as shown in Figure 5-10.

The Topology Table

EIGRP uses its topology table to store all of the information it needs to calculate a set of distances and vectors to all reachable destinations. EIGRP maintains a separate topology table for each routed protocol, as shown in Example 5-4.

Example 5-4 *EIGRP Topology Tables*

```
Router#show ip eigrp topology
IP-EIGRP Topology Table for process 100


Codes: P - Passive, A - Active, U - Update, Q - Query, R - Reply,
    r - Reply Status


P 32.0.0.0/8, 1 successors, FD is 2195456 via 200.10.10.10   (2195456/281600),
    Serial1
P 170.32.0.0/16, 1 successors, FD is 2195456 via 199.55.32.10
    (2195456/2169856), Ethernet0 via 200.10.10.5 (2169856/2169856), Serial0
P 200.10.10.8/30, 1 successors, FD is 2169856 via Connected, Serial1
P 200.10.10.12/30, 1 successors, FD is 2681856 via 200.10.10.10
    (2181856/2169856), Serial1
P 200.10.10.0/24, 1 successors, FD is 2169856 via summary (2199856/0), Null0
P 200.10.10.4/30, 1 successors, FD is 2169856 via Connected, Serial0
```

The topology table is made up of all the EIGRP routing tables in the autonomous system. By tracking this information, EIGRP routers can find alternative routes quickly. The topology table includes the following fields:

- **Feasible distance (FD is *xxxx*)**—The feasible distance is the lowest calculated metric to each destination. In Example 5-4, the feasible distance to 32.0.0.0 is 2195456, as indicated by FD.

- *Route source* **(via or by way of *xxx.xxx.xxx.xxx*)**—The route's source is the identification number of the router that originally advertised that route. This field is populated only for routes learned externally from the EIGRP network. Connected routes and learned routes appear the same in Example 5-4, except connected routers have "via Connected" instead of "via *xxx.xxx.xxx.xxx*." Route tagging can be particularly useful with policy-based routing. In Example 5-4, the route source to 32.0.0.0 is 200.10.10.10.

- *Reported distance (RD)*—The path's reported distance is the distance reported by an adjacent neighbor to a specific destination. In Example 5-4, the reported distance to 32.0.0.0 is 281600, as indicated by 2195456/281600.

In addition to these fields, each entry includes the interface through which the destination can be reached.

EIGRP sorts the topology table so that the successor routes are at the top, followed by feasible successors. At the bottom, EIGRP lists routes that DUAL believes to be loops in the topology table.

How does an EIGRP router determine which routers are successors and which routers are feasible successors? Assume that the routing table for RTA includes a route to Network Z through RTB, as shown in Figure 5-11. From RTA's point of view, RTB is the current successor for Network Z. RTA forwards packets destined for Network Z to RTB. RTA must have at least one successor for Network Z for DUAL to place it in the routing table.

Figure 5-11 EIGRP Successor

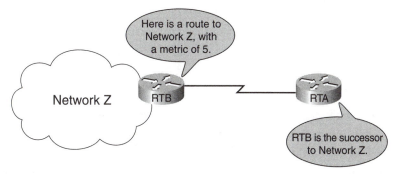

Can RTA have more than one successor for Network Z? If RTC claims to have a route to Network Z with the exact same metric as RTB, RTA also considers RTC a successor. DUAL then installs a second route to Network Z through RTC, as shown in Figure 5-12.

Figure 5-12 Multiple EIGRP Successors

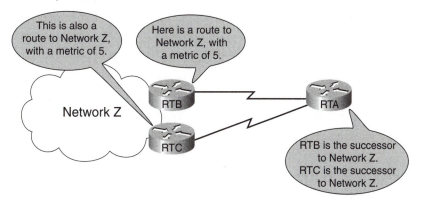

Any of the other neighbors of RTA that advertise a loop-free route to Network Z are identified as feasible successors in the topology table, as shown in Figure 5-13. However, they must be higher than the best-route metric and lower than the FD.

Figure 5-13 EIGRP Successors and Feasible Successors

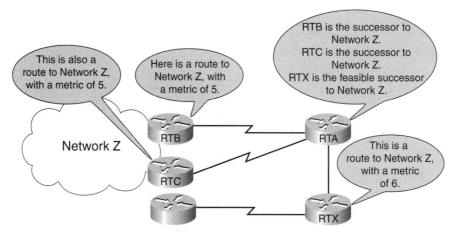

A router views its feasible successors as neighbors that are downstream, or closer, to the destination than it is. If something goes wrong with the successor, DUAL can quickly identify a feasible successor from the topology table and install a new route to the destination. If no feasible successors to the destination exist, DUAL places the route in the active state. Entries in the topology table can be in one of two states: active or passive. These states identify the status of the route indicated by the entry, rather than the status of the entry itself.

A passive route is one that is stable and available for use. An active route is a route in the process of being recomputed by DUAL. Recomputation happens if a route becomes unavailable and DUAL cannot find any feasible successors. When this occurs, the router must ask neighbors for help in finding a new, loop-free path to the destination. Neighbor routers are compelled to reply to this query. If a neighbor has a route, it replies with information about the successor(s). If not, the neighbor notifies the sender that it does not have a route to the destination either.

Excess recomputation is a symptom of network instability and results in poor performance. To prevent convergence problems, DUAL always tries to find a feasible successor before resorting to a recomputation. If a feasible successor is available, DUAL can quickly install the new route and avoid recomputation.

"Stuck in Active" Routes

If one or more routers to which a query is sent do not respond with a reply within the active time of 180 seconds or 3 minutes, the route(s) in question are placed in the "stuck in active" state. When this happens, EIGRP clears the neighbors that did not send a reply and logs a "stuck in active" error message for the route(s) that went active.

Interactive Media Activity   Point and Click: EIGRP Neighbor Table

After completing this activity, you will be able to identify the key elements of the EIGRP neighbor table.

Route Tagging with EIGRP

Not only does the topology table track information regarding route states, but it also can record special information about each route. EIGRP classifies routes as either internal or external. EIGRP uses a process called route tagging to add special tags to each route. These tags identify a route as internal or external and may include other information as well.

Internal routes originate from within the EIGRP AS. External routes originate from outside the system. Routes learned (redistributed) from other routing protocols, such as RIP, OSPF, and IGRP, are external. Static routes originating from outside the EIGRP AS and redistributed inside are also external routes.

All external routes are included in the topology table and are tagged with the following information:

- The identification number (called the router ID) of the EIGRP router that redistributed the route into the EIGRP network
- The destination's AS number
- The protocol used in that external network
- The cost or metric received from that external protocol
- The configurable administrator tag

Example 5-5 shows a specific topology table entry for an external route.

Example 5-5 *EIGRP Route Tag Information*

```
RTX#show ip eigrp top 204.100.50.0
IP-EIGRP topology entry for 204.100.50.0/24
   State is Passive, Query origin flag is 1, 1 Successor(s), FD is 2297856
   Routing Descriptor Blocks:
   10.1.0.1 (Serial0), from 10.1.0.1, Send flag is 0x0
       Composite metric is (2297856/128256), Route is External
       Vector metric:
          Minimum bandwidth is 1544 Kbit
          Total delay is 25000 microseconds
```

Example 5-5 *EIGRP Route Tag Information (Continued)*

```
        Reliability is 255/255
        Load is 1/255
        Minimum MTU is 1500
        Hop count is 1
    External data:
        Originating router is 192.168.1.1
        AS number of route is 0
        External protocol is Connected, external metric is 0
        Administrator tag is 0 (0x00000000)
```

Using route tagging, particularly the administrator tag, gives you an advantage when developing a precise routing policy. The administrator tag can be any number between 0 and 255. This is a custom tag that can be used to implement a special routing policy. External routes can be accepted, rejected, or propagated based on any of the route tags, including the administrator tag. Configuring an administrator tag in this way affords you a high degree of control. This level of precision and flexibility proves especially useful when EIGRP networks interact with BGP networks, which themselves are policy-based. BGP is covered in depth in Chapter 9, "BGP."

EIGRP Operation

The sophisticated algorithm of DUAL results in exceptionally fast EIGRP convergence. To better understand convergence when using DUAL, consider the scenario shown in Figure 5-14. RTA can reach Network 24 via three different routers: RTX, RTY, or RTZ. In Figure 5-14, RTA can reach Network 24 via three different routers, but RTY is used as the successor because it provides the lowest-cost path.

Convergence Using EIGRP

In Figure 5-14, the composite metric of EIGRP is replaced by a link cost to simplify calculations. The RTA topology table includes a list of all routes advertised by neighbors. For each network, RTA keeps the real, computed cost of getting to the network. RTA keeps the computed cost, or feasible distance, and advertised cost, or reported distance, from its neighbor, as shown in Table 5-2.

At first, RTY is the successor to Network 24 by virtue of its lowest computed cost. The lowest calculated metric from RTA to Network 24 is 31. This value is the FD to Network 24. What if the successor to Network 24, RTY, becomes unavailable, as shown in Figure 5-15? With the successor down, RTA tries to use a feasible successor to reach Network 24.

Figure 5-14 Convergence Using EIGRP

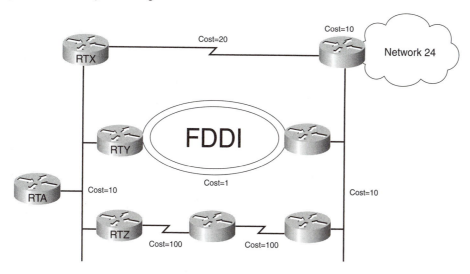

Table 5-2 Neighbor Computed Cost and Reported Distance

Neighbor	Computed Cost to NETWORK 24	Reported Distance to NETWORK 24
RTY	31	21
RTZ	230	220
RTX	40	30

Figure 5-15 Successor Route Goes Down

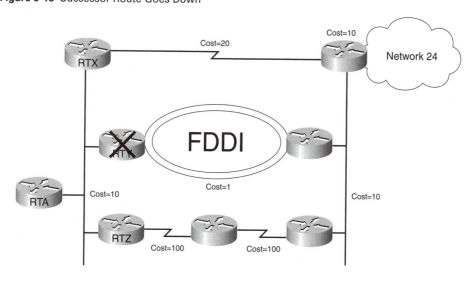

RTA follows a three-step process to select a feasible successor to become a successor for NETWORK 24:

1. Determine which neighbors have a reported distance (RD) to NETWORK 24 that is less than the FD reported by RTA to NETWORK 24. The FD is 31. The RD for RTX is 30, and the RD for RTZ is 220. Therefore, the RD for RTX is less than the current FD, and the RD for RTZ is not.

2. Determine the minimum computed cost to NETWORK 24 from among the remaining routes available. The computed cost by way of RTX is 40, and the computed cost by way of RTX is 230. Therefore, RTX provides the lowest computed cost.

3. Determine whether any routers that meet the criterion in Step 1 also meet the criterion in Step 2. RTX does both, so it is the feasible successor.

With RTY down, RTA immediately uses RTX, which is the feasible successor, to forward packets to NETWORK 24. The capability to make an immediate switchover to a backup route gives EIGRP exceptionally fast convergence time. However, what happens if RTX also becomes unavailable, as shown in Figure 5-16? With no routers advertising costs less than the FD, RTA places NETWORK 24 in the active state and queries neighbors for alternative routes.

Figure 5-16 RTX Goes Down

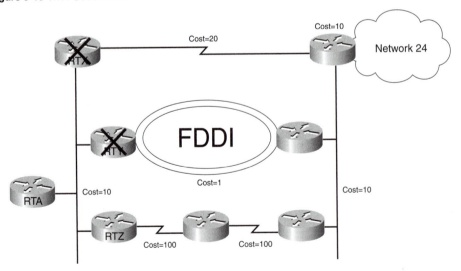

Can RTZ be a feasible successor? Using the same three-step process as before, RTA finds that RTZ is advertising a cost of 220, which is greater than the FD of 31 for RTA. Therefore, RTZ cannot be a feasible successor as of yet. The FD can change only during an active-to-passive transition, and this did not occur, so it remains at 31. At this point, because no transition to active state for NETWORK 24 has occurred, DUAL has been performing what is called a local computation.

RTA cannot find any feasible successors, so it finally transitions from passive to active state for NETWORK 24 and queries its neighbors about NETWORK 24. This process is called a diffusing computation. When NETWORK 24 is in an active state, the FD is reset. This allows RTA to at last accept RTZ as the successor to NETWORK 24.

Configuring EIGRP

The following section covers the steps and commands to configure an EIGRP routing scenario.

Configuring EIGRP for IP Networks

Despite DUAL's complexity, configuring EIGRP can be relatively simple. EIGRP configuration commands vary depending on the protocol that is to be routed, such as IP, IPX, or AppleTalk.

Perform the following steps to configure EIGRP for IP:

Step 1   Use the following command to enable EIGRP and define the autonomous system:

```
Router(config)#router eigrp autonomous-system-number
```

The *autonomous-system-number* is the number that identifies the autonomous system. It is used to indicate all routers that belong in the internetwork. This value must match all routers in the internetwork.

Step 2   Indicate which networks belong to the EIGRP autonomous system on the local router:

```
Router(config-router)#network network-number
```

The *network-number* determines which interfaces of the router are participating in EIGRP and which networks are advertised by the router.

The **network** command configures only connected networks. For example, network 3.1.0.0, located on the far left of Figure 5-17, is not directly connected to Router A. Consequently, that network is not part of the configuration for Router A.

Figure 5-17 Configuring EIGRP and Network Numbers for IP

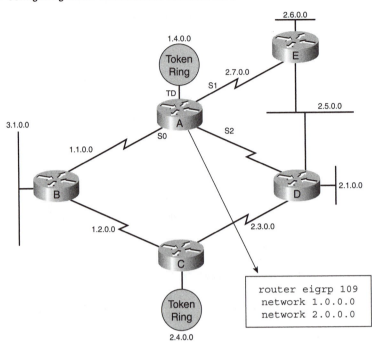

```
router eigrp 109
network 1.0.0.0
network 2.0.0.0
```

Step 3   When configuring serial links using EIGRP, it is important to configure the bandwidth setting on the interface. If the bandwidth setting is not changed for these interfaces, EIGRP assumes the default bandwidth on the link instead of the true bandwidth. If the link is slower, the router might not be able to converge, routing updates might become lost, or suboptimal path selection might result.

Router(config-if)#**bandwidth** *kilobits*

The value for *kilobits* indicates the intended bandwidth in kilobits per second. For generic serial interfaces, such as PPP or HDLC, set the bandwidth to the line speed.

Cisco also recommends adding the following command to all EIGRP configurations:

Router(config-router)#**eigrp log-neighbor-changes**

This command enables the logging of neighbor adjacency changes to monitor the routing system's stability and help detect problems.

Lab 5.7.1   Configuring EIGRP

In this lab, EIGRP is configured on three Cisco routers within the International Travel Agency WAN so that you can observe basic behaviors of the protocol.

EIGRP and the bandwidth Command

You should adhere to the following three rules when configuring EIGRP over an NBMA cloud, such as Frame Relay:

- EIGRP traffic should not exceed the virtual circuit's (VC) CIR capacity.
- The aggregated traffic that EIGRP has over all of the VCs should not exceed the interface's access line speed.
- The bandwidth allocated to EIGRP on each VC must be the same in both directions.

If you understand and follow these rules, EIGRP works well over the WAN. If you aren't careful when configuring the WAN, EIGRP can swamp the network.

Configuring Bandwidth over a Multipoint Network

Configuring the **bandwidth** command in an NBMA cloud depends on the design of the VCs. If the serial line has many VCs in a multipoint configuration, and all the VCs share bandwidth evenly, set the bandwidth to the sum of all the CIRs. In Figure 5-18, the CIR for each VC is set to 56 Kbps. Because there are four VCs, the bandwidth is set to 224 (4 * 56).

Figure 5-18 EIGRP WAN Configuration: Pure Multipoint

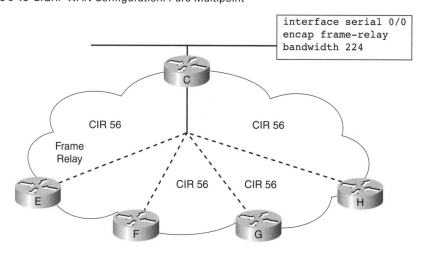

Configuring Bandwidth over a Hybrid Multipoint Network

If differing speeds are allocated to the VCs in the multipoint network, a more complex solution is needed. The following are the two main approaches:

- Take the lowest CIR and multiply it by the number of VCs, as shown in Figure 5-19. This is applied to the physical interface. The problem with this configuration is that the higher-bandwidth links might be underutilized.

- Use subinterfaces. The **bandwidth** command may be configured on each subinterface, which allows different speeds on each VC. In this case, subinterfaces are configured for the links with the differing CIRs. The links that have the same configured CIR are presented as a single subinterface with a bandwidth reflecting the aggregate CIR of all the circuits. Three of the VCs have the same CIR, 256 Kbps, as shown in Figure 5-20. All three VCs are grouped as a multipoint subinterface, serial 0/0.1. The single remaining VC, which has a lower CIR, 56 Kbps, can be assigned a point-to-point subinterface, serial0/0.2.

Figure 5-19 EIGRP WAN Configuration: Hybrid Multipoint

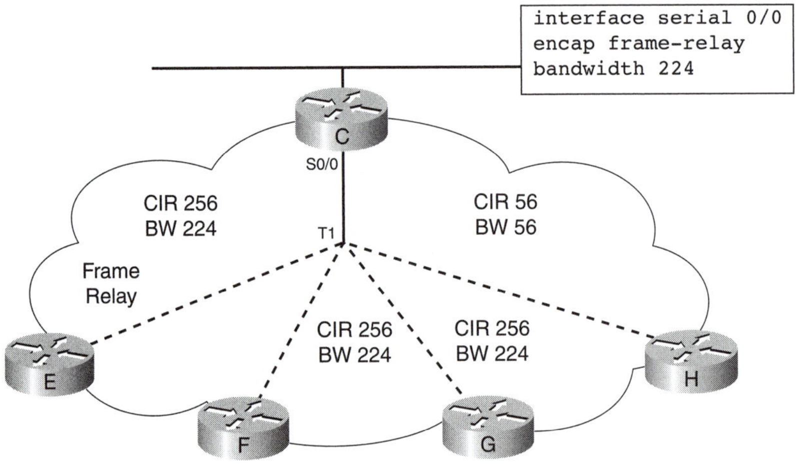

The bandwidth-percent Command

The **bandwidth-percent** command configures the percentage of bandwidth that EIGRP may use on an interface. By default, EIGRP is set to use only up to 50% of an interface's bandwidth to exchange routing information. To calculate the percentage, the **bandwidth-percent** command relies on the value set by the **bandwidth** command.

Figure 5-20 EIGRP WAN Configuration: Hybrid Multipoint with Subinterfaces

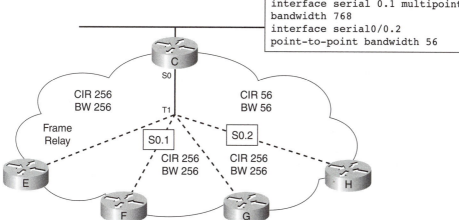

```
interface serial 0.1 multipoint
bandwidth 768
interface serial0/0.2
point-to-point bandwidth 56
```

Use the **bandwidth-percent** command when a link's bandwidth setting does not reflect its true speed. The bandwidth value might be artificially low for a variety of reasons, such as to manipulate the routing metric or to accommodate an oversubscribed multipoint Frame Relay configuration. Regardless of the reasons, configure EIGRP to overcome an artificially low bandwidth setting by setting the bandwidth-percent to a higher number. In some cases, it might even be set to a number greater than 100.

NOTE

You can change the EIGRP percentage of bandwidth for IP with the following command:

```
Router(config-if)
#ip bandwidth-
percent eigrp
```

For example, assume that the actual bandwidth of a router serial link is 64 Kbps, but the bandwidth value is set artificially low, to 32 Kbps. Figure 5-21 shows how to modify EIGRP's behavior so that it limits routing protocol traffic according to the serial interface's actual bandwidth. The sample configuration sets the bandwidth-percent on serial 0/0 to 100 percent for the EIGRP process running in AS 24. Because 100 percent of 32 Kbps is 32, EIGRP is allowed to use half of the actual bandwidth of 64 Kbps.

Figure 5-21 Using the **ip bandwidth-percent eigrp** Command

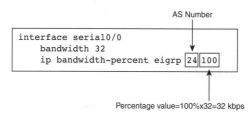

Lab 5.7.2   Configuring EIGRP Fault Tolerance

In this lab, EIGRP is configured over a full-mesh topology so that you can test and observe DUAL replacing a successor with a feasible successor after a link failure.

Summarizing EIGRP Routes: no auto-summary

EIGRP automatically summarizes routes at the classful boundary, the boundary where the network address ends as defined by class-based addressing. This means that even though RTC is connected only to the subnet 2.1.1.0, as shown in Figure 5-22, it advertises that it is connected to the entire Class A network, 2.0.0.0. In most cases, autosummarization is a good thing, keeping the routing tables as compact as possible.

Figure 5-22 Summarizing Automatically Based on Class

In the presence of discontiguous subnetworks, autosummarization must be disabled for routing to work properly, as shown in Figure 5-23. To turn off autosummarization, use the following command:

```
Router(config-router)#no auto-summary
```

Figure 5-23 Autosummarization Issues with Discontiguous Subnets

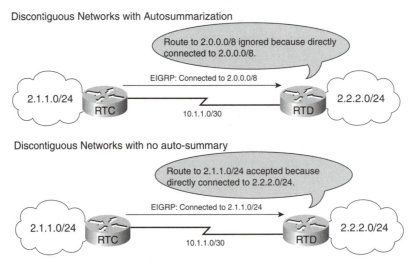

Autosummarization prevents routers from learning about discontiguous subnets. With summarization turned off, EIGRP routers advertise subnets.

Summarizing EIGRP Routes: Interface Summarization

EIGRP also lets you manually configure a prefix to use as a summary address. Manual summary routes are configured on a per-interface basis. You select the interface that will propagate the route summary and then define it with the **ip summary-address eigrp** command, which has the following syntax:

```
Router(config-if)#ip summary-address eigrp autonomous-system-number
  ip-address mask administrative-distance
```

EIGRP summary routes have an administrative distance of 5 by default. Optionally, they can be configured for a value between 1 and 255.

In Figure 5-24, RTC can be configured using the commands shown in Example 5-6.

Figure 5-24 Manual Summarization with EIGRP

Example 5-6 *Configuring Manual Summarization with EIGRP*

```
RTC(config)#router eigrp 2446
RTC(config-router)#no auto-summary
RTC(config-router)#exit
RTC(config)#interface serial0/0
RTC(config-if)#ip summary-address eigrp 2446 2.1.0.0 255.255.0.0
```

Therefore, RTC adds a route to its table, as follows:

```
D 2.1.0.0/16 is a summary, 00:00:22, Null0
```

Notice that the summary route is sourced from Null0, not an actual interface. This is because this route is used for advertisement purposes and does not represent a path that RTC can take to reach that network. On RTC, this route has an administrative distance of 5.

In Figure 5-24, RTD is oblivious to the summarization but accepts the route. It assigns the route the administrative distance of a "normal" EIGRP route, which is 90 by default. In the configuration for RTC, automatic summarization is turned off, with **no auto-summary** command. Otherwise, RTD would receive two routes—the manual summary address of 2.1.0.0/16 and the automatic, classful address of 2.0.0.0/8.

In most cases, when you use manual summarization, the **no auto-summary** command should be configured.

Lab 5.7.3 Configuring EIGRP Summarization

In this lab, you configure and test EIGRP over discontiguous (nonsequential) subnets by disabling automatic route summarization. Then you manually configure EIGRP to use specific summary routes.

Lab 5.8.1 EIGRP Challenge Lab

In this lab, you configure an EIGRP network with Network Address Translation (NAT) and Dynamic Host Configuration Protocol (DHCP) services provided by the routers. You also configure EIGRP interface address summarization to reduce the number of routes in the EIGRP routing tables.

Monitoring EIGRP

Proper verification of EIGRP is necessary to ensure that the configuration was done correctly. The following section explains some the commands that are used to verify EIGRP operation.

Verifying EIGRP Operation

Throughout this chapter, the EIGRP **show** commands have been used to verify EIGRP operation. The Cisco IOS software debug feature also provides useful EIGRP monitoring commands, as shown in Table 5-3. Table 5-4 lists the key EIGRP **show** commands and briefly describes their functions.

Table 5-3 EIGRP **debug** Commands

Command	Description
debug eigrp fsm	This command helps you observe EIGRP feasible successor activity and determine whether route updates are being installed and deleted by the routing process.
debug eigrp packet	This command's output shows transmission and receipt of EIGRP packets. These packet types may be hello, update, request, query, or reply packets. The sequence and acknowledgment numbers by the EIGRP reliable transport algorithm are shown in the output.

Table 5-4 EIGRP **show** Commands

Command	Description
show ip eigrp neighbors [*type number*] [**details**]	Displays the EIGRP neighbor table. Uses the *type* and *number* options to specify an interface. The **details** keyword expands the output.
show ip eigrp interfaces [*type number*] [*as-number*] [**details**]	Shows EIGRP information for each interface. The optional keywords limit the output to a specific interface or AS. The **details** keyword expands the output.
show ip eigrp topology [*as-number*	[*ip-address*] *mask*]	Displays all feasible successors in the EIGRP topology table. The optional keywords can filter output based on AS number or specific network address.
show ip eigrp topology [**active**	**pending**	**zero-successors**]	Depending on which keyword is used, displays all routes in the topology table that are either active, pending, or without successors.
show ip eigrp topology all-links	Displays all routes, not just feasible successors, in the EIGRP topology.
show ip eigrp traffic [*as-number*]	Displays the number of EIGRP packets sent and received. You can filter the output by including an optional AS number.

Summary

EIGRP, a Cisco-proprietary routing protocol, is an advanced distance vector protocol that uses the DUAL algorithm. It includes features such as rapid convergence, reduced bandwidth usage, and multiple network layer support.

EIGRP converges rapidly, performs incremental updates, routes IP, and summarizes routes. The labs demonstrated how to configure and verify EIGRP configuration for various protocols.

Key Terms

acknowledgment packet   An EIGRP router uses acknowledgment packets to indicate receipt of any EIGRP packet during a reliable exchange.

feasible distance (FD)   The lowest calculated metric to each destination.

feasible successor   A backup route. These routes are selected at the same time the successors are identified, but they are kept in the topology table. Multiple feasible successors for a destination can be retained in the topology table.

hello packet   EIGRP relies on hello packets to discover, verify, and rediscover neighbor routers.

hold time (hold uptime)   How long to wait without receiving anything from a neighbor before considering the link unavailable. Originally, the expected packet was a hello packet. However, in current Cisco IOS software releases, any EIGRP packets received after the first hello reset the timer.

neighbor address   The network layer address of the neighbor router. This is Address in the EIGRP neighbor table.

neighbor table   Each EIGRP router maintains a neighbor table that lists adjacent routers. This table is comparable to the adjacency database used by OSPF. A neighbor table exists for each protocol EIGRP supports.

query packet   An EIGRP router uses a query packet whenever it needs specific information from one or all of its neighbors.

queue count (Q Cnt)   The number of packets waiting in queue to be sent. If this value is constantly higher than 0, a congestion problem might exist at the router. A 0 means that no EIGRP packets are in the queue.

reported distance (RD)   A path's RD is the distance reported by an adjacent neighbor to a specific destination.

route source   The identification number of the router that originally advertised that route. This field is populated only for routes learned externally from the EIGRP network.

routing table   EIGRP chooses the best routes to a destination from the topology table and places them in the routing table. Each EIGRP router maintains a routing table for each network protocol.

Smooth Round-Trip Timer (SRTT)   The average amount of time it takes to send and receive packets to and from a neighbor. This timer is used to determine the retransmit interval or retransmission timeout (RTO).

successor   A route selected as the primary route to use to reach a destination. Successors are the entries kept in the routing table. Multiple successors for a destination can be retained in the routing table.

topology table   Every EIGRP router maintains a topology table for each configured network protocol. This table includes route entries for all destinations the router has learned. All learned routes to a destination are maintained in the topology table.

update packet   Used to update a router when the router discovers a new neighbor.

Check Your Understanding

Complete all of the review questions to test your understanding of the topics and concepts in this chapter. The answers appear in Appendix B, "Answers to the Check Your Understanding Questions."

For additional, more in-depth questions, refer to the chapter-specific study guides on the companion CD-ROM.

1. How do you configure automatic redistribution between IGRP and EIGRP?

   A. Configure the two protocols with different AS numbers

   B. Configure the two protocols with different DS numbers

   C. Configure the two protocols with the same AS number

   D. Configure the two protocols with the same DS number

2. What protocol combines the advantages of link-state and distance vector routing protocols?

   A. RIP

   B. OSPF

   C. IGRP

   D. EIGRP

3. What command shows the neighbors that EIGRP has discovered?

   A. **show eigrp neighbors**

   B. **show ip eigrp neighbors**

   C. **show router eigrp process-id**

   D. **show ip eigrp networks**

4. What multicast IP address does EIGRP use?

   A. 224.0.0.110

   B. 224.0.0.100

   C. 224.0.0.11

   D. 224.0.0.10

5. What table includes route entries for all destinations that the router has learned and is maintained for each configured routing protocol?

   A. Topology table

   B. Routing table

   C. Neighbor table

   D. Successor table

6. What establishes adjacencies in EIGRP?

   A. DUAL finite-state machine

   B. Hello packets

   C. Topology table

   D. Reliable Transport Protocol

7. What guarantees ordered delivery of EIGRP packets to all neighbors?

   A. DUAL finite-state machine

   B. Hello packets

   C. Topology table

   D. Reliable Transport Protocol

8. What does DUAL do after it tracks all routes, compares them, and guarantees that they are loop-free?

   A. Inserts lowest-cost paths into the routing table

   B. Determines the optimal path and advertises it to the neighbor routers using hello packets

   C. Supports other routed protocols through PDMs

   D. Sends a unicast query to the neighboring routers

9. How does EIGRP prevent routing loops from occurring with external routes?

   A. By rejecting external routes tagged with a router ID identical to their own

   B. By storing the identities of neighbors that are feasible successors

   C. By rejecting all neighboring routers that have an advertised composite metric that is less than a router's best current metric

   D. By storing in a special table all neighboring routes that have loops identified

10. On higher-bandwidth connections, such as point-to point serial links or multipoint circuits, how long is the hello interval used by EIGRP?

    A. 5 seconds

    B. 10 seconds

    C. 60 seconds

    D. 120 seconds

Objectives

Upon completing this chapter, you will be able to

- Describe the characteristics and operation of OSPF
- Configure and verify OSPF routing
- Configure OSPF over NBMA
- Describe multiarea OSPF operation
- Configure and verify multiarea OSPF
- Configure stubby, totally stubby, and not-so-stubby areas
- Configure virtual links

You can reinforce your understanding of the objectives covered in this chapter by opening the interactive media activities on the CD accompanying this book and performing the lab activities collected in the *Cisco Networking Academy Program CCNP 1: Advanced Routing Lab Companion*. Throughout this chapter, you will see references to these activities by title and by icon. They look like this:

    Interactive Media Activity

    Lab Activity

Chapter 6

OSPF

Open Shortest Path First (OSPF) is a link-state routing protocol based on open standards. Described in several RFCs, most recently RFC 2328, the Open in Open Shortest Path First means that OSPF is open to the public and is nonproprietary. Among nonproprietary routing protocols, such as RIPv1 and RIPv2, OSPF is preferred because of its remarkable scalability. Recall that both versions of Routing Information Protocol (RIP) are very limited. RIP cannot scale beyond 15 hops. It converges slowly, and it chooses suboptimal routes that ignore critical factors such as bandwidth. OSPF addresses all of these limitations and proves to be a powerful, scalable routing protocol.

OSPF's considerable capability to scale is achieved through hierarchical design and the use of areas. By defining areas in a properly designed network, an administrator can reduce routing overhead and improve performance. To achieve scalability, OSPF relies on complex communications and relationships to maintain a comprehensive link-state database. However, as an OSPF network scales to 100, 500, or even 1000 routers, link-state databases can balloon to include thousands of links. To help OSPF routers route more efficiently and to preserve their CPU and memory resources for the business of switching packets, network engineers divide OSPF networks into multiple areas.

This chapter describes how to create and configure OSPF. Specifically, it examines the different OSPF area types, including stubby, totally stubby, and not-so-stubby areas (NSSAs). Each of these different area types uses a special advertisement to exchange routing information with the rest of the OSPF network. Therefore, link-state advertisements (LSAs) are covered in detail. The Area 0 backbone rule and how virtual links can work around backbone connectivity problems also are reviewed. Finally, this chapter surveys important **show** commands you can use to verify multiarea OSPF operations.

OSPF Overview

OSPF uses link-state technology, which uses factors such as speed or the link's shortest path. For example, in Figure 6-1, OSPF chooses the faster path via the T3 links between the left-most and rightmost routers. This is opposed to distance vector technology, which uses factors such as hop count to determine the path to the destination. Distance vector technology is used by protocols such as RIP. For example, in Figure 6-2, RIP chooses the path via the slower 64 Kbps links because it has fewer hops.

Figure 6-1 Link-State Path Determination

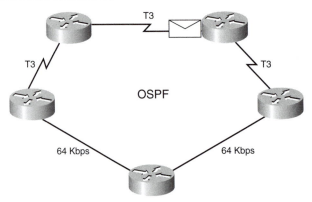

Figure 6-2 Distance Vector Path Determination

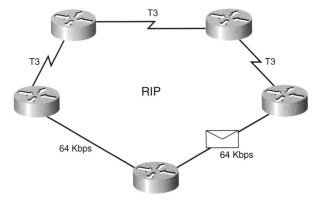

Issues Addressed by OSPF

Link-state routers maintain a common picture of the network and exchange link information upon initial discovery of network changes. Link-state routers do not broadcast their routing tables periodically like distance vector routing protocols do. Although RIP is appropriate for small networks, OSPF was written to address the needs of large, scalable internetworks. OSPF addresses the following issues:

- **Speed of convergence**—In large networks, RIP convergence can take several minutes, because the entire routing table of each router is copied and shared with directly connected neighboring routers. In addition, a distance vector routing algorithm might experience hold-down or route aging periods. With OSPF, convergence is faster because only the routing changes, not the entire routing table, are flooded rapidly to other routers in the OSPF network.

- **Support for variable-length subnet masking (VLSM)**—RIPv1 is a classful protocol and does not support VLSM. In contrast, OSPF, a classless protocol, supports VLSM.

- **Network size**—In a RIP environment, a network that is more than 15 hops away is considered unreachable. Such limitations restrict the size of a RIP network to small topologies. On the other hand, OSPF has virtually no distance limitations and is appropriate for medium to large networks.

- **Use of bandwidth**—RIP broadcasts full routing tables to all neighbors every 30 seconds. This is especially problematic over slow WAN links, because these updates consume bandwidth. Alternatively, OSPF multicasts minimize the size of link-state updates (LSUs) and send the updates only when there is a network change.

- **Path selection**—RIP selects a path by measuring the hop count, or distance, to other routers. It does not take into consideration the available bandwidth on the link or delays in the network. In contrast, OSPF selects optimal routes using cost as a factor.

- **Grouping of members**—RIP uses a flat topology, and all routers are part of the same network. Therefore, communication between routers at each end of the network must travel through the entire network. Unfortunately, changes in even one router affect every device in the RIP network. OSPF, on the other hand, uses the concept of areas and can effectively segment a network into smaller clusters of routers. By narrowing the scope of communication within areas, OSPF limits traffic regionally and can prevent changes in one area from affecting performance in other areas. This use of areas allows a network to scale efficiently.

> **NOTE**
>
> RIP v2 supports VLSM.

> **NOTE**
>
> Cost is a metric based on bandwidth.

Although OSPF was written for large networks, implementing it requires proper design and planning, which is especially important if the network has more than 50 routers. At this size, it is important to configure the network to let OSPF reduce traffic and combine routing information whenever possible.

OSPF Terminology

As a link-state protocol, OSPF operates differently from the distance vector routing protocols. Link-state routers identify and communicate with their neighbors so that they can gather firsthand information from other routers in the network. The OSPF terminology is shown in Figure 6-3. A description of each term follows.

Figure 6-3 OSPF Terminology

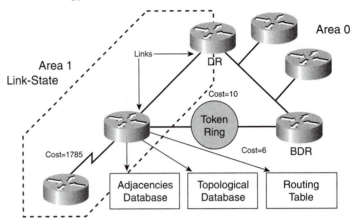

The information gathered from OSPF neighbors is not a complete routing table. Instead, OSPF routers tell each other about the status of their connections or links to the internetwork, as shown in Figure 6-4. A link, in OSPF terminology, is defined as a network communications channel that consists of a circuit or transmission path. In other words, OSPF routers advertise their link states.

Figure 6-4 OSPF Terminology: Links

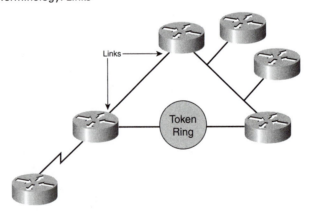

In the link between the routers shown in Figure 6-4, the routers process information exchanged between them about the link and build link-state databases. The link state, in OSPF terminology, is defined as the status of a link between two routers or the router's interface and its relationship to its neighboring routers.

Figure 6-5 shows what is connected to what. This is called the topological or link-state data-base, which is a list of information about all other routers in the internetwork, to show them the internetwork topology.

Figure 6-5 OSPF Terminology: Topological Database

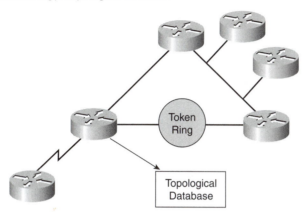

All routers within an area have identical topological or link-state databases. For example, all routers in a given area should have identical link-state or topological databases, as shown in Figure 6-6. An area, in OSPF terminology, is defined as a collection of routers that have the same area identification. Each router within the defined area has the same link-state informa-tion. Routers located in the defined area are called internal routers.

Figure 6-6 OSPF Terminology: Area

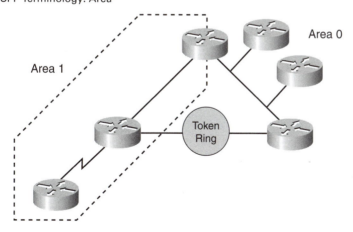

Independently, each router then runs the shortest path first (SPF) algorithm, also known as the Dijkstra algorithm, on the link-state database to determine the best routes to a destination. The SPF algorithm adds up the cost, which is a value usually based on bandwidth, of each link between the router and the destination, as shown in Figure 6-7. The cost is the value that is assigned to the link. Rather than hops, link-state protocols assign a cost, which is based on the medium's speed. The router then chooses the lowest-cost path to add to its routing table, also called a forwarding database, as shown in Figure 6-8. The routing table is generated when the SPF algorithm is run on the topological or link-state database. Each routing table on a router is unique.

Figure 6-7 OSPF Terminology: Cost

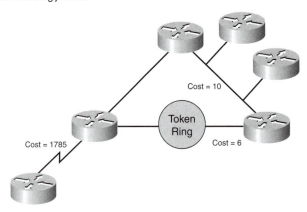

Figure 6-8 OSPF Terminology: Routing Table

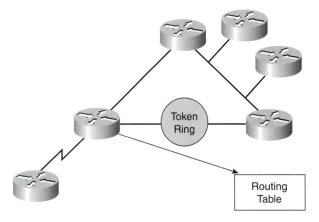

Figure 6-9 shows how OSPF routers keep track of their neighbors in their adjacencies database. The adjacencies database lists all of the neighbors to which a router has established bidirectional communication. To simplify the exchange of routing information among several neighbors on the same network, OSPF routers may elect a *designated router (DR)* and a *backup designated router (BDR)*, as shown in Figure 6-10, to serve as focal points for routing updates. These are routers that are elected by all other routers on the same LAN to represent all the routers. The DR and BDR have special responsibilities that are discussed in later sections of this chapter.

Figure 6-9 OSPF Terminology: Adjacencies Database

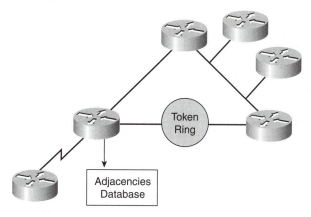

Figure 6-10 OSPF Terminology: DR and BDR

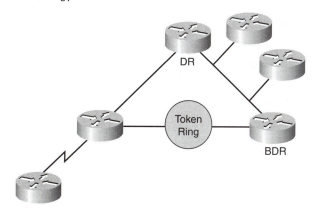

OSPF States

OSPF routers establish relationships, or states, with their neighbors to efficiently share link-state information. In contrast, distance vector routing protocols, such as RIP, blindly broadcast or multicast their complete routing table out every interface, hoping that a router is out there to receive it. Every 30 seconds, by default, RIP routers send only one kind of message. This message is their complete routing table. OSPF routers, on the other hand, rely on five different kinds of packets to identify their neighbors and to update link-state routing information, as shown in Table 6-1.

Table 6-1 OSPF Packet Types

Packet Type	Name	Description
Type 1	*Hello*	Establishes and maintains adjacency information with neighbors.
Type 2	*Database description (DBD) packet*	Describes the contents of the link-state database on an OSPF router.
Type 3	*Link-state request (LSR)*	Requests specific pieces of a link-state database.
Type 4	*Link-state update (LSU)*	Transports LSAs to neighbor routers.
Type 5	*Link-state acknowledgment (LSAck)*	Acknowledgment receipt of a neighbor's LSA.

These five packet types make OSPF capable of sophisticated and complex communications. These packet types are discussed in more detail later in this chapter. At this point, become familiar with the different relationships, or states, possible between OSPF routers, the different OSPF network types, and the OSPF Hello protocol.

The key to effectively designing and troubleshooting OSPF networks is to understand the relationships, or states, that develop between OSPF routers. OSPF interfaces can be in one of seven states. OSPF neighbor relationships progress through these states, one at a time, in the following order:

1. **Down state**—In the *Down state*, the OSPF process has not exchanged information with any neighbor. OSPF is waiting to enter the next state—the Init state.

2. **Init state**—OSPF routers send Type 1 packets, or Hello packets, at regular intervals to establish a relationship with neighbor routers. These intervals are usually 10 seconds. When an interface receives its first Hello packet, the router enters the *Init state*. This means that the router knows a neighbor is out there and is waiting to take the relationship to the next step.

   The two kinds of relationships are the *two-way state* and adjacency. A router must receive a Hello from a neighbor before it can establish any relationship.

3. **Two-way state**—Using Hello packets, every OSPF router tries to establish a two-way state, or bidirectional communication, with every neighbor router on the same IP network. Among other things, Hello packets include a list of the sender's known OSPF neighbors. A router enters the two-way state when it sees itself in a neighbor's Hello. When RTB learns that RTA knows about it, it declares a two-way state to exist with RTA, as shown in Figure 6-11.

Figure 6-11 OSPF Two-Way State or Bidirectional Communication

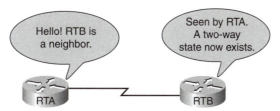

The two-way state is the most basic relationship that OSPF neighbors can have, but routing information is not shared between routers in this relationship. To learn about the link states of other routers and eventually build a routing table, every OSPF router must form at least one adjacency. An adjacency is an advanced relationship between OSPF routers that involves a series of progressive states that rely not just on Hellos, but also on the other four types of OSPF packets. Routers attempting to become adjacent to one another exchange routing information even before the adjacency is fully established. The first step toward *full adjacency* is the ExStart state, which is described next.

4. **ExStart state**—Technically, when a router and its neighbor enter the *ExStart state*, their conversation is characterized as an adjacency, but they have not become fully adjacent. ExStart is established using Type 2 DBD packets, also known as DDPs. The two neighbor routers use Hello packets to negotiate who is the "master" and who is the "slave" in their relationship and use DBD packets to exchange databases, as shown in Figure 6-12.

Figure 6-12 Route Discovery

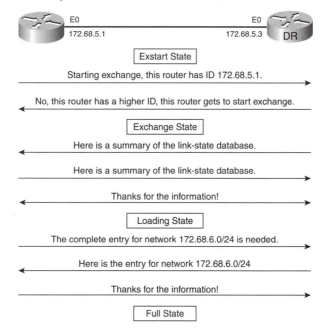

The router with the highest OSPF *router ID* "wins" and becomes the master. The OSPF router ID is discussed later in this chapter. When the neighbors establish their roles as master and slave, they enter the Exchange state, and begin sending routing information.

5. **Exchange state**—In the *Exchange state*, neighbor routers use Type 2 DBD packets to send each other their link-state information, as shown in Figure 6-12. In other words, the routers describe their link-state databases to each other. The routers compare what they learn with their existing link-state databases and explicitly acknowledge each DBD packet. If either of the routers receives information about a link that is not already in its database, the router requests a complete update from its neighbor. Complete routing information is exchanged in the *Loading state*.

6. **Loading state**—After the databases have been described to each router, they may request information that is more complete by using Type 3 packets, LSRs. When a router receives an LSR, it responds with an update by using a Type 4 LSU packet. These Type 4 LSU packets contain the actual LSAs, which are the heart of link-state routing protocols, as shown in Figure 6-12. Type 4 LSUs are acknowledged using Type 5 packets, called LSAcks.

7. **Full adjacency**—With the Loading state complete, the routers are fully adjacent. Each router keeps a list of adjacent neighbors, called the adjacencies database. Do not confuse the adjacencies database with the link-state database or the forwarding database. The forwarding database is a list of routes generated when an algorithm is run on the link-state database. The routing table on each router is unique and contains information on how and where to send packets to other routers.

 Interactive Media Activity   Drag and Drop: OSPF States

After completing this activity, you will be able to list in order the different states of OSPF.

OSPF Network Types

Adjacency is required to allow OSPF routers to share routing information. A router will try to become adjacent to at least one other router on each IP network to which it is connected. Some routers might try to become adjacent to all of their neighbor routers, and others might try with only one or two. OSPF routers determine which routers to become adjacent to based on what type of network connects them.

OSPF interfaces automatically recognize three types of networks: broadcast multiaccess, nonbroadcast multiaccess (NBMA), and point-to-point networks, which are illustrated in Figure 6-13. An administrator can configure a fourth network type, a point-to-multipoint network.

Figure 6-13 OSPF Network Types

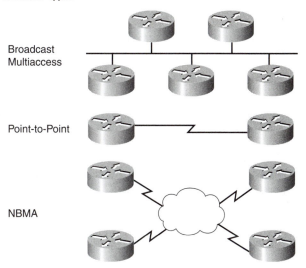

Table 6-2 summarizes some various types of networks that are associated with these four OSPF network types.

Table 6-2 OSPF Network Types

OSPF Network Type	Network Example
Broadcast multiaccess	Ethernet, Token Ring, or FDDI
Nonbroadcast multiaccess	Frame Relay, X.25, SMDS
Point-to-point	PPP, HDLC
Point-to-multipoint	Configured by an administrator

The type of network dictates how OSPF routers should relate to each other. An administrator might have to override the detected network type for OSPF to operate properly.

Some networks are defined as multiaccess because it cannot be predicted just how many routers are connected to them. There might be one, two, or more routers. A campus that uses a switched Ethernet core might have half a dozen routers connected to the same backbone network. A school district might have 10, 12, or 25 remote-site routers connected by way of Frame Relay PVCs to the same IP subnet.

A significant number of routers can exist on a multiaccess network. The designers of OSPF developed a system to avoid the overhead that would be created if every router established full adjacency with every other router. This system restricts who can become adjacent to whom by employing the services of one of the following:

- **Designated router (DR)**—For every multiaccess IP network, one router is elected the DR. The DR has two main functions—becoming adjacent to all other routers on the network and acting as a spokesperson for the network. As spokesperson, the DR sends network LSAs for all other IP networks to every other router. Because the DR becomes adjacent to all other routers on the IP network, it is the focal point for collecting routing information (LSAs).

- **Backup designated router (BDR)**—The DR could represent a single point of failure, so a second router is elected as the BDR to provide fault tolerance. Therefore, the BDR must also become adjacent to all routers on the network and must serve as a second focal point for LSAs, as shown in Figure 6-14. However, unlike the DR, the BDR is not responsible for updating the other routers or sending network LSAs. Instead, the BDR keeps a timer on the DR's update activity to ensure that it is operational. If the BDR does not detect activity from the DR before the timer expires, the BDR takes over the role of DR, and a new BDR is elected.

Figure 6-14 DR and BDR Receive LSAs

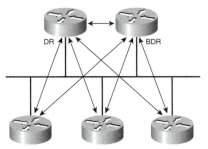

On point-to-point networks, only two nodes exist. Therefore, a focal point for routing information is not needed. No DR or BDR is elected. Both routers become fully adjacent to one another.

The OSPF Hello Protocol

When a router starts an OSPF routing process on an interface, it sends a Hello packet and continues to send Hellos at regular intervals. The rules that govern the exchange of OSPF Hello packets are collectively referred to as the Hello protocol.

At Layer 3 of the OSI model, Hello packets are addressed to the multicast address 224.0.0.5. This address in effect means all OSPF routers. OSPF routers use Hello packets to initiate new adjacencies and to ensure that adjacent neighbors have not disappeared. Hellos are sent every 10 seconds by default on multiaccess and point-to-point networks. On interfaces that connect to NBMA networks, such as Frame Relay, Hellos are sent every 30 seconds.

Although the Hello packet is small, often less than 50 bytes, it contains plenty of vital information. Like other OSPF packet types, Hello packets include an OSPF packet header, which has the form shown in Figure 6-15.

Figure 6-15 OSPF Packet Header

Version	Type	Packet Length
Router ID		
Area ID		
Checksum		Authentication Type
Authentication Data		

All five types of OSPF packets use the OSPF packet header, which consists of eight fields.

- *Version, Type, and Packet Length*—The first three fields of the OSPF packet let the recipients know the version of OSPF that is being used by the sender, the OSPF packet type, and the length. The OSPF version can be either 1 or 2. OSPF version 2 was introduced in 1991 (RFC 1247) and is incompatible with version 1, which is obsolete. The Cisco IOS software uses OSPF version 2 and cannot be configured to use OSPF version 1.

- *Router ID*—The function of the Hello packet is to establish and maintain adjacencies. So the sending router signs the fourth field with its router ID, which is a 32-bit number used to identify the router to the OSPF protocol. A router uses its IP address as its ID because both the router ID and the IP address must be unique within a network. Because routers support multiple IP addresses, a loopback IP address is used as the router ID. In the absence of a loopback IP address, the highest value address interface IP is used as the router ID. This is regardless of whether that interface is involved in the OSPF process.

  If the interface associated with that IP address goes down, the router can no longer use that IP address as its router ID. When a router's ID changes for any reason, the router must reintroduce itself to its neighbors on all links. To avoid the unnecessary overhead caused by reestablishing adjacency and readvertising link states, an administrator typically assigns an IP address to a loopback interface. Unless an administrator shuts down a loopback interface, it always stays up, so loopback interfaces make ideal router IDs.

- *Area ID*—Multiple areas can be defined within an OSPF network to reduce and summarize route information. This allows large and complex networks to continue growing. When configuring a single-area OSPF network, always use Area 0, because it is defined as the "backbone" area. There must be a backbone area to scale or add other OSPF areas.

NOTE

If a loopback interface is configured with an IP address, the Cisco IOS software uses that IP address as the router ID. This happens even if the other interfaces have higher addresses.

- *Checksum*—A 2-byte checksum field is used to check the message for errors, as seen with other protocols. Good packets are retained, and damaged packets are discarded.

- *Authentication Type and Authentication Data*—OSPF supports different methods of authentication so that OSPF routers do not believe just anyone sending Hellos to 224.0.0.5. Routers with unequal authentication fields do not accept OSPF information from each other.

The Hello header, shown in Figure 6-16, is found only in Type 1 Hello packets. It carries essential information.

Figure 6-16 OSPF Hello Header

Network Mask		
Hello Interval	Options	Router Priority
Dead Interval		
Designated Router		
Backup Designated Router		
Neighbor Router ID		
Neighbor Router ID		
(Additional Neighbor Router ID Fields Can Be Added to the End of the Header, If Necessary)		

The following are the fields in the Hello header:

- **Network Mask**—The *network mask* is a 32-bit field that carries subnet mask information for the network.

- **Hello Interval and Dead Interval**—The *Hello interval* is how many seconds an OSPF router waits to send the next Hello packet. The default for multiaccess broadcast and point-to-point networks is 10 seconds. The *dead interval* is how many seconds a router waits before it declares a neighbor down—that is, if the neighbor's Hello packets are no longer being received. The dead interval is four times the Hello interval by default, or 40 seconds. Both of these intervals can be configured, which is why they are advertised. If two routers have different Hello intervals, or if they have different dead intervals, they do not accept OSPF information from each other.

- **Options**—The router can use this field to indicate optional configurations, including the stubby area flag.

- **Router Priority**—The *router priority* field contains a value that indicates this router's priority when selecting a DR and BDR. The default priority is 1, but you can set this to a higher number to ensure that a specified router becomes the DR.

- *Designated Router (DR) and Backup Designated Router (BDR)*—The router IDs of the DR and BDR are listed here if they are known by the source of the Hello packet.
- *Neighbor router ID*—If the source of the Hello packet receives a valid Hello from any neighbor within the dead interval, its router ID is included here.

OSPF Operation

The following sections discuss some of the details of OSPF operation:

- Steps of OSPF operation
- Establish router adjacencies
- Elect a DR and a BDR
- Discover routes
- Select appropriate routes
- Maintain routing information

Steps of OSPF Operation

OSPF routers progress through the following five distinct steps of operation:

1. Establish router adjacencies.
2. Elect a DR and BDR if necessary.
3. Discover routes.
4. Select the appropriate routes to use.
5. Maintain routing information.

 Interactive Media Activity   Drag and Drop: OSPF Operation

After completing this activity, you will be able to list the steps of OSPF operation.

Step 1: Establish Router Adjacencies

The first step a router takes in the OSPF operation is to establish router adjacencies. Each of the three routers shown in Figure 6-17 attempts to become adjacent to another router on the same IP network.

Figure 6-17 OSPF Topology Example

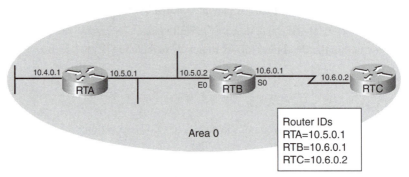

Router IDs
RTA=10.5.0.1
RTB=10.6.0.1
RTC=10.6.0.2

To become adjacent to another router, RTB sends Hello packets, advertising its own router ID. Because no loopback interfaces are present, RTB chooses its highest IP address, 10.6.0.1, as its router ID.

Assuming that RTB is appropriately configured, RTB multicasts Hello packets out both S0 and E0. RTA and RTC should both receive the Hello packets. These two routers then add RTB to the Neighbor ID field of their respective Hello packets and enter the Init state with RTB.

RTB receives Hello packets from both its neighbors and sees its own ID number, 10.6.0.1, in the Neighbor ID field. RTB declares a two-way state between itself and RTA and a two-way state between itself and RTC.

At this point, RTB determines which routers to establish adjacencies with, based on the type of network a particular interface resides on. If the network type is point-to-point, the router becomes adjacent with its sole link partner. If the network type is multiaccess, RTB enters the election process to become a DR or BDR. This happens unless both roles are already established, as advertised in the Hello packet header.

If an election is necessary, OSPF routers proceed as described in the next section. However, if an election is unnecessary, the routers enter the ExStart state, as described in the section "Step 3: Discover Routes."

Step 2: Elect a DR and a BDR

Because multiaccess networks can support more than two routers, OSPF elects a DR to be the focal point of all LSUs and LSAs. The role of the DR is critical, so a BDR is elected to "shadow" the DR. If the DR fails, the BDR can smoothly take over.

Like any election, the DR/BDR selection process can be rigged to change the outcome. The "ballots" are Hello packets, which contain the router's ID and priority fields. The router with the highest priority value among adjacent neighbors wins the election and becomes the DR. The router with the second-highest priority is elected the BDR. When the DR and BDR have been elected, they keep their roles until one of them fails, even if additional routers with higher priorities show up on the network. Hello packets inform newcomers of the identity of the existing DR and BDR.

By default, all OSPF routers have the same priority value of 1. A priority number from 0 to 255 can be assigned on any given OSPF interface. A priority of 0 prevents the router from winning any election on that interface. A priority of 255 ensures at least a tie. The router ID field is used to break ties. If two routers have the same priority, the router with the highest ID is selected. You can manipulate the router ID by configuring an address on a loopback interface, but that is not the preferred way to control the DR/BDR election process. The priority value should be used instead because each interface can have its own unique priority value. A router can be easily configured to win an election on one interface and lose an election on another.

How does the DR election process affect the sample network? RTB and RTC are connected by way of PPP on a point-to-point link, as shown in Figure 6-18. Therefore, there is no need for a DR on the network 10.6.0.0/16, because only two routers can exist on this link.

Figure 6-18 DR and BDR Election Process

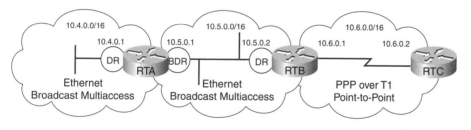

NOTE

DRs and BDRs are elected on a per-network basis. An OSPF area can contain more than one IP network. Therefore, each area can, and usually does, have multiple DRs and BDRs.

Because the 10.4.0.0/16 and 10.5.0.0/16 networks are multiaccess Ethernet networks, they may potentially connect more than two routers. Even if only one router is connected to a multiaccess segment, a DR is still elected. This is because the potential exists for more routers to be added to the network. Therefore, a DR must be elected on both 10.4.0.0/16 and 10.5.0.0/16.

In the sample topology, RTA serves a dual role as both the DR and the BDR. Because it is the only router on the 10.4.0.0/16 network, RTA elects itself as the DR. After all, the 10.4.0.0/16 network is a multiaccess Ethernet network. A DR is elected because multiple routers can potentially be added to this network. RTA is also the runner-up in the election for 10.5.0.0/16 and, therefore, is the BDR for that network. Despite claiming equal priority value with RTA, RTB is elected as the DR for 10.5.0.0/16 by virtue of the tiebreaker. The tiebreaker is having a higher router ID of 10.5.0.2 versus 10.5.0.1.

With elections complete and bidirectional communication established, routers are ready to share routing information with adjacent routers and build their link-state databases. This process is discussed in the next section.

Lab 6.9.2a Examining the DR/BDR Election Process

In this lab, you observe the OSPF DR and BDR election process using **debug** commands. Then you assign each OSPF interface a priority value to force the election of a specific router as a DR.

Step 3: Discover Routes

On a multiaccess network, the exchange of routing information occurs between the DR or BDR and every other router on the network. As the DR and BDR on the 10.5.0.0/16 network, RTA and RTB exchange link-state information, as shown in Figure 6-18.

Link partners on a point-to-point or point-to-multipoint network also engage in the exchange process. That means that RTA and RTB share link-state data, as shown in Figure 6-19.

Figure 6-19 Route Discovery

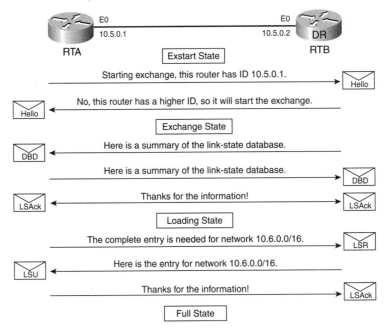

However, who goes first? This question is answered in the first stage of the exchange process, the ExStart state, as shown in Figure 6-19. The purpose of ExStart is to establish a master/slave relationship between the two routers. The router that announces the highest router ID in the Hello packet acts as master. The master router orchestrates the exchange of link-state information, and the slave router responds to prompts from the master. RTB engages in this process with both RTA and RTB.

After the routers define their roles as master and slave, they enter the Exchange state, shown in Figure 6-19. The master leads the slave through a swap of DBDs that describe the link-state database in limited detail for each router. These descriptions include the link-state type, the address of the advertising router, the link's cost, and a sequence number.

The routers acknowledge the receipt of a DBD by sending an LSAck (Type 5) packet, which echoes the DBD's sequence number. Each router compares the information it receives in the DBD with the information it already has. If the DBD advertises a new or more up-to-date link state, the router enters the Loading state by sending an LSR (Type 3) packet about that entry, as shown in Figure 6-19. In response to the LSR, a router sends the complete link-state information using an LSU (Type 4) packet. LSUs carry LSAs.

With the Loading state complete, the routers have achieved full adjacency and have entered the Full state. Figure 6-19 shows that RTB is now adjacent to RTA and to RTC. Adjacent routers must be in the Full state before they can create their routing tables and route traffic. At this point, the neighbor routers should all have identical link-state databases.

Step 4: Select Appropriate Routes

After a router has a complete link-state database, it is ready to create its routing table so that it can forward traffic. As mentioned earlier, OSPF uses the metric value called cost. It is used to determine the best path to a destination, as shown in Figure 6-20. The default cost value is based on media bandwidth. In general, cost decreases as the speed of the link increases. For example, the 10-Mbps Ethernet interface used by RTB has a lower cost than its T1 serial line because 10 Mbps is faster than 1.544 Mbps.

Figure 6-20 Selecting the Best Route

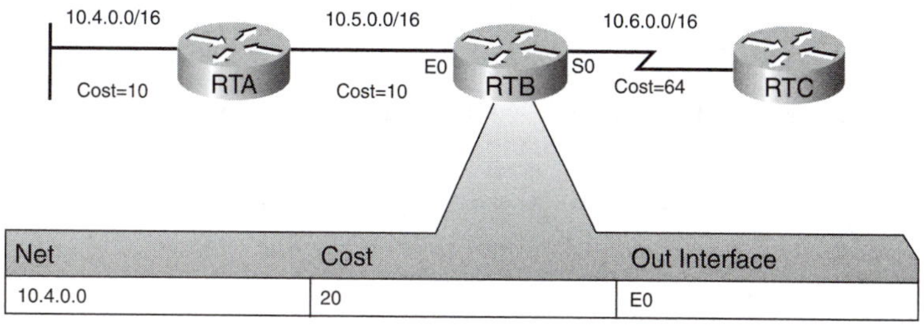

Net	Cost	Out Interface
10.4.0.0	20	E0

To calculate the lowest cost to a destination, RTB uses the SPF algorithm. In simple terms, the SPF algorithm adds up the total costs between the local router, called the root, and each destination network, as shown in Figure 6-20. If there are multiple paths to a destination, the lowest-cost path is preferred. By default, OSPF keeps up to four equal-cost route entries in the routing table for load balancing.

Sometimes a link, such as a serial line, goes up and down rapidly. This condition is called flapping. If a flapping link causes LSUs to be generated, routers that receive those updates must rerun the SPF algorithm to recalculate routes. Prolonged flapping can severely affect performance. Repeated SPF calculations can overtax the router CPU. Also, the constant updates might prevent link-state databases from converging.

To resist this problem, the Cisco IOS software uses an SPF hold timer. After receiving an LSU, the SPF hold timer determines how long a router waits before running the SPF algorithm. The timer defaults to 10 seconds. You can adjust it using the **timers spf** command.

After RTB has selected the best routes using the SPF algorithm, it moves into the final phase of OSPF operation.

Step 5: Maintain Routing Information

When an OSPF router has installed routes in its routing table, it must diligently maintain routing information. When there is a change in a link state, OSPF routers use a flooding process to notify other routers on the network of the change. The dead interval from the Hello protocol provides a simple mechanism for declaring a link partner down. If RTB does not hear from RTA for a time period exceeding the dead interval, usually 40 seconds, RTB declares its link to RTA down.

RTB then sends an LSU packet containing the new link-state information, but to whom?

- On a point-to-point network, no DR or BDR exists. New link-state information is sent to the 224.0.0.5 multicast address. All OSPF routers listen at this address.

- On a multiaccess network, a DR and BDR exist and maintain adjacencies with all other OSPF routers on the network. If a DR or BDR needs to send a LSU, it sends it to all OSPF routers at 224.0.0.5. However, the other routers on a multiaccess network form adjacencies only with the DR and the BDR and, therefore, can send LSUs only to them. For that reason, the DR and BDR have their own multicast address, 224.0.0.6. Non-DR and non-BDR routers send their LSUs to 224.0.0.6, or all DR and BDR routers. For example, in the sample topology shown in Figure 6-21, the DR acknowledges the receipt of the change and floods an LSU to advertise this change to others on the network using the OSPF multicast address 224.0.0.5.

Figure 6-21 Link-State Information

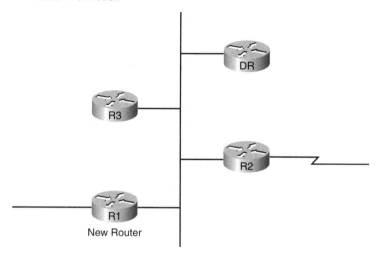

New Router

If an OSPF router is connected to another network, such as R2 in Figure 6-21, it floods the LSU to that network by forwarding the LSU to the DR of the multiaccess network or an adjacent router in a point-to-point network. The DR of that network, in turn, multicasts the LSU to the other OSPF routers in that network.

Upon receiving an LSU that includes the changed LSA and new information, an OSPF router updates its link-state database. It then runs the SPF algorithm using the new information to recalculate the routing table, as shown in Figure 6-22. After the SPF hold timer expires, the router switches over to the new routing table.

If a route already exists in a Cisco router, the old route is used while the SPF algorithm calculates the new information. If the SPF algorithm is calculating a new route, the router does not use that route until after the SPF calculation is complete.

It is important to note that even if a change in link state does not occur, OSPF routing information is periodically refreshed. Each LSA entry has its own age timer. The default timer value is 30 minutes. After an LSA entry ages out, the router that originated the entry sends an LSU to the network to verify that the link is still active.

Figure 6-22 LSUs and Routing Table Updates

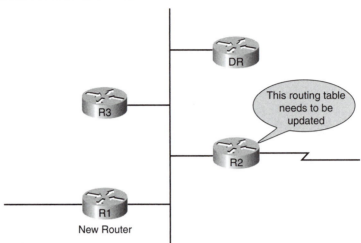

OSPF Configuration and Verification

In this section, you learn how to configure OSPF on routers within a single area.

Configuring OSPF on Routers Within a Single Area

To configure OSPF, enable OSPF on Routers A and B, as shown in Figure 6-23.

Figure 6-23 Basic OSPF Topology Configuration

Configure the network addresses and area information for the router by following these steps:

Step 1   Enable OSPF on the routers using the following command:

```
Router(config)#router ospf process-id
```

The process ID is a process number on the local router. The process ID is used to identify multiple OSPF processes on the same router. The number can be any value between 1 and 65,535. The OSPF processes do not need to start at 1. Most network administrators keep the same process ID throughout the entire AS. It is possible to run multiple OSPF processes on the same router, but this is not recommended because it creates multiple database instances that add overhead to the router.

Enter the following OSPF process commands on the routers shown in Figure 6-23:

```
RouterA(config)#router ospf 1
RouterB(config)#router ospf 1
```

Step 2   Identify IP networks on the router using the following command. Table 6-3 describes the parameters.

```
Router(config-router)#network address wildcard-mask area area-id
```

Table 6-3 network area Command Description

Parameter	Description
address	Can be the network address, subnet, or interface address. Instructs the router to know which links and networks to advertise and which links to listen to advertisements on.
wildcard-mask	An inverse mask used to determine how to read the address. The mask has wildcard bits where 0 is a match and 1 is "do not care." For example, 0.0.255.255 indicates a match in the first two octets. The equivalent *regular* subnet mask is a 16-bit mask of 255.255.0.0. If you're specifying the interface address, use mask 0.0.0.0.
area-id	Specifies the OSPF area to be associated with the address. Can be a number or can be similar to an IP address *A.B.C.D.* For a backbone area, the ID must equal 0.

Enter the following network area commands on the routers shown in Figure 6-23:

```
RouterA(config)#network 10.0.0.0 0.255.255.255 area 0
RouterB(config)#network 10.2.1.2 0.0.0.0 area 0
RouterB(config)#network 10.64.0.2 0.0.0.0 area 0
```

For each network, identify the area to which the network belongs. The network address value can be the network address, subnet, or interface address. The router interprets the address by comparing it to the wildcard mask. A wildcard mask is necessary because OSPF supports CIDR and VLSM, unlike RIPv1 and IGRP. The **area** argument is needed even when you're configuring OSPF in a single area. Again, note that more than one IP network can belong to the same area.

The wildcard mask is essentially an inverse subnet mask. For Router A, the entire 10.0.0.0 network is advertised by specifying the 0.255.255.255 mask. On Router B, the interface addresses are advertised using a 0.0.0.0 mask. All interfaces are in area 0.

Table 6-4 provides other examples of addresses, subnet masks, and inverse masks. The first example advertises the entire network address 172.16.0.0. The second advertises the entire network address 192.168.45.0. The third advertises a small subnet with four hosts (two of which are useable) as might be found on a WAN link. The fourth advertises a subnet with 16 hosts (14 of which are useable). The fifth example advertises an interface address.

Table 6-4 Network Area Command Examples

Interface Address	Subnet Mask	AdvertisedAddress	Wildcard Mask
172.16.0.8	255.255.0.0	172.16.0.0	0.0.255.255
192.168.45.147	255.255.255.0	192.168.45.0	0.0.0.255
192.168.45.5	255.255.255.252	192.168.45.4	0.0.0.3
192.168.45.17	255.255.255.240	192.168.45.16	0.0.0.15
192.168.45.1	255.255.255.0	192.168.45.1	0.0.0.0

Lab 6.9.1   Configuring OSPF

In this lab, you configure OSPF on three Cisco routers.

Optional Configuration Commands

Optional commands exist for doing the following:

- Configuring a loopback address
- Modifying OSPF router priority
- Configuring authentication
- Configuring OSPF timers

Configuring a Loopback Address

When the OSPF process starts, the Cisco IOS software uses the highest local IP address as its OSPF router ID. If a loopback interface is configured, that address is used, regardless of its value. You can assign an IP address to a loopback interface with the following commands:

```
Router(config)#interface loopback number
Router(config-if)#ip address ip-address subnet-mask
```

A loopback-derived router ID ensures stability because that interface is immune to link failure. The loopback interface must be configured before the OSPF process starts, to override the highest interface IP address.

It is recommended that the loopback address be used on all key routers in the OSPF-based network. To avoid routing problems, it is good practice to use a 32-bit subnet mask when configuring a loopback IP address, as shown here:

```
Router(config)#interface loopback0
Router(config-if)#ip address 192.168.1.1 255.255.255.255
```

A 32-bit mask is sometimes called a host mask because it specifies a single host and not a network or subnetwork.

Modifying OSPF Router Priority

You can manipulate the DR or BDR elections by configuring the priority value to a number other than the default value (1). A value of 0 guarantees that the router will not be elected as a DR or BDR. Each OSPF interface can announce a different priority. Configure the priority value, a number from 0 to 255, with the **ip ospf priority** command, which has the following syntax:

```
Router(config-if)#ip ospf priority number
```

To set the fa0 FastEthernet interface on a router with a priority of 0, use the following commands:

```
RTB(config)#interface fa0
RTB(config-if)#ip ospf priority 0
```

For the priority value to figure into the election, it must be set before the election takes place. The priority value and other key information on the interface can be displayed with the **show ip ospf interface** command. The output shown in Example 6-1 tells you which routers have been elected as the DR and BDR, the network type, the link's cost (10), and the timer intervals specific to this interface. In this case, the network type is broadcast multiaccess. The timer intervals configured are Hello (10), Dead (40), Wait (40), and Retransmit (5).

Example 6-1 *Monitoring OSPF with the* **show ip ospf interface** *Command*

```
Router>show ip ospf interface e0
Ethernet0 is up, line protocol is up
  Internet Address 10.5.0.2, Area 0
  Process ID 1, Router ID 10.6.0.1, Network Type BROADCAST, Cost: 10
  Transmit Delay is 1 sec, State DR, Priority 1
  Designated Router (ID) 10.6.0.2, Interface address 10.6.0.1
  Backup Designated Router (ID) 10.5.0.1, Interface address 10.5.0.1
  Timer intervals configured, Hello 10, Dead 40, Wait 40,
     Retransmit 5 Hello due in 00:00:03
  Index 1/1, flood queue length 0
  Next 0x0 (0) (0)/0x0(0)
  Last flood scan length i 1, maximum is 1
  Last flood scan time is 0 msec, maximum is 0 msec
  Neighbor Count is 2, Adjacent neighbor count is 2
    Adjacent with neighbor 10.5.0.1 (Backup Designated Router)
  Suppress hello for 0 neighbor(s)
```

NOTE

To prevent propagation of bogus or fake routes, OSPF always advertises loopback addresses as host routes, with a 32-bit mask.

NOTE

Set 0 priority so that the router cannot win DR/ BDR elections on that network.

OSPF routers use costs associated with interfaces to determine the best route. The Cisco IOS software automatically determines cost based on an interface's bandwidth in bits per second using the following formula:

10^8 / bandwidth value

Table 6-5 shows common default path costs for a variety of media. For OSPF to calculate routes properly, all interfaces connected to the same link must agree on that link's cost. In a multivendor routing environment, an interface's default cost may be overridden to match another vendor's value with the **ip ospf cost** command, which has the following syntax:

```
Router(config-if)#ip ospf cost number
```

Table 6-5 Cisco IOS Software Default OSPF Costs

Medium	Cost
56-kbps serial link	1785
T1 (1.544-Mbps serial link)	64
E1 (2.048-Mbps serial link)	48
4-Mbps Token Ring	25
Ethernet	10
16-Mbps Token Ring	6
100-Mbps Fast Ethernet, FDDI	1

The new cost can be a number between 1 and 65,535. To override the default cost on a router's Serial0 interface, use the following commands:

```
Router(config)#interface s0
Router(config-if)#ip ospf cost 1000
```

The **ip ospf cost** command can also be used to manipulate a route's desirability. This is because routers install the lowest-cost paths in their tables.

For the Cisco IOS software cost formula to be accurate, serial interfaces must be configured with appropriate bandwidth values. Cisco routers default to T1 (1.544 Mbps) on most serial interfaces and require manual configuration for any other bandwidth, as shown in the following example:

```
Router(config)#interface s1
Router(config-if)#bandwidth 56
```

The default reference bandwidth of 100,000,000 does not account for new technologies such as Gigabit and 10 Gigabit Ethernet. The cost of these links would still be 1, which is the same as that of a Fast Ethernet link. Beginning with Cisco IOS Release 11.2, OSPF configuration lets you adjust the reference bandwidth using the **auto-cost reference-bandwidth** command.

The number entered is the number of Mbps. In the following, the reference bandwidth is set to 1000 megabits, or 1 gigabit.

```
Router(config-router)#auto-cost reference-bandwidth 1000
% OSPF: Reference bandwidth is changed.
Please ensure reference bandwidth is consistent across all routers.
```

Configuring Authentication

Authentication is another interface-specific configuration. Each OSPF interface on a router can present a different authentication key, which functions as a password among OSPF routers in the same area. You use the following command syntax to configure OSPF authentication:

```
Router(config-if)#ip ospf authentication-key password
```

After a password is configured, you enable authentication on an area-wide basis with the following syntax, which must be entered on all participating routers:

```
Router(config-router)#area number authentication [message-digest]
```

Although the **message-digest** keyword is optional, it is recommended that you always use it with this command. By default, authentication passwords are sent in clear text over the wire. A packet sniffer could easily capture an OSPF packet and decode the unencrypted password. However, if the **message-digest** argument is used, a message digest, or hash, of the password is sent over the wire in place of the password itself. Unless the recipient is configured with the proper authentication key, that person cannot make sense of the message digest.

If message digest authentication is used, the authentication key is not used. Instead, configure a message digest key on the interface of the OSPF router. The syntax for this command is as follows:

```
Router(config-if)#ip ospf message-digest-key key-id md5 [encryption-type] password
```

Table 6-6 describes the **ip ospf message-digest-key** command parameters.

Table 6-6 ip ospf message-digest-key Command Parameters

Parameter	Description
key-id	An identifier in the range 1 to 255 that allows for multiple keys. The key's ID configuration on each router must match to authenticate.
md5	A required value that specifies that the MD5 algorithm will be used.
[*encryption-type*]	An optional value that specifies the type of encryption to use (0 to 7). An *encryption-type* value of 7 indicates Cisco-proprietary encryption. Type 0 is the default.
password	An alphanumeric password to be used as the message digest key.

Example 6-2 sets the message digest key to "itsasecret" and enables message digest authentication within Area 0.

Example 6-2 *Setting the Message Digest Key*

```
Router(config)#int s0
Router(config-if)#ip ospf message-digest-key 1 md5 0 itsasecret
Router(config-if)#int e0
Router(config-if)#ip ospf message-digest-key 1 md5 0 itsasecret
Router(config-if)#router ospf 1
Router(config-router)#area 0 authentication message-digest
```

Remember, the same parameters would have to be configured on the other routers in the same area.

Configuring OSPF Timers

For OSPF routers to exchange information, they must have the same Hello intervals and the same Dead intervals. By default, the dead interval is 4 times the value of the Hello interval. That way, a router has four chances to send a Hello packet before being declared dead.

On broadcast OSPF networks, the default Hello interval is 10 seconds, and the default Dead interval is 40 seconds. On nonbroadcast networks, the default Hello interval is 30 seconds, and the default Dead interval is 120 seconds.

These default values typically result in efficient OSPF operation and, therefore, do not need to be modified. A situation might arise in which the Hello and Dead intervals need to be adjusted either to improve performance or to match the timers on another router. The syntax of the commands needed to configure both the Hello and Dead intervals is as follows:

```
Router(config-if)#ip ospf hello-interval seconds
Router(config-if)#ip ospf dead-interval seconds
```

Example 6-3 sets the Hello interval to 5 seconds and the dead interval to 20 seconds.

Example 6-3 *Setting the Hello Interval*

```
Router(config)#interface e0
Router(config-if)#ip ospf hello-interval 5
Router(config-if)#ip ospf dead-interval 20
```

Notice that, although it is advised, the Cisco IOS software does not require the dead interval to be configured as 4 times the Hello interval. If the dead interval is set to less than that, the risk is increased that a router could be declared dead. In fact, a congested or flapping link might prevent one or two Hello packets from reaching their destination.

show Commands

Use the commands shown in Table 6-7 to verify that OSPF is working properly. Become familiar with these commands to ensure that the routers are configured correctly and are performing the way they should.

Table 6-7 OSPF Operation and Statistics Commands

Command	Description
show ip protocols	Displays parameters about timers, filters, metrics, networks, and other information for the entire router.
show ip route	Displays the routes known to the router and how they were learned. This is one of the best ways to determine connectivity between the local router and the rest of the internetwork.
show ip ospf interface	Verifies that interfaces have been configured in the intended areas. If no loopback address is specified, the interface with the highest address is taken as the router ID. It also gives the timer intervals, including the hello interval, and shows the neighbor adjacencies.
show ip ospf	Displays the number of times the SPF algorithm has been executed. It also shows the LSU interval, assuming that no topological changes have occurred.
show ip ospf neighbor detail	Displays detailed lists of neighbors, their priorities, and their state, such as Init, ExStart, or Full.
show ip ospf database	Displays the contents of the topological database maintained by the router. Also shows the router ID and the OSPF process ID. A number of database types can be shown with this command using keywords.

clear and debug Commands

You can use the commands described in this section and their associated options when troubleshooting OSPF.

To clear all routes from the IP routing table, use this command:

```
Router#clear ip route *
```

To clear a specific route from the IP routing table, use this command:

```
Router#clear ip route A.B.C.D
```

where *A.B.C.D* is the destination network route to delete.

To debug OSPF operations, use the following **debug** options:

```
Router#debug ip ospf ?
  adj              OSPF adjacency events
  database-timer   OSPF database timer
  events           OSPF events
  flood            OSPF flooding
  hello            OSPF hello events
  lsa-generation   OSPF lsa generation
  mpls             OSPF MPLS
  nsf              OSPF non-stop forwarding events
  packet           OSPF packets
  retransmission   OSPF retransmission events
  spf              OSPF spf
  tree             OSPF database tree
```

Configuring OSPF over NBMA

This chapter has focused on two types of OSPF networks in detail—broadcast multiaccess and point-to-point. Even if there is only one router, broadcast multiaccess networks elect a DR to serve as a focal point for routing information. If there is more than one router, they elect a DB and a BDR. In contrast, point-to-point OSPF networks do not elect a DR because they can never include more than two nodes.

NBMA Overview

Another type of OSPF network, NBMA, can include more than two nodes, as shown in Figure 6-24. Therefore, NBMA tries to elect a DR and a BDR. Common NBMA implementations include Frame Relay, X.25, and Switched Multimegabit Data Service (SMDS). NBMA networks follow rules at Layer 2 that prevent the delivery of broadcasts and multicasts. Table 6-8 summarizes the OSPF network types.

Figure 6-24 Neighbor Status in Different Network Types

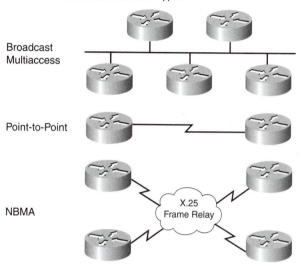

Table 6-8 Types of OSPF Networks

OSPF Network Type	Characteristics	DR Election?
Broadcast multiaccess	Ethernet, Token Ring and FDDI	Yes
Nonbroadcast multiaccess	Frame Relay, X.25 and SMDS	Yes
Point-to-point	PPP and HDLC	No
Point-to-multipoint	Configured by an administrator	No

NBMA networks can create problems with OSPF operation—specifically, with the exchange of multicast Hello packets. RTA, RTB, and RTC belong to the same IP subnetwork and attempt to elect a DR and a BDR, as shown in Figure 6-25. However, these routers cannot hold a valid election if they cannot receive multicast Hellos from every other router on the network. Without administrative intervention, a strange election takes place. As far as RTA is concerned, RTC is not participating. Likewise, RTC goes through the election process oblivious to RTA. This botched election can lead to problems if the central router, RTB, is not elected the DR.

Figure 6-25 DR and BDR Election

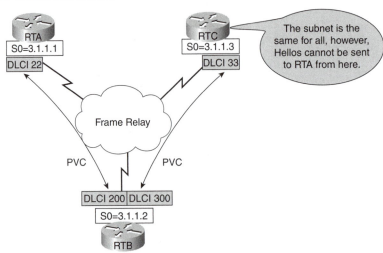

The Cisco IOS software offers several options for configuring OSPF to overcome NBMA limitations, including the OSPF **neighbor** command, point-to-point subinterfaces, and point-to-multipoint configuration. The solutions that are available depend on the current NBMA network topology.

You must understand the different NBMA topologies before selecting an OSPF configuration strategy for a Frame Relay network or a legacy X.25 network. Fundamentally, two possible physical topologies exist for Frame Relay networks, as illustrated in Figure 6-26:

- Full-mesh topology
- Partial-mesh topology, including the hub-and-spoke topology

Figure 6-26 Frame Relay Topologies

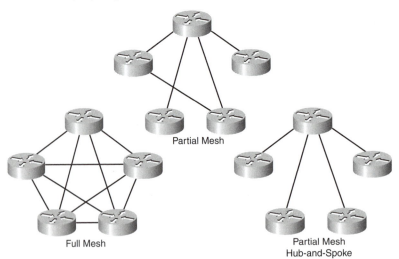

The following sections describe how to configure OSPF in both full-mesh and partial-mesh Frame Relay networks.

Full-Mesh Frame Relay

Organizations use Frame Relay primarily because it supports more than one logical connection over a single interface, as shown in Figure 6-27. This makes it an affordable and flexible choice for WAN links. A full-mesh topology takes advantage of Frame Relay's capability to support multiple permanent virtual circuits (PVCs) on a single serial interface. In a full-mesh topology, every router has a PVC to every other router.

Figure 6-27 Full-Mesh Frame Relay Topologies

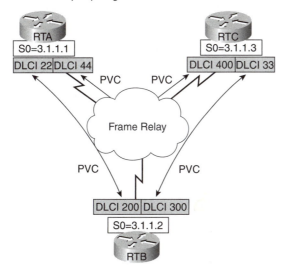

For OSPF to work properly over a multiaccess full-mesh topology that does not support broadcasts, you must manually enter each OSPF neighbor address on each router, one at a time. The OSPF **neighbor** command tells a router about the IP addresses of its neighbors so that it can exchange routing information without multicasts. Example 6-4 illustrates how the **neighbor** command is used.

Example 6-4 **neighbor** *Command*

```
RTA(config)#router ospf 1
RTA(config-router)#network 3.1.1.0 0.0.0.255 area 0
RTA(config-router)#neighbor 3.1.1.2
RTA(config-router)#neighbor 3.1.1.3
```

Specifying the neighbors for each router is not the only option to make OSPF work in this type of environment. The following section explains how configuring subinterfaces can eliminate the need for the **neighbor** command.

Configuring Subinterfaces to Create Point-to-Point Networks

The Cisco IOS software subinterface feature can be used to break a multiaccess network into a collection of point-to-point networks.

In Figure 6-28, a different IP subnet is assigned to each PVC. OSPF automatically recognizes this configuration as point-to-point, not NBMA, even with Frame Relay configured on the interfaces. Recall that OSPF point-to-point networks do not elect a DR. Instead, the Frame Relay router uses Inverse ARP or a Frame Relay map to obtain the link partner's address so that routing information can be exchanged.

Figure 6-28 Neighbor Status in Different Network Types

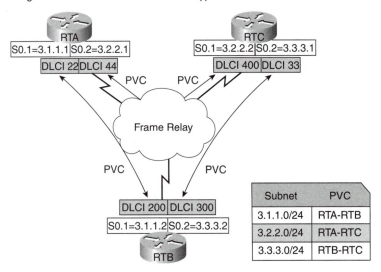

A full-mesh topology offers numerous advantages, including maximum fault tolerance. Unfortunately, full-mesh topologies can get expensive, because each PVC must be leased from a provider. An organization would have to lease 45 PVCs to support just ten fully meshed routers. If subinterfaces are used to create point-to-point networks, the 45 IP subnets must also be allocated and managed, which is an additional expense.

Partial-Mesh Frame Relay

Because a full-mesh topology is costly, many organizations implement a partial-mesh topology instead. A partial-mesh topology is any configuration in which at least one router maintains multiple connections to other routers without being fully meshed. The most cost-effective partial-mesh topology is a hub-and-spoke topology. This is where a single router, the hub, connects to multiple spoke routers.

The hub-and-spoke topology is a cost-effective WAN solution that introduces a single point of failure, the hub router. Organizations typically use Frame Relay because it is inexpensive, not because it is fault-tolerant.

Unfortunately, the **neighbor** command that worked with a full-mesh topology does not work as well with the hub-and-spoke topology. The hub router shown in Figure 6-29 sees all of the spoke routers and can send routing information to them using the **neighbor** command, but the spoke routers can send Hellos only to the hub.

Figure 6-29 Hub-and-Spoke Topology

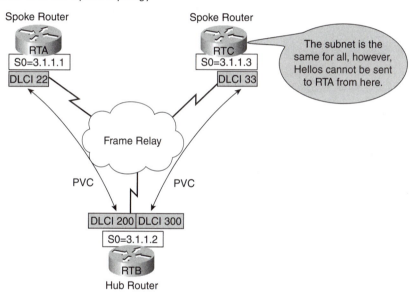

The DR or BDR election is held, but only the hub router sees all of the candidates. Because the hub router must act as the DR for this OSPF network to function properly, configure an OSPF interface priority of 0 on all of the spoke routers. Recall that a priority of 0 makes it impossible for a router to be elected as a DR or a BDR for a network.

A second approach to dealing with this topology is to avoid the DR and BDR issue altogether by breaking the network into point-to-point connections, as shown in Figure 6-30. Point-to-point networks do not elect a DR or BDR.

Figure 6-30 Hub-and-Spoke Topology with Subinterfaces

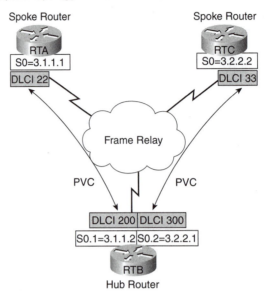

Although they make OSPF configuration straightforward, point-to-point networks have major drawbacks when used with a hub-and-spoke topology. Subnets must be allocated for each link. This can lead to WAN addressing that is complex and difficult to manage. You can avoid the WAN addressing issue by using IP unnumbered, but many organizations have WAN-management policies that prevent using this feature. Are there any possible alternatives to a point-to-point configuration? Fortunately, the Cisco IOS software offers a relatively new alternative. A hub-and-spoke physical topology can be manually configured as a point-to-multipoint network type, as described in the following section.

Lab 6.9.2b   Configuring Point-to-Multipoint OSPF over Frame Relay

In this lab, you configure OSPF as a point-to-multipoint network type so that it operates efficiently over a hub-and-spoke Frame Relay topology.

Point-to-Multipoint OSPF

In a point-to-multipoint network, a hub router is directly connected to multiple spoke routers, but all of the WAN interfaces are addressed on the same subnet, as illustrated in Figure 6-31.

Figure 6-31 Hub-and-Spoke Topology with OSPF Point-to-Multipoint

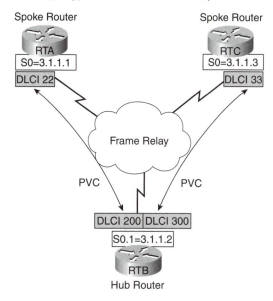

You saw this logical topology earlier in this chapter. However, you also learned that OSPF does not work properly as an NBMA OSPF network type. If you manually change the OSPF network type to point-to-multipoint, this logical topology can then work. Routing between RTA and RTC goes through the router that has virtual circuits to both routers, RTB. Notice that it is not necessary to configure neighbors when using this feature. Inverse ARP discovers them.

Point-to-multipoint networks have the following properties:

- Adjacencies are established between all neighboring routers. There is no DR or BDR for a point-to-multipoint network. No network LSA is originated for point-to-multipoint networks. Router priority is not configured for point-to-multipoint interfaces or for neighbors on point-to-multipoint networks.

- When a router LSA is originated, the point-to-multipoint interface is reported as a collection of point-to-point links to all of the adjacent neighbors on the interface. This is together with a single stubby link advertising the IP address of the interface with a cost of 0.

When flooding out a nonbroadcast interface, the LSU or LSAck packet must be replicated to be sent to each of the neighbors on the interface.

To configure point-to-multipoint, manually override the detected OSPF network type with the following syntax:

```
Router(config-if)#ip ospf network point-to-multipoint
```

Also configure the interface with a **frame-relay map ip** command:

```
Router(config-if)#frame-relay map ip address dlci broadcast
```

The **broadcast** keyword permits the router to send broadcasts by way of the specified DLCI to the mapped neighbor or neighbors. If you're applying the point-to-multipoint configuration to the sample network shown in Figure 6-31, two separate **frame-relay map** statements would have to be configured on the hub router, RTB, as shown in Example 6-5.

Example 6-5 *Configurations for Point-to-Multipoint OSPF*

```
RTA>show running configuration
<output omitted>
!
interface Serial0
  encapsulation frame-relay
  ip address 3.1.1.1 255.255.255.0
  ip ospf network point-to-multipoint
  frame-relay map ip 3.1.1.2 22 broadcast
!
router ospf 1
  network 3.1.1.0 0.0.0.255 area 0

RTB>show running configuration
<output omitted>
!
interface Serial0
  encapsulation frame-relay
  ip address 3.1.1.2 255.255.255.0
  ip ospf network point-to-multipoint
  frame-relay map ip 3.1.1.1 200 broadcast
frame-relay map ip 3.1.1.3 300 broadcast
!
router ospf 1
  network 3.1.1.0 0.0.0.255 area 0

RTC>show running configuration
<output omitted>
```

Example 6-5 *Configurations for Point-to-Multipoint OSPF (Continued)*

```
!
interface Serial0
  encapsulation frame-relay
  ip address 3.1.1.3 255.255.255.0
  ip ospf network point-to-multipoint
frame-relay map ip 3.1.1.2 33 broadcast
!
router ospf 1
  network 3.1.1.0 0.0.0.255 area 0
```

In a point-to-multipoint configuration, OSPF treats all router-to-router connections on the nonbroadcast network as if they were point-to-point links. No DR is elected for the network. Neighbors can be manually specified using the **neighbor** command or can be dynamically discovered using Inverse ARP. Ultimately, point-to-multipoint OSPF offers efficient operation without administrative complexity.

Multiarea OSPF Operation

Three issues can overwhelm an OSPF router in a heavily populated OSPF network:

- High demand for router processing and memory resources
- Large routing tables
- Large topology tables

Creating Multiple OSPF Areas

In a very large internetwork, changes are inevitable. OSPF routers are likely to run SPF calculations frequently, which deprive the router of precious CPU cycles and memory resources, as shown in Figure 6-32.

Not only is the routing table frequently recalculated in a large OSPF network, but it also risks being overstuffed with multiple paths and hundreds of routes. Full routing tables make routers less efficient. Finally, the link-state database, which must contain a complete topology of the network, also threatens to consume resources and slow down the router.

Fortunately, OSPF allows large areas to be separated into smaller, more manageable areas. These smaller areas can exchange summaries of routing information rather than exchange every detail. By splitting the network into manageable pieces, OSPF routers can scale gracefully.

Figure 6-32 Issues with Maintaining a Large OSPF Network

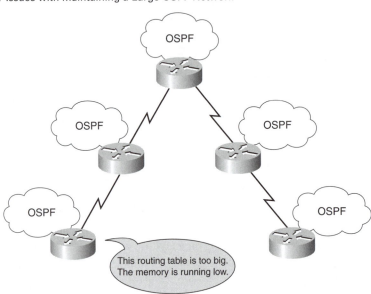

Just how many routers can an OSPF area support? Field studies have shown that a single OSPF area should not stretch beyond 50 routers, although there is no set limit. Some areas might do fine with more than 50 routers. Other areas, particularly those with unstable links, might need to operate with fewer than 50 routers. Ultimately, you must determine just how many routers a particular OSPF area can handle. Knowing the network by tracking performance and monitoring usage is the only way to accurately gauge whether an OSPF area can support 20, 30, or 60 routers.

OSPF's capability to separate a large internetwork into multiple areas is called *hierarchical routing*. Hierarchical routing enables the separation of large internetworks into smaller internetworks that are called *interareas*. With this technique, interarea routing still occurs. Interarea routing is the process of exchanging routing information between OSPF areas. However, interarea routing allows OSPF to summarize and contain area-specific information so that many of the smaller internal routing operations, such as recalculating the database, are restricted within an area.

For example, if Area 1 is having problems with a link going up and down (flapping), routers in other areas do not need to run their SPF calculation, because they are isolated from the problems in Area 1, as shown in Figure 6-33.

Figure 6-33 OSPF Hierarchical Routing

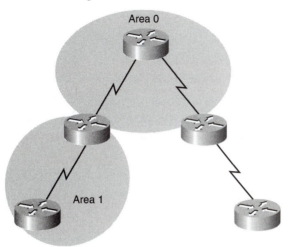

OSPF's hierarchical topology possibilities have the following important advantages:

- **Reduced frequency of SPF calculations**—Because detailed route information is kept within each area, it is not necessary to flood all link-state changes to all other areas. Therefore, only routers affected by a change need to run the SPF calculation.

- **Smaller routing tables**—When multiple areas are used, detailed route entries for specific networks within an area are kept inside the area. Rather than advertise these explicit routes outside the area, the routes can be summarized into one or more summary routes. Advertising these summaries reduces the number of LSAs propagated between areas but allows all networks to remain reachable.

- **Reduced LSU overhead**—LSUs can contain a variety of LSA types, including link-state information and summary information. Rather than send an LSU about each network to every area, advertise a single route or a few summarized routes between areas to reduce the overhead associated with LSUs that cross multiple areas.

Hierarchical routing increases routing efficiency because it lets you control the type of routing information that flows into and out of an area. OSPF provides for different types of routing updates, depending on the type and number of areas a router connects to. The following sections describe the different roles an OSPF router can play, the types of LSAs it can use, and the types of areas it can connect to.

 Interactive Media Activity   Drag and Drop: Comparison of OSPF and EIGRP Features

After completing this activity, you will be able to identify and compare the different features of OSPF and EIGRP.

OSPF Router Types

Four different types of OSPF routers exist, as shown in Figure 6-34:

- **Internal router**—As discussed previously, routers that have all of their interfaces within the same area are called internal routers. Internal routers in the same area have identical link-state databases and run a single copy of the routing algorithm.

- **Backbone router**—Routers that are attached to the backbone area of the OSPF network are called backbone routers. They have at least one interface connected to Area 0, the backbone area. These routers maintain OSPF routing information using the same procedures and algorithms as internal routers.

- **Area Border Router (ABR)**—ABRs are routers with interfaces attached to multiple areas. They maintain a separate link-state database for each area to which they are connected, and they route traffic destined for or arriving from other areas. ABRs are exit points for the area, which means that routing information destined for another area can travel there only by way of the of the local area ABR. ABRs summarize information about the attached areas from their link-state databases and distribute the information into the backbone. The backbone ABRs then forward the information to all other connected areas. An area can have one or more ABRs.

- **Autonomous System Boundary Router (ASBR)**—ASBRs are routers that have at least one interface connected to an external internetwork—another autonomous system, such as a non-OSPF network. These routers can import non-OSPF network information to the OSPF network and OSPF to non-OSPF. This is called *redistribution*.

Figure 6-34 OSPF Multiarea Components

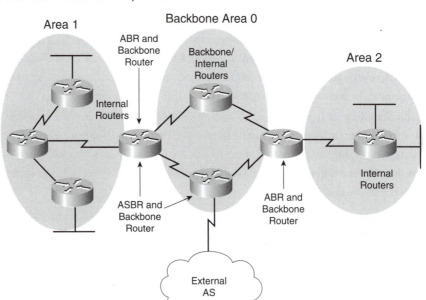

A router can be more than one router type. For example, if a router interconnects to Area 0 and Area 1, as well as to a non-OSPF network, it is both an ABR and an ASBR.

OSPF LSA and Area Types

Multiarea OSPF is scalable because a router's link-state database can include multiple types of LSAs, as shown in Figure 6-35.

Figure 6-35 OSPF Sample OSPF Database

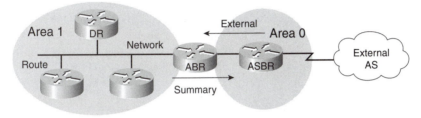

OSPF LSA Types

DRs and routers that reside in multiple areas or autonomous systems use special LSAs to send or summarize routing information. The OSPF LSA types are described in Table 6-9.

Table 6-9 OSPF LSA Types

LSAType	Name	Description
1	Router link entry (O-OSPF)	Generated by each router for each area it belongs to. It describes the states of the link from the router to the area. These are flooded only within a particular area. The link status and cost are two of the descriptors provided. Routes learned by way of Type 1 LSAs are denoted by an O in the routing table.
2	Network link entry (O-OSPF)	Generated by the DR in multiaccess networks. A Type 2 LSA describes the set of routers attached to a particular network. Type 2 LSAs are flooded only within the area that contains the network. Routes learned by way of Type 2 LSAs are denoted by an O in the routing table.
3	Summary link entry (IA-OSPF)	Originated by ABRs. A Type 3 LSA describes the links between the ABR and the internal routers of a local area. These entries are flooded throughout the backbone area to the outer ABRs. Type 3 LSAs describe routes to networks within the local area and are sent to the backbone area. Routes learned by way of Type 3 LSAs are denoted by an O in the routing table.

continues

Table 6-9 OSPF LSA Types (Continued)

LSAType	Name	Description
4	Summary link entry (O-OSPF)	Originated by ABRs. Type 4 LSAs are flooded throughout the backbone area to the outer ABRs. Type 4 LSAs describe reachability to ASBRs. These link entries are not flooded through totally stubby areas. Routes learned by way of Type 4 LSAs are denoted by an IA in the routing table.
5	Autonomous system external link entry (E1-OSPF external Type 1 and E2-OSPF external Type 2)	Originated by ASBRs. A Type 5 LSA describes routes to destinations external to the autonomous system. These are flooded throughout an OSPF autonomous system except for stubby and totally stubby areas. Routes learned by way of Type 5 LSAs are denoted by either an E1 or E2 in the routing table.
6	Multicast OSPF (MOSPF)	Not implemented by Cisco. MOSPF enhances OSPF by letting routers use their link-state data-bases to build multicast distribution trees for the forwarding of multicast traffic.
7	Autonomous system external link entry (N1-OSPF NSSA external Type 1, N2-OSPF external Type 2)	Originated by an ASBR connected to an NSSA. Type 7 messages can be flooded throughout NSSAs and translated into LSA Type 5 messages by ABRs. Routes learned by way of Type 7 LSAs are denoted by either an N1 or an N2 in the routing table.

OSPF Area Type

The characteristics assigned to an area control the type of route information it can receive. For example, the size of routing tables might need to be minimized in an OSPF area. In this case, configure the routers to operate in an area that does not accept external routing information, Type 5 LSAs.

The following are several area types that are possible, as shown in Figure 6-36:

- **Standard area**—A standard area can accept link updates and route summaries.
- **Backbone area (transit area)**—When interconnecting multiple areas, the backbone area is the central entity to which all other areas connect. The backbone area is always Area 0. All other areas must connect to this area to exchange route information. The OSPF backbone has all of the properties of a standard OSPF area.
- **Stubby area**—A stubby area is an area that does not accept information about routes external to the autonomous system, the OSPF internetwork, such as routes from

non-OSPF sources. If routers need to reach networks outside the autonomous system, they use a default route. A default route is denoted as 0.0.0.0/0.

■ **Totally stubby area**—A totally stubby area is an area that does not accept external autonomous system routes or summary routes from other areas internal to the autonomous system. Instead, if the router needs to send a packet to a network external to the area, it sends it using a 0.0.0.0/0 default route. Totally stubby areas are a Cisco-proprietary feature.

■ **Not-so-stubby area (NSSA)**—An NSSA is an area that is similar to a stubby area but allows for importing external routes as Type 7 LSAs and translating specific Type 7 LSA routes into Type 5 LSAs.

Figure 6-36 Types of Areas

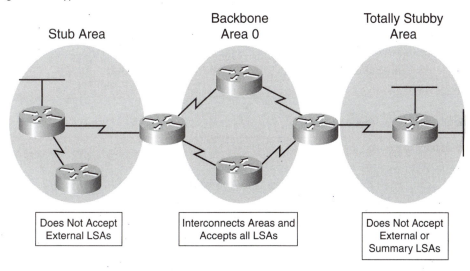

A key difference among these OSPF area types is how they handle external routes. An ASBR injects external routes into OSPF. The ASBR may learn these routes from RIP or some other routing protocol.

An ASBR can be configured to send two types of external routes into OSPF. These types are denoted in the routing table as E1 for Type 1 and E2 for Type 2. Depending on the type, OSPF calculates the cost of external routes differently:

■ If a packet is an E1, the metric is calculated by adding the external cost to the internal cost of each link the packet crosses. Use this packet type when multiple ASBRs are advertising a route to the same autonomous system.

■ If a packet is an E2, the packet always has the external cost assigned, no matter where in the area it crosses; this is the default setting on ASBRs. Use this packet type if only one router is advertising a route to the autonomous system. Type 2 routes are preferred over Type 1 routes, unless two equal-cost routes to the destination exist.

For example, consider the network shown in Figure 6-37.

Figure 6-37 OSPF LSA

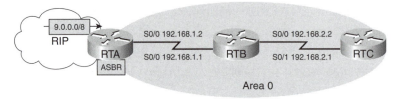

In this network, RTB receives external RIP routes, including 9.0.0.0/8 from RTA. By default, RTA sends external routing information using Type 2 metrics. Therefore, when RTB sends this route to RTC, the metric for the external route remains the same—in this case, 20. Compare the E2 routing table entries for RTB in Example 6-6 to the E2 entries for RTC in Example 6-7.

Example 6-6 *Routing Table Entries for RTB*

```
RTB#show ip route
<output omitted>
O E2 9.0.0.0/8 [110/20] via 192.168.1.2, 00:00:07, Serial0/0
C    192.168.1.0/24 is directly connected, Serial0/0
C    192.168.2.0/24 is directly connected, Serial0/1
```

Example 6-7 *Routing Table Entries for RTC*

```
RTC#show ip route
<output omitted>
O E2 9.0.0.0/8 [110/20] via 192.168.2.1, 00:00:46, Serial0/0
C    192.168.1.0/24 [110/1171] via 192.168.2.1, 00:03:09, Serial0/0
C    192.168.2.0/24 is directly connected, Serial0/0
```

If RTA is configured to use a Type 1 metric with external routes, OSPF increments the metric value of the external route according to its standard cost algorithm. In the **show ip route** output shown in Example 6-8, you can see that the same routes are now listed as E1 and have very different metrics in each table. RTB now increments the metric for the external route, as shown in Example 6-9.

Example 6-8 *Routing Table Entries for RTB*

```
RTB#show ip route
<output omitted>
O E2 9.0.0.0/8 [110/20] via 192.168.2.1, 00:00:05, Serial0/0
C    192.168.1.0/24 is directly connected, Serial0/0
C    192.168.2.0/24 is directly connected, Serial0/1
```

Example 6-9 *Routing Table Entries for RTC*

```
RTC#show ip route
<output omitted>
O E2 9.0.0.0/8 [110/1191] via 192.168.2.1, 00:00:47, Serial0/0
C    192.168.1.0/24 [110/1171] via 192.168.2.1, 00:04:50, Serial0/0
C    192.168.2.0/24 is directly connected, Serial0/0
```

Interactive Media Activity   Drag and Drop: OSPF LSA Types

After completing this activity, you will be able to identify the different OSPF LSA types.

Configuring OSPF Operation Across Multiple Areas

Internal routers, ABRs, ASBRs, and backbone routers each play a role in communicating OSPF routing information in a multiarea network. This section summarizes how the different types of OSPF routers flood information and how they build their routing tables when operating within a multiarea environment.

You've seen that a packet destined for a network within an area is merely forwarded from one internal router to another until it reaches the destination network. However, what if a packet must traverse multiple areas, as shown in Figures 6-38, 6-39, and 6-40?

Figure 6-38 Packet Forwarding in a Multiarea Network to ABR1

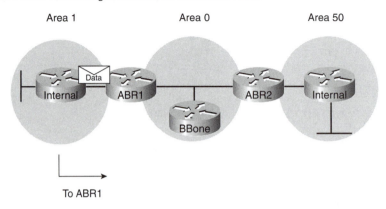

Figure 6-39 Packet Forwarding in a Multiarea Network to the Backbone

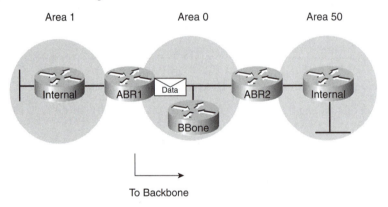

Figure 6-40 Packet Forwarding in a Multiarea Network to the Destination Network

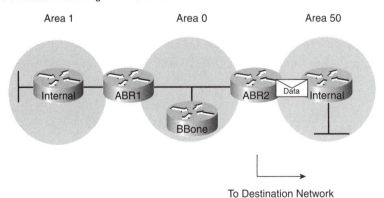

In this case, the packet must exit Area 1 by way of ABR1. ABR1 then sends the packet through the backbone area to ABR2. Finally, ABR2 can forward the packet to an internal router in Area 50. The internal router then delivers the message to the appropriate host on that network.

In this example, for the OSPF routers to make these routing decisions, they must build sufficient routing tables by exchanging LSUs. The LSU exchange process within a single OSPF area relies on just two LSA types—Type 1 and Type 2. To distribute routing information to multiple areas efficiently, ABRs must use Type 3 and Type 4 LSAs. The following sections describe how LSUs containing the various LSA types are flooded to multiple areas and how OSPF routers use this information to update their routing tables.

Lab 6.9.3   Configuring Multiarea OSPF

In this lab, you configure a multiarea OSPF operation, interarea summarization, external route summarization, and default routing.

Flooding LSUs to Multiple Areas

An ABR is responsible for generating routing information about each area to which it is connected. Then it floods the information through the backbone area to the other areas to which the backbone is connected, as shown in Figures 6-41, 6-42, and 6-43.

Figure 6-41 Flooding Type 1 LSUs to Multiple Areas

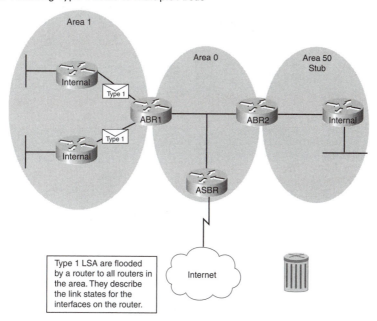

Figure 6-42 Flooding Type 3 LSUs to Multiple Areas

Area 1
Area 0
Area 50
Stub
Internal
ABR1
Type 3
ABR2
Internal
Internal
ASBR
Type 3 LSAs are used to summarize link advertisements generated by ABRs describing interarea routes. Type 3 LSAs describe routers to networks and are used for summarization.
Internet

Figure 6-43 Flooding Type 5 LSUs to Multiple Areas

Area 1
Area 0
Area 50
Stub
Internal
Type 5
ABR1
ABR2
Default
Internal
Type 5
Internal
ASBR
Type 5
Type 5 LSAs are generated by the ASBR and describe links external to the autonomous system. Type 5 LSAs are flooded to all areas except sub areas.
Internet

The general flooding process follows these steps:

1. The routing processes occur within the area. The entire area must be synchronized before the ABR can begin sending summary LSAs to other areas.
2. The ABR reviews the resulting link-state database and generates summary LSAs using Type 3 or Type 4. By default, the ABR sends summary LSAs for each network it knows

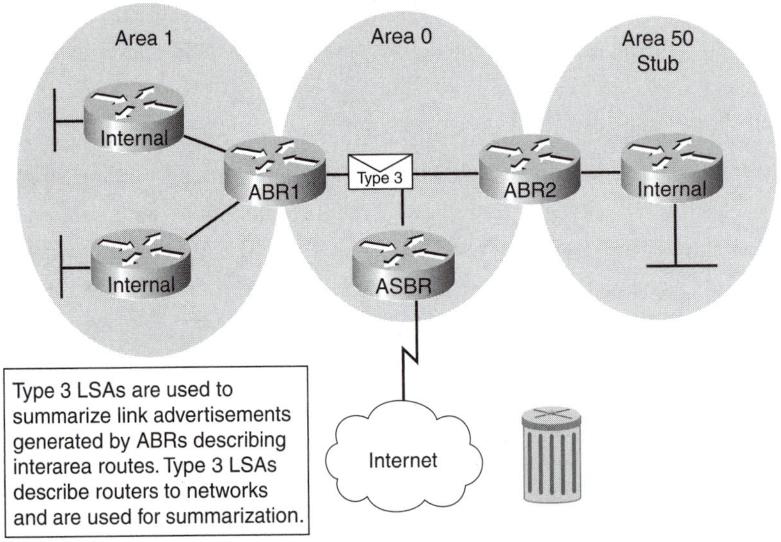

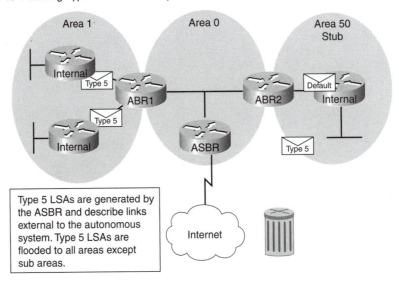

about. To reduce the number of summary LSA entries, configure route summarization so that a single IP address can represent multiple networks. To use route summarization, the areas need to use contiguous IP addressing, as discussed in Chapter 2, "Advanced IP Addressing Management." The better this IP address plan is, the fewer summary LSA entries an ABR advertises.

3. The summary LSAs are placed in an LSU and are distributed through all ABR interfaces, with the following exceptions:

— If the interface is connected to a neighboring router that is in a state below the exchange state, the summary LSA is not forwarded.

— If the interface is connected to a totally stubby area, the summary LSA is not forwarded.

— If the summary LSA includes a Type 5 (external) route and the interface is connected to a stubby or totally stubby area, the LSA is not sent to that area.

4. After an ABR or ASBR receives summary LSAs, it adds them to its link-state databases and floods them to the local area. The internal routers then assimilate the information into their databases. Remember that OSPF lets you configure different area types so that you can reduce the number of route entries that internal routers maintain. To minimize routing information, define the area as a stubby area, a totally stubby area, or an NSSA.

Updating the Routing Table

After all routers receive the routing updates, they add them to their link-state databases and recalculate their routing tables. Paths are calculated in this order:

1. All routers calculate the paths to destinations within their area and add these entries to the routing table. These are learned by way of Type 1 and Type 2 LSAs.

2. All routers calculate the paths to the other areas within the internetwork. These paths are learned by way of interarea route entries, or Type 3 and Type 4 LSAs. If a router has an interarea route to a destination and an intra area route to the same destination, the intra area route is kept.

3. All routers, except those that are in any of the stubby area types, calculate the paths to the AS external (Type 5) destinations.

At this point, a router can reach any network within or outside the OSPF autonomous system.

Opaque LSAs

Opaque LSAs allow for the future extensibility of OSPF. The information contained in opaque LSAs may be used directly by OSPF or indirectly by applications that want to distribute information throughout an OSPF domain. For example, the OSPF opaque LSA may be used for traffic engineering with Multiprotocol Label Switching (MPLS).

Opaque LSAs are Types 9, 10, and 11 LSAs. Opaque LSAs consist of a standard LSA header followed by a 32-bit aligned application-specific information field. Like any other LSA, the opaque LSA uses the link-state database distribution mechanism to flood this information throughout the topology. The opaque LSA's link-state type field identifies the LSA's topological distribution range. This range is called the *flooding scope*.

The flooding scope associated with each opaque link-state type is defined as follows:

- Link-state Type 9 denotes a link-local scope. Type 9 opaque LSAs are not flooded beyond the local network or subnetwork.
- Link-state Type 10 denotes an area-local scope. Type 10 opaque LSAs are flooded only within their associated area.
- Link-state Type 11 denotes that the LSA is flooded throughout the entire autonomous system. The flooding scope of Type 11 LSAs is equivalent to the flooding scope of AS-external (Type 5) LSAs.

Multiarea OSPF Configuration and Verification

The following sections discuss some of the details of OSPF configuration and verification:

- Using and configuring OSPF multiarea components
- Configuring OSPF route summarization
- Verifying multiarea OSPF operation

Using and Configuring OSPF Multiarea Components

The following sections cover some of the multiarea OSPF capabilities and associated configurations in more detail. You will learn how to configure an ABR and route summarization.

Configuring an ABR

No special commands make a router an ABR or an ASBR. The router becomes an ABR as soon as two of its interfaces are configured to operate in different areas, as shown in Figure 6-44. Example 6-10 shows the configuration for the routers shown in Figure 6-44.

Figure 6-44 Configuring OSPF ABRs

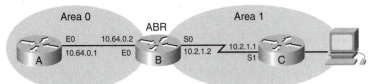

Example 6-10 *Configuring OSPF ABRs*

```
RouterA#show running configuration
<output omitted>
!
ip address 10.64.0.1 255.255.255.0
!
<output omitted>
router ospf 77
network 10.0.0.0 0.255.255.255 area 0

RouterB#show running configuration
<output omitted>
interface Ethernet0
ip address 10.64.0.2 255.255.255.0
!
interface Serial0
ip address 10.2.1.2 255.255.255.0
<output omitted>
router ospf 50
network 10.0.0.0 0.255.255.255 area 1
network 10.0.0.0 0.255.255.255 area 0
```

Configuring an ASBR

ASBRs are created when OSPF is configured to import, or redistribute, external routes into OSPF, as shown in Figure 6-45. Notice that the ASBR configuration commands include the command **redistribute rip subnets**, which is shown in Example 6-11. This command tells OSPF to import RIP routing information. A detailed discussion of route redistribution can be found in Chapter 8, "Route Optimization." The **subnets** option tells the OSPF process to include RIP subnets in redistribution.

Figure 6-45 Configuring OSPF ASBRs

Example 6-11 *Configuring OSPF ASBR*

```
RTA(config)#router rip
RTA(config-router)#network 10.0.0.0
RTA(config-router)#exit
RTA(config)#router ospf 1
RTA(config-router)#network 192.168.1.0 0.0.0.255 area 0
RTA(config-router)#redistribute rip subnets
RTA(config-router)#^Z

RTA#show ip ospf
Routing Process "ospf 1" with ID 192.168.1.2
Supports only single TOS(TOS0) routes
 Supports opaque LSA
 It is an autonomous system boundary router
 Redistributing external routes from rip, including subnets in redistribution.
<output omitted>
```

Configuring OSPF Route Summarization

Recall that summarization is the consolidation of multiple routes into one single, supernet advertisement. See Chapter 2, "Objectives," for more details. Proper summarization requires contiguous (sequential) addressing. 200.10.0.0, 200.10.1.0, 200.10.2.0, and so on are examples of contiguous addressing. OSPF routers can be manually configured to advertise a supernet route, which is different from an LSA summary route.

Route summarization directly affects the amount of bandwidth, CPU, and memory resources that the OSPF process consumes. With summarization, if a network link fails or flaps, the topology change is not propagated into the backbone and other areas by way of the backbone. As discussed in previous chapters, route summarization protects routers from needless routing table recalculations. Because the SPF calculation places a significant demand on a router CPU, proper summarization is an important part of OSPF configuration. OSPF supports the following two types of summarization:

- **Interarea route summarization**—Interarea route summarization is done on ABRs and applies to routes from within each area. It does not apply to external routes injected into OSPF by way of redistribution. To take advantage of summarization, network numbers within areas should be contiguous.

- **External route summarization**—External route summarization is specific to external routes that are injected into OSPF by way of redistribution. Here again, it is important to ensure that external address ranges that are being summarized are contiguous.

Summarization of overlapping ranges from two different routers can cause packets to be sent to the wrong destination. Only ASBRs can summarize external routes.

To configure an ABR to summarize routes for a specific area before injecting them into a different area, use the following syntax:

```
Router(config-router)#area area-id range address mask
```

To configure an ASBR to summarize external routes before injecting them into the OSPF domain, use the following syntax:

```
Router(config-router)#summary-address address mask
```

Use the following commands to configure RTA for external router summarization, as shown in Figure 6-46.

```
RTA(config)#router ospf 1
RTA(config-router)#summary-address 200.9.0.0 255.255.0.0
```

Figure 6-46 OSPF Route Summarization

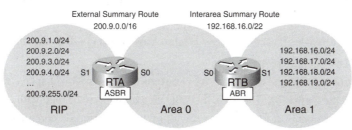

After it is configured, RTA sends only a single summary route, 200.9.0.0/16, into the OSPF domain.

Because RTB sits on the border between Area 0 and Area 1, it should be configured to perform interarea summarization, as follows:

```
RTB(config)#router ospf 1
RTB(config-router)#area 1 range 192.168.16.0 255.255.252.0
```

Notice that the **area 1 range** command in this example specifies the area containing the range to be summarized before being injected into Area 0. In this example, the four networks in the area, 192.168.16.0/24 through 192.168.19.0/24, are summarized to the single summary route 192.168.16.0/22 using the common bits.

Also, depending on the network topology, you might not want to summarize Area 0 networks. If there is more than one ABR between an area and the backbone area, for example, sending a summary LSA with the explicit network information ensures that the shortest path is selected. If the addresses are summarized, suboptimal path selection might occur.

Verifying Multiarea OSPF Operation

In addition to the **show** commands discussed earlier, several key OSPF commands can be used to verify multiarea operation:

- **show ip ospf border-routers**—Displays the internal OSPF routing table entries to an ABR.

- **show ip ospf virtual-links**—Displays parameters about the current state of OSPF virtual links.

- **show ip ospf** *process-id*—Displays information about each area to which the router is connected and indicates whether the router is an ABR, ASBR, or both. The process ID is a user-defined identification parameter. It is locally assigned and can be any positive integer. The number used here is the number assigned administratively when enabling the OSPF routing process.

- **show ip ospf database**—Displays the contents of the topological database maintained by the router. Several keywords can be used with this command to get specific information about the following links:

    - **show ip ospf** [*process-id area-id*] **database** [**router**]—Displays individual router link-state information.

    - **show ip ospf** [*process-id area-id*] **database** [**network**]—Displays network link-state information. The *area ID* is the area number associated with the OSPF address range defined in the network router configuration command when defining a particular area.

    - **show ip ospf** [*process-id area-id*] **database** [**summary**]—Displays summary information about ABR link states.

    - **show ip ospf** [*process-id area-id*] **database** [**asbr-summary**]—Displays information about ASBR link states.

    - **show ip ospf** [*process-id area-id*] **database** [**external**]—Displays information about autonomous system external link states.

    - **show ip ospf** [*process-id area-id*] **database** [**database-summary**]—Displays database summary information and totals.

Stub, Totally Stubby, and Not-So-Stubby Areas

An OSPF router interface can be configured to operate as either a stubby area or a totally stubby area. A stubby area does not accept information about routes external to the AS. A totally stubby area does not accept external AS routes and summary routes from other areas internal to the AS.

Using Stub and Totally Stubby Areas

If you configure an area as stubby, you can greatly reduce the size of the link-state database inside that area. As a result, this reduces the area routers' memory requirements. Remember that stubby areas do not accept Type 5 (external) LSAs.

Because OSPF routers internal to a stubby area do not learn about external networks, routing to the outside world is based on a 0.0.0.0/0 default route. When configuring a stubby area, the ABR on the stub automatically propagates a 0.0.0.0/0 default route within the area.

Stubby areas are typically created when using a hub-and-spoke topology, with the spokes configured as stubby areas. The spokes could be the branch offices. In the case of a hub-and-spoke topology, the branch office might not need to know about every network at the headquarters site. It can instead use a default route to get there.

To further reduce the number of routes in a table, create a totally stubby area, which is a Cisco-specific feature. A totally stubby area is a stubby area that blocks external (Type 5) LSAs and summary (Type 3 and Type 4) LSAs from entering the area. This way, intra area routes and the default of 0.0.0.0/0 are the only routes known to the stubby area. ABRs inject the default summary link 0.0.0.0/0 into the totally stubby area.

Therefore, totally stubby areas further minimize routing information and increase stability and scalability of OSPF internetworks. This is typically a better solution than creating stubby areas, unless the target area uses a mix of Cisco and non-Cisco routers. The following sections describe the criteria for determining whether an area should be configured as stubby or totally stubby and the configuration commands necessary to implement these area types.

Stub and Totally Stubby Area Criteria

An area can be qualified as stubby or totally stubby when it meets the following criteria, which are illustrated in Figure 6-47.

- There is a single exit point from that area.
- The area is not needed as a transit area for virtual links. Virtual links are discussed near the end of this chapter.
- No ASBR is internal to the stubby area.
- The area is not the backbone area (Area 0).

Figure 6-47 Using Stubby and Totally Stubby Area Criteria

These criteria are important because a stubby or totally stubby area is configured primarily to exclude external routes. If these criteria are not met, external links may be injected into the area, invalidating their stubby nature.

Interactive Media Activity   Drag and Drop: ID the Area

After completing this activity, you will be able to identify the difference between stubby and totally stubby areas in OSPF.

Configuring Stub and Totally Stubby Areas

To configure an area as stubby or totally stubby, use the following syntax on all OSPF areas that are configured to belong to a specific area:

```
Router(config-router)#area area-id stub [no-summary]
```

The optional **no-summary** keyword is used only on ABRs. This keyword configures the ABR to block interarea summaries (Type 3 and Type 4 LSAs). The **no-summary** keyword creates a totally stubby area. The **area stub** command is configured on each router in the stub location, which is essential for the routers to become neighbors and exchange routing information. When this command is configured, the stub routers exchange Hello packets with the E bit set to 0. The E bit is in the Hello packet's Options field. It indicates that the area is stubby. The state of this bit must be agreed on; otherwise, the routers do not become neighbors.

On ABRs only, there is the option of defining the cost of the default route that is automatically injected into the stubby or totally stubby area. Use the following syntax to configure the cost of the default route:

```
Router(config-router)#area area-id default-cost cost
```

OSPF Stub Area Configuration Example

In Figure 6-48, Area 2 is configured as stubby. No routes from the external autonomous system are forwarded into the stub.

Figure 6-48 OSPF Stubby Area Configuration

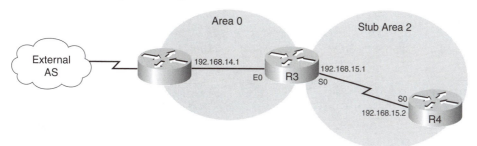

The last line in each configuration shown in Example 6-12, **area 2 stub**, defines the stubby area. The **area stub default-cost** has not been configured on R3, so this router advertises 0.0.0.0, the default route, with a default cost metric of 1 plus any internal costs.

Example 6-12 *Stubby Area Configuration*

```
R3(config)#router ospf 100
R3(config-router)#network 192.168.14.0 0.0.0.255 area 0
R3(config-router)#network 192.168.15.0 0.0.0.255 area 2
R3(config-router)#area 2 stub


R4(config)#router ospf 15
R4(config-router)#network 192.168.15.0 0.0.0.255 area 2
R4(config-router)#area 2 stub
```

Notice that the OSPF process number on each router can be different.

The only routes that appear on the routing table for R4 are intra area routes, the default route, and interarea routes. intra area routes are designated with an O in the routing table. Both the default and interarea routes are designated with an IA in the routing table. The default route is denoted with an asterisk (*).

Notice that each router in the stub must be configured with the **area stub** command. The **area stub** command determines whether the routers in the stub become neighbors. This command must be included on all routers in the stubby area if they are to exchange routing information.

OSPF Totally Stubby Area Configuration Example

To create a totally stubby area, the keyword **no-summary** is added to the **area stub** command configuration, as shown in Example 6-13, on R3 in Figure 6-49. This keyword causes summary routes, delivered by both Type 3 and Type 4 LSAs, to also be blocked from the stub. Each router in the stub picks the closest ABR as a gateway to all other networks outside the area.

Figure 6-49 OSPF Totally Stubby Area Configuration Example

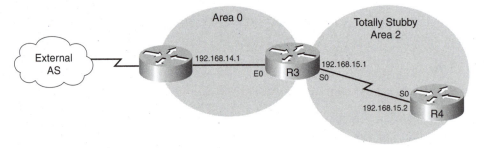

Example 6-13 *Totally Stubby Area Configuration*

```
R3(config)#router ospf 100
R3(config-router)#network 192.168.14.0 0.0.0.255 area 0
R3(config-router)#network 192.168.15.0 0.0.0.255 area 2
R3(config-router)#area 2 stub no-summary
```

The only routes that appear on the routing table for R4 are intra area routes, designated with an O in the routing table, and the default route. No interarea routes, designated with an IA in the routing table, are included.

Notice that it is necessary to configure the **no-summary** keyword only on the totally stubby border routers, because the area is already configured as stubby.

 Lab 6.9.4   Configuring a Stubby Area and a Totally Stubby Area

In this lab, you configure an OSPF stubby area and a totally stubby area.

NSSA Overview

NSSAs are a relatively new, standards-based OSPF enhancement. To understand how to use NSSAs, consider the network shown in Figure 6-50.

Figure 6-50 Connecting OSPF to an External Autonomous System

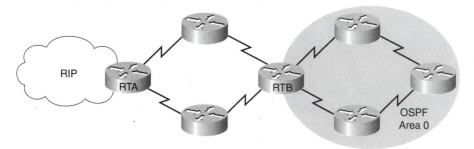

RTA is an ASBR that connects to an external RIP domain, and RTB currently serves as an ABR for Area 0, as shown in Figure 6-51. If the RIP domain is not under the same administrative control, what options are there to exchange routing information between these two domains? If dynamic routing will be used, an OSPF standard area could be created.

Figure 6-51 Using an OSPF Standard Area to Connect to an External AS

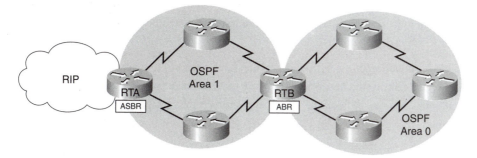

However, what if the routers that are placed in Area 1 do not have the required processing power or memory to run OSPF? You have learned that you can reduce the burden on OSPF routers by configuring them to participate in a stubby or totally stubby area. Figure 6-52 illustrates what would happen in this case.

Figure 6-52 Using an OSPF Stubby Area to Connect to an External AS

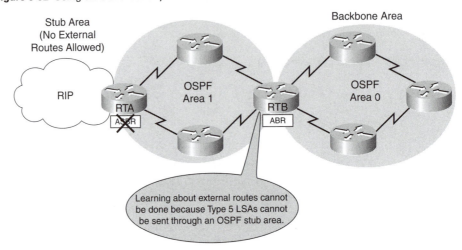

A stubby area cannot include an ASBR because Type 5 (external) LSAs are not allowed in a stub domain. The configuration shown in Figure 6-52 would fail miserably.

So how is external routing information dynamically exchanged without creating a standard OSPF area? Another routing protocol could be configured, such as RIP or IGRP, in place of creating an Area 1. This might prove to be a disadvantage. This is because an additional routing protocol must be maintained and imported into OSPF and because the RIP domain is not under the same administrative control.

With the introduction of the NSSA, there is another, easier option, as shown in Figure 6-53. An NSSA acts like a stub network in the sense that it does not allow Type 5 LSAs. It can also be configured to prevent floods of Type 3 and Type 4 summary LSAs, just as a totally stubby area would. However, an NSSA does allow Type 7 LSAs, which can carry external routing information and be flooded throughout the NSSA.

How NSSA Operates

By configuring an area as an NSSA, you can minimize routing tables within the area but still import external routing information into OSPF.

Figure 6-53 illustrates the sample network, including an NSSA implementation. RTA can import external routes as Type 7 LSAs, and ABRs translate Type 7 LSAs into Type 5 LSAs as they leave the NSSA. A benefit of Type 7 LSAs is that they can be summarized. The OSPF specification prohibits the summarizing or filtering of Type 5 LSAs. It is an OSPF requirement that Type 5 LSAs always be flooded throughout a routing domain. When defining an NSSA, specific external routes can be imported as Type 7 LSAs into the NSSA. In addition, when translating Type 7 LSAs to be imported into nonstub areas, the LSAs can be summarized or filtered before importing them as Type 5 LSAs.

NOTE

NSSAs are supported in Cisco IOS Release 11.2 and later.

Figure 6-53 Using an OSPF NSSA to Connect an External AS

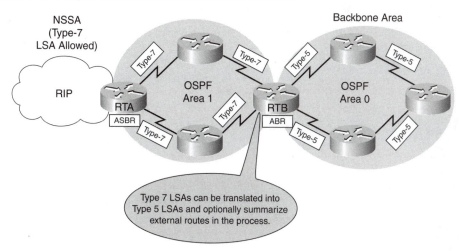

NSSAs are often used when a remote site that uses RIP or IGRP must be connected to a central site using OSPF. Use NSSA to simplify the administration of this kind of topology. Before NSSA, the connection between the corporate site ABR and the remote router used RIP or EIGRP. This meant maintaining two routing protocols. Now, with NSSA, OSPF can be extended to handle the remote connection by defining the area between the corporate router and the remote router as an NSSA.

Figure 6-54 shows the central site and branch offices interconnected through a slow WAN link. The branch office is not using OSPF, but the central site is. If a standard OSPF area between the two networks is configured, the slow WAN link could be overwhelmed by the ensuing flood of LSAs. This is especially true for Type 5 external LSAs. As an alternative, you could configure a RIP domain between the two networks, but that would mean running two routing protocols on the central site routers. A better solution is to configure an OSPF area and define it as an NSSA, as shown in Example 6-14.

Figure 6-54 Configuring OSPF NSSA

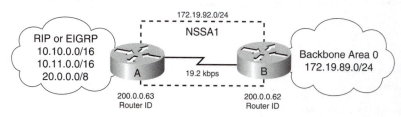

Example 6-14 *NSSA Configuration*

```
RTA(config)#router ospf 1
RTA(config-router)#redistribute rip subnets
RTA(config-router)#network 172.19.92.0 0.0.0.255 area 1
RTA(config-router)#area 1 nssa


RTB(config)#router ospf 1
RTB(config-router)#summary-address 10.0.0.0 255.0.0.0 tag 8
RTB(config-router)#network 172.19.92.0 0.0.0.255 area 1
RTB(config-router)#network 172.19.89.0 0.0.0.255 area 0
RTB(config-router)#area 1 nssa
```

In this scenario, RTA is defined as an ASBR. It is configured to redistribute any routes within the RIP or EIGRP domain to the NSSA. The following describes what happens when the area between the connecting routers is defined as an NSSA:

- RTA receives RIP or EIGRP routes for networks 10.10.0.0/16, 10.11.0.0/16, and 20.0.0.0/8.
- Because RTA is also connected to an NSSA, it redistributes the RIP or EIGRP routes as Type 7 LSAs into the NSSA.
- RTB, an ABR between the NSSA and the backbone Area 0, receives the Type 7 LSAs.
- After the SPF calculation on the forwarding database, RTB translates the Type 7 LSAs into Type 5 LSAs and then floods them throughout Area 0.

At this point, RTB can summarize routes 10.10.0.0/16 and 10.11.0.0/16 as 10.0.0.0/8 or filter one or more of the routes.

Configuring NSSA

To configure an OSPF area as an NSSA, configure all OSPF router interfaces that belong to the area using the following command syntax:

```
Router(config-router)#area area-id nssa [no-summary]
```

Typically, you use the optional keyword **no-summary** when configuring NSSA on an ABR. This prevents Type 3 and Type 4 summary routes from flooding the NSSA area and minimizing the routing tables within the area. In effect, the **no-summary** keyword makes the NSSA totally stubby.

Optionally, you can control the summarization or filtering during the translation using the following syntax:

```
Router(config)#summary-address prefix mask [not-advertise] [tag tag]
```

The **not-advertise** keyword is used to suppress routes that match the prefix and mask pair. This keyword applies to OSPF only. The **tag** value can also be assigned but is not required. Route tags can be used in policy routing; they are discussed in Chapter 5, "EIGRP."

To verify that NSSA is defined on a given router, use the **show ip ospf** command. This command shows the general OSPF configured parameters, including the number of NSSAs to which the router is attached and whether the router is performing LSA translation.

Lab 6.9.5   Configuring an NSSA

In this lab, you configure an OSPF NSSA to import external routing information while retaining the benefits of a stubby area.

Virtual Links

OSPF has certain restrictions when multiple areas are configured. One area must be defined as Area 0, the backbone area. It is called the backbone because all interarea communication must go through it. Therefore, all areas should be physically connected to Area 0 so that the routing information injected into this backbone can be disseminated to other areas. The backbone area must always be configured as Area 0. No other area ID can function as the backbone.

There are situations, however, when a new area is added after the OSPF internetwork has been designed, and it is not possible to give that new area direct access to the backbone. In these cases, a virtual link can be defined to provide the needed connectivity to the backbone area.

Meeting the Backbone Area Requirements

The virtual link gives the disconnected area a logical path to the backbone. All areas must connect directly to the backbone area or through a transit area, as shown in Figure 6-55.

Figure 6-55 Meeting the Backbone Area Requirements

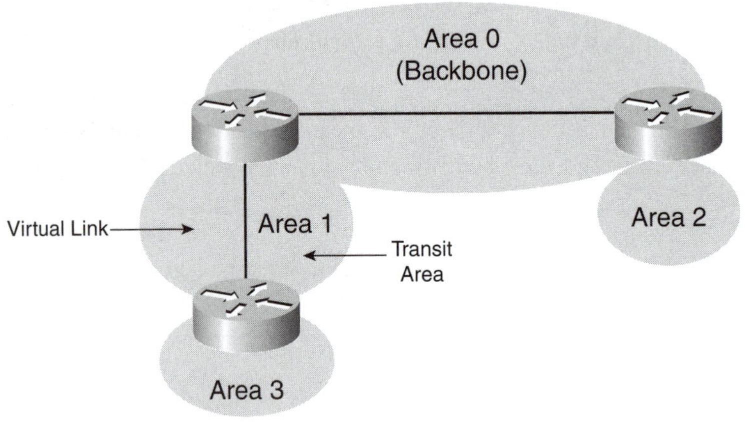

The virtual link has the following two requirements:

- It must be established between two routers that share a common area.
- One of these two routers must be connected to the backbone.

When virtual links are used, they require special processing during the SPF calculation. That is, the "real" next-hop router must be determined so that the true cost to reach a destination across the backbone can be calculated. Virtual links serve the following purposes:

- They can link an area that does not have a physical connection to the backbone. This linking could occur, for example, when two organizations merge.
- They can patch the backbone if discontinuity in Area 0 occurs. Discontinuity of the backbone might occur, for example, if two companies merge their two separate OSPF networks into a single one with a common Area 0. The only alternative for the companies is to redesign the entire OSPF network and create a unified backbone.

Another reason for creating a virtual link is to add redundancy in cases when router failure might cause the backbone to be split in two.

In Figure 6-56, the disconnected Area 0s are linked through a virtual link through the common area, Area 3. If a common area does not already exist, one can be created to become the transit area. Area 0 could become partitioned, for example, if two OSPF networks were merged.

Figure 6-56 Meeting the Backbone Area Requirements

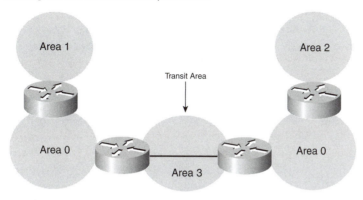

Configuring Virtual Links

To configure a virtual link, follow these steps:

Step 1   Configure OSPF, as described in the "Using and Configuring OSPF Multiarea Components" section.

Step 2   On each router that will use the virtual link, create the "virtual link" configuration. The routers that make the links are the ABR that connects the remote area to the transit area and the ABR that connects the transit area to the backbone area.

```
Router(config-router)#area area-id virtual-link router-id
```

If the neighbor's router ID is unknown, Telnet to it and enter the **show ip ospf** command.

Virtual Link Configuration Example

In Figure 6-57, Area 3 does not have a direct physical connection to the backbone, Area 0, which is an OSPF requirement. This is because the backbone is a collection point for LSAs. ABRs forward summary LSAs to the backbone, which, in turn, forward the traffic to all areas. All interarea traffic transits the backbone. Examples 6-15 and 6-16 show the configurations.

Figure 6-57 *Virtual Link Example*

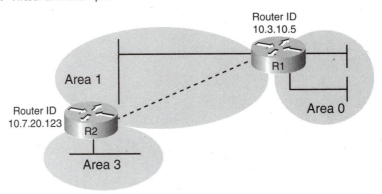

Example 6-15 *Virtual Link Configuration: R1*

```
router ospf 100
network 10.2.0.0 0.0.0.255 area 0
network 10.3.0.0 0.0.0.255 area 1
area 1 virtual-link 10.7.20.123
```

Example 6-16 *Virtual Link Configuration: R2*

```
router ospf 63
network 10.3.0.0 0.0.0.255 area 0
network 10.7.0.0 0.0.0.255 area 3
area 1 virtual-link 10.3.10.5
```

To provide connectivity to the backbone, a virtual link must be configured between R2 and R1. Area 1 is the transit area, and R1 is the entry point into Area 0. R2 has a logical connection to the backbone through the transit area.

Both sides of the virtual link must be configured as follows:

- With the following command on R2, Area 1 is defined as the transit area, and the router ID of the other side of the virtual link is configured:

  ```
  R2(config-router)#area 1 virtual-link 10.3.10.5
  ```

- With the following command on R1, Area 1 is defined as the transit area, and the router ID of the other side of the virtual link is configured:

  ```
  R1(config-router)#area 1 virtual-link 10.7.20.123
  ```

Lab 6.9.6   Configuring Virtual Links

In this lab, you configure an OSPF virtual link so that a disconnected area can reach the backbone, as required by OSPF.

 Lab 6.10.1   OSPF Challenge Lab

In this lab, you create a multiarea OSPF autonomous system that includes a totally stubby area and a persistent default route toward the ISP.

Summary

OSPF is a scalable, standards-based link-state routing protocol. Its benefits include no hop count limitation, the capability to multicast routing updates, faster convergence rates, and optimal path selection. The basic steps of OSPF operation are as follows:

1. Establish router adjacencies.
2. Select a DR and a BDR.
3. Discover routes.
4. Select appropriate routes to use.
5. Maintain routing information.

The following is a summary of the topics you have learned in this chapter:

- The advantages of multiarea OSPF configurations
- The OSPF components used in a large multiarea OSPF internetwork
- The benefits of multiarea configurations include reduced frequency of SPF calculations, smaller routing tables, and reduced LSU overhead.
- The types of areas, including stubby, totally stubby, and NSSA
- OSPF router types, including ABRs and ASBRs
- Link-state advertisements
- Virtual links

Key Terms

area ID   Multiple areas can be defined within an OSPF network to reduce and summarize route information.

authentication type and authentication data   OSPF supports different methods of authentication so that OSPF routers do not believe just anyone sending Hellos to 224.0.0.5.

backup designated router (BDR)   The DR could represent a single point of failure, so a second router is elected as the BDR to provide fault tolerance.

checksum   This 2-byte field is used to check the message for errors.

dead interval   How many seconds a router waits before it declares a neighbor down. The dead interval is 4 times the Hello interval by default, or 40 seconds.

designated router (DR)   For every multiaccess IP network, one router is elected the DR. The DR has two main functions—to become adjacent to all other routers on the network and to act as a spokesperson for the network.

Down state   In the Down state, the OSPF process has not exchanged information with any neighbor.

Exchange state   In the Exchange state, neighbor routers use Type 2 DBD packets to send each other their link-state information. In other words, the routers describe their link-state databases to each other. The routers compare what they learn with their existing link-state databases.

ExStart state   Technically, when a router and its neighbor enter the ExStart state, their conversation is characterized as an adjacency, but they have not become fully adjacent.

full adjacency   With the Loading state complete, the routers are fully adjacent. Each router keeps a list of adjacent neighbors, called the adjacencies database.

Hello interval   How many seconds an OSPF router waits to send the next Hello packet.

Init state   OSPF routers send Type 1 packets, or Hello packets, at regular intervals to establish a relationship with neighbor routers.

Loading state   After the databases have been described to each router, they may request information that is more complete by using Type 3 packets, link-state requests (LSRs).

network mask   This 32-bit field carries subnet mask information for the network.

router ID   The function of the Hello packet is to establish and maintain adjacencies. So the sending router signs the fourth field with its router ID, which is a 32-bit number used to identify the router to the OSPF protocol.

router priority   This field contains a value that indicates this router's priority when selecting a designated router (DR) and backup designated router (BDR).

two-way state   Using Hello packets, every OSPF router tries to establish a two-way state, or bidirectional communication, with every neighbor router on the same IP network.

Type 1: Hello packet   Establishes and maintains adjacency information with neighbors.

Type 2: database description packet (DBD)   Describes the contents of the link-state database on an OSPF router.

Type 3: link-state request (LSR)   Requests specific pieces of a link-state database.

Type 4: link-state update (LSU)   Transports link-state advertisements (LSAs) to neighbor routers.

Type 5: link-state acknowledgment (LSAck)   Acknowledgment receipt of a neighbor's LSA.

version, type, and packet length   The first three fields of the OSPF packet let the recipients know the version of OSPF that is being used by the sender, the OSPF packet type, and length.

Check Your Understanding

Complete all of the review questions to test your understanding of the topics and concepts in this chapter. The answers appear in Appendix B, "Answers to the Check Your Understanding Questions."

For additional, more in-depth questions, refer to the chapter-specific study guides on the companion CD-ROM.

1. Which state are the routers in an OSPF network in after the DR and BDR are elected?

    A. ExStart

    B. Full

    C. Loading

    D. Exchange

2. What is the default cost metric for OSPF based on?

    A. Delay

    B. Media bandwidth

    C. Efficiency

    D. Network traffic

3. What command can you use to change the OSPF priority on an interface?

    A. **ip priority number ospf**

    B. **ip ospf priority number**

    C. **ospf priority number**

    D. **set priority ospf number**

4. What IP address is used to send a multicast to only OSPF DRs and BDRs?

    A. 224.0.0.6

    B. 224.0.0.1

    C. 224.0.0.4

    D. 224.0.0.5

5. Which of the following is a common feature associated with NBMA networks?

    A. Support for only two routers

    B. Support for more than two routers

    C. No election of DRs

    D. Full support for broadcast and multicast packets

6. While troubleshooting a communication problem between two OSPF routers, you find that mismatched hello interval timers on the interfaces have caused the problem. Which command allows you to set the hello interval on the interfaces?

A. **hello-interval**

B. **ospf hello-interval**

C. **ip hello-interval**

D. **ip ospf hello-interval**

7. What type of OSPF router generates routing information about each area to which it is connected and floods that information through the backbone?

A. BR

B. BDR

C. Backbone

D. ABR

8. What type of OSPF router has at least one interface connected to an external autonomous system?

A. ABR

B. ASBR

C. Backbone

D. Internal

9. What command configures a virtual link?

A. Router#**area** *area-id router-id* **virtual-link**

B. Router(config)#**ip-area** *area-id* **virtual-link** *router-id*

C. Router(config-router)#**ip area virtual-link** *router-id area-id*

D. Router(config-router)#**area** *area-id* **virtual-link** *router-id*

10. What type of summarization occurs on ABRs and applies to routes from within each area?

A. Internal summarization

B. Interarea route summarization

C. External router summarization

D. Backbone summarization

11. What command configures an area as an NSSA?

    A. Router(config)#**area** *area-id* **nssa**

    B. Router(config-router)#**area** *area-id* **nssa**

    C. Router(config-router)#*area-id* **nssa**

    D. Router(config)#**area nssa** *area-id*

12. What command displays information about each area to which a router is connected and indicates whether the router is an ABR, ASBR, or both?

    A. show ip ospf border-routers

    B. show ip ospf virtual-links

    C. show ip ospf *process-id*

    D. show ip ospf database

Objectives

Upon completing this chapter, you will be able to

- Understand IS-IS fundamentals
- Understand ISO addressing
- Describe IS-IS operation
- Understand IP routing with Integrated IS-IS
- Configure Integrated IS-IS
- Describe Integrated IS-IS operation in a WAN environment

You can reinforce your understanding of the objectives covered in this chapter by opening the interactive media activities on the CD accompanying this book and performing the lab activities collected in the *Cisco Networking Academy Program CCNP 1: Advanced Routing Lab Companion*. Throughout this chapter, you will see references to these activities by title and by icon. They look like this:

 Interactive Media Activity

 Lab Activity

Chapter 7

IS-IS

In recent years, the *Intermediate System-to-Intermediate System (IS-IS)* routing protocol has become increasingly popular, with widespread usage among Internet service providers (ISPs). IS-IS enables very fast convergence and is very scalable. It is also a very flexible protocol and has been extended to incorporate leading-edge features such as Multiprotocol Label Switching/ Traffic Engineering (MPLS/TE).

The features of IS-IS include the following:

- Hierarchical routing
- Classless behavior
- Rapid flooding of new information
- Fast convergence
- Very scalable
- Flexible timer tuning

The Cisco IOS software implementation of IS-IS also supports the following features:

- Multiarea routing
- Route leaking
- Overload bit

IS-IS Fundamentals

IS-IS is an Open System Interconnection (OSI) routing protocol originally specified by International Organization for Standardization (ISO) 10589. IS-IS is a dynamic, link-state, intradomain interior gateway protocol (IGP). It is designed to operate in an OSI Connectionless Network Service (CLNS) environment. IS-IS selects routes based on a cost metric assigned to links in the IS-IS network. The cost is an arbitrary value assigned by a network engineer as the value of the path to a neighbor router.

A two-level hierarchy is used to support large routing *domains*. A large domain can be administratively divided into *areas*. Each system resides in exactly one area. Routing within an area is called Level 1 routing. Routing between areas is called Level 2 routing. A Level 2 *intermediate system (IS)* keeps track of the paths to destination areas. A Level 1 IS keeps track of the routing in its own area. For a packet destined for another area, a Level 1 IS sends the packet to the nearest Level 2 IS in its own area, regardless of the level of the destination area. Then the packet travels by way of Level 2 routing to the destination area, where it might travel by way of Level 1 routing to the destination. It should be noted that selecting an exit from an area based on Level 1 routing to the closest Level 2 IS might result in suboptimal routing.

On broadcast multiaccess media, a designated intermediate system (DIS) is elected and conducts the flooding over the media. The DIS is analogous to the designated router (DR) in OSPF, even though details such as the election process and adjacencies within a multiaccess media differ significantly. The DIS is elected by priority. The highest priority becomes the DIS. This can be configured on an interface basis using the **isis priority** command. In the case of a tie, the router with the highest *subnetwork point of attachment (SNPA)* address becomes the DIS. In the case of Ethernet, the SNPA address is just the MAC address.

OSI Protocols

The *OSI protocols* are the product of an international program formed to develop data networking protocols and other standards that facilitate multivendor equipment interoperability. The OSI program grew out of a need for international networking standards. It is designed to facilitate communication between hardware and software systems despite differences in underlying architectures.

The OSI specifications were conceived and implemented by two international standards organizations—the ISO and the International Telecommunication Union Telecommunication Standardization Sector (ITU-T). The world of OSI internetworking includes various network services with the following characteristics:

- Independent of underlying communications infrastructure
- End-to-end transfer
- Transparency
- Quality of service (QoS) selection
- Addressing

The OSI protocol suite supports numerous standard protocols at the physical, data link, network, transport, session, presentation, and application layers, as shown in Figure 7-1.

Figure 7-1 OSI Protocol Suite

OSI Reference Model	OSI Protocol Suite				
Application		CMIP DS FTAM MHS VTP			
		ASES ACSE ROSE RTSE CCRSE ...			
Presentation	Presentation Service/Presentation Protocol				
Session	Session Service/Session Protocol				
Transport	TP0 TP1 TP2 TP3 TP4				
Network	CONP/CMNS IS-IS		CLNP/CLNS ES-IS		
Data Link	IEEE 802.2	IEEE 802.3	IEEE 802.5/ Token Ring	FDDI	X.25
Physical	IEEE 802.3 Hardware	Token Ring Hardware	FDDI Hardware	X.25 Hardware	

OSI CLNS is a network layer service similar to bare IP service, as shown in Table 7-1.
A CLNS entity communicates over Connectionless Network Protocol (CLNP) with its peer
CLNS entity. CLNP is the OSI equivalent of IP.

Table 7-1 Comparing TCP/IP to OSI

TCP/IP	OSI
Basic connectionless service: IP (RFC 791)	CLNP (ISO 8473)
Neighbor greeting and error reports to source about packet delivery: ICMP (RFC 792) ARP (RFC 826) IRDP (RFC 1256)	CLNP (ISO 8473) ES-IS (ISO 9542)
Routing: Integrated IS-IS (RFC 1195) Participants are routers and hosts	IS-IS (ISO 10589) Participants are ISs and *end systems (ESs)*
IP autonomous system	ISO routing domain
Interior Gateway Protocol (IGP)	Intradomain Routing Protocol
Exterior Gateway Protocol (EGP) Border Gateway Protocol (BGP) for IP (RFC 1105) Static IP routes	Intradomain Routing Protocol ISO IDRP (proposal) Static CLNS routes

CLNP is an OSI network layer protocol that carries upper-layer data and error indications over connectionless links. CLNP provides the interface between CLNS and the upper layers. CLNS does not perform connection setup or termination because paths are determined independently for each packet that is transmitted through a network. In addition, CLNS provides best-effort delivery, which means that no guarantee exists that data will not be lost, corrupted, misordered, or duplicated. CLNS relies on transport layer protocols to perform error detection and correction.

OSI network layer addressing is implemented by using two types of hierarchical addresses—*network service access point (NSAP)* and *network entity title (NET)*.

The OSI protocol suite specifies two routing protocols at the network layer—*End System-to-Intermediate System (ES-IS)* and IS-IS, as shown in Table 7-1. In addition, the OSI suite implements two types of network service—connectionless and connection-oriented.

OSI Terminology

An OSI network has four significant architectural entities—hosts, areas, a backbone, and a domain. A domain is any portion of an OSI network that is under a common administrative authority. Within any OSI domain, one or more areas can be defined. An area is a logical entity. An area is formed by a set of contiguous routers and the data links that connect them. All routers in the same area exchange information about all of the hosts they can reach. The areas are connected to form a backbone. All routers on the backbone know how to reach all areas. The term end system refers to any nonrouting host or node. The term intermediate system refers to a router. These terms are the basis of the OSI ES-IS and IS-IS protocols.

An NSAP is a conceptual point on the boundary between the network and transport layers. The NSAP is the location where OSI network services are provided to the transport layer. Each transport layer entity is assigned a single NSAP. The NSAP address identifies any system in an OSI network. The last byte in an NSAP identifies a process on the device, similar to a port or socket in TCP/IP.

A NET is an NSAP in which the last byte is 0. The NET identifies a device. Therefore, each router has a unique NET address.

An SNPA is the point at which subnetwork services are provided. This is the equivalent of the Layer 2 address corresponding to the Layer 3 (NET or NSAP) address. This is usually a MAC address on a LAN or virtual circuit ID in X.25, Frame Relay, or ATM.

A circuit is an interface. A link is the path between two neighbor ISs. It is defined as being up when communication is possible between the two neighbors' SNPAs.

ES-IS and IS-IS

ISO has developed standards for two types of network protocols used in routing—ES-IS and IS-IS. The ES-IS discovery protocols are used for routing between end systems and intermediate systems. The IS-IS routing protocols are used for hierarchical routing between intermediate systems.

ES-IS is analogous to Address Resolution Protocol (ARP) in IP. Although technically it isn't a routing protocol, ES-IS is included here because it is commonly used with routing protocols to provide end-to-end data movement through an internetwork. Routing between end systems and intermediate systems is sometimes called Level 0 routing, as shown in Figure 7-2.

Figure 7-2 ES-IS and IS-IS

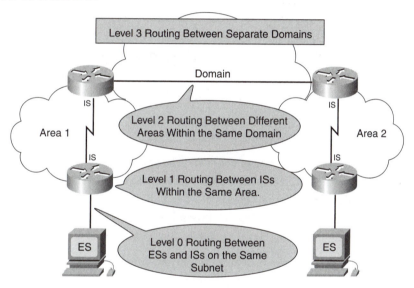

With IS-IS routing, OSI distinguishes between Level 1, Level 2, and Level 3 routing to simplify router design and operation. Level 1 ISs communicate with other Level 1 ISs in the same area. Level 2 ISs route between Level 1 areas and form an intradomain routing backbone. Level 3 routing is done between separate domains. Hierarchical routing simplifies backbone design, because Level 1 ISs only need to know how to get to the nearest Level 2 IS.

Each ES lives in a particular area. OSI routing begins when the ESs discover the nearest IS by listening to Intermediate System Hello (ISH) packets. When an ES wants to send a packet to another ES, it sends it to one of the ISs on its directly attached network, Level 0 routing. The router then looks up the destination address and forwards the packet along the best route. If the destination ES is on the same subnetwork, the local IS knows this from listening to End System Hello (ESH) packets and forwards the packet appropriately. The IS also might provide a redirect message to the source to tell it that a more direct route is available. If the destination address is an ES on another subnetwork in the same area, the IS knows the correct route and forwards the packet appropriately. If the destination address is an ES in another area, the Level 1 IS sends the packet to the nearest Level 2 IS, Level 2 routing. Forwarding through Level 2 ISs continues until the packet reaches a Level 2 IS in the destination area. Within the destination area, ISs forward the packet along the best path until the destination ES is reached.

Integrated IS-IS

For routing in the ISO CLNS environment, Cisco routers support the IS-IS routing protocol. Routers usually operate as ISs and can exchange reachability information with other ISs using the IS-IS protocol. As an IS, a Cisco router can operate at Level 1 only, at Level 2 only, or at both levels. In the last case, the router can advertise itself at Level 1 as an exit point from the area. *Integrated IS-IS* allows the IS-IS protocol to propagate routing information for protocols other than CLNP. IS-IS can route CLNP, IP, or both when in dual mode.

IS-IS is the dynamic link-state routing protocol for the OSI protocol stack. As such, it distributes routing information for routing CLNP data for the ISO CLNS environment. When IS-IS is used strictly for the ISO CLNS environment, it is called ISO IS-IS.

Integrated IS-IS is an implementation of the IS-IS protocol for routing multiple network protocols. Integrated IS-IS tags CLNP routes, upon which IS-IS bases its link-state database, with information on IP networks and subnets. IS-IS provides an alternative to OSPF in the IP world, mixing ISO CLNS and IP routing in one protocol. Again, IS-IS can be used purely for IP routing, purely for ISO routing, or for a combination of the two, as shown in Figure 7-3.

Integrated IS-IS is deployed extensively in an IP-only environment in the top-tier ISP networks. The IS-IS working group of the Internet Engineering Task Force (IETF) developed the specification for Integrated IS-IS, RFC 1195. Integrated IS-IS differs from the approach taken by IS-IS routing, in which completely independent routing protocols are used for each of the two protocol suites. Integrated IS-IS uses a single integrated protocol for interior routing. The single integrated protocol is used to calculate routes within a routing domain for both protocol suites.

IS-IS is one of the few protocols that provides an integrated framework for concurrent processing of more than one network layer protocol. Other routing protocols, such as OSPF, usually support routing for only one type of Layer 3 protocol. This chapter focuses mostly on the use of IS-IS in an IP environment.

NOTE

IS-IS was originally designed for routing DECnet Phase V and was subsequently adopted for ISO CLNP. DECnet is a routed protocol, like IP, IPX, and AppleTalk, used in Digital Equipment Corporation networking. IS-IS was proposed for use with TCP/IP in the late 1980s and early 1990s. IS-IS was ultimately specified for this context in RFC 1195, *Use of OSI IS-IS for Routing in TCP/IP and Dual Environments*.

Figure 7-3 Dual IS-IS

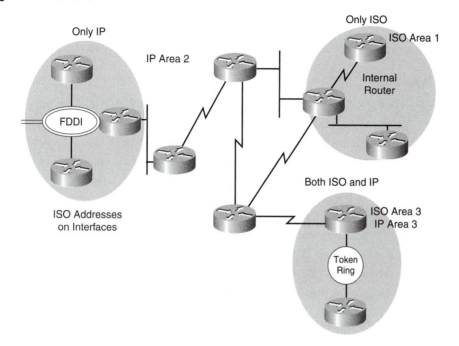

IS-IS was not designed specifically to route IP. However, its successful widespread deployment for IP routing on the Internet has led the IETF to revisit RFC 1195. The point is to incorporate proprietary features outside the scope of RFC 1195 designed to improve usability and to provide flexibility and scalability. MPLS traffic engineering stands out as a recent technology that has driven advances in IS-IS feature sets, possibly vendor-specific.

The Integrated IS-IS protocol provides dynamic routing for an IP and ISO internetworking environment. Integrated IS-IS has the following features:

- It uses ISO IS-IS to distribute routing information.
- It provides ISO and IP routing services.
- It routes only within one ISO domain.
- It provides link-state distribution of routing information.
- It is based on the shortest path first (SPF) routing algorithm.

Integrated IS-IS provides IP routing capability by

- Defining links with IP addresses, subnets, and metrics
- Forwarding IP routing information within the PDUs of the ISO IS-IS packets
- Configuring an area to support IP or both IP and CLNP

NOTE

For routing in the ISO CLNS environment, Cisco routers, also support static CLNS routes as well as the proprietary ISO IGRP routing protocol. ISO IGRP is, as its name suggests, based on Cisco's Interior Gateway Routing Protocol (IGRP). It uses distance vector technology to propagate routing information. As such, ISO IGRP shares some of the limitations of its IP counterpart, including long convergence times. This is because of periodic updates and long invalid times and hold times.

Interactive Media Activity Checkbox: IS-IS Terminology Quiz

After completing this activity, you will have a firm grasp on the IS-IS terminology.

OSPF Versus IS-IS

The configuration of OSPF is based on a central backbone, Area 0, with all other areas being physically attached to Area 0. Because of this, certain design constraints inevitably exist. A good, consistent IP addressing structure is necessary when this type of hierarchical model is used. It is used to summarize addresses into the backbone and reduce the amount of information that is carried in the backbone and advertised across the network. In comparison, IS-IS also has a hierarchy with Level 1 and Level 2 routers. With IS-IS, the area borders lie on the links. However, significantly fewer *link-state PDUs (LSPs)* are used. Therefore, many more routers, up to 100, can reside in a single area. This capability makes IS-IS more scalable than OSPF. IS-IS allows a more flexible approach to extending the backbone. Adding Level 2 routers can extend the backbone. This process is less complex than with OSPF.

Here are some of the similarities between OSPF and IS-IS:

- Classless
- Link-state databases and Dijkstra's Algorithm
- Hello packets to form and maintain adjacencies
- Use areas to form hierarchical topologies
- Support address summarization between areas
- Elect a designated router on multiaccess networks
- Link-state representation, aging, and metrics
- Update, decision, and flooding processes
- Convergence capabilities
- Deployed on ISP backbones

Here are some of the differences between OSPF and IS-IS:

- IS-IS does not elect a backup designated router
- IS-IS repeats the election process whenever a new router becomes active:
  - If a new router has a higher priority or the same priority and a higher *system ID*, it takes over as the DR.
  - IS-IS is designed to be deterministic: The same set of routers always produces the same DR.
- Every time the DR changes, a new set of LSPs must be flooded.
- IS-IS routers form adjacencies with all neighbors, not just the DR.

With regard to CPU use and the processing of routing updates, IS-IS is more efficient. Not only are there fewer LSPs to process as compared to OSPF link-state advertisements (LSAs), but the mechanism by which IS-IS installs and withdraws prefixes is less intensive.

Both OSPF and IS-IS are link-state protocols and therefore provide fast convergence. The convergence time depends on a number of factors, such as timers, number of nodes, and types of routers. Based on the default timers, IS-IS detects a failure more quickly than OSPF and therefore should converge more rapidly. If there are many neighbors and adjacencies to consider, the convergence time depends on the router's processing power. IS-IS is typically less CPU-intensive than OSPF. OSPF and IS-IS handle resource usage differently as well. For example, IS-IS uses one link-state packet per router in one area, including redistributed prefixes, compared to many OSPF LSAs. Here are some other differences between OSPF and IS-IS areas:

- OSPF is based on a central backbone with all other areas attached to it:
    - In OSPF, the border lies within the area border router (ABR).
    - Each link (interface) belongs to one area.
- In IS-IS, the area border lies on the link:
    - Each IS-IS router belongs to exactly one Level 2 area.
    - IS-IS allows a more flexible approach to extending the backbone.

Here are some of the differences between OSPF and IS-IS scalability:

- OSPF supports up to 50 routers per area.
- IS-IS supports up to 100 routers per area.
- OSPF has more features, including route tags, stubby areas/not-so-stubby areas (NSSAs), and demand circuit.

The timers in IS-IS allow more tuning than those in OSPF. There are more timers to adjust, so finer granularity can be achieved. By tuning the timers, you can significantly decrease convergence time. However, this speed might come at the expense of stability, so you might have to compromise. A network engineer should understand the implications of adjusting these timers.

 Interactive Media Activity   Checkbox: OSPF Versus IS-IS

After completing this activity, you will be able to identify the differences between OSPF and IS-IS.

ISO Addressing

OSI network layer addressing is implemented by using two types of hierarchical addresses—NSAP and NET.

NSAPs

The NSAP is a conceptual point on the boundary between the network and the transport layers. The NSAP is the location at which OSI network services are provided to the transport layer. Each transport layer entity is assigned a single NSAP. The NSAP address identifies any system in an OSI network. Various NSAP formats are used for various systems. Different protocols might use different representations of the NSAP.

The NSAP address is the network layer address for CLNS packets. As with DECnet Phase V, one NSAP address is used for each device, not for each interface. LSPs, *Hello PDUs*, and other routing PDUs are OSI-formatted PDUs. Therefore, every IS-IS router requires an OSI address. IS-IS uses the OSI address in the LSPs to identify the router, build the topology table, and build the underlying IS-IS routing tree. NSAP addresses contain the device's OSI address and provide a link to upper-layer processes. The NSAP address can be thought of as equivalent to the combination of an IP address and upper-layer protocol identifier in an IP header. The Cisco implementation supports all NSAPs defined by ISO 8348/Addendum 2 and ISO 10589. The NSAP addressing structure is shown in Figure 7-4. Its fields are as follows:

- The NSAP is formed by the *Interdomain Part (IDP)* and the *Domain-Specific Part (DSP)*.
- The IDP is composed of
  - 1-byte *Authority and Format Identifier (AFI)*
  - Variable-length initial domain identifier (IDI)
- The DSP is composed of a
  - 2-byte area
  - 6-byte station ID
  - 1-byte selector

Figure 7-4 NSAP Addressing Structure

IDP		DSP		
AFI	IDI	AREA	STATION ID	SEL

A DSP address has three parts—area address, system ID, and *NSAP selector* (N-selector) byte. The total length is between 8 and 20 bytes. The area address is a variable-length field composed of high-order octets, excluding the system ID and the N-selector byte. The system ID is the ES or IS identifier in an area, similar to the OSPF router ID. The system ID has a fixed length of 6 bytes, as engineered in the Cisco IOS software (see Figure 7-5). The N-selector byte is a service identifier. The role of the N-selector byte is analogous to that of a port or socket in TCP/IP.

Figure 7-5 NSAP Addressing Structure

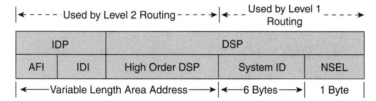

Cisco routers can route CLNS data that uses addressing that conforms to the ISO 10589 standard. The fields specified in this standard are as follows (see Figure 7-5):

- **Authority and Format ID (AFI)**—1 byte, actually a binary value between 0 and 99, used to specify the IDI format and DSP syntax of the address and the authority that assigned the address.

- **Initial domain identifier (IDI)**—Identifies the domain.

- **Interdomain Part (IDP)**—Consists of the AFI and IDI together. This is roughly equivalent to a classful IP network in decimal format.

- *High-Order Domain-Specific Part (HODSP)*—Used to subdivide the domain into areas. This is roughly equivalent to a subnet in IP.

- **System ID**—Identifies an individual OSI device. In OSI, a device has an address, just as it does in DECnet. In IP, an interface has an address.

- **NSAP selector (NSEL)**—Identifies a process on the device. It is roughly equivalent to a port or socket in TCP/IP. The NSEL is not used in routing decisions.

- **Domain-Specific Part (DSP)**—Comprised of the HODSP, the system ID, and the NSEL in binary format.

IS-IS uses a simple two-layer architecture. IS-IS joins the IDP and HODSP and treats them as the Level 2 area ID, with the remaining system ID used for Level 1 routing. Restated, in IS-IS, everything to the left of the system ID is used as the area ID. The minimum length of this area ID is a single byte. The maximum is the remaining 13 bytes permitted by the ISO standard. Therefore, an NSAP for an IS-IS network could be as little as 8 bytes in length. The length is normally longer to permit some granularity in the allocation of areas.

There are three NSAP formats, as shown in Figure 7-6. The first is a simple 8-byte area ID and system ID format. The second is an OSI NSAP format, and the third is a Government OSI Profile (GOSIP) NSAP format. Cisco supports all NSAP formats that are defined by ISO 8348/Ad2, as described in this section.

Figure 7-6 ISO Addressing

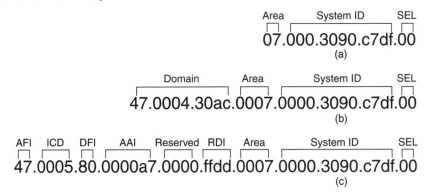

NETs

An NSAP address with an NSEL value of 00 is used to identify the device. This is the device's network address. In this case, the NSAP is called a NET. So a NET is determined by the area ID and system ID.

All router NETs have an N-selector of 00, implying the network layer of the IS itself. The 00 indicates that no transport layer entity is associated with this address. For this reason, a router's NSAP is always called a NET. The NSEL is like a TCP port number.

Routers are identified with NETs of 8 to 20 bytes. ISO/IEC 10589 distinguishes only three fields in the NSAP address format—a variable-length area address beginning with a single octet, a system ID, and a 1-byte N-selector. Cisco implements a fixed length of 6 bytes for the system ID, which is similar to the OSPF router ID. This is further clarified in RFC 941.

In general, the big difference between NSAP style addressing and IP style addressing is that there will be a single NSAP address for the entire router. However, IP has one IP address per interface. NSAP address allocation is shown in Table 7-2.

Table 7-2 NSAP AFI Allocations

Address	Description
00–09	Reserved—is not allocated
10–35	Reserved for future allocation by joint agreement of ISO and CCITT
36–37	X.121
38–39	ISO DCC

Table 7-2 NSAP AFI Allocations (Continued)

40–41	F.69
42–43	E.163
44–45	E.164
46–47	ISO 6523-ICD
48–51	LOCAL
52–59	Reserved for future allocation by joint agreement of ISO and CCITT
60–69	Allocated for assignment to new IDI formats by ISO
70–79	Allocated for assignment to new IDI formats by CCITT
80–99	Reserved for future allocation by joint agreement of ISO and CCITT

The following are some guidelines for NETs:

- All ISs and ESs in a routing domain must have system IDs of the same length.
- All routers in an area must have the same area address.
- All Level 2 routers must have a unique system ID domain-wide.
- All Level 1 routers must have a unique system ID area-wide.
- All ESs in an area form an adjacency with a Level 1 router on a shared media segment if they share the same area address.
- If multiple NETs are configured on the same router, they must all have the same system ID.

Routers use the NET to identify themselves in the LSPs. The NET forms the basis of OSI route calculation. Addresses starting with value 49 (AFI = 49) are considered private. Private or local addresses are analogous to those specified by RFC 1918 for IP addresses. These addresses are routed by IS-IS. However, this group of addresses should not be advertised to other CLNS networks.

Addresses starting with AFI values of 38 or 39 represent the ISO Data Country Code. Addresses starting with AFI values of 46 or 47 represent the ISO International Code Designator. RFC 941 allocates NSAP addresses. The division of the global network addressing domain according to IDI format and the numbers adjacent to each line in Table 7-2 are AFI values.

It is possible to configure multiple NETs on a router, but no router is ever in more than one area. Configuring multiple NETs causes the areas to merge into a common area, leaking the Level 1 databases into each other. The only reasons to have multiple NETs are for splitting, merging, or renumbering areas. This method should be used only in periods of transition. Using multiple NETs is analogous to using secondary addresses with IP. Cisco limits the number of configurable NETs to three per router.

ISO Addressing with Cisco Routers

NETs and NSAPs are composed entirely of hexadecimal digits and must start and end on a byte boundary.

Cisco IOS software interprets the NSAP address starting at the right. The last byte is the NSEL and must be specified as a single byte in length preceded by a period (.). A NET definition must set the N-selector to 00.

The preceding 6 bytes form the system ID. The IOS fixes this length at 6 bytes. It is customary to code either a Media Access Control (MAC) address from the router or an IP address, such as a loopback address, into the system ID. With Integrated IS-IS, a loopback IP address is commonly used for this purpose. In this case, the system ID is obtained by converting a loopback address: 192.168.111.3 to 192.168.111.003 to 1921.6811.1003. This is further explained as follows:

- NET must begin with an octet:
    - 47.xxxx...
    - 0111.xxxx, not 111.xxxx...
- NET must end with a single octet set to 00, identifying the network entity itself, such as a router:
    - ...xxxx.00
- The station ID is normally 6 octets. It's always 6 with Cisco, and it has to be the same length everywhere.
- The following are real examples:
    - 47.0001.0000.0c12.3456.00
    - 01.1921.6811.1003.00 (note the imbedded IP address)
    - 1047.0001.1234.5678.9101.00

IOS treats the rest of the address as the area ID. The area ID can be as small as 1 byte and as large as 13 bytes. It is customary to use 3 bytes for the area ID field, with an AFI of 1 byte, such as the 47, as just shown. There are also 2 additional bytes for area IDs, shown as 0001, and the effective area ID is 47.0001. The IOS attempts to summarize the area ID as far as possible. For example, if an IS-IS network is organized with major areas subdivided into minor areas, and this is reflected in the area ID assignments, the IOS does the following:

- Between minor areas, it bases the route on the whole area ID.
- Between major areas, it summarizes into the area ID portion up to the major area boundary.

The following two examples illustrate the use of NSAP addresses with the Cisco IOS software:

- Example 1: NSAP 47.0001.aaaa.bbbb.cccc.00

  The IS-IS area ID is 47.0001.

  The system ID is aaaa.bbbb.cccc.

  The NSAP selector byte is 00.

- Example 2: NSAP 39.0f01.0002.0000.0c00.1111.00

  The IS-IS area ID is 39.0f01.0002.

  The system ID is 0000.0c00.1111.

  The NSAP selector byte is 00.

Identifying Systems in IS-IS

The router assigns a circuit ID of one octet to each interface on the router. In the case of point-to-point interfaces, this is the sole identifier for the circuit, such as 03.

In the case of LAN interfaces, the circuit ID is tagged to the end of the system ID of the designated IS to form a 7-byte LAN ID, such as 1921.6811.1001.03. The SNPA is taken from the following:

- MAC address on a LAN interface
- Virtual circuit ID for X.25 or ATM
- Data-link connection identifier (DLCI) for Frame Relay
- High-Level Data Link Control (HDLC) for interfaces

For convenience, the NET restrictions listed previously for devices used in IS-IS routing are repeated here:

- All ISs and ESs in a routing domain must have system IDs of the same length. Cisco fixes the system ID length at 6 bytes.
- All ISs in an area must have the same area address. This defines the area.
- All ESs and Level 1 ISs must have a unique system ID area-wide. Level 1 routing is based on system IDs.
- All Level 2 ISs must have a unique system ID domain-wide. It is recommended that, in general, all system IDs remain unique across a domain. That way, there can never be a conflict at Level 1 or Level 2 if a device is moved into a different area.
- All ESs in an area form an adjacency with a Level 1 IS on a shared media segment if they share the same area address. ESs recognize only ESs and ISs on the same subnetwork that share the same area address.
- If multiple NETs are configured on the same IS, they must all have the same system ID.

The following are several techniques used to create unique system IDs:

- Start numbering 1, 2, 3, 4, and so on.
- Use MAC addresses.
- Convert and use the loopback IP address, 192.168.11.1 to 192.168.011.001 to 1921.6801.1001. This is how most ISPs define system IDs.

The practice of using a modified loopback IP address as the system ID is becoming outdated because of the dynamic host name feature available in Cisco IOS releases beginning with Release 12.1.

IS-IS and ES-IS PDUs contain variable-length fields, depending on the PDU's function. Each field contains a type code and length, followed by the appropriate values. For that reason, the abbreviation TLV is used for Type, Length, and Value fields. The dynamic host name feature is specified in RFC 2763. It uses a new TLV—namely, TLV 137—to map the router's host name to the system ID, as shown in Table 7-3. In the LSP flooding process, a dynamic distribution of host name to NET mappings takes place. This prevents having to maintain a huge database of static mappings for system IDs on all of the IS-IS routers. Maintaining such a database has been a very real issue faced by ISPs running Integrated IS-IS.

Table 7-3 New TLVs

TLV Name	Type	Origin
Extended IS Reachability Information	22	Used in place of TLV 2 for traffic engineering (TE).
Router-ID	134	TE extension to IS-IS.
Extended IP Reachability Information	135	TE extension to IS-IS. Used in place of TLV 128 or 130.
Dynamic Hostname Information	137	For dynamic distribution of host name-to-NET mapping through LSP flooding.
Point-to-Point Adjacency State	240	Reliable point-to-point adjacency formation.

Finally, when routing CLNS, request an official NSAP address for use in addressing areas. When routing only IP, just use AFI 49, which indicates local or private addressing. Then the area numbering appears as 49.0001, 49.0002, 49.0003, and so on.

The 1-byte N-selectors are set to 00, indicating that these are NETs. The 6-byte system IDs are unique across the network. Additionally, the 3-byte area IDs are common to each area and are distinct between areas, as shown in Figure 7-7.

Figure 7-7 Identifying Systems in IS-IS

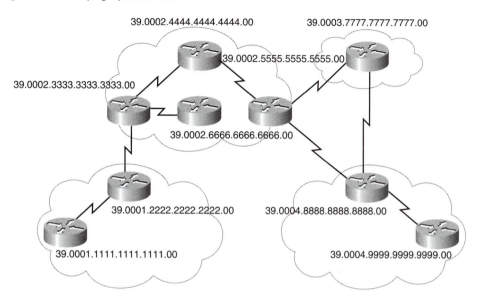

IS-IS Operation

The following sections discuss some of the details of IS-IS operation. Topics that are covered include

- High-level view of IS-IS operation
- OSI PDUs
- IS-IS hello messages
- IS-IS link-state PDU formats
- IS-IS routing levels
- IS-IS adjacencies
- DIS and pseudonodes
- IS-IS data flow
- LSP flooding and synchronization
- IS-IS metrics
- IS-IS network types
- SPF algorithm

High-Level View of IS-IS Operation

From a high level, IS-IS operates as follows:

- Routers running IS-IS send Hello packets out all IS-IS enabled interfaces to discover neighbors and establish adjacencies.
- Routers sharing a common data link become IS-IS neighbors if their Hello packets contain information that meets the criteria for forming an adjacency. The criteria differ slightly depending on the type of media being used, whether point-to-point or broadcast. The main criteria are matching authentication, IS type, and MTU size.
- Routers build an LSP based on their local interfaces that are configured for IS-IS and prefixes learned from other adjacent routers.
- Routers flood LSPs to all adjacent neighbors except the neighbor from which they received the same LSP. However, there are different forms of flooding and also a number of scenarios in which the flooding operation might differ.
- All routers construct their link-state database from these LSPs.
- Each IS calculates a shortest-path tree (SPT). The routing table is built from this SPT.

OSI PDUs

The OSI stack defines a unit of data as a protocol data unit (PDU). OSI therefore regards a frame as a data-link PDU. Three types of PDUs have 802.2 Logical Link Control (LLC) encapsulation, as shown in Table 7-4. From these you can see that the IS-IS and ES-IS PDUs are encapsulated directly in a data-link PDU, whereas CLNP data packets contain a full CLNP header between the data-link header and any higher-layer CLNS information. The IS-IS and ES-IS PDUs contain variable-length fields, depending on the PDU's function. Each field contains a type code, a length, and the appropriate values. The TLV fields contain the following information:

- The neighbor ISs for the router used to build the map of the network
- The neighbor ESs for the router
- Authentication information, used to secure routing updates
- Attached IP subnets if Integrated IS-IS is being run

Table 7-4 OSI PDUs

IS-IS	Data-link header (OSI family 0xFEFE)	IS-IS fixed header (first byte is 0x83)	IS-IS TLVs
ES-IS	Data-link header (OSI family 0xFEFE)	ES-IS fixed header (first byte is 0x81)	ES-IS TLVs
CLNS	Data-link header (OSI family 0xFEFE)	CLNS fixed header (first byte is 0x80)	User data

IS-IS PDUs are encapsulated directly into an OSI data-link layer frame. There is no CLNP header and no IP header. The IS-IS protocol family is OSI, and values such as 0xFE and 0xFEFE are used by the data-link protocol to identify the Layer 3 protocol as OSI. This chapter focuses on the OSI PDUs specific to IS-IS.

There are four categories of IS-IS PDUs, as shown in Figure 7-8:

- **Hello PDU (ESH, ISH, IS-IS Hello [IIH])**—Used to establish and maintain adjacencies. ESHs are sent from ESs to ISs. ISHs are sent from ISs to ESs. IIHs are sent between ISs. Note that ESH and ISH PDUs are ES-IS PDUs, not IS-IS PDUs.

- **LSP**—Used by IS-IS to distribute link-state information. There are independent pseudonode (PSN) and nonpseudonode LSPs for both Level 1 and Level 2.

- *Complete Sequence Number PDU (CSNP)*—Used to distribute a complete link-state database on the router. CSNPs are used to inform other routers of LSPs that might be outdated or missing from their own database. This ensures that all routers have the same information and are synchronized. The packets are similar to an OSPF database description packet.

- *Partial Sequence Number PDU (PSNP)*—Used to acknowledge and request link-state information.

Figure 7-8 Identifying Systems in IS-IS

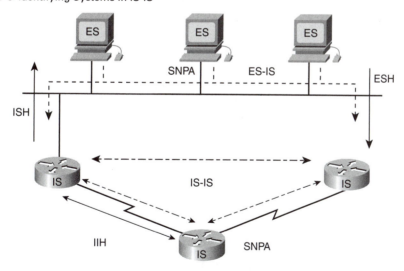

There are nine IS-IS PDU types, as shown in Table 7-5. The value codes 1 through 10 are defined in ISO 10589, and 128 through 133 are defined in RFC 1195. TLV Code 133, for authentication information, is specified in RFC 1195, but Cisco technology uses the ISO

Code of 10 instead. TLV Code 4 is used for partition repair and is not supported by Cisco technology.

Table 7-5 Valid Code Values for Nine Types of IS-IS PDUs

IS-IS PDUs	Code Value
Level 1 LAN IS-to-IS Hello PDU Type 15	Code 1 = Area addresses Code 6 = IS neighbors (hellos) Code 8 = Padding Code 10 = Authentication information Code 129 = Protocols supported Code 132 = IP interface address
Level 2 LAN IS-to-IS Hello PDU Type 16	Code 1 = Area addresses Code 6 = IS neighbors (hellos) Code 8 = Padding Code 10 = Authentication information Code 129 = Protocols supported Code 132 = IP interface address
Point-to-Point IS-to-IS Hello PDU Type 17	Code 1 = Area addresses Code 8 = Padding Code 10 = Authentication information Code 129 = Protocols supported Code 132 = IP interface address
Level 1 Link-State PDU Type 18	Code 1 = Area addresses Code 2 = IS neighbors (LSPs) Code 3 = ES neighbors Code 6 = IS neighbors Code 10 = Authentication information Code 128 = IP internal reachability information Code 129 = Protocols supported Code 132 = IP interface address
Level 2 Link-State PDU Type 20	Code 1 = Area addresses Code 2 = IS neighbors (LSPs) Code 2 = IS neighbors Code 4 = Partition designated Level 2 IS Code 5 = Prefix neighbors Code 10 = Authentication information Code 128 = IP internal reachability information Code 129 = Protocols supported Code 130 = IP external reachability information Code 131 = IDRP information Code 132 = IP interface address

Table 7-5 Valid Code Values for Nine Types of IS-IS PDUs (Continued)

IS-IS PDUs	Code Value
Level 1 Complete Sequence Number PDU Type 24	Code 9 = LSP entries Code 10 = Authentication information
Level 2 Complete Sequence Number PDU Type 25	Code 9 = LSP entries Code 10 = Authentication information
Level 1 Partial Sequence Number PDU Type 26	Code 9 = LSP entries Code 10 = Authentication information
Level 2 Partial Sequence Number PDU Type 27	Code 9 = LSP entries Code 10 = Authentication information

IS-IS Hello Messages

Table 7-6 lists the various IS-IS Hello message types. The following information is included in IIH PDUs:

- **Type of PDU**—Whether the PDU is a point-to-point WAN PDU or a LAN PDU.
- **Source ID**—The sending router's system ID.
- **Holding time**—The amount of time to wait to hear a Hello before declaring the neighbor dead. Similar to the OSPF dead interval, the default value is 3 times the Hello interval but can be changed with the **isis hello-multiplier** command.
- **Circuit type**—Indicates whether the interface on which the PDU was sent is Level 1, Level 2, or Level 1 and Level 2.
- **PDU length**—Length of PDU packets.
- **Circuit ID**—Local circuit ID on the sending interface in point-to-point Hello PDUs.
- **LAN ID**—System ID of the DIS plus the PSN ID (1-byte circuit ID) to differentiate LAN IDs on the same DIS. On broadcast multiaccess media LANs, a DIS is elected and conducts the flooding over the media. The DIS is analogous to the designated router in OSPF, even though the election process and the definition of adjacencies on multiaccess media differ significantly. The DIS is elected by priority; the highest priority becomes the DIS. Priority can be configured on an interface basis. In the case of a tie, the router with the highest SNPA address becomes the DIS. Unlike OSPF, there is no backup DIS.
- **Priority**—Higher priority takes precedence. Used in DIS election in LAN Hello PDUs. There is no DIS election on a point-to-point link.

Table 7-6 IS-IS Hello Message Types

Number	Description	
1	Point-to-point IIH	Part of the IS-IS spec 10589. Used by routers to form adjacencies.
2	Point-to-point IIH	Part of the IS-IS spec 10589. Used by routers to form adjacencies.
3	Point-to-point IIH	Part of the IS-IS spec 10589. Used by routers to form adjacencies.
4	ESH	Part of the ES-IS spec. Similar to ICMP Router Discovery Protocol (IRDP) in TCP/IP. Lets routers (ISs) and ESs detect each other.
5	ISH	Part of the ES-IS spec. Similar to IRDP in TCP/IP. Lets routers (ISs) and ESs detect each other.

Author Query:

both one and two are the same. Is this OK?

The IS-IS LAN Hello PDU is shown in Figure 7-9.

The IS-IS LAN Hello fields are as follows:

- **Intradomain Routing Protocol Discriminator**—Network layer identifier assigned to IS-IS in ISO 9577. The binary value is 10000011 (0x83).
- **Length Indicator**—Length of the fixed header in octets.
- **Protocol ID Ext**—Currently has a value of 1.
- **ID Length**—Length of the System ID field. This must be the same for all nodes in the domain. If this is set to 0, it implies six octets.
- **PDU Types**—Values are 15 and 16 for Level 1 and Level 2 LSPs, respectively.
- **Version**—Value is 1.
- **Maximum Area Addresses**—Number of area addresses permitted for this IS area. Values are between 1 and 254 for the actual number. 0 implies a maximum of three.
- **Reserved/Circuit Type**—The top 6 bits are reserved. The bottom 2 bits with a value of 0 indicates reserved. A value of 1 indicates Level 1, a value of 2 indicates Level 2, and a value of 3 indicates Levels 1 and 2.
- **Source ID**—Transmitting router's system ID.
- **Holding Time**—Holding time as configured on this router.
- **PDU Length**—Length of the entire PDU, fixed header, and TLVs.
- **Reserved/Priority**—Bit 8 is reserved. Bit 1 is used for priority for being the Level 1 or Level 2 DIS. The value is copied from the IIH of the DIS.
- **LAN ID**—A field composed of the system ID of the DIS, 1 to 8 bytes, plus a low-order octet assigned by the LAN Level 1 DIS.

Figure 7-9 IS-IS Hello PDU

Number of Octets

Intradomain Routing Protocol Discriminator	1
Length Indicator	1
Vision/Protocol ID EXT	1
ID Length	1
R R R Type	1
Version	1
Reserved	1
Maximum Area Address	1
Reserved Circuit Type	1
Source ID	6
Holding Timer	2
PDU Length	2
RES Priority	1
LAN ID	7
Variable-Length Fields	Variable

Notice the variable-type length fields at the bottom of the packet. This is where the TLV information is stored. Different types of PDUs have a set of currently defined codes. Any codes that are not recognized are supposed to be ignored and passed through unchanged.

By default, IS-IS Hellos are padded to the full MTU size. The benefit of padding IIHs to the full MTU is the early detection of errors caused by transmission problems with large frames or MTU mismatches on adjacent interfaces. The drawbacks of IIH padding are that on high-speed interfaces it could be a strain on huge buffers, and on low-speed interfaces, large Hello PDUs waste bandwidth. This could affect time-sensitive applications such as voice over IP (VoIP). The padding of IS-IS Hellos can be turned off for all interfaces on a router, beginning with Cisco IOS Releases 12.0(5)S and 12.0(5)T, with the **no hello padding** command in IS-IS router configuration mode. The padding of IS-IS Hellos can be turned off selectively for point-to-point or multipoint interfaces with the **no hello padding multipoint** command or the **no hello padding point-to-point** command, respectively, in IS-IS router configuration mode. Hello padding can also be turned off on an individual interface basis using the **no isis hello padding** interface configuration command.

 Interactive Media Activity   Drag and Drop: IS-IS Hello Messages

After completing this activity, you will be able to identify the fields in an IS-IS LAN Hello PDU.

IS-IS Link-State PDU (LSP) Formats

The contents of the TLV fields, shown in Figure 7-10, include the following:

- The neighbor ISs of the router that are used to build the map of the network
- The neighboring router ESs for the router
- Authentication information, used to secure routing updates
- Attached IP subnets if Integrated IS-IS is being run

Figure 7-10 TLV Field Contents

The complete list of LSP fields for Level 1 and Level 2 PDUs is shown in Figure 7-11.

Figure 7-11 IS-IS Level 1 and Level 2 Link-State PDU Format

				Number of Octets
Intradomain Routing Protocol Discriminator				1
Length Indicator				1
Vision/Protocol ID EXT				1
ID Length				1
R	R	R	PDU Type	1
Version				1
Reserved				1
Maximum Area Address				1
PDU Length				2
Remaining Lifetime				2
LSP ID				ID Length + 2
Sequence Number				4
Checksum				2
P	ATT	LSPDBOL	IS	Type	1
Type Length Fields				Variable

These fields are as follows:

- **Intradomain Routing Protocol Discriminator**—The network layer identifier assigned to IS-IS in ISO 9577. Its binary value is 10000011, hexadecimal 0x83.

- **Length Indicator**—Length of the fixed header in octets.

- **Protocol ID Ext**—Currently has a value of 1.

- **ID Length**—Length of the System ID field. Must be the same for all nodes in the domain. If set to 0, it implies six octets.

- **PDU Types**—Assumes decimal values. For example, values of 17, 18, and 20 are for point-to-point, Level 1, and Level 2 LSPs, respectively.

- **Version**—Value is 1.

- **Maximum Area Addresses**—Number of area addresses permitted for this IS area. Values are between 1 and 254 for the actual number. 0 implies a maximum of three.

- **PDU Length**—Length of the entire PDU, fixed header, and TLVs.

- **Remaining Lifetime**—Time in seconds before LSP expires. Used to age out LSPs. Outdated and invalid LSPs are removed from the topology table after a suitable period. It is a count-to-zero operation with a default 1200-second start value, or MaxAge. If the remaining lifetime expires, the first router that notices purges the LSP, removes the LSP body, keeps the LSP header, and sets the age to 0. It floods this modified LSP in the usual way throughout the network. Zero-lifetime LSPs are newer than nonzero-lifetime LSPs. After a while, all routers remove the purged LSP from their LSP database.

- **LSP ID**—Consists of the system ID, PSN ID, and LSP fragmentation number, as shown in Figure 7-12. The PSN ID is 0 for a router LSP. Length is ID length plus 2 bytes.

Figure 7-12 LSP ID

- **Sequence Number**—Used for synchronization. A higher sequence number indicates a newer LSP. Allows receiving routers to ensure that they use only the latest LSPs in their route calculations. Used to avoid duplicate LSPs being entered into the topology tables.

  When a change occurs, the sequence number is incremented, and a new version of the LSP is generated with the new sequence number.

  When a router reloads, the sequence number is initially set to 1. The router might then receive its own old LSPs back from its neighbors, which will have the last good sequence number before the router reloaded. It records this number and reissues its own LSPs with the next-highest sequence number.

- **Checksum**—Computed from the source ID to the end of the PDU. Used to detect LSP corruption during flooding. It might be that the Layer 2 CRC is insufficient for error checking. Corruption happens in routers and switches. The checksum is computed upon receipt of the LSP and is checked against the checksum inside the LSP. If corrupt, the LSP is dropped, and the sender retransmits. If two LSPs have the same LSP ID, the same sequence number, and the same remaining lifetime, the LSP with the highest checksum is kept. This guarantees consistent LSP databases across the network. This scenario can happen after a router reboots or is reconnected to the network.

- **Partition (P)**—Bit 8 of the octet. When set, this means that the originator of LSP supports partition repair.
- **Attached Bit (ATT)**—Bits 4 through 7 of the octet. When any of these bits is set, the originator is attached to another area using the referred metric. For example, as shown in Figure 7-13, bit 4 set implies attached using the default metric. Set in the Level 1 LSP by an L1L2 router if it has connectivity to another area, it indicates to the area routers, Level 1, that it is a potential exit point for the area. Level 1 routers select the closest, best metric Level 2 router with the ATT bit set.

Figure 7-13 Attached Bit

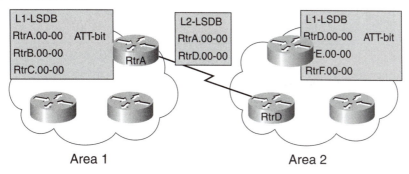

- **LSPDBOL (Overload Bit)**—Bit 3. When set, this indicates that the originator's LSP database is overloaded and should be circumvented in path calculations to other destinations. Indicates that the router has an incomplete LS database and, therefore, cannot be trusted to compute any correct routes. It is used in the LSP database, but the topology behind it is not calculated. Therefore, other routers do not compute routes that would require the PDU to pass through the overloaded router. An exception to this is ES neighbors, because these paths are guaranteed to be nonlooping.
- **IS Type**—Bits 1 and 2 indicate a Level 1 or Level 2 LSP type. When only Bit 1 is set, it indicates Level 1 IS. If both bits are set, it indicates Level 2 IS.

Section 9 of RFC 1142, a rewrite of ISO 10589, gives details about the packet layouts for each type of IS-IS PDU. It also gives the TLV information supported for each type. The first eight octets of all IS-IS PDUs are header fields that are common to all PDU types. The Level 1 and Level 2 LAN Hello PDUs are identical, except for the PDU type, which differentiates them as either Level 1 or Level 2, as shown in Figure 7-14. Figure 7-15 shows that the point-to-point Hello PDU is very similar to the Level 1 and Level 2 LAN Hello PDUs.

Figure 7-14 Level 1 and Level 2 IS-IS Hello PDU

Number of Octets

Field	Octets
Intradomain Routing Protocol Discriminator	1
Length Indicator	1
Vision/Protocol ID EXT	1
ID Length	1
Type / R / R / R	1
Version	1
Reserved	1
Maximum Area Address	1
Reserved/Circuit Type	1
Source ID	6
Holding Timer	2
PDU Length	2
RES / Priority	1
LAN ID	7
Variable-Length Fields	Variable

The lengths of the various ID fields in the PDUs—the LSP ID, source ID, and so on—all assume that the length of the system ID is fixed at 6 bytes. Under the column for the number of octets in Figure 7-11, an 8 would mean ID length + 2, a 7 would mean ID length + 1, and a 6 would mean ID length. Don't confuse the value of the ID length variable with the size of the ID Length field, which is fixed at 1 byte. The CLNS protocol allows the system ID, part of the NSAP address, to vary from 3 to 8 bytes. However, in practice, a 6-byte system ID is always used (ID length = 0). If the ID length field is 0, it means that the system ID is using the default length of 6 bytes.

Figure 7-15 Point-to-Point IS-IS Hello PDU

Number of Octets

Intradomain Routing Protocol Discriminator	1
Length Indicator	1
Vision/Protocol ID EXT	1
ID Length	1
Type | R | R | R	1
Version	1
Reserved	1
Maximum Area Address	1
Reserved/Circuit Type	1
Source ID	6
Holding Timer	2
PDU Length	2
Local Circuit ID	1
Variable-Length Fields	Variable

IS-IS Routing Levels

An IS-IS network is called a domain, analogous to an autonomous system in TCP/IP. The following shows IS-IS within the domain as a two-level hierarchy:

- Level 1 (L1) ISs, closely equivalent to OSPF internal nonbackbone routers, are responsible for routing to ESs inside an area. L1 ISs enable communication between ESs in an area.
- Level 2 (L2) ISs, closely equivalent to backbone routers in OSPF, route between areas only.

■ Level 1 and Level 2 (L1L2) intermediate ISs, closely equivalent to ABRs in OSPF, route between areas and the backbone. They participate in L1 intrarea routing and L2 interarea routing.

L1 routers are also called station routers because they allow stations to communicate with each other and the rest of the network. A contiguous group of L1 routers defines an area. The L1 routers maintain the L1 link-state PDU database (LSPD), which defines the picture of the area itself and the exit points to neighboring areas.

L2 routers are also called area routers because they interconnect the L1 areas. L2 routers store a separate LSPD that contains only the interarea topology information.

L1L2 routers act as if they were two IS-IS routers, as shown in Figures 7-16 and 7-17. Physically, an L1L2 router connects to L1 routers inside its area and to L2 routers in the backbone. Notice that the boundary between areas in IS-IS exists on a link between routers and not on an ABR, as in OSPF. Logically, the L1L2 router acts, for the purposes of IS-IS routing, as if it were two logical routers. An L1L2 router operates an L1 routing process, with its own L1 topology table and adjacency table, to handle its association with other L1 routers and ESs. An L1L2 router also operates an L2 routing process, with a separate L2 topology table and a separate L2 adjacency table, to handle its association with its neighbor backbone routers.

Figure 7-16 IS-IS Routing Levels

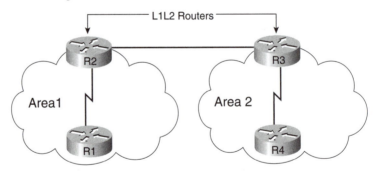

L1L2 routers support an L1 function to communicate with the other L1 routers in their area and maintain the L1 LSP information in an L1 LSPD. They inform other L1 routers that they are an exit point for the area. They also support an L2 function to communicate with the rest of the backbone and maintain an L2 topology database separately from their L1 LSPD. IS-IS does not have the concept of an Area 0, as does OSPF. An IS-IS domain appears as a set of distinct areas interconnected by a chain of L2 routers, weaving their way through and between the Level 1 areas.

Figure 7-17 IS-IS Routing Levels

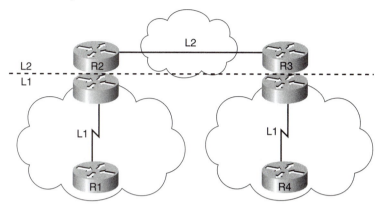

An L1 area is a collection of L1 and L1L2 routers. The backbone area is a collection of L2 and L1L2 routers and has to be contiguous. IS-IS does not have a backbone area such as OSPF Area 0. The IS-IS backbone is a contiguous collection of L2-capable routers, each of which can be in a different area, as shown in Figure 7-18.

NOTE

By default, all Cisco routers behave as L1L2 routers. You can override this default behavior by using the **is-type** router global configuration mode command or the **isis circuit-type** interface configuration mode command or both.

Figure 7-18 IS-IS Backbone

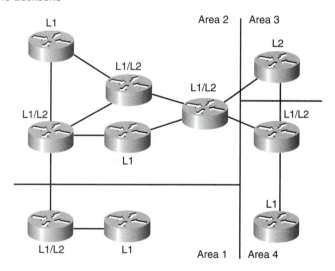

Useful examples of the L1, L2, and L1L2 concepts are discussed in this section. As shown in Figure 7-19, Area 1 contains two routers. One router borders Area 2 and, therefore, is an L1L2 IS. The other router is an L1-only.

NOTE

Figure 7-19 IS-IS Backbone

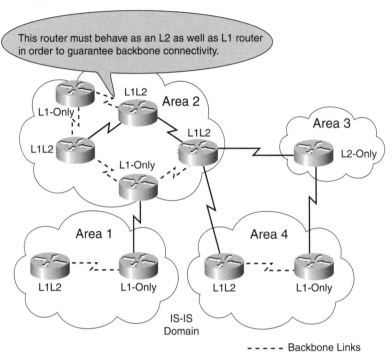

Previously, each Cisco router could participate in only one area. The router would perform L1, intra-area routing locally. The router would perform L2, interarea routing to other areas in the network. This limitation meant that when the network was divided into a large number of L1 areas, a correspondingly large number of L1L2 routers were required to route between all areas. The need for redundancy increases the number of routers needed. With Cisco IOS Release 12.0(5)T, support was added for configuring multiple L1 areas within a single router. A single Cisco router can now participate in routing in up to 29 areas, as well as perform L2 routing in the backbone. In other words, expanding an IS-IS network that consists of many small areas is simpler than before because multiple L1 areas can now be configured on the same Cisco router. You can do this without needing to add and configure physical units for each additional local area. This feature provides connectivity between L1 areas local to the router. Previously, L1 areas could only be connected using the L2 backbone. However, it should be emphasized that multiarea support per IS was introduced in later implementations of IS-IS to accommodate OSI tele-communications management network needs. This functionality generally is not useful or recommended for IP network design.

Area 2 has many routers. Some are specified as L1-only and can route internally to that area only and to the exit points. L1L2 routers form a chain across the area linking to the neighbor areas. Even though the middle of these three L1L2 routers does not link directly to another area, it must support Level 2 routing so that the backbone is contiguous. If that middle router fails, the other L1-only routers, although they provide a physical path across the area, cannot perform the L2 function. This causes the backbone to fail.

Area 3 contains one router that borders Area 2 and Area 4 but that has no intra area neighbors, so this router is an L2-only router. If another router were added to Area 3, the border router would revert to L1L2.

Interactive Media Activity   Matching: IS-IS Level 1 Adjacencies

After completing this activity, you will be able to identify the Level 1 adjacencies between routers in an IS-IS network.

IS-IS Adjacencies

IS-IS uses Hello PDUs to establish adjacencies with other routers (ISs) and ESs. Hello PDUs carry information about the system, its parameters, and its capabilities.

ISs use IIHs to establish and maintain neighbor relationships. As soon as an adjacency is established, the ISs exchange link-state information with LSPs.

ISs also send out ISHs. ESs listen for these ISHs and randomly pick an IS—the first one heard—to forward all of their packets to. OSI ESs require no configuration to forward packets to the rest of the network.

ISs listen to the ESHs and learn about all of the ESs on a segment. ISs include this information in their LSPs. For particular destinations, ISs might send redirect messages to ESs to provide them with an optimal route off the segment.

Now consider adjacencies between ISs. Separate adjacencies are established for Level 1 and Level 2. If two neighboring routers in the same area run both Level 1 and Level 2, they establish two adjacencies, one for each level. The L1 and L2 adjacencies are stored in separate L1 and L2 adjacency tables.

On LANs, two adjacencies are established with specific L1 and L2 IIH PDUs. Routers on a LAN establish adjacencies with all other routers on the LAN with the same area ID and level. This is unlike OSPF, where routers establish adjacencies only with the designated router. On LANs, IS-IS PDUs are multicast to the well-known MAC addresses, as shown in Table 7-7. IIH PDUs announce the area ID. Separate IIH PDUs announce the Level 1 and Level 2 neighbors. For example, where a LAN has routers from two areas attached, the routers from one area accept Level 1 IIH PDUs only from their own area. Therefore, they establish adjacencies with only their own area routers, as shown in Figure 7-20. The routers from a second area similarly accept Level 1 IIH PDUs only from their own area. The L2 routers, or the L2 process within any L1L2 router, accept only L2 IIH PDUs and establish only L2 adjacencies, as shown in Figure 7-21.

Table 7-7 IS-IS Layer 2 Multicast Addresses

Name	Address
AllL1ISs	01-80-C2-00-00-14
AllL2ISs	01-80-C2-00-00-15
AllIntermediateSystems	09-00-2B-00-00-05
AllEndSystems	09-00-2B-00-00-04

Figure 7-20 L1 and L2 Adjacencies In Area

Author Query:

Figure Titles
are the same.

Figure 7-21 L1 and L2 Adjacencies In and Out of Area

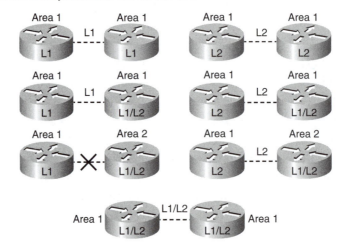

Point-to-point WAN links have a common IIH format, part of which specifies whether the Hello message relates to Level 1, Level 2, or both. The area ID is also announced in the Hello messages.

By default, Hello PDUs are sent every 10 seconds. The timeout to declare a neighbor down is 30 seconds, which equals three missing Hello packets. These timers can be reconfigured using the **isis hello-interval** and **isis hello-multiplier** interface configuration commands.

Various combinations are possible for links between L1, L2, and L1L2 routers. L1 routers in the same area, which include links between L1-only and L1L2 routers, exchange IIH PDUs specifying L1 and establish an L1 adjacency. L2 routers, when in the same area or between areas, and including links between L2-only and L1L2 routers, exchange IIH PDUs specifying L2 and establish an L2 adjacency. Two L1L2 routers in the same area establish both L1 and L2 adjacencies. The two routers maintain these with a common IIH PDU specifying both the L1 and L2 information. Two L1 routers that might be physically connected but, that are not in the same area, exchange L1 IIH PDUs. This includes an L1-only router to an L1L2 router in a different L1 area. However, they ignore these because the area IDs do not match. Therefore, they do not establish an adjacency.

L1-only routers establish L1 adjacencies. L2 routers establish L2 adjacencies between areas. L1L2 routers establish both L1 and L2 adjacencies with their L1L2 neighbors in the same area. L2 adjacencies exist independent of areas and must be contiguous; for example, Area 2 is not the backbone area, as shown in Figure 7-22. The backbone in IS-IS is exactly the contiguous set of routers and connections between L2 and L1L2 routers. The backbone might traverse multiple areas.

Figure 7-22 L2 Adjacencies Connect the Backbone Area

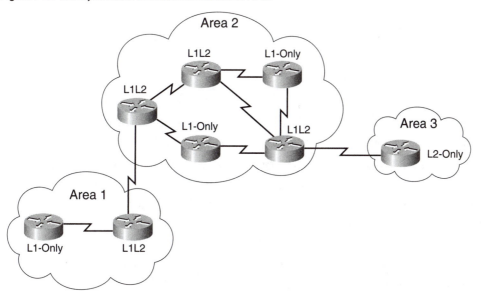

 Interactive Media Activity   Matching: IS-IS Level 2 Adjacencies

After completing this activity, you will be able to identify the Level 2 adjacencies between routers in an IS-IS network.

Designated Intermediate Systems (DIS) and Pseudonodes (PSN)

The idea behind the DIS is similar to the one behind the DR in OSPF. The DIS creates and acts on behalf of a PSN, a virtual node, as shown in Figure 7-23. All the routers on the LAN, including the DIS, form an adjacency with the PSN. Instead of flooding and database synchronization taking place over $n * (n - 1)$ adjacencies, the PSN lets the reduction in flooding and database synchronization occur only over the adjacencies formed with the pseudonode. On a LAN, one of the routers is elected the DIS, based on interface priority. The default priority is 64. The configurable range is 0 to 127. If all interface priorities are the same, the router with the highest SNPA is selected. MAC addresses are the SNPAs on LANs. On Frame Relay networks, the local DLCI is the SNPA. If the SNPA is a DLCI and is the same on both sides of a link, the router with the higher system ID in the NSAP address becomes the DIS.

Figure 7-23 Pseudonode

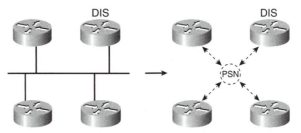

A pseudonode LSP represents a LAN, including all ISs attached to that LAN. A nonpseudonode LSP represents a router, including all ISs and LANs connected to the router.

The DIS election is preemptive, unlike DR election with OSPF. If a new router boots on the LAN with a higher interface priority, it becomes the DIS and purges the old pseudonode LSP, and a new set of LSPs is flooded. The DIS Hello interval, at 3.3 seconds, is 3 times faster than the interval for other routers on the LAN. This allows for quick detection of DIS failure and immediate replacement on the LAN. Remember that IS-IS has no concept of backup DIS.

In IS-IS, a DIS does not synchronize LSPs with its neighbors through acknowledgments. Reliability is ensured when the DIS creates the pseudonode for the LAN. It sends L1 and L2 Hello PDUs every 10 seconds and CSNPs every 10 seconds. The Hello PDUs indicate that it is the DIS on the LAN for that level. The CSNPs describe the summary of all the LSPs, including the LSP ID, sequence number, checksum, and remaining lifetime. The LSPs are always flooded to the multicast address. The CSNP mechanism only corrects for any lost PDUs. For example, a router can ask the DIS for a missing LSP using a PSNP or, in turn, give the DIS a new LSP. CSNPs are used to tell other routers about all the LSPs in another router's database. Similar to an OSPF database descriptor packet, PSNPs are used to request an LSP and acknowledge receipt of an LSP.

To restate, the DIS is responsible for conducting flooding over the LAN and also for maintaining synchronization. A router might need an LSP because it is older than the LSP advertised by the DIS in its CSNP. A router might need an LSP if it is missing an LSP that is listed in the CSNP. If either of these is the case, the router sends a PSNP to the DIS and receives the LSP in return. This mechanism can work both ways. If a router sees that it has a newer version of an LSP, or if it has an LSP that the DIS does not advertise in its CSNP, the router sends the newer or missing LSP to the DIS.

IS-IS Data Flow

In IS-IS, routers might have adjacencies with other routers on point-to-point links. In a LAN environment, routers report their adjacencies to the DIS, which generates an additional LSP, commonly known as the pseudonode LSP. The DIS is responsible for conducting flooding over the LAN and also for maintaining synchronization.

The flow of information within the IS-IS routing function is shown in Figure 7-24. This consists of four processes—receiver, update, decision, and forward—and a Routing Information Base (RIB). The RIB consists of the link-state database and the forwarding database.

Figure 7-24 IS-IS Data Flow Diagram

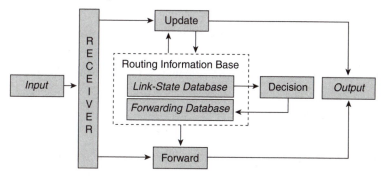

The receive process is the entry point for all data, including user data, error reports, routing information, and control packets. The receive process passes user data and error reports to the forward process. It passes routing information and control packets, such as Hello messages, LSPs, and sequence number packets, to the update process.

The update process generates local link information that is flooded to adjacent routers. In addition, the update process receives, processes, and forwards link information received from adjacent routers. This process manages the L1 and L2 link-state databases and floods L1 and L2 LSPs throughout an area. Each LSP that resides in the link-state database has a remaining lifetime, a checksum, and a sequence number. The LSP remaining lifetime counts down from 1200 seconds to 0. The MaxAge is 20 minutes. The LSP originator must periodically refresh its LSPs to prevent the remaining lifetime from reaching 0. The refresh interval is 15 minutes, with a random jitter of up to 25 percent. If the remaining lifetime reaches 0, the expired LSP is kept in the database for an additional 60 seconds before it is purged. This additional 60 seconds is called ZeroAgeLifetime. If a router receives an LSP with an incorrect checksum, the router causes a purge of the LSP. The router does this by setting the remaining lifetime value to 0, removing the LSP data, and reflooding it. This triggers the LSP originator to send a new LSP. This behavior is different from that of OSPF, where only the originating router can purge an LSP. IS-IS can be configured so that LSPs with incorrect checksums are not purged, but the router that originated the LSP does not know that the LSP was not received.

The decision process runs the SPF algorithm on the link-state database and creates the forwarding database. It computes next-hop information and computes sets of equal-cost paths, creating an adjacency set that is used for load balancing. On a Cisco router, IS-IS supports load balancing with up to six equal-cost paths.

The forward process gets its input from the receive process and uses the forwarding database to forward data packets to their destination. It also redirects load sharing and generates error reports.

LSP Flooding and Synchronization

The following are the two types of link-state PDUs:

- Nonpseudonode PDUs represent a router, including all ISs and LANs connected to the router.
- Pseudonode PDUs represent a LAN, including all ISs attached to that LAN, and are generated by the DIS.

An L1 router creates an L1 LSP, an L2 router creates an L2 LSP, and an L1L2 router creates both an L1 and an L2 LSP.

The DIS creates one pseudonode LSP for L1, one for L2, and one for each LAN. The use of pseudonode LSPs reduces the number of adjacencies on a LAN and, therefore, reduces the flooding of LSPs on the LAN, as shown in Figures 7-25 and 7-26.

The DIS creates and floods a new pseudonode LSP when the following happens:

- A new neighbor comes up or an existing neighbor goes away
- The refresh interval timer expires

The DIS generates the pseudonode LSP. The DIS reports all LAN neighbors, including the DIS, in the pseudonode LSP with a metric of 0. All LAN routers, including the DIS, report connectivity to the pseudonode in their LSPs. This is similar in concept to the network LSA in OSPF.

Figure 7-25 LSP Database Without a Pseudonode

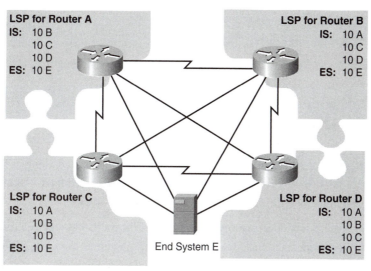

LSP for Router A
IS: 10 B
      10 C
      10 D
ES: 10 E

LSP for Router B
IS: 10 A
      10 C
      10 D
ES: 10 E

LSP for Router C
IS: 10 A
      10 B
      10 D
ES: 10 E

End System E

LSP for Router D
IS: 10 A
      10 B
      10 C
ES: 10 E

Figure 7-26 LSP Database with a Pseudonode

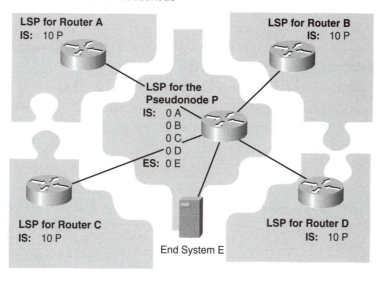

LSP for Router A
IS: 10 P

LSP for Router B
IS: 10 P

LSP for the Pseudonode P
IS: 0 A
      0 B
      0 C
      0 D
ES: 0 E

LSP for Router C
IS: 10 P

End System E

LSP for Router D
IS: 10 P

Each IS creates and floods a nonpseudonode LSP when the following happens:

- A new neighbor comes up or an existing neighbor goes away
- New IP prefixes are inserted or removed
- A link's metric changes
- The refresh interval timer expires

For L1 LSP databases, L1 CSNPs and L1 PSNPs are used. For L2 LSP databases, L2 CSNPs and L2 PSNPs are used.

The following are true of a CSNP:

- It describes all LSPs in the LSP database. It contains an address range, LSP ID, sequence number, checksum, and remaining lifetime.
- It is used in two cases—periodic multicast by DIS every 10 seconds and on point-to-point links when the link comes up.
- If the LSP database is large, multiple CSNPs are sent.

Each router floods its LSPs to adjacent neighbors. The LSPs are passed along unchanged to other adjacent routers until all of the routers in the area have received them. All of the L1 LSPs received by one router in an area describe the area's topology.

The IS-IS link-state database consists of all of the LSPs the router has received. Each node in the area maintains an identical link-state database. A change in the topology means a change in one or more of the LSPs. The router that has experienced a link going up or down resends its LSP to inform the other routers of the change. The LSP sequence number is increased by 1 to let the other routers know that the new LSP supersedes the older LSP. When a router originates an LSP, the LSP sequence number is 1. If the sequence number increases to the maximum of 0xFFFFFFFF, the IS-IS process must shut down. IS-IS must shut down for at least 21 minutes, which is MaxAge + ZeroAgeLifetime. This allows the old LSPs to age out of all the router databases.

Flooding is the process by which these new LSPs are sent throughout the area to ensure that the databases in all routers remain identical. If the LSP database is not synchronized, routing loops might occur. When a router receives a new LSP, it floods this LSP to its neighbors, except the neighbor that sent it.

On point-to-point links, the neighbors acknowledge the new LSP with a PSNP, which holds the LSP ID, sequence number, checksum, and remaining lifetime. When the acknowledgment PSNP is received from a neighbor, the originating router stops sending the new LSP to that particular neighbor, although it might continue sending the new LSP to other neighbors that have not yet acknowledged it.

On LANs, there is no explicit acknowledgment with a PSNP. Missing LSPs are detected when a CSNP is received and the list of LSPs within the CSNP is compared to the LSPs in that router's database. If any LSPs are missing or outdated, the router sends a request for these in the form of a PSNP.

If a router receives an LSP that has an older sequence number than the one in its IS-IS database, it sends the newer LSP to the router that sent the old LSP. The router keeps resending it until it receives an acknowledgment PSNP from the originator of the old LSP.

LSPs must be flooded throughout an area in order for the databases to synchronize and the SPF tree to be consistent within an area. It is not possible to control which LSPs are flooded by using a distribute list, although it is possible to use a route map to control which routes are redistributed into IS-IS from another routing protocol.

New LSPs are flooded when there is a change in the topology. These changes are triggered by the following:

- Adjacency comes up or goes down
- Interface comes up or goes down
- Redistributed IP routes change
- Interarea IP routes change
- An interface is assigned a new metric
- Most other configuration changes

When a new LSP is received, it is installed in the LSP database and is marked for flooding. It is sent to all neighbors. Neighbors, in turn, flood the LSP further. Only new LSPs are flooded. Old LSPs are simply acknowledged. This is because "state" is already maintained for this LSP, and infinite looping of LSPs is avoided. It is also important to note that the LSP isn't flooded back to the router it was received from.

On a point-to-point link, as soon as an adjacency is established, both ISs send a CSNP packet. Missing LSPs are sent by both ISs if they are not present in the received CSNP. Missing LSPs might be requested with a PSNP, as shown in Figures 7-27 and 7-28. The ACK is communicated with a PSNP.

NOTE

Point-to-point is sometimes abbreviated P2P.

Figure 7-27 P2P LSP Flooding

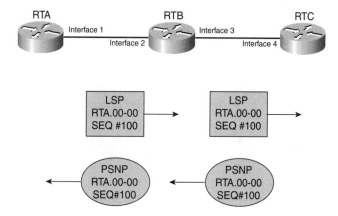

Figure 7-28 The Link Goes Down

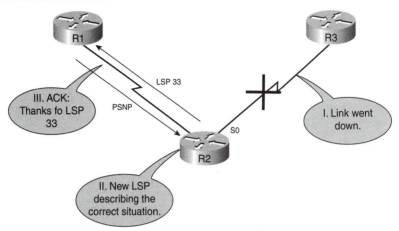

A LAN has a DIS. The DIS has two tasks—creating and updating the pseudonode LSP and flooding LSPs over the LAN (see Figure 7-29). Recall that a DIS is elected for each LAN based on priority, with the highest SNPA (MAC) address breaking the tie. DIS election is deterministic.

Figure 7-29 LAN LSP Flooding

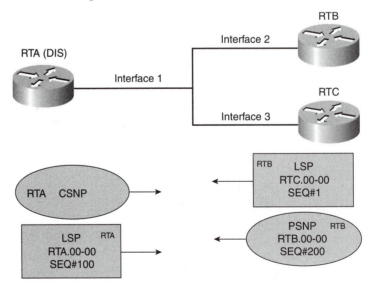

Every 10 seconds, the DIS sends CSNPs listing the LSPs it holds in its link-state database. This is a multicast to all IS-IS routers on the LAN. R1 compares this list of LSPs with its topology table and realizes it is missing one LSP, as shown in Figure 7-30. Therefore, it sends a PSNP to the DIS (R2) to request the missing LSP. The DIS reissues that LSP, and R2 acknowledges it with a PSNP.

Figure 7-30 LAN LSP Flooding

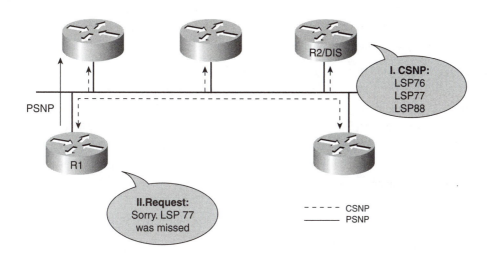

IS-IS Metrics

The original IS-IS specification defines four different types of metrics. All routers support the default metric of cost. Delay, expense, and error are optional metrics. The delay metric measures transit delay, the expense metric measures the monetary cost of link utilization, and the error metric measures the residual error probability associated with a link.

The Cisco implementation uses cost only. If the optional metrics were implemented, there would be a link-state database for each metric, and SPF would be run for each link-state database.

NOTE

Try to avoid confusing the IS-IS metric range and default with the IS-IS priority range of 0 to 127 and default of 64.

Default Metric

Some routing protocols calculate the link metric automatically based on bandwidth, OSPF, EIGRP, or bandwidth/delay. However, IS-IS has no automatic calculation. Using old-style metrics, an interface cost is between 1 and 63, a 6-bit metric value.

All links use a metric of 10 by default. The total cost to a destination is the sum of the costs on all outgoing interfaces along a particular path from the source to the destination. Least-cost paths are preferred. The total path metric is limited to 1023. This is the sum of all link metrics along a path between the calculating router and any other node or prefix. This small metric value proved insufficient for large networks and provided too little granularity for new features, such as traffic engineering and other applications. This is especially true with high-bandwidth links. Wide metrics are also required if route leaking is used.

Extended Metric

Cisco IOS software addresses this issue by supporting a 24-bit metric field called the wide metric. Using this new metric style, link metrics now have a maximum value of 16,777,215 ($2^{24}-1$) with a total path metric of 4,261,412,864 ($2^{32}-2^{25}$). The wide metric formulation can be found in IETF Internet Draft document draft-ietf-isis-traffic-02.txt.

Deploying IS-IS in the IP network with wide metrics is recommended to enable finer granularity and to support applications such as traffic engineering. Running different metric styles within one network can cause a major problem. Link-state protocols calculate loop-free routes. This is because all routers within one area calculate their routing table based on the same link-state database. This principle is violated if some routers look at the old, narrow style and some look at the new, wider-style TLVs. However, if the same interface cost is used for both the old and new-style metrics, SPF computes a loop-free topology.

IS-IS Network Types

IS-IS defines point-to-point and broadcast networks.

Point-to-point networks, such as serial lines, connect a single pair of routers. A router running IS-IS forms an adjacency with the neighbor on the other side of a point-to-point interface. A DIS is not elected on this type of link. The basic mechanism defined in the standard is that each side of a point-to-point link declares the other side to be reachable if a Hello packet is received from it. When this occurs, each side then sends a CSNP to trigger database synchronization.

Broadcast networks, such as Ethernet, Token Ring, and Fiber Distributed Data Interface (FDDI), are multiaccess in that they can connect more than two devices. All devices connected to routers receive a packet sent by one router. On broadcast networks, one IS is elected the DIS. Hello packets on broadcast networks are sent to the AllL1ISs or AllL2ISs MAC-layer broadcast addresses. The DIS is responsible for flooding. It creates and floods a new pseudonode LSP for each routing level it participates in, whether L1 or L2, and for each LAN to which it is connected. A router can be the DIS for all connected LANs or a subset of connected LANS. This depends on the configured priority or, if no priority is configured, the Layer 2 address. The DIS also creates and floods a new pseudonode LSP when a neighbor adjacency is established or torn down or the refresh interval timer for this LSP expires. The DIS mechanism reduces the amount of flooding on LANs.

Nonbroadcast multiaccess (NBMA) networks, such as Frame Relay, ATM, and X.25, can connect multiple devices but have no broadcast capability. None of the other routers attached to the network receive a packet sent by a router. Special consideration should be taken when configuring IS-IS over NBMA networks. IS-IS has no concept of an NBMA network. IS-IS considers these media to be just like any other broadcast media, such as Ethernet or Token Ring. In general, it is better to configure point-to-point networks for IS-IS on WAN interfaces and subinterfaces, such as with ATM, Frame Relay, and X.25. Unlike OSPF, no configuration is necessary to tell IS-IS what the network type is.

SPF Algorithm

After the link-state database is updated, the router still needs to populate the routing table or forwarding table. Just as with OSPF, IS-IS uses the Dijkstra algorithm, also called the SPF algorithm, to compute the best path to a given destination in the link-state database. This is the critical decision-making process that determines what routes, of those appearing in the link-state database, will populate the routing table as IS-IS routes.

Edsger Dijkstra's SPF algorithm is used to calculate routes with the IS-IS routing protocol, for support of both TCP/IP and OSI. This is based on an extension to the algorithm specified in ISO/IEC 10589.

The SPF algorithm computes the shortest paths from a single-source vertex to all other vertices in a weighted, directed graph. In the Cisco IOS software implementation, the weight assigned to the branches of a tree is a configurable metric with 2^{24} possible values for each link and 2^{32} possible values for each path from the root to a leaf.

The main difference between link-state and distance vector routing protocols is that a link-state protocol provides full visibility of the network topology, and a distance vector protocol uses learned information to build forwarding tables. The visibility provided by a link-state protocol is achieved through the use of a flooding mechanism. This mechanism ensures that each router in a specified area of a network receives information that can be used to build a network map. In IS-IS this information is flooded through the use of LSP data units. Each intermediate system, or router, then advertises information that pertains to itself and its links. After the information is flooded and all routers obtain the same information, the SPF algorithm is applied separately to each router. This is done to determine the topology and to extract the shortest paths for each router from the tree's root to all its leaves. The information derived from this process is used to create the forwarding table on the router.

IP Routing with Integrated IS-IS

Integrated IS-IS supports the following three types of networks:

- OSI
- IP
- Dual, made up of both OSI and IP

The LSPs can contain many variable-length TLV fields describing OSI and IP state information.

OSI, IP, and Dual

Integrated IS-IS LSPs describe IP information similar to how IS-IS describes ESs. There are specific TLV types for IP information. Like all modern routing protocols, Integrated IS-IS supports the following:

- Variable-length subnet masks (VLSMs)—The mask is sent with the prefix in the updates
- Redistribution of IP routes into and out of IS-IS
- Summarization of IP routes

Even if Integrated IS-IS is being used only for IP routing, a NET address is required for L2 forwarding and Dijkstra algorithm computation. OSI protocols are used to form the neighbor relationship between routers. SPF calculations rely on a configured NET address to identify the routers. The next paragraph describes IS-IS routing in a pure OSI environment. If IP routing with IS-IS is required, the same process described still takes place. TLVs are used to carry IP routing information, enabling IP routing by way of OSI routing.

To build the OSI forwarding database, the CLNS routing table, the synchronized link-state database is used to calculate the SPF tree to OSI destinations or NETs. The link metrics are totaled along each path to find the shortest way to any given destination. L1 and L2 routes have separate link-state databases. Therefore, SPF is run twice, once for each level, and separate SPF trees are created for each level, as shown in Figure 7-31. ES reachability is calculated with a partial route calculation (PRC) based on the L1 and L2 SPF trees. There are no OSI ESs if it is a pure IP Integrated IS-IS environment. The best paths are inserted in the CLNS routing table, OSI forwarding database.

Routing inside an L1 area is based on the system ID of the destination ISO (NSAP) address. OSI packets to other areas are routed to the nearest L1L2 router. L2 routing is based on the area ID and considers only the area cost. If an L1L2 router receives a packet from an L2 neighbor destined for its own area, it routes it based on the system ID, the L1 routing.

Figure 7-31 L1 and L2 SPF Tree Calculations

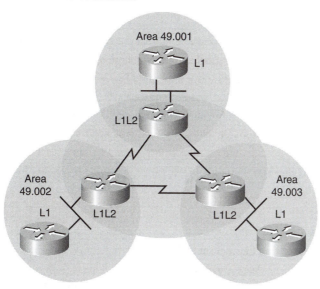

When routing a packet from one area to another, the L1 routers route the packet to the nearest L1L2 router. L1 routers find the closest exit point from the area based on receipt of default routes from the L1L2 routers in their area. The L1L2 router routes the packets into the L2 backbone based on the destination area ID. The packet travels across the L2 backbone to the destination area. After the packet arrives at the destination area, L1 routing is again used to route the packet to its final destination inside that area. The interface between the L1 world and the L2 world takes place on an L1L2 router. The L1L2 router behaves as if it were both an L1 router, by routing to L1 destinations, and an L2 router, by routing between areas.

An IS-IS domain is the equivalent of an IP AS. IS-IS can support the interconnection of multiple domains. In a pure OSI environment, ISO IGRP interprets the IDI portion of CLNS routes and allows routing between domains. ISO-IGRP is a Cisco-proprietary routing protocol. A standard OSI IDRP, specified in ISO/IEC 10747, provides the same function, but it is not supported by Cisco. IDRP is used for L3 routing in an OSI environment. This protocol has never been deployed in a production environment. This is because by the time the ISO formalized IDRP, IP had already become the dominant routed protocol for the Internet. The current standard for interdomain routing in an IP environment is Border Gateway Protocol (BGP) version 4. Chapter 9, "BGP", discusses this further.

Suboptimal IS-IS Routing

An L1 router knows the topology of only its own area and has L1 or L1L2 neighbors within this area. An L1 router has an L1 link-state database with all of the information for intra-area routing. It uses the closest L2-capable router in its own area to send packets out of the area, a scenario that might result in suboptimal routing.

An L1L2 router that is attached to another area sets the attached bit in its L1 LSP. All of the L1 ISs in an area get a copy of this LSP and know where to forward packets to destinations outside the area. If the routers are running Integrated IS-IS, a default IP route is automatically installed in the L1 routers pointing toward the nearest L1L2 router that set the attached bit in its L1 LSP. An L1L2 router that is not attached to another area can also detect that an L2-only neighbor is attached to another area and can set the attached bit on behalf of this L2-only neighbor. If there is more than one point to exit the area, the closest L1L2 router is selected based on the cost. If there are two equal-cost paths, the traffic might load-balance over the two paths.

Suboptimal Routing

In Figure 7-32, assume that the cost on all links is 10. Router A, an L1, in Area X sends all traffic destined for outside Area X to Router B, an L1L2. This is because Router B is the clos-est L1L2 neighbor. Router B is directly connected to Area Y. Router C, also an L1L2, is in Area X and is directly connected to Area Z. Router A sends packets destined for Area Z to Router B. Because Router B, Router E, and Router C are backbone routers, Router B sends this packet to Router C through Router E for delivery into Area Z. The more optimal path would be for Router A to send the packet directly to Router C through Router D.

Figure 7-32 Suboptimal IS-IS Routing

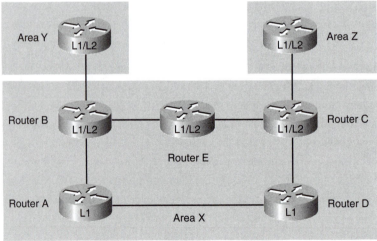

Figure 7-33 shows a second example of suboptimal routing. Router R1 routes packets des-tined for Router R2 to its L1L2 router. This router looks at the destination area and routes directly to Area 2. After they reach Area 2, the packets are routed as L1 to Router R2. Even though the initial next hop is another L1L2 router, the routing is still L1. Return packets from Router R2 to Router R1 are routed by R2 to its nearest L1L2 router. This router sees the best route to Area 1 as being by way of Area 4 and routes the return packets by a different route to the incoming packets. The path taken is not actually the least-cost path from R2 to R1. Asymmetric routing (packets in different directions taking different paths) is not necessarily detrimental to the network, but it can make troubleshooting difficult.

Figure 7-33 Suboptimal IS-IS Routing

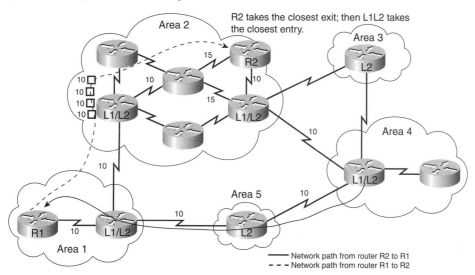

A feature available since Cisco IOS Release 12.0 allows L2 routes to be leaked in a controlled manner into the L1 area to help avoid this situation. All IS-IS areas are "stub" areas. However, with the route-leaking feature, leaking L2 routes into L1, a sort of IS-IS NSSA is created. Route leaking helps reduce suboptimal routing by providing a mechanism for leaking, or redistributing, L2 information into L1 areas. By having more details about interarea routes, an L1 router can make a better choice about which L1L2 router to forward the packet. Route leaking is defined in RFC 2966 for use with the narrow metric TLV types 128 and 130, as shown in Figure 7-34. IS-IS extensions for traffic engineering (see IETF Internet Draft document draft-ietf-isis-traffic-04.txt) define route leaking for use with the wide metric TLV Type 135, as shown in Figure 7-35. Both define an up/down bit to indicate whether the route defined in the TLV has been leaked. If the up/down bit is set to 0, the route was originated within that L1 area. If the up/down bit is set to 1, the route has been redistributed into the area from L2. The up/down bit is used to prevent routing loops. An L1L2 router does not readvertise into L2 any L1 routes that have the up/down bit set. You configure route leaking with the

IS-IS router configuration mode command **redistribute isis ip level-2 into level-1 distribute-list** *100–199*.

Figure 7-34 TLV Type 128 and Type 130

TLV Type 128 and Type 130		
1	1	6
Up/Down	Int/Ext	Default Metric
Supported	Rsvd	Delay Metric
Supported	Rsvd	Expense Metric
Supported	Rsvd	Error Metric
IPAddress		
Subnet Mask		

Figure 7-35 TLV Type 135

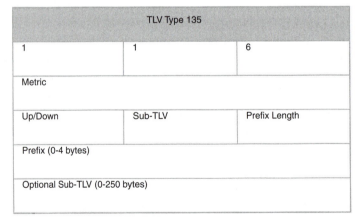

TLV Type 135		
1	1	6
Metric		
Up/Down	Sub-TLV	Prefix Length
Prefix (0-4 bytes)		
Optional Sub-TLV (0-250 bytes)		

Interactive Media Activity   Drag and Drop: Identifying IS-IS Routers

After completing this activity, you will be able to identify the different types of IS-IS routers in a network.

Intra-Area and Interarea Integrated IS-IS Routing Example

An array of useful IS-IS commands in the context of the topology shown in Figure 7-36 are introduced and analyzed in this section.

Figure 7-36 Routing in a Two-Level Area Structure

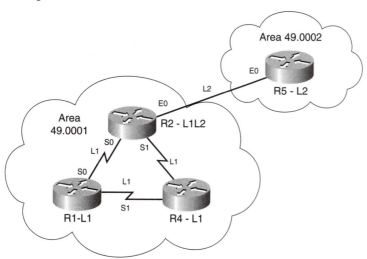

The **show isis topology** command is explored first. This command displays the least-cost paths to the destination NETs, as shown in Example 7-1. The system ID shows the NET of the destination. IOS uses dynamic host name mapping, described in RFC 2763, to map this system ID to a host name when that host name is available to the router. The router's host name is included in its outgoing LSP.

Example 7-1 show isis topology *Command*

```
R1#show isis topology
IS-IS paths to level-1 routers
System Id       Metric    Next-Hop    Interface    SNPA
R1              - -
R2              10        R2          Se0          *HDLC*
R4              10        R4          Se1          *HDLC*


R2#show isis topology
IS-IS paths to level-1 routers
System Id       Metric    Next-Hop    Interface    SNPA
R1              10        R1          Se0          *HDLC*
```

continues

Example 7-1 show isis topology *Command (Continued)*

```
R2                 --
R4                 10       R4        Se1       *HDLC*
IS-IS paths to level-2 routers
System Id     Metric    Next-Hop    Interface    SNPA
R2                 --
R5                 10       R5        Et0       0010.7bb5.9e20
```

The metric shows the sum of the metrics on the least-cost path to the destination. The next-hop router, IS, is shown. Also shown is the interface through which that next hop is reached and the SNPA of that next hop. HDLC is shown as the next hop across a serial line. The output for Router R2 shows that separate topology databases exist for L1 and L2.

Recall that the SNPA is taken from the following:

- MAC address on a LAN interface
- Virtual circuit ID for X.25 or ATM
- DLCI for Frame Relay
- HDLC for interfaces

The **show clns routes** and **show isis routes** commands are the next commands to be looked at. There is a common source of confusion for those learning about Integrated IS-IS. That confusion comes from the frequent use of commands directly referencing CLNS but that are used to verify and troubleshoot IP routing.

The **show clns routes** command displays the CLNS destinations to which this router can route packets, as shown in Example 7-2. R1 shows only its local NET entry, because it is an L1-only router and, therefore, has no L2 area routes to display. The **show isis routes** command shows the L1 routes to IS-IS neighbors. R1 has visibility of the other L1 routers in its area. The L1L2 routers appear in the L1 routing table by virtue of their L1 connection. There is a note at the end of their entry to show that they also act as L2. The closest L1L2 router also appears as the default route out of area. Again, the next-hop IS, its SNPA, is the interface over which that next hop is reached. The cumulative metric to that destination is shown for all IS routes. The neighbors show that their state is up and that the Hello process has established an adjacency.

Example 7-2 show clns routes *and* show isis routes *Commands*

```
R1#show clns routes
CLNS Prefix Routing Table
49.0001.0000.0000.0001.00, Local NET Entry
```

Example 7-2 show clns routes *and* show isis routes *Commands (Continued)*

```
R1#show isis routes
IS-IS Level-1 Routing Table - version 312
System Id       Next-Hop      SNPA      Interface    Metric      State
R2              R2            *HDLC*    Se0          10          Up    L2-IS
R4              R4            *HDLC*    Se1          10          Up
R1              - -
Default Route out of Area - (via 2 L2-atached ISs)
System Id       Next-Hop      SNPA      Interface    Metric      State
                R2            *HDLC*    Se0          10          Up
```

The command **show clns routes** shows the local NET entry. This command also shows the L2 routes to its own area and the neighbor areas. Notice in Example 7-3 that R2 regards the route to the area of R2 as being through itself. This further emphasizes that the L1 and L2 processes operate separately. The command **show isis routes** shows the IS-IS neighbors.

Example 7-3 show clns routes *and* show isis routes *Commands*

```
R2#show clns routes
Codes: C - connected, S - static, d - DecnetIV
I - ISO-IGRP, i - IS-IS, e - ES-IS

ICLNS Prefix Routing Table
49.0001.0000.0000.0002.00, Local NET Entry

C   49.0002 [110/10], via R5, IS-IS, Up, Ethernet0
C   49.0001 [110/0], via R2, IS-IS, Up

R2#show isis routes
IS-IS Level-1 Routing Table - version 47
System Id       Next-Hop      SNPA      Interface    Metric      State
R4              R4            *HDLC*    Se1          10          Up
R1              R1            *HDLC*    Se0          10          Up
```

Next, the **which-route** command in the context of L1 and L2 will be explored. The **which-route** command is an alternative method of finding the route to a destination NET or NSAP, as shown in Example 7-4. You enter this command on the L1-only router, R1. This command returns the next hop to the destination and states whether the destination can be reached by L1 or by the default exit point to L2. Executing the **which-route** command on an L2 router specifies the next hop. It also states that the route was matched by an entry from the CLNS L2 routing table, as shown in Example 7-5.

Example 7-4 which-route *Command*

```
R1#which-route 49.0001.0000.0000.0002.00
Route look-up for destination 49.0001.0000.0000.0002.00
Found route in IS-IS Level-1 routing table
Adjacency entry used:
System Id       Interface    SNPA     State    Holdtime    Type    Protocol
0000.0000.0002  Se0          HDLC*    Up       26          L1      IS-IS
  Area Address(es); 49.0001
   Uptime: 00:09:50


R1#which-route 49.0002.0000.0000.0005.00
Route look-up for destination 49.0001.0000.0000.0002.00
Using route to closest IS-IS Level-2 router
Adjacency entry used:
System Id       Interface    SNPA     State    Holdtime    Type    Protocol
0000.0000.0002  Se0          HDLC*    Up       27          L1      IS-IS
   Area Address(es); 49.0001
    Uptime: 00:09:57
```

Example 7-5 which-route *Command*

```
R5#which-route 49.0001.0000.0000.0002.00
Found route in CLNS L2 Prefix routing table
Route entry used:
49.0001 [110/10], via R2, Ethernet 0/0
Adjacency entry used:
System Id    Interface    SNPA            State    Hold    Type    Protocol
R2           Ethernet0/0  0000.0c92.e515  Up       24      L2      IS-IS
   Area Address(es); 49.0001



R5#which-route 49.0002.0000.0000.0005.00
Found route in CLNS L2 Prefix routing table
```

Example 7-5 which-route *Command (Continued)*

```
Route entry used:
49.0001 [110/10], via R2, Ethernet 0/0
Adjacency entry used:
System Id    Interface    SNPA           State   Hold   Type   Protocol
R2           Ethernet0/0  0000.0c92.e515  Up      21     L2     IS-IS
   Area Address(es); 49.0001
```

Building the IP Forwarding Table

So far, the process and outputs have referred to the OSI part of the IS-IS process. However, in the IP world, when running Integrated IS-IS, IP information is included in the LSPs. IP reachability behaves in IS-IS as if it were ES information. IP information takes no part in the calculation of the SPF tree. It is simply information about leaf connections to the tree. Therefore, updating the IP reachability is only a PRC. This is similar to ES reachability. IP routes are generated by the PRC and are offered to the routing table. Here they are accepted based on routing table rules that compare, for example, administrative distance. When entered in the routing table, IP IS-IS routes are shown as being by way of Level 1 or Level 2, as appropriate. The separation of IP reachability from the core IS-IS network architecture gives Integrated IS-IS better scalability than, for example, OSPF. OSPF sends LSAs for individual IP subnets. If an IP subnet fails, the LSA is flooded through the network. In all circumstances, all routers must run a full SPF calculation. In Integrated IS-IS, the SPF tree is built from CLNS information. If an IP subnet fails in Integrated IS-IS, the LSP is flooded, as it is for OSPF. However, if this is a leaf IP subnet, meaning that the loss of the subnet has not affected the underlying CLNS architecture, the SPF tree is unaffected. Only a PRC takes place.

The IP routing table, a pure entity, will now be looked at. The output for the **show ip routes** command shows the IS-IS routes chosen by the SPF algorithm, from the IS-IS LSP database, to populate the IP routing table, as shown in Example 7-6. The IP addresses on loopbacks of routers are 1.0.0.1/8-R1, 2.0.0.1/8-R2, 4.0.0.1/8-R4, and 5.0.0.1/8-R5. The "i" indicates that the route was sourced from IS-IS. L1 and L2 show whether the IS-IS path to these destination IP networks is by way of IS-IS L1 or L2 routing. The next-hop IP addresses are matched from the corresponding next-hop IS-IS neighbor routers. Notice that the metric is 10 for each route because 10 is the Cisco default for the IS-IS metric over a link.

Example 7-6 show ip route *Command*

```
R2#show ip route
i L1 1.0.0.0/8 [115/10] via 10.12.0.1, Ser0 -(R1)
i L1 4.0.0.0/8 [115/10] via 10.24.0.4, Ser1 -(R4)
i L2 5.0.0.0/8 [115/10] via 11.0.0.10, Eth0 -(R5)
```

Configuration of Integrated IS-IS

As with any routing protocol, the first step is to plan the logical topology, the addressing scheme, and the participating interfaces. After this initial step is complete, Integrated IS-IS can be configured on the network.

Basic Configuration of Integrated IS-IS

Enabling Integrated IS-IS on a router for IP routing is easy. Many more commands are used to tune the IS-IS processes. However, only the following three commands are required to start Integrated IS-IS:

- Enable IS-IS as an IP routing protocol, using the command **router isis**, and assign a tag if there are multiple IS-IS processes. If the tag is omitted, a tag of 0 is assumed.
- Identify the router for IS-IS by assigning a NET to the router with the **net** command.
- Enable IS-IS on the interfaces participating in IS-IS using the command **ip router isis**. This command is configured on the interface and not on the routing process. This is slightly different from most other IP routing protocols, in which the participating interfaces are specified by **network** statements. The IS-IS process has no **network** statement. If multiple IS-IS processes exist, interfaces must state which process they belong to by specifying the appropriate tag.

These commands enable Integrated IS-IS on the router. However, further commands might be required to tune IS-IS operation.

Troubleshooting Integrated IS-IS, even in an IP-only world, requires some investigation of CLNS data. For example, the IS-IS neighbor relationships are established over OSI, not over IP. To view IS-IS neighbors, you use the **show clns neighbors** command. Two ends of a CLNS adjacency can actually have IP addresses on different subnets, with no impact on the operation of IS-IS. However, IP next-hop resolution could be an issue.

Figure 7-37 shows a simple topology with three routers in area 49.0001. The pertinent configuration for each router is shown in Examples 7-7, 7-8, and 7-9.

Figure 7-37 Basic Configuration of Integrated IS-IS

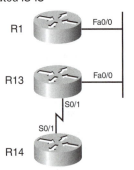

Example 7-7 *Basic Configuration of Integrated IS-IS: R1 Configuration*

```
interface Loopback0
 ip address 172.16.1.1 255.255.255.255
!
interface FastEthernet 0/0
 ip address 172.16.113.1 255.255.255.0
 ip router isis
!
router isis
 passive-interface Loopback0
 net 49.0001.1720.1600.1001.00
```

Example 7-8 *Basic Configuration of Integrated IS-IS: R13 Configuration*

```
interface Loopback0
 ip address 172.16.13.13 255.255.255.255
!
interface FastEthernet 0/0
 ip address 172.16.113.13 255.255.255.0
 ip router isis
!
interface serial 0/1
 ip address 172.16.34.13 255.255.255.252
 ip router isis
!
router isis
 passive-interface Loopback0
 net 49.0001.1720.1601.3013.00
```

Example 7-9 *Basic Configuration of Integrated IS-IS: R14 Configuration*

```
interface Loopback0
 ip address 172.16.14.14 255.255.255.255
!
interface serial 0/1
 ip address 172.16.34.14 255.255.255.252
 ip router isis
 clockrate 2000000
!
```

continues

Example 7-9 *Basic Configuration of Integrated IS-IS: R14 Configuration (Continued)*

```
router isis
 passive-interface Loopback0
 net 49.0001.1720.1601.4014.00
```

Here are some informative **show** commands for this topology:

- **show clns neighbors**—Lists the ES neighbors that the router knows about.
- **show clns interface**—Lists the CLNS-specific information about each interface.
- **show isis database** [**detail**]—Displays the database of the configuration server.
- **show ip route isis**—Displays the current state of the IS-IS routing table.
- **show isis spf-log**—Displays how often and why the router has run a full SPF calculation.
- **show isis lsp-log**—Displays the Level 1 and Level 2 IS-IS LSP log of the interfaces that triggered the new LSP.

For added security, configure IS-IS passwords for areas or domains. The area authentication password is inserted in L1, which is the station router level, LSPs, CSNPs, and PSNPs. The routing domain authentication password is inserted in L2, which is the area router level, LSPs, CSNPs, and PSNPs. To configure area or domain authentication passwords, respectively, use the following commands in router configuration mode:

```
area-password password
domain-password password
```

You can configure authentication for an interface using the **isis password** interface configuration command. This command lets you prevent unauthorized routers from forming adjacencies with this router. Therefore, it protects the network from intruders. The password is exchanged as plain text and, therefore, provides only limited security. You can assign different passwords to different routing levels using the **level-1** and **level-2** keyword arguments. Specifying the **level-1** or **level-2** keyword enables the password only for L1 or L2 routing, respectively.

Last, as with OSPF, aggregate addresses can be created with IS-IS. They are represented in the routing table by a summary address. One summary address can include multiple groups of addresses for a given level. Routes learned from other routing protocols can also be summarized. The metric used to advertise the summary is the smallest metric of all the more-specific routes. To create a summary of addresses for a given level, use the command **summary-address address mask** {**level-1** | **level-1-2** | **level-2**} in router configuration mode.

 Interactive Media Activity   Drag and Drop: Basic IS-IS Configuration

After completing this activity, you will be able to perform basic IS-IS configuration on a Cisco router.

Lab 7.7.1   Configuring Basic Integrated IS-IS

In this lab, you configure basic Integrated IS-IS. You also implement IS-IS authentication for security purposes.

Multiarea Integrated IS-IS Configuration

This section explores a simple multiarea Integrated IS-IS scenario, shown in Figure 7-38. The output in Example 7-10 shows the correct behavior for IS-IS. The IS-IS configuration commands shown in Examples 7-11 through 7-14 successfully route IP by way of IS-IS. For example, the routing tables of both Rtr-A and Rtr-D are automatically populated with a default route.

Figure 7-38 Multiarea Integrated IS-IS Configuration

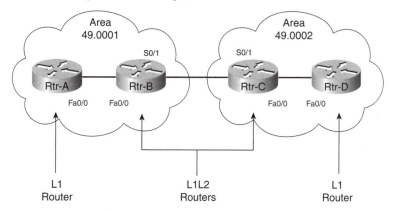

Example 7-10 *Sample IS-IS Configuration*

```
Rtr-A#show ip route
Gateway of last resort is 192.168.120.10 to network 0.0.0.0
C 192.168.120.0/24 is directly connected, FastEthernet0/0
192.168.1.0/32 is subnetted, 2 subnets
i L1 192.168.1.1 [115/10] via 192.168.120.10, FastEthernet0/0
C 192.168.1.5 is directly connected, Loopback0
i L1 192.168.222.0/24 [115/20] via 192.168.120.10, FastEthernet0/0
i*L1 0.0.0.0/0 [115/10] via 192.168.120.10, FastEthernet0/0
Rtr-D#show ip route
Gateway of last resort is 192.168.111.2 to network 0.0.0.0
C 192.168.111.0/24 is directly connected, FastEthernet0/0
```

continues

Example 7-10 *Sample IS-IS Configuration (Continued)*

```
192.168.2.0/32 is subnetted, 2 subnets
i L1 192.168.2.2 [115/10] via 192.168.111.2, FastEthernet0/0
C 192.168.2.4 is directly connected, Loopback0
i*L1 0.0.0.0/0 [115/10] via 192.168.111.2, FastEthernet0/0
```

Example 7-11 *Multiarea Integrated IS-IS Configuration: Rtr-A Configuration*

```
interface Loopback0
 ip address 192.168.1.5 255.255.255.255
 no ip directed-broadcast
!
interface FastEthernet 0/0
 ip address 192.168.120.5 255.255.255.0
 ip router isis
!
router isis
 passive-interface Loopback0
 net 49.0001.1921.6800.1005.00
 is-type level-1
```

Example 7-12 *Multiarea Integrated IS-IS Configuration: Rtr-B Configuration*

```
interface Loopback0
 ip address 192.168.1.1 255.255.255.255
!
interface FastEthernet 0/0
 ip address 192.168.120.10 255.255.255.0
 ip router isis

!
interface serial 0/1
 ip address 192.168.222.1 255.255.255.0
 ip router isis

!
router isis
 passive-interface Loopback0
 net 49.0001.1921.6800.1001.00
```

Example 7-13 *Multiarea Integrated IS-IS Configuration: Rtr-C Configuration*

```
interface Loopback0
 ip address 192.168.2.2 255.255.255.255
!
interface FastEthernet 0/0
 ip address 192.168.111.2 255.255.255.0
 ip router isis
 isis circuit-type level-1
!
interface serial 0/1
 ip address 192.168.222.2 255.255.255.0
 ip router isis
 clockrate 2000000
 isis circuit-type level-2-only
!
router isis
 passive-interface Loopback0
 net 49.0002.1921.6800.2002.00
```

Example 7-14 *Multiarea Integrated IS-IS Configuration: Rtr-D Configuration*

```
interface Loopback0
 ip address 192.168.2.4 255.255.255.255
!
interface FastEthernet 0/0
 ip address 192.168.112.2 255.255.255.0
 ip router isis
!
router isis
 passive-interface Loopback0
 net 49.0002.1921.6800.2004.00
 is-type level-1
```

By default, Cisco IOS software enables both L1 and L2 operations on IS-IS routers. If a router is to operate only as an area router or only as a backbone router, you can specify this by entering the **is-type** command in IS-IS router configuration mode. To specify that the router will act only as an area or L1 router, specify **is-type level-1**. To specify that the router will act only as a backbone or L2 router, specify **is-type level-2-only**. Rtr-A and Rtr-D use the **is-type level-1** command.

Although the router might be an L1L2 router, it might be required to establish only L1 adjacencies over certain interfaces and only L2 adjacencies over other interfaces. The interface command **isis circuit-type** can specify **level-1**, **level-1-2**, or **level-2-only**. If a level is not specified, the IOS attempts to establish both types of adjacencies over the interface. The Rtr-C configuration uses the **isis circuit-type** command. Notice that L1 adjacencies cannot form between areas. No **isis circuit-type** command is applied to interface Fa0/0 on Rtr-B. The optimal configuration would include the **isis circuit-type level-1** command on this interface to avoid an attempt by Rtr-B to form an L2 adjacency with Rtr-A. This would fail, though, because Rtr-A is configured with the IS-IS router mode command **is-type level-1**.

Unlike some other IP protocols, IS-IS does not consider line speed or bandwidth when setting its link metrics. All interfaces are assigned a metric of 10. To change this value, use the interface command **isis metric** *value* **level-1 | level-2**. The metric can have different values for Level 1 and Level 2 over the same interface. The **isis metric** interface command is not used in the scenario presented in this section.

The **show clns** command, shown in Example 7-15, indicates that Rtr-B is running IS-IS in IP-only mode. This is because none of the interfaces are configured with the **clns router isis** command. This would force the router to begin forwarding CLNP packets. Despite the fact that CLNS is not being routed, the **show protocol** output, shown in Example 7-16, appears to contradict this. The output says CLNS routing is enabled and says CLNS enabled on each of the FastEthernet0/0 and Serial0/1 interfaces. However, CLNP packets are not being routed, as verified by the **show clns traffic** output, shown in Example 7-17.

Example 7-15 show clns *Command*

```
Rtr-B#show clns
Global CLNS Information:
  2 Interfaces Enabled for CLNS
  NET: 49.000101921.6800.1001.00
  Configuration Timer: 60, Default Holding Timer: 300, Packet Lifetime 64
  ERPDU's requested on locally generated packets
  Running IS-IS in IP-only mode with CLNS forwarding not allowed
```

Example 7-16 show clns protocol *Command*

```
Rtr-B#show protocol
Global values:
  Internet protocol routing is enabled
  CLNS routing is enabled (address 49.0001.1921.6800.1001.00)
Fastethernet0/0 is up, line protocol is up
```

Example 7-16 show clns protocol *Command (Continued)*

```
   Internet address is 192.168.120.10/24
   CLNS enabled
Serial0/0 is administratively down, line protocol is down
Serial0/1 is up, line protocol is up
   Internet address is 192.168.222.1/24
   CLNS enabled
Loopback0 is up, line protocol is up
   Internet address is 192.168.1.1/32


Rtr-B#show clns protocol
IS-IS Router: <Null Tag>
   System Id: 1921.6800.1001.00 IS-TypeL: level-1-2
   Manual area address(es):
       49.0001
   Routing for area address(es):
       49.0001
   Interfaces supported by IS-IS:
       Serial 0/1 - IP
         FastEthernet 0/0 - IP
   Next global update in 530 seconds
   Redistributing:
     static
     iso-igrp (remote)
   Distance: 110
```

Example 7-17 show clns traffic *Command*

```
Rtr-B#show clns traffic
CLNS & ESIS Output: 139885, Input: 90406
CLNS Local: 0, Forward: 0
CLNS Discards:
   Hdr Syntax: 150, Checksum: 0, Lifetime: 0, Output cngstn: 0
   No Route: 0, Dst Unreachable 0, Encaps. Failed: 0
   NLP Unknown: 0, Not an IS: 0
CLNS Options: Packets 19, total 19, bad 0, GQOS 0, cngstn exprncd 0
CLNS Segments: Segmented: 0, Failed: 0
CLNS Broadcasts: sent: 0, rcvd: 0
```

continues

Example 7-17 show clns traffic *Command (Continued)*

```
Echos: Rcvd 0 requests, 69679 replies
  Sent 69701 requests, 0 replies
ESIS(sent/rcvd): ESHs: 0/34, ISHs: 483/1839, RDs: 0/0, QCF: 0/0
ISO IGRP: Querys (sent/rcvd): 0/0 Updates (sent/rcvd): 1279/1402
ISO IGRP: Router Hellos: (sent/rcvd): 1673/1848
ISO IGRP Syntax Errors: 0
IS-IS: Level-1 Hellos (sent/rcvd): 0/0
IS-IS: Level-2 Hellos (sent/rcvd): 0/0
IS-IS: PTP Hellos (sent/rcvd): 0/0
IS-IS: Level-1 LSPs (sent/rcvd): 0/0
IS-IS: Level-2 LSPs (sent/rcvd): 0/0
IS-IS: Level-1 CSNPs (sent/rcvd): 0/0
IS-IS: Level-2 CSNPs (sent/rcvd): 0/0
IS-IS: Level-1 PSNPs (sent/rcvd): 0/0
IS-IS: Level-2 PSNPs (sent/rcvd): 0/0
IS-IS: Level-1 DR Elections: 0
IS-IS: Level-2 DR Elections: 0
IS-IS: Level-1 SPF Calculations: 0
IS-IS: Level-2 SPF Calculations: 0
```

The **show isis database** output, shown in Examples 7-18 and 7-19, demonstrates the automatic setting of the ATT by the L1L2 router, Rtr-B. This tells the L1 routers that it is a potential exit point for the area.

Example 7-18 show isis database *Command*

```
Rtr-B#show isis database
ISIS Level-1 Link State Database:
LSPID         LSP Seq Num  LSP Checksum  LSP Holdtime   ATT/P/OL
Rtr-B.00-00   0x0000008B   0x6843        55             0/0/0
Rtr-A.00-00   0x00000083   0x276E        77             0/0/0
Rtr-B.01-00   0x00000004   0x34E1        57             0/0/0

ISIS Level-2 Link State Database:
LSPID         LSP Seq Num  LSP Checksum  LSP Holdtime   ATT/P/OL
Rtr-B.00-00   0x00000092   0x34B2        41             0/0/0
Rtr-C.00-00   0x0000008A   0x7A59        115            0/0/0
```

Example 7-19 show isis database detail *Command*

```
Rtr-B#show isis database detail
ISIS Level-1 link-state database:
LSPID           LSP Seq Num  LSP Checksum  LSP Holdtime  ATT/P/OL
Rtr-B.00-00    0x00000093    0x077E         71            0/0/0
  Area Address: 49.0001
  NLPID:        0xCC
  Hostname: R2
  IP Address:   192.168.1.1
  Metric: 10         IP 192.168.120.0 255.255.255.0
  Metric: 10          IP 192.168.220.0 255.255.255.255
  Metric: 0          IP 192.168.1.1 255.255.255.255
  Metric: 10          IS Rtr-B.01
ISIS Level-2 LSP R2.00-00
LSPID           LSP Seq Num  LSP Checksum  LSP Holdtime  ATT/P/OL
Rtr-B.00-00    0x0000009A    0x5A69         103           0/0/0
  Area Address: 49.0001
  NLPID:        0xCC
  Hostname: Rtr-B
  IP Address:   192.168.1.1
  Metric: 10         IS Rtr-B.01
  Metric: 10         IS Rtr-C.00
  Metric: 10         IP 192.168.120.0 255.255.255.0
  Metric: 0          IP 192.168.1.1 255.255.255.255
  Metric: 10         IP 192.168.1.5 255.255.255.255
  Metric: 10         IP 192.168.220.0 255.255.255.0
```

The **show clns traffic** output lets you analyze CLNS traffic statistics. For this command output, keep the following in mind:

- LSPs sourced indicate IS stability.
- LSP retransmissions should stay low.
- PRCs cannot be checked elsewhere.
- LSP checksum errors are a bad sign.
- The update queue should not stay full.
- The update queue should not drop much.

The **debug isis spf-triggers** command is useful for determining the cause, or trigger, for an SPF calculation.

 Lab 7.7.2   Configuring Multiarea Integrated IS-IS

In this lab, you configure multiarea Integrated IS-IS and level-specific routers.

Integrated IS-IS Operation in a WAN Environment

WANs are typically implemented as either point-to-point or point-to-multipoint. WAN technologies, such as Frame Relay, do not support broadcasts—thus the term nonbroadcast multi-access (NBMA).

Point-to-Point and Point-to-Multipoint Operation with IS-IS

Point-to-point WANs can be leased circuits between two routers. A point-to-point WAN has two devices attached, one device at each end of the circuit. Such links commonly run Cisco HDLC or PPP. These WAN links correspond exactly to the Integrated IS-IS classification of a point-to-point network.

Dialup networks using dial-on-demand routing (DDR) can be configured as either point-to-point or point-to-multipoint WANs. Legacy DDR connections using **dialer map** statements are NBMA networks, despite the fact that they might use PPP as their line protocol. This is because a single dialer interface can support multiple destinations. Dialer profiles and dialer virtual profiles are point-to-point connections, in which one dialer profile equates to one remote profile. These connections can suffer from the same loss-of-neighbor delays as other NBMA networks. Dialer virtual profiles are point-to-point connections in which the interface drops immediately if the remote end disconnects, leading to faster neighbor loss detection and faster convergence. Dial interfaces and dialer profiles are not dealt with in this book. As a general rule, avoid using IS-IS over dialup, except to provide dial backup functionality.

IS-IS can work only over NBMA clouds, such as Frame Relay, configured with a full mesh. Anything less than a full mesh could create serious connectivity and routing issues. However, even if a full mesh is configured, this is no guarantee that it will exist at all times. A failure in the underlying switched WAN network, or a misconfiguration on one or more routers, could break the full mesh either temporarily or permanently. Avoid NBMA multipoint configurations for IS-IS networks. Use point-to-point subinterfaces instead.

Point-to-point interfaces should usually be explicitly configured with an IP subnet. In this case, a 31-bit mask (which requires Cisco IOS Release 12.2) or a 30-bit mask is applied. In modern IP networks using private addressing and variable-length subnetting, there are usually plenty of spare IP addresses to apply to point-to-point interfaces. Alternatively, in conformance with RFC 1195, an unnumbered IP can be used with IS-IS on point-to-point interfaces.

NOTE

A point-to-point circuit is still regarded as an NBMA network, just as a back-to-back Ethernet connection is still a LAN. Both are examples of multiaccess networks that have only two devices attached.

Recall that, on a point-to-point link, a single IIH PDU type is used. These IIHs specify whether the adjacency is L1, L2, or both. When the adjacency is established, each neighbor sends a CSNP describing the contents of its link-state database. Each router then requests any missing LSPs from the neighbor using PSNPs and acknowledges the receipt of the LSPs with PSNPs. This activity reduces the amount of routing traffic across the point-to-point link. Each router exchanges only the information missing from its link-state database, rather than the entire link-state database of its neighbor router.

Configuring Integrated IS-IS in a WAN Environment

To enable IS-IS over switched WAN media, do the following:

- Start the IS-IS process, and assign NETs as usual.
- On each NBMA interface, do the following:
  — Design a mesh between the NBMA peers, whether full or partial.
  — Configure point-to-point subinterfaces for each NBMA virtual circuit (VC), and assign IP addresses.
  — Define the mapping of network protocols and addresses to the VC. If manual mappings are used, such as **x25 map** or **frame-relay map**, the CLNS mapping must specify broadcast. This is to support routing updates. However, the IP mapping does not require this. It is used only for next-hop resolution.
  — Start IS-IS processing on the subinterface with the **ip router isis** command. This command must not be used on the main interface, or that multipoint interface generates a pseudonode LSP for itself.
- Use Integrated IS-IS timer and blocking commands to control flooding of link-state information.

To illustrate IS-IS configuration in a WAN environment, this IS-IS chapter ends with a Frame Relay point-to-point scenario and a Frame Relay point-to-multipoint scenario.

Frame Relay Point-to-Point Scenario with Integrated IS-IS

Look at the example of a router network connected over Frame Relay using point-to-point subinterfaces shown in Figure 7-39. Each Frame Relay PVC is treated as its own point-to-point network, with its own IP addresses. The example is of a hub-and-spoke network topology. It is important to note that the spoke routers are also configured with point-to-point subinterfaces, even though, unlike the hub router, they use only one VC. This is the best practice in general for all routing protocols. It allows further VCs to be added without affecting the existing VC. This practice is imperative for IS-IS. A main interface is a multipoint interface, even if it has only one VC configured. If the single VC were configured under a main interface, IS-IS would treat this as a broadcast network and attempt to elect a DIS. Also, an adjacency would not be established, because the multipoint end would send broadcast network-style Hello PDUs, but the point-to-point end would send point-to-point Hello PDUs.

Figure 7-39 Frame Relay Point-to-Point Scenario with Integrated IS-IS

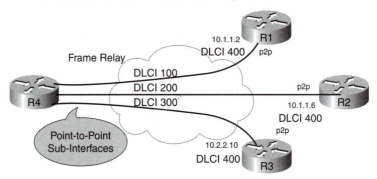

The hub router R4 configuration is shown in Example 7-20.

Example 7-20 *R4 Configuration*

```
interface Serial0/0
 encapsulation frame-relay
!
interface Serial0/0.1 point-to-point
 ip address 10.1.1.1 255.255.255.252
 ip router isis
 frame-relay interface-dlci 100
!
interface Serial0/0.2 point-to-point
 ip address 10.1.1.5 255.255.255.252
 ip router isis
 frame-relay interface-dlci 200
!
interface Serial0/0.3 point-to-point
 ip address 10.1.1.9 255.255.255.252
 ip router isis
 frame-relay interface-dlci 300
```

The encapsulation type, Frame Relay, is set under the main interface of Serial0/0. No IP or IS-IS configuration is included under the main interface. Three subinterfaces are defined, one for each VC. Each subinterface specifies the following:

- The IP address for that point-to-point link, which is a different subnet for each subinterface.

- Integrated IS-IS, **ip router isis**, as the routing protocol over that subinterface.

- The VC to use for that point-to-point subinterface, using the **frame-relay interface-dlci** command. This is the only command needed to enable both IP and CLNS across this VC. The router automatically enables, across this VC, all the protocols that are enabled on the point-to-point subinterface. With this configuration, the subinterface automatically forwards routing updates, as is the case when using the **broadcast** keyword with a Frame Relay map.

Notice that no Frame Relay maps are used in this scenario, because point-to-point interfaces are used.

As shown in Example 7-21, the **show frame-relay map** command displays the status of each Frame Relay VC as follows:

- "Status defined" means it has been configured on the Frame Relay switch, and "active" indicates that this VC is operational.

- The type is point-to-point, meaning it has been assigned to a point-to-point subinterface.

- Assigned subinterface, such as Serial0/0.1

- VC identification, such as DLCI 100.

- Whether it supports broadcast packets, such as RIPv1 routing packets.

Example 7-21 **show frame-relay map** *Command*

```
R4#show frame-relay map
Serial0/0.1 (up): point-to-point dlci, Dlci 100(0x64, 0x1840,
    broadcast Status defined,        active
Serial0/0.2 (up): point-to-point dlci, Dlci 200(0xC8, 0x3080,
    broadcast Status defined,        active
Serial0/0.3 (up): point-to-point dlci, Dlci 300(0xA4, 0x4580,
    broadcast Status defined,        active
```

The **debug isis adj-packet** command in Example 7-22 shows neighbor relationship establishment across one of the subinterfaces, Serial0/0.1, sending and receiving point-to-point IIH PDUs and declaring the adjacency up. Ongoing Hello conversations for the other subinterfaces are also shown.

Example 7-22 **debug isis adj-packet** *Command*

```
R4#debug isis adj-packet
ISIS-Adj: Sending serial IIH on Serial0/0.1, length 1499
ISIS-Adj: Rec serial IIH from DLCI 100 (Serial0/0.1), cir type L1L2,
    cir id 00, length 1499
ISIS-Adj: rcvd state UP, old state UP, new state UP
ISIS-Adj: Action = ACCEPT


ISIS-Adj: Sending serial IIH on Serial0/0.2, length 1499
ISIS-Adj: Rec serial IIH from DLCI 200 (Serial0/0.2), cir type L1L2,
    cir id 01, length 1499
ISIS-Adj: Sending serial IIH on Serial0/0.3, length 1499
ISIS-Adj: Rec serial IIH from DLCI 300 (Serial0/0.3), cir type L1L2,
    cir id 01, length 1499
```

Frame Relay Point-to-Multipoint Scenario with Integrated IS-IS

In this scenario, all of the Frame Relay ports are configured as multipoint interfaces. They are configured either as a multipoint subinterface, on the hub router R4, or as a main interface on the other routers. All interfaces share the same IP subnet in a multipoint configuration. In a multipoint environment with IS-IS, it is important that a full mesh be implemented. Therefore, all other routers also are interconnected by VCs, although these are not shown in Figure 7-40. If this were a true hub-and-spoke environment, and the spoke sites had no need to communicate with each other, this topology could work with only the indicated DLCIs. In this case, the hub router must become the DIS for the NBMA network, because it is the only router visible to all others. A suitable IS-IS priority should be set on the hub router's Frame Relay interface using the **isis priority** command. Routes would be installed in each spoke router toward the other spoke routers by way of their local IP addresses. However, packets to these destinations would be dropped, because there are no direct VCs between the spokes, as shown in Figure 7-40.

Figure 7-40 Frame Relay Point-to-Multipoint Scenario with Integrated IS-IS

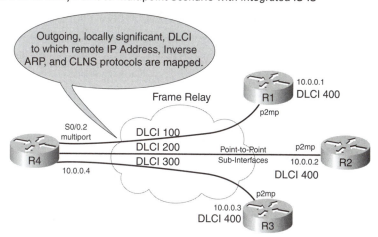

This point-to-multipoint scenario shows the configuration of the multipoint interface on the R4 hub router in Example 7-23.

Example 7-23 *Multipoint Interface Configuration*

```
interface Serial0/0.1
 encapsulation frame-relay

interface Serial0/0.2 multipoint
 ip address 10.0.0.4 255.255.0.0
 ip router isis
 frame-relay map clns 100 broadcast
 frame-relay map clns 200 broadcast
 frame-relay map clns 300 broadcast
 frame-relay interface-dlci 100
 frame-relay interface-dlci 200
 frame-relay interface-dlci 300

router isis
 net 00.0001.000.000.0004.00
```

In a multipoint environment, IP and CLNS maps must be configured separately. The **frame-relay interface-dlci** command is used to enable IP across the Frame Relay PVCs. Inverse ARP automatically resolves the remote-end IP addresses. On a point-to-point subinterface, this command enables all traffic, but in a multipoint environment it enables only IP. Alternatively, the IP maps could be entered explicitly using **frame-relay map ip** *ip address dlci*. In this case, the **broadcast** keyword is not necessary for IP, because only directed IP packets use this VC. To enable CLNS, which must be done separately from IP in a multipoint environment, the **frame-relay map clns** command is used. CLNS is used for the IS-IS routing packets, so the **broadcast** keyword must be specified.

Finally, the same monitoring commands used for the point-to-point example yield slightly different output in the point-to-multipoint environment. The **show frame-relay map** command, shown in Example 7-24, displays the status of each Frame Relay VC. These time separate entries are created as follows for the IP and CLNS mappings, even though they use the same VC:

- The CLNS map shows that it is created as a static map and that **broadcast** was specified.
- The IP map is dynamic because the IP address was resolved by inverse ARP.

Example 7-24 show frame-relay map *Command*

```
R4#show frame-relay map
Serial0/0.4 (up): CLNS dlci 400(0x190, 0x6400), static, broadcast, CISCO,
    status defined, active
Serial0/0.4 (up): ip 10.1.4.3 dkcu 400 (0x190, 0x6400), static, broadcast,
    status defined, active
```

The **debug isis adj-packet** command shown in Example 7-25 again shows the neighbor relationship establishment. However, this time the adjacency uses LAN IIH PDUs because this is a multipoint environment. Keep in mind that the preferred configuration for Integrated IS-IS in a WAN environment is to configure all interfaces as point-to-point subinterfaces. This avoids the full mesh required with the point-to-multipoint option. The point-to-multipoint option results in weak network stability. Having one PVC go down can have a domino effect on the WAN. This points out one major difference between OSPF and IS-IS configuration.

Example 7-25 debug isis adj-packet *Command*

```
R4#debug isis adj-packet
ISIS-Adj: Sending L2 LAN IIH on Serial0/0.2,
    length 1500
ISIS-Adj: Rec L2 IIH from DLCI 400 (Serial0/0.2), cir type L1L2,
    cir id 0000.0000.0004.03, length 1500
ISIS-Adj: Sending L1 LAN IIH on Serial0/0.2, length 1500
ISIS-Adj: Rec L1 IIH from DLCI 400 (Serial0/0.2), cir type L1L2,
    cir id 0000.0000.0004.03, length 1500
```

Lab 7.7.3   Configuring IS-IS over Frame Relay

In this lab, you configure IS-IS over a hub-and-spoke Frame Relay topology using P2P subinterfaces. Multipoint configurations are not used with IS-IS, as they are in OSPF.

Detecting Mismatched Interfaces with Integrated IS-IS

One important skill to develop with Integrated IS-IS configuration and troubleshooting is to be able to identify a problem resulting from mismatched interfaces in an NBMA environment.

An example of a misconfiguration is configuring one end of a link, on router R2, to be specified as a point-to-point subinterface. The other end, router R4, is to be used as a point-to-multipoint interface. Issuing the **show clns neighbor** command on each router, as shown in Example 7-26, shows a mismatch. R2, the point-to-point end router, shows the adjacency as up. R4, the multipoint end, shows the adjacency as stuck in the init state. The misconfiguration results from the fact that the two ends of the VC are set to different network types. The point-to-point end sends serial IIH PDUs, and the multipoint end sends LAN IIH PDUs, so an adjacency cannot form.

Example 7-26 **show clns neighbor** *Command*

```
R2#show clns neighbor

System Id          Interface    SNPA             State  Holdtime  Type  Protocol
0000.0000.0004     Se0/0.2      DLCI 300         Up     8         L1    IS-IS
R5                 Et0/0        0050.3ef1.5690   Up     8         L2    IS-IS
R1                 Se0/0.1      DLCI 100         Up     23        L1    IS-IS


R4#show clns neighbor

System Id          Interface    SNPA             State  Holdtime  Type  Protocol
R6                 Et0/0        0010.117e.74a8   Up     26        L2    IS-IS
R3                 Se0/0.3      DLCI 400         Up     28        L1    IS-IS
0000.0000.0002     Se0/0.2      DLCI 300         Init   29        L1    IS-IS
0000.0000.0001     Se0/0.1      DLCI 200         Up     290       IS    IS-IS
```

The ISO standard defines a three-way handshake (an agreement) for initiating LAN adjacencies as follows:

■ The adjacency starts in the Down state. The IS sends out LAN IIH PDUs, identifying itself.

■ If a LAN IIH PDU is received, the adjacency is installed in the init state. This router then sends an IIH PDU to the neighbor, including the SNPA of the neighbor in the Hello packet. The neighbor does the same thing with the SNPA on this router.

■ The IS receives a second IIH from the neighbor router with its own SNPA identified in the packet. After receiving the IIH, the IS understands that the new neighbor knows of its presence and, therefore, declares the adjacency up.

According to the ISO standard ISO 10589, this process is omitted for a point-to-point adjacency. However, the Cisco IOS software implements the same three-way handshake by adding a point-to-point adjacency state TLV, TLV 240, in the serial Hello PDUs. In a manner similar to the LAN adjacency, the router checks for its own SNPA in the neighbor's Hello PDU before declaring the adjacency up.

The result of the sample mismatch depends on the IOS release. Before Release 12.1(1)T, the results were as follows:

■ R4, the multipoint router, receives the point-to-point Hello PDU from R2 but treats it as a LAN Hello PDU and puts the adjacency in the init state. R4 looks for its own SNPA in the received Hello PDUs but never finds it. In a LAN Hello PDU this would be identified in TLV 6 as IS Neighbors, but this TLV is not present in a serial Hello PDU. Therefore, the adjacency remains in the init state.

■ R2, the point-to-point router, receives a LAN Hello PDU and treats it as a point-to-point Hello PDU. It checks the Hello PDU for a TLV 240, point-to-point adjacency state, and fails to find one. For backward compatibility, or perhaps to allow the link to be made to a non-Cisco IS-IS device, the router assumes that this is an ISO-specified point-to-point link. R2 ignores the Cisco three-way handshake and allows the adjacency to be established, setting it to "up."

Since Release 12.1(1)T, the results are as follows:

■ R4, the multipoint router, receives the point-to-point Hello PDU, realizes it is the wrong Hello type, and installs the neighbor as an ES. R4 shows R2 in the **show clns neighbors** with protocol ES-IS.

■ R2, the point-to-point router, receives the LAN Hello PDU, recognizes the mismatch, and ignores the neighbor. R4 does not appear at all in the **show clns neighbors** output of R2, as shown in Example 7-27. The **debug isis adj-packets** output shows the incoming LAN IIH PDU and R2 declaring the mismatch.

Example 7-27 **show clns neighbors** *Command*

```
R2#show clns neighbors
System Id          SNPA           Interface    State  Holdtime  Type Protocol
0000.0000.0004     DLCI 300       Serial0/0.2  Up     8         L1   IS-IS
R5                 0050.3ef1.5960 Ethernet0/0  Up     8         L1   IS-IS
R1                 DLCI 100       Serial0/0.1  Up     23        L1   IS-IS

R2#show clns neighbors
System Id          SNPA           Interface    State  Holdtime  Type Protocol
R6                 0010.1117e.74a8 Ethernet0/0 Up     26        L2   IS-IS
R3                 DLCI 400       Serial0/0.3  Up     28        L2   IS-IS
0000.0000.0002     DLCI 300       Serial0/0.2  Init   29        L1   IS-IS
0000.0000.0001     DLCI 200       Serial0/0.1  Up     230       IS   ES-IS
```

Summary

After reading this chapter, you should have a firm understanding of the following concepts:

- CLNS addressing
- IS-IS operation in a CLNS environment
- Types and functions of PDUs in IS-IS routing
- Integrated IS-IS operation in an IP and CLNS environment
- Default behavior of Integrated IS-IS routing and the role of the attached bit, the overload bit, and route leaking
- Integrated IS-IS in an NBMA environment
- Configuration of IS-IS in single and multiple areas, L1 and L2 circuit types, authentication, and route summarization
- Monitoring an Integrated IS-IS network with **show** and **debug** commands

IS-IS is a versatile routing protocol used by many very large ISPs. The natural scalability of IS-IS makes it a great choice for modern large-scale IGP network deployments. IS-IS uses the SPF algorithm, just as OSPF does, but it requires fewer SPF calculations as a result of its ability to handle PRCs. IS-IS has established a firm foothold in many networks comprising the Internet, and it will not be surprising if its presence expands in the years to come.

Key Terms

area   A logical set of network segments (either CLNS-, DECnet-, or OSPF-based) and their attached devices. Areas are usually connected to other areas via routers, making up a single autonomous system or domain.

Authority and Format ID (AFI)   1 byte, actually a binary value between 0 and 99, used to specify the IDI format and DSP syntax of the address and the authority that assigned the address.

Complete Sequence Number PDU (CSNP)   Used to distribute a complete link-state database on the router. CSNPs are used to inform other routers of LSPs that might be outdated or missing from their own database. This ensures that all routers have the same information and are synchronized. The packets are similar to an OSPF database description packet.

domain   In IS-IS, this refers to a logical set of networks or any portion of an OSI network that is under a common administrative authority.

Domain-Specific Part (DSP)   Composed of the HODSP, the system ID, and the NSEL in binary format.

end system (ES)   Any nonrouting host or node.

End System-to-Intermediate System (ES-IS)   ES-IS discovery protocols are used for routing between end systems and intermediate systems.

Hello PDU   Used to establish and maintain adjacencies. ESHs are sent from ESs to ISs. ISHs are sent from ISs to ESs. IIHs are sent between ISs. Note that ESH and ISH PDUs are ES-IS PDUs, not IS-IS PDUs.

High-Order Domain-Specific Part (HODSP)   Used for subdividing the domain into areas. This is roughly equivalent to a subnet in IP.

Integrated IS-IS   An implementation of the IS-IS protocol for routing multiple network protocols. Integrated IS-IS tags CLNP routes, upon which IS-IS bases its link-state database, with information about IP networks and subnets.

initial domain identifier (IDI)   Identifies the domain.

Interdomain Part (IDP)   Consists of the AFI and IDI together. This is roughly equivalent to a classful IP network in decimal format.

intermediate system (IS)   Another name for a router in an IS-IS system.

Intermediate System-to-Intermediate System (IS-IS)   The IS-IS routing protocols are used for hierarchical routing between intermediate systems.

link-state PDU (LSP)   Used by IS-IS to distribute link-state information. There are independent pseudonode and nonpseudonode LSPs for both Level 1 and Level 2.

network entity title (NET)   An NSAP whose last byte is 0. The NET is used to identify a device.

network service access point (NSAP)   A conceptual point on the boundary between the network and transport layers. The NSAP is the location where OSI network services are provided to the transport layer. Similar to an IP address.

NSAP selector (NSEL)   Identifies a process on the device. It is roughly equivalent to a port or socket in TCP/IP. The NSEL is not used in routing decisions.

OSI protocols   The product of an international program formed to develop data networking protocols and other standards that facilitate multivendor equipment interoperability.

Partial Sequence Number PDU (PSNP)   Used to acknowledge and request link-state information.

subnetwork point of attachment (SNPA)   The point at which subnetwork services are provided. This is the equivalent of the Layer 2 address corresponding to the Layer 3 (NET or NSAP) address.

system ID   Identifies an individual OSI device. In OSI, a device has an address, just as it does in DECnet, whereas in IP an interface has an address.

Check Your Understanding

Complete all of the review questions to test your understanding of the topics and concepts in this chapter. The answers appear in Appendix B, Answers to the Check Your Understanding Questions.

For additional, more in-depth questions, refer to the chapter-specific study guides on the companion CD-ROM.

1. Which type of location is most likely to use the IS-IS protocol?

    A. Branch office

    B. SOHO

    C. Service provider

    D. PSTN

2. Which of the following are features of the IS-IS protocol? (Choose three.)

    A. Classful behavior

    B. Slow convergence

    C. Fast convergence

    D. Scalable

    E. Distance vector

    F. IGP

3. OSI networking design and proper implementation provide which of the following? (Choose two.)

    A. Quality of service

    B. Proprietary architectures

    C. Transparency

    D. Four-layer model

4. CLNS is located at which layer of the OSI model?

    A. Data-link layer

    B. Transport layer

    C. Application layer

    D. Network layer

5. IS-IS was originally designed to route which protocol?

    A. IPX

B. AppleTalk

C. IP

D. DECnet Phase V

E. SNA

6. How many routers can exist in a single IS-IS area?

A. 15

B. 50

C. 100

D. 500

E. 1000

7. What is identified by the information contained in the CLNS system ID field?

A. A process on a device

B. The domain

C. A single OSI device

D. Port or socket information

8. How many addresses does an NSAP have?

A. A single address for the entire router

B. An address for each configured interface

C. Multiple addresses for each configured interface

D. The number of addresses depends on the routing protocol chosen

9. Which of the following is the equivalent of using more than one NET with the IS-IS protocol?

A. Using CIDR

B. Using secondary addresses with IP

C. Using VLSM

D. Implementing dynamic routing

10. What command displays the least-cost paths to a destination NET?

A. **which-route**

B. **show isis topology**

C. **show clns route**

D. **show isis routes**

Objectives

Upon completing this chapter, you will be able to

- Understand methods of controlling routing update traffic
- Describe policy-based routing
- Understand methods and guidelines for route redistribution
- Analyze a redistribution and summarization example
- Apply route optimization techniques, such as routing update control, policy-based routing, and route redistribution

You can reinforce your understanding of the objectives covered in this chapter by opening the interactive media activities on the CD accompanying this book and performing the lab activities collected in the *Cisco Networking Academy Program CCNP 1: Advanced Routing Lab Companion*. Throughout this chapter, you will see references to these activities by title and by icon. They look like this:

 Interactive Media Activity

 Lab Activity

Chapter 8

Route Optimization

Dynamic routing, even in small internetworks, can involve much more than just enabling a routing protocol's default behavior. A few simple commands might be enough to get dynamic routing started. However, more advanced configuration must be done to enable such features as routing update control and exchanges among multiple routing protocols. You can optimize routing in a network by controlling when a router exchanges routing updates and what those updates contain. This chapter examines the key Cisco IOS software route optimization features, including routing update control, policy-based routing, and route redistribution.

Controlling Routing Update Traffic

The following sections discuss some of the details of controlling routing update traffic. The topics covered are

- Controlling routing updates
- Passive interfaces
- Filtering routing updates with **distribute-list**

Controlling Routing Updates

Router RTA, as shown in Figure 8-1, is running a simple distance vector routing protocol called RIP.

The RIP configuration command **network 10.0.0.0** serves two functions. First, it tells RIP where to send and receive advertisements, and on which interfaces to send and receive updates. The **network 10.0.0.0** command enables RIP updates on all interfaces that have an IP address belonging to the 10.0.0.0 network, such as Bri0, S1, S2, and E0. Second, this command tells the RIP process what to advertise. All directly connected subnets belonging to the major network 10.0.0.0 are included in RIP updates in addition to any dynamically learned routes. This means that RTA advertises the networks 10.1.1.0, 10.2.2.0, 10.3.3.0, and 10.4.4.0.

Figure 8-41 Controlling Routing Updates

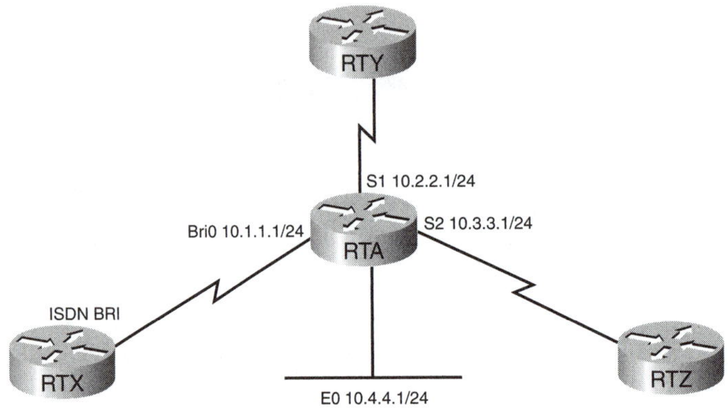

Unfortunately, RIP's default behavior, or that of any routing protocol, might not be the best thing for an internetwork. Is it useful for RTA to send updates on all four interfaces?

Updating out E0 is a waste of resources. No other routers on the 10.4.4.0 subnetwork can receive the updates, so they serve no purpose. Meanwhile, sending updates creates slight, but needless, overhead and is a potential security risk. A malicious user could use a packet sniffer to capture routing updates and, therefore, glean key network information.

For these reasons, it is necessary to configure passive interfaces or route filters to control routing updates. Both strategies are discussed in the following sections.

Passive Interfaces

You should configure LAN interfaces as passive interfaces when enabling a routing protocol unless multiple routers are attached to the LAN. A *passive interface* receives updates but does not send them. The **passive-interface** command can be used with all IP interior gateway protocols. It can be used with RIP, IGRP, EIGRP, OSPF, and IS-IS. Its syntax is as follows:

```
Router(config-router)#passive-interface type number
```

This command can be used to configure the E0 interface on RTA as a passive interface, as shown in Figure 8-2.

Use the **passive-interface** command on WAN interfaces to prevent routers from sending updates to link partners.

There might be several reasons to prevent updates on the WAN. If RTA and RTX, shown in Figure 8-3, are connected by a dial-on-demand ISDN link, regular RIP updates keep the link up constantly. This results in an unnecessarily large bill from the provider. Instead, a static route can be configured on both routers with Bri0 on RTA configured as a passive interface, as shown in Example 8-1.

Figure 8-42 Configuring Passive Interfaces

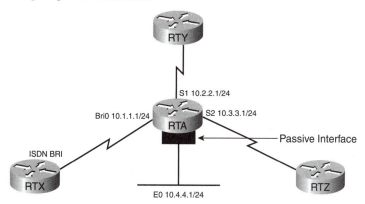

Figure 8-43 Configuring Passive Interfaces—Updates Prevented

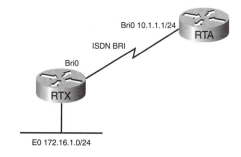

Example 8-1 *Configuring Passive Interfaces on a WAN Link*

```
RTA(config)#router rip
RTA(config-router)#network 10.0.0.0
RTA(config-router)#passive-interface bri0
RTA(config-router)#redistribute static
RTA(config-router)#exit
RTA(config)#ip route 172.16.1.0 255.255.255.0 bri0


RTX(config)#ip route 0.0.0.0 0.0.0.0 bri0
```

Notice that for RTA to update RTY and RTZ in Figure 8-2 about the route to 172.16.1.0, it must be configured to redistribute static routes into RIP. The **redistribute static** command tells RIP to import the static routes into RIP and advertise them as part of a RIP update. Route redistribution is covered in more detail later in this chapter.

The **passive-interface** command works differently with the different IP routing protocols that support it. In OSPF, the network address of the passive interface appears as a stub network. OSPF routing information is neither sent nor received by way of a passive interface. In EIGRP and OSPF, the router stops sending Hello packets on passive interfaces. When this happens, the router cannot form neighbor adjacencies. Therefore, the router cannot send and receive routing updates on the interface. You will see later in this chapter that the passive effect can be achieved for an EIGRP interface by using the **distribute-list** command. This can be done without preventing adjacency relationships. It is also important to point out that distribute lists can be used for all routing protocols, not just EIGRP.

In some networks, there might be cases in which the user does not want the router to send routing updates. The **passive-interface** command can be used to prevent routing updates from being sent over a certain WAN or LAN interface.

For instance, the user might not want RIP updates to be sent over an ISDN (DDR) interface. Different routing protocols behave differently with a passive interface. You can set an interface to passive with the **passive-interface** command. When a passive interface is used with RIP, routing updates are not sent over that interface. The RIP routing protocol continues to receive routing updates over a passive interface, as shown in Figure 8-4.

Figure 8-44 RIP

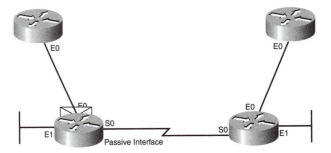

In Figure 8-5, the network is running OSPF. The serial interface on the left router is set to passive. OSPF does not send routing updates out of a passive interface. Unlike RIP, OSPF does not accept any updates over a passive interface. Passive interface behavior is similar to a stub network.

Before EIGRP can send routing updates, it needs to build neighbor relationships. EIGRP uses routing transport protocol (RTP). RTP uses *keepalive messages* for communication. Passive interfaces do not allow keepalives to be sent. This prevents EIGRP from discovering its neighbors. Because of the passive interface over the serial link, EIGRP is unable to discover its neighbor. The router does not send router updates over the serial interface. Even though the passive interface is set on the bottom-left router, the bottom-right router does not send any EIGRP routing updates, as shown in Figure 8-6. EIGRP needs to discover its neighbor before sending routing updates.

Figure 8-45 OSPF

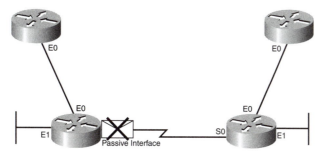

Figure 8-46 EIGRP

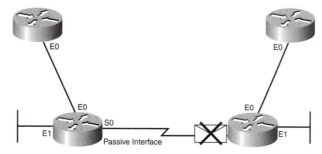

Filtering Routing Updates with distribute-list

Configuring an interface as passive prevents it from sending updates entirely. However, sometimes you need to suppress only certain routes in the update from being sent or received. In Figure 8-7, if RTA is configured with the **network 10.0.0.0** command, all four directly connected subnets are advertised in the updates from RTA, along with any dynamically learned routes. However, RTZ might need to be prevented from learning about network 10.1.1.0 from RTA, as shown in Example 8-2.

Figure 8-47 Using Outbound Route Filters

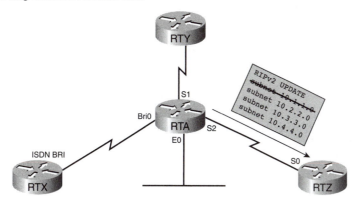

Example 8-2 *Configuring Outbound Route Filters*

```
RTA(config)#router rip
RTA(config-router)#network 10.0.0.0
RTA(config-router)#distribute-list 24 out
RTA(config-router)#exit
RTA(config)#access-list 24 deny 10.1.1.0 0.0.0.225
RTA(config)#access-list 24 permit any
```

This might be needed to enforce a routing policy that is based on an external factor, such as link expense, administrative jurisdiction, or security concerns. In some cases, you want to reduce needless overhead by preventing access routers from receiving the complete, and possibly immense, core routing table. Just assume that for one of these reasons, RTZ should not learn the route to 10.1.1.0 from RTA.

Use the **distribute-list** command to pick and choose which routing updates a router sends or receives. By referencing an access list, the distribute list creates a route filter. This is a set of rules that precisely controls what routes a router sends or receives in a routing update. This command is available for all IP routing protocols and can be applied to either inbound or outbound routing updates. When applied to inbound updates, the syntax for configuring a route filter is as follows:

```
Router(config-router)#distribute-list access-list-number in [interface-name]
```

When applied to outbound updates, the syntax can be more complicated:

```
Router(config-router)#distribute-list access-list-number out
    [interface-name | routing-process | as-number]
```

The *routing-process* and *as-number* options are invoked when routes are exchanged between different routing protocols. This is covered in the section "Route Redistribution."

In Example 8-2, access list 24 matches the route to 10.1.1.0 and results in a deny. When referenced by the **distribute-list** command, this match results in the removal of the route to network 10.1.1.0 in the outbound update. However, there is a drawback. The **distribute-list 24 out** command has a global effect on RIP updates out every interface, not just out the interface connected to RTZ. The intent is to suppress the 10.1.1.0 route from updates to RTZ only. This level of specificity can be accomplished by using the optional *interface-name* argument with the command:

```
RTA(config-router)#distribute-list 24 out serial2
```

Conversely, RTZ could be told to globally filter network 10.1.1.0 from any incoming updates, as shown in Example 8-3.

Example 8-3 *Configuring Inbound Route Filters*

```
RTZ(config)#router rip
RTZ(config-router)#network 10.0.0.0
RTZ(config-router)#distribute-list 16 in
RTZ(config-router)#exit
RTZ(config)#access-list 16 deny 10.1.1.0 0.0.0.225
RTZ(config)#access-list 16 permit any
```

Or, 10.1.1.0 could be precisely filtered from the specific interface on RTZ:

```
RTZ(config-router)#distribute-list 16 in serial0
```

The **distribute-list** command can filter any routes in either an outbound or inbound update globally or for a specific interface. The Cisco IOS software permits one incoming and one outgoing global distribute list for each routing process. It also permits one incoming and one outgoing distribute list for each interface involved in a routing process. You can keep track of which routing filters are applied globally and which are applied on specific interfaces with the **show ip protocols** command.

Configuring a Passive EIGRP Interface Using the distribute-list Command

A passive interface cannot send EIGRP Hello packets, which prevents adjacency relationships with link partners. A pseudo or false passive EIGRP interface can be created by using a route filter that suppresses routes from the EIGRP routing update, as shown in Example 8-4.

Example 8-4 *Configuring a Passive EIGRP Interface Using the* **distribute-list** *Command*

```
RTA(config)#router eigrp 364
RTA(config-router)#network 10.0.0.0
RTA(config-router)#distribute-list 5 out s2
RTA(config-router)#exit
RTA(config)#access-list 5 deny any
```

With this configuration, RTA can send EIGRP Hello packets and establish adjacencies, but no routes appear in any updates sent out of s2. This applies to OSPF as well as EIGRP.

Policy Routing

The following sections discuss some of the details of policy routing.

Policy Routing Overview

You use the **ip route** command to dictate which path to a given destination a router selects. However, through *policy routing*, a router can be programmed to choose a route based not only on destination, but on source as well.

Concerns such as monetary expense, organizational jurisdiction, or security issues can lead administrators to establish policies or rules that routed traffic should follow. Left to their default behavior, routing protocols might arrive at path decisions that conflict with these policies. For that reason, administrators use policy routing to override dynamic routing and to take precise control of how their routers handle certain traffic.

Although policy routing can be used to control traffic within an *autonomous system* (AS), it is typically used to control routing between autonomous systems. For that reason, policy routing is used extensively with *exterior gateway protocols (EGPs)*, such as Border Gateway Protocol (BGP).

The **route-map** command is used to configure policy routing, which is often a complicated task. A route map is defined using the following syntax:

```
Router(config)#route-map map-tag [permit | deny] [sequence-number]
Router(config-map-router)#
```

The *map-tag* is the name, or ID, of the route map. This map tag can be set to something easily recognizable, such as route2ISP or CHANGEROUTE. The **route-map** command changes the mode on the router to route-map configuration mode. From there, you can configure conditions for the route map.

Route maps operate similar to access lists, by examining one line at a time. When a match is found, an action is taken. Route maps are different from numbered access lists because you can modify them without changing the entire list. Each route map statement is given a number. If a sequence number is not specified, the first route map condition is automatically numbered as 10. The second condition is automatically numbered as 20, and so on. The optional sequence number can be used to indicate the position that a new route map is to have in the list of route maps already configured with the same name.

After you enter the **route-map** command, enter **set** and **match** commands in route-map configuration mode. Each **route-map** command has a list of **match** and **set** commands associated with it. The **match** commands specify the **match** criteria. They are the conditions that should be tested to determine whether to take action. The **set** commands specify the **set** actions. They are the actions to be performed if the match criteria are met.

Policy Routing Example

Figure 8-8 presents a policy routing scenario. A route map can be used at RTA to implement policy routing. Assume for this example that the policy to be enforced is as follows:

- Route Internet-bound traffic from 192.168.1.0/24 to ISP 1
- Route Internet-bound traffic from 172.16.1.0/24 to ISP 2

Figure 8-48 Policy Routing Example

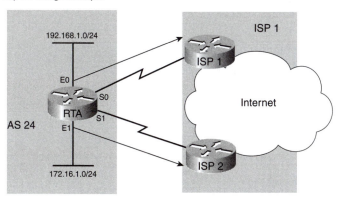

First, define the access lists that will be used in the route maps to match IP addresses. Then configure the route map itself using the syntax shown in Example 8-5.

Example 8-5 *Configuring a Route Map*

```
RTA(config)#access-list 1 permit 192.168.1.0 0.0.0.255
RTA(config)#access-list 2 permit 172.16.1.0 0.0.0.255
RTA(config-router)#route-map ISP1 permit 10
RTA(config-route-map)#match ip address 1
RTA(config-route-map)#set interface serial 0
RTA(config-route-map)#exit
RTA(config-router)#route-map ISP2 permit 20
RTA(config-route-map)#match ip address 2
RTA(config-route-map)#set interface serial 1
```

The commands shown in Example 8-5 have actually configured two policies. The ISP1 route map matches access list 1 and routes traffic out S0 toward ISP1. The ISP2 route map matches access list 2 and routes that traffic out S1 toward ISP2.

The final step is to apply each route map to the appropriate interface on RTA using the **ip policy route-map** command, as shown in Example 8-6. The appropriate interface is the interface that the traffic uses to enter the router. With the route maps applied to the appropriate LAN interfaces, policy routing is successfully implemented.

Example 8-6 *Applying a Route Map to an Interface*

```
RTA(config)#interface ethernet 0
RTA(config-if)#ip policy route-map ISP1
RTA(config-if)#interface ethernet 1
RTA(config-if)#ip policy route-map ISP2
```

Frequently, route maps are used to control the exchange of routing information during redistribution. Route redistribution is detailed in the next section.

Route Redistribution

The following sections discuss some of the details of route redistribution:

- Redistribution overview
- Administrative distance
- Modifying administrative distance by using the **distance** command
- Redistribution guidelines
- Configuring one-way redistribution
- Configuring two-way redistribution
- Redistributing connected and static routes
- Verifying redistribution operation

Redistribution Overview

To support multiple routing protocols within the same internetwork efficiently, routing information must be shared among the different routing protocols. For example, routes learned from a RIP process might need to be imported into an IGRP process. This process of exchanging routing information between routing protocols is called *route redistribution* . Such redistribution can be one-way or two-way. With one-way routes, one protocol receives the routes from another. With two-way routes, both protocols receive routes from each other. Routers that perform redistribution are called boundary routers because they border two or more autonomous systems or routing domains. This section examines route redistribution in detail, including the use of administrative distance, guidelines for redistribution implementation, and issues with redistribution configuration.

Using multiple routing protocols typically results in increased administrative complexity and overhead. So why would this be done? Actually, there are several scenarios in which using multiple routing protocols solves more problems than it creates, especially in medium- and large-sized networks.

Consider a large, mixed-vendor routing environment in which Cisco routers work alongside other routers, as shown in Figure 8-9. An administrator might create an all-Cisco domain, where the advantages of proprietary protocols, such as IGRP and EIGRP, can be retained. Meanwhile, other areas of the network run a nonproprietary protocol, such as OSPF or RIP.

Figure 8-49 Redistribution Example

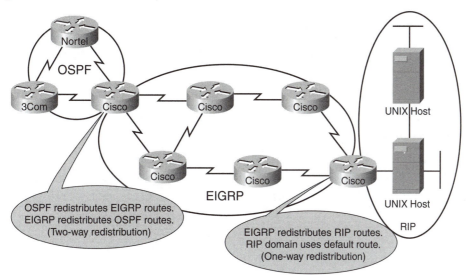

Multiple routing protocols may also be effectively deployed to support legacy UNIX systems that support RIP only. These systems might represent a significant financial investment and might not be readily upgradeable. An administrator might elect to run RIP on subnets popu- lated by the UNIX systems but might use a more scalable protocol elsewhere, as shown in Figure 8-9. Also, running multiple routing protocols can be seen as a temporary fix during a prolonged upgrade from older protocols and hardware to newer, more scalable solutions.

On some occasions, redistribution is implemented even when compatible routing platforms are being run. For example, consider an organization with all Cisco routers running EIGRP. If the organization is exchanging routing information with a domain outside its administrative control, it might choose to configure route redistribution as a means of logically separating the different routing processes, which might have different policies.

Cisco routers support up to 30 dynamic routing processes. This means that a router can run RIP, OSPF, IGRP, IS-IS, EIGRP, IPX RIP, RTMP, AppleTalk, and other protocols simulta- neously. Most of these routing protocols enable the configuration of multiple processes of the same routing algorithm. RIP is a notable exception. For example, multiple IGRP processes can be defined by using different AS numbers, or different OSPF processes can be defined by using different process ID numbers, as shown in Example 8-7.

Example 8-7 *Multiple OSPF and IGRP Processes*

```
RTA#show running-config
<output omitted>

router ospf 24
 network 10.2.0.0 0.0.255.255 area 0
!
router ospf 46
 network 192.168.2.0 0.0.0.255 area 2
!
router igrp 53
 network 172.16.0.0
 network 172.17.0.0
!
router igrp 141
 network 10.0.0.0
 network 192.168.3.0
```

Notice that the OSPF processes for RTA, 24 and 46, do not share routing information unless route redistribution is configured. Each routing process places substantial demands on the router memory and CPU resources. Because of this, only boundary routers should run more than one routing process for the same routed protocol and only when absolutely necessary.

Administrative Distance

If a boundary router is running multiple IP routing protocols, it might learn about the same network from more than one routing protocol. For example, RTZ might learn about the 10.0.0.0 network from both RIP and IGRP, as shown in Figure 8-10. Which route will RTZ install in its routing table?

Figure 8-50 Administrative Distance Example

A router looks at the metric value to determine the best route. However, in this case, the router would have to compare the simple metric of RIP, its hop count, with the composite metric of IGRP, this being derived from bandwidth and delay by default. As noted in Chapter 3, "Routing Overview," the metrics are not based on the same factors, so this is an unreliable comparison. The metric of 10576 from IGRP cannot be accurately measured against the metric of 3 from RIP for the same route. Instead, routers use *administrative distance* to choose between routes to the same network offered by different routing protocols.

A routing protocol's administrative distance provides a rate of trustworthiness as a source of routing information. Administrative distance is an integer from 0 to 255. The lowest administrative distance has the highest trust rating. An administrative distance of 255 means that the routing information source cannot be trusted and should be ignored. An administrative distance of 0 is reserved for directly connected interfaces and is always preferred.

Specifying administrative distance values allows the Cisco IOS software to discriminate between sources of routing information. If two routes have the same network number, and possibly the same subnet information, the Cisco IOS software always picks the route whose routing protocol has the lowest administrative distance. Table 8-1 shows the default administrative distances for some routing information sources.

Table 8-8 Administrative Distance

Route Source	Default Distance
Connected interface	0
Static route	1
EIGRP summary route	5
External BGP	20
Internal EIGRP	90
IGRP	100
OSPF	110
IS-IS	115
RIP	120
EGP	140
External EIGRP	170
Internal BGP	200
Unknown	255

The IGRP route is preferred, or trusted, over the RIP route to the same network. This is because of IGRP's lower administrative distance, which is 100, as opposed to RIP, which is 120. There might be a time when you need the router to believe RIP over IGRP. Fortunately, the Cisco IOS software allows the administrative distance to be manually configured, as discussed in the next section.

 Interactive Media Activity   Drag and Drop: Administrative Distance

After completing this activity, you will be able to identify the administrative distances for all entries in a routing table.

Modifying Administrative Distance by Using the distance Command

When you use multiple IP routing protocols on a router, the default administrative distance of each is usually sufficient. However, some circumstances call for changing the administrative distance values on a router.

For example, if a router is running both IGRP and OSPF, it might receive routes to the same network from both protocols. The default administrative distance favors IGRP routes over OSPF routes. However, because IGRP does not support CIDR, the router needs to use the OSPF route instead. In this case, configure the local router to apply a custom administrative distance to all OSPF routes.

With the **distance 95** OSPF configuration command, RTZ compares the IGRP and OSPF routes and comes up with a different result, as shown in Example 8-8. The beginning of Example 8-8 shows route comparison with default administrative distances. The end of Example 8-8 shows route comparison with manually configured administrative distances.

Example 8-8 *Using the* **distance** *Command*

```
I  10.0.0.0  [100/10576] via 192.168.0.1, Serial 0
O  10.0.0.0  [110/192] via 172.17.0.1, Serial 1


RTZ(config)#router ospf 1
RTZ(config-router)#distance 95


I  10.0.0.0  [100/10576] via 192.168.0.1, Serial 0
O  10.0.0.0  [95/192] via 172.17.0.1, Serial 1
```

In its broadest application, the **distance** command can be used to modify the administrative distance value applied to all routes learned by way of a specific routing process. The commands shown in Example 8-8 assign the value of 95 to all routes learned by the OSPF 1 process. Notice that these values are local to the router. Although RTZ assigns the 10.0.0.0 network an administrative distance of 95, all other Cisco OSPF routers apply a value of 110, unless otherwise configured.

The **distance** command can also be applied with optional arguments to make changes to selected routes based on where they originate. The expanded syntax of the **distance** command is as follows:

```
Router(config-router)#distance weight [source-ip-address source-mask
    {access-list-number | name}]
```

After running multiple protocols on a boundary router, you might discover that one or two suboptimal paths have been installed because of their lower administrative distance. Rather than assigning a new distance value to all routes learned by a process, you can identify specific routes based on their source IP. Using the optional arguments, configure a router as follows to apply an administrative distance of 105 to all RIP routes received from 10.4.0.2:

```
RTZ(config)#router rip
RTZ(config-router)#distance 105 10.4.0.2 255.255.255.255
```

Alternatively, you can apply an administrative distance value to only certain routes from that same source by specifying an access list.

Remember that the administrative distance defaults exist for a reason and that they serve a network well in most circumstances. Use the **distance** command only when you're sure it's necessary to guarantee optimal routing.

Redistribution Guidelines

Route redistribution can be complicated and has several disadvantages:

- **Routing loops**—Depending on how redistribution is used, routers can send routing information received from one AS back into the AS. The feedback is similar to the split-horizon problem that occurs in distance vector technologies.

- **Incompatible routing information**—Each routing protocol uses different metrics. Because these metrics cannot be translated exactly into a different protocol, path selection using the redistributed route information might not be optimal.

- **Inconsistent convergence time**—Different routing protocols converge at different rates. For example, RIP converges slower than EIGRP, so if a link goes down, the EIGRP network learns about it before the RIP network.

You can avoid these potential trouble spots with careful planning and implementation. Follow these important guidelines when configuring route redistribution:

- **Be familiar with the network**—There are many ways to implement redistribution. Being familiar with the network helps you make the best decisions.

- **Do not overlap routing protocols**—Do not run two different protocols in the same internetwork. Instead, have distinct boundaries between networks that use different routing protocols.

- **Use one-way redistribution with multiple boundary routers**—If more than one router serves as a redistribution point, use one-way redistribution to avoid routing loops and convergence problems. Consider using default routes in the domains that do not import external routes.

- **Use two-way redistribution with a single boundary router**—Two-way redistribution works smoothly when it is configured on a single boundary router in the internetwork. If there are multiple redistribution points, do not use two-way redistribution unless a mechanism to reduce the chances of routing loops is enabled. You can use a combination of default routes, route filters, and distance modifications to combat routing loops.

Configuring One-Way Redistribution

Although the **redistribute** command is available for all IP routing protocols, it behaves differently depending on the IP routing protocols involved. However, the underlying principles are the same. Therefore, you can use the examples in this section as a starting point for any redistribution scheme.

This section closely examines examples of one-way and two-way redistribution and then focuses on specific redistribution issues, including connected, static routes and the **default-metric** command.

In Figure 8-11, RTB injects routes learned by way of RIP into the EIGRP domain. However, the RIP routers do not learn about the EIGRP routes. This is one-way route distribution. In this example, the RIP routers can use a default route to handle any traffic bound for nonlocal destinations.

As the AS boundary router, RTB must run two routing processes, one for the RIP domain and one for the EIGRP AS, as shown in Example 8-9. The syntax of the **redistribute** command is as follows:

```
Router(config-router)# redistribute protocol [process-id]
    {level-1 | level-1-2 | level-2} [as-number] [metric metric-value]
    [metric-type type-value] [match {internal | external 1 | external 2}]
    [tag tag-value] [route-map map-tag] [subnets]
```

Figure 8-51 One-Way Redistribution Example

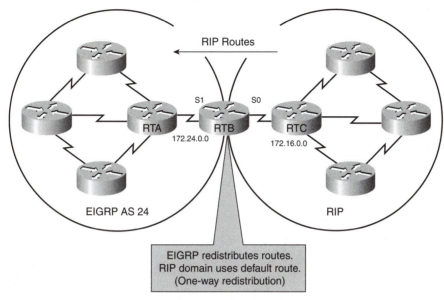

Example 8-9 *Configuring One-Way Route Redistribution*

```
RTB(config)#router rip
RTB(config-router)#network 172.16.0.0
RTB(config-router)#router eigrp 24
RTB(config-router)#network 172.24.0.0
RTB(config-router)#redistribute rip metric 10000 100 255 1 1500
```

The **redistribute rip** command enables route redistribution. RIP routes learned by RTB are imported into the EIGRP process. The **metric** argument sets up the values used by EIGRP to translate the metric from the hop count on RIP to the composite metric on EIGRP. When used with IGRP/EIGRP, the **metric** keyword sets the bandwidth value, the delay, the reliability, the load, and the maximum transmission unit (MTU). The bandwidth value is in Kbps, the delay is in tenths of microseconds, and the reliability and load are out of 255.

These five values constitute the seed metric. The seed metric is the initial metric value of an imported route. After it is imported into the EIGRP AS, the RIP route becomes an EIGRP route with a composite metric derived from these seed values. Using the configuration shown in Example 8-9, RIP routes with metrics of 2, 6, and 14 are redistributed with the same EIGRP metric value of 2195456. However, as the imported route propagates to other EIGRP routers, its metric values increment according to EIGRP rules.

The routing table on RTA includes not only the EIGRP routes from AS 24 but also the redistributed routes from the RIP domain, as shown in Example 8-10. The internal EIGRP routes are denoted by a D. The redistributed RIP routes that have been learned from RTB are denoted by D EX because EIGRP considers them external. As discussed in Chapter 5, "EIGRP," EIGRP differentiates between internal routes and external routes. Internal routes are learned from within the AS, and external routes are imported from outside the AS. Internal EIGRP routes have an administrative distance of 90. The Cisco IOS software assigns a different administrative distance of 170 to the external EIGRP routes, which is much less desirable.

Example 8-10 *Routing Table for RTA*

```
RTA#show ip route
<output omitted>
C     172.24.0.0/16 is directly connected, Serial 0
C     172.25.0.0/16 is directly connected, Serial 1
C     172.26.0.0/16 is directly connected, Serial 2
C     172.27.0.0/16 is directly connected, Serial 3
D     172.28.0.0/16 [90/2681856] via 172.20.0.0, 00:00:02, Serial1
D     172.29.0.0/16 [90/2681856] via 172.21.0.0, 00:00:02, Serial3
D EX 172.17.0.0/16 [170/2195456] via 172.24.0.1. 00:00:02, Serial0
D EX 172.18.0.0/16 [170/2195456] via 172.24.0.1. 00:00:02, Serial0
D EX 172.19.0.0/16 [170/2195456] via 172.24.0.1. 00:00:02, Serial0
D EX 172.20.0.0/16 [170/2195456] via 172.24.0.1. 00:00:02, Serial0
D EX 172.21.0.0/16 [170/2195456] via 172.24.0.1. 00:00:02, Serial0
```

The routing table from RTB, shown in Example 8-11, shows that RTB is running two routing protocols and has learned routes by way of RIP and EIGRP. RIP is denoted by an R, and EIGRP is denoted by a D.

Example 8-11 *Routing Table for RTB*

```
RTB#show ip route
<output omitted>
C     172.16.0.0/16 is directly connected, Serial 0
C     172.24.0.0/16 is directly connected, Serial 1
R     172.17.0.0/16 [120/1] via 172.16.0.2, 00:00:02, Serial0
R     172.18.0.0/16 [120/1] via 172.16.0.2, 00:00:02, Serial0
```

Example 8-11 *Routing Table for RTB (Continued)*

```
R    172.19.0.0/16 [120/1] via 172.16.0.2, 00:00:02, Serial0
R    172.20.0.0/16 [120/1] via 172.16.0.2, 00:00:02, Serial0
R    172.21.0.0/16 [120/1] via 172.16.0.2, 00:00:02, Serial0
D    172.25.0.0/16 [90/2681856] via 172.24.0.2, 00:00:02, Serial1
D    172.26.0.0/16 [90/2681856] via 172.24.0.2, 00:00:02, Serial1
D    172.37.0.0/16 [90/2681856] via 172.24.0.2, 00:00:02, Serial1
D    172.28.0.0/16 [90/3193856] via 172.24.0.2, 00:00:02, Serial1
D    172.29.0.0/16 [90/3193856] via 172.24.0.2, 00:00:02, Serial1
```

In Example 8-12, RTC does not have a default route and has not learned about any routes from the boundary router, RTB. This means that RTC cannot route to six of the 12 networks shown in the output from RTB.

Example 8-12 *Routing Table for RTC*

```
RTC#show ip route
<output omitted>
C    172.16.0.0/16 is directly connected, Serial 0
C    172.17.0.0/16 is directly connected, Serial 1
C    172.18.0.0/16 is directly connected, Serial 2
C    172.19.0.0/16 is directly connected, Serial 3
R    172.20.0.0/16 [120/1] via 172.17.0.2, 00:00:02, Serial1
R    172.21.0.0/16 [120/1] via 172.19.0.2, 00:00:02, Serial3
*S   0.0.0.0/0 S* is directly connected, Serial0
```

You might decide that the best solution in this scenario is to use a default route that points to RTB. This can easily be accomplished statically:

```
RTC(config)#ip route 0.0.0.0 0.0.0.0 172.16.0.1
```

Because RTC is running RIP, it can dynamically propagate its 0.0.0.0/0 route to the other routers in the RIP domain. If you choose to implement this default route configuration, there is no need for the boundary router, RTB, to send updates into the RIP domain. Therefore, the RIP interface on RTB should be configured as passive:

```
RTB(config)#router rip
RTB(config-router)#passive-interface s0/0
```

A more complex topology might require that you employ a two-way, or mutual, redistribution. You do this by importing the EIGRP routes into the RIP domain, as described in the next section.

Lab 8.5.1 Configuring Distribute Lists and Passive Interfaces

In this lab, you configure a combination of advanced routing features to optimize routing. These features include distribute lists, passive interfaces, default routes, and route redistribution.

Configuring Two-Way Redistribution

The boundary router can be configured for two-way redistribution, as shown in Figure 8-12. Notice that in Example 8-13, the syntax of the **metric** keyword varies depending on which routing protocol it uses. For RIP, OSPF, and BGP, the **metric** option is followed by a single number that represents the metric value (hop count, cost, and so on). For IGRP and EIGRP, the **metric** option is followed by five values that represent bandwidth, delay, reliability, load, and MTU.

Figure 8-52 Two-Way Redistribution Example

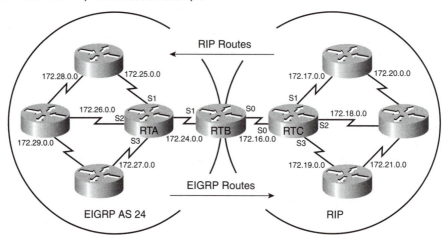

Example 8-13 *Configuring Two-Way Route Redistribution*

```
RTB(config)#router eigrp 24
RTB(config-router)#network 172.24.0.0
RTB(config-router)#redistribute rip metric 10000 100 255 1 1500
RTB(config-router)#router rip
RTB(config-router)#network 172.16.0.0
RTB(config-router)#redistribute eigrp 24 metric 2
```

In Example 8-13, RIP is configured to import EIGRP routes and distribute them into the RIP domain with a seed metric of two hops.

Mutual redistribution causes RTC to install 11 routes in its table, as shown in Example 8-14.

Example 8-14 *Routing Table for RTC*

```
RTC#show ip route
<output omitted>
C    172.16.0.0/16 is directly connected, Serial 0
C    172.17.0.0/16 is directly connected, Serial 1
C    172.18.0.0/16 is directly connected, Serial 2
R    172.19.0.0/16 is directly connected, Serial 3
R    172.20.0.0/16 [120/1] via 172.20.0.2, 00:00:02, Serial1
R    172.21.0.0/16 [120/1] via 172.21.0.2, 00:00:02, Serial3
R    172.25.0.0/16 [120/1] via 172.16.0.1, 00:00:02, Serial0
R    172.26.0.0/16 [120/1] via 172.16.0.1, 00:00:02, Serial0
R    172.27.0.0/16 [120/1] via 172.16.0.1, 00:00:02, Serial0
R    172.28.0.0/16 [120/1] via 172.16.0.1, 00:00:02, Serial0
R    172.29.0.0/16 [120/1] via 172.16.0.1, 00:00:02, Serial0
```

NOTE

Whenever a major network is subnetted, use the keyword **subnets** to redistribute other routing protocols into OSPF. Without this keyword, OSPF redistributes only major networks that are not subnetted. For example, to inject EIGRP routes, including subnets, into an OSPF area, use the command **redistribute eigrp 24 metric 100 subnets**

Unlike EIGRP, RIP does not differentiate between external and internal routes. Also, note that the RTB seed metric results in a metric of two hops for all of the redistributed routes, even though two of these networks are actually three hops away.

After configuring two-way redistribution, RTC and RTA have only 11 routes, whereas the boundary router (RTB) has 12. What is happening? The answer lies in RTB's directly connected routes:

- 172.16.0.0/16 (missing from the RTA table)
- 172.24.0.0/16 (missing from the RTC table)

Recall that the **network** command identifies not only which interfaces to run the routing protocol, but also which directly connected networks are included in routing updates. Look carefully at Example 8-14. RTB's RIP process is configured to advertise the connected network 172.16.0.0, whereas its EIGRP process is configured to advertise the connected network 172.24.0.0.

To bring RTA and RTC routing tables up to a complete 12 routes, you can configure both RTB routing processes to include the two connected networks using the **network** command. However, this results in a RIP process running in the EIGRP AS and an EIGRP process running in the RIP domain. This solution generates needless overhead. Redistribution offers a much more efficient and elegant solution. RTB can be configured to redistribute its connected routes using a default metric, as discussed in the following sections.

Lab 8.5.2a   Configuring Route Maps

In this lab, apply a routing policy by configuring a route map.

Lab 8.5.2b   NAT: Dynamic Translation with Multiple Pools Using Route Maps

In this lab, you configure dynamic Network Address Translation (NAT) with multiple pools using route maps.

Redistributing Connected and Static Routes

You can redistribute directly connected routes into a routing protocol by using the **redistribute connected** command with a seed metric:

```
RTB(config-router)#router eigrp 24
RTB(config-router)#redistribute connected metric 10000 100 255 1 1500
```

When you use the **connected** keyword, redistribution injects all connected routes into the updates from the routing protocol. This is done without configuring a **network** statement.

Static routes can be redistributed in the same way. The following example illustrates how RTB can be configured to redistribute static routes:

```
RTB(config-router)#router eigrp 24
RTB(config-router)#redistribute static metric 10000 100 255 1 1500
```

In Figure 8-12, RTB is configured for two-way redistribution. Notice that, in Example 8-15, the seed metric is included each time the **redistribute** command is issued. The **default-metric** command can be used as a shortcut in this situation.

Example 8-15 *Configuration for RTB*

```
RTB#show running-config
<output omitted>


router eigrp 24
  network 172.24.0.0
  redistribute rip metric 10000 100 255 1 1500
  redistribute connected metric 10000 100 255 1500
router rip
  network 172.16.0.0
  redistribute eigrp 24 metric 2
  redistribute connected metric 2

<output omitted>
```

The default-metric Command

An alternative to this redistribution configuration is to use the **default-metric** command instead of including the same seed metric with each **redistribute** statement. Whenever the **redistribute** command is used and the metric is not specified, the router uses the default metric value as the seed metric. The default metric value can be administratively configured for each routing protocol, as shown in the **show running-config** output in Example 8-16. In this example, all EIGRP **redistribute** commands use the default metric, 10000 100 255 1 1500. Meanwhile, all RIP **redistribute** commands use a default metric of 2.

Example 8-16 *Configuration for RTB*

```
RTB#show running-config
<output omitted>


router eigrp 24
  network 172.24.0.0
  redistribute rip
  redistribute connected
  default-metric 10000 100 255 1 1500
router rip
  network 172.16.0.0
  redistribute eigrp 24
  redistribute connected
  default-metric 2

<output omitted>
```

Lab 8.5.3 Redistributing RIP and OSPF with Distribution Lists

In this lab, you configure mutual redistribution between RIPv1 and OSPF.

Verifying Redistribution Operation

The commands shown in Example 8-17 are used to verify the route redistribution operation, as shown in Figure 8-13. Example 8-17 shows the running configurations of the two routers shown in Figure 8-13.

Figure 8-53 Redistribution Operation

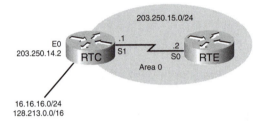

Example 8-17 *Verifying Redistribution Operation*

```
RouterC#show running-config
interface Ethernet 0
ip address 203.250.14.2 255.255.255.0

interface Serial 1
ip address 203.250.15.1 255.255.255.252

router ospf 10
redistribute static metric 50 subnets
network 203.250.15.0 0.0.0.255 area 0
network 203.250.14.0 0.0.0.255

ip route 16.16.16.0 255.255.255.0 Ethernet 0
ip route 128.213.0.0 255.255.0.0 Ethernet 0

RouterE#show running-config
interface Serial 0
ip address 203.250.15.2 255.255.255.252

router ospf 10
network 203.250.15.0 0.0.0.255 area 0
```

The following list provides some rules to follow when verifying route redistribution operation:

- Know the network topology, particularly where redundant routes exist.

- Display the routing table of the appropriate routing protocol on a variety of routers in the internetwork using the **show ip route** command. For example, check the routing table on the Autonomous System Boundary Router (ASBR) as well as some of the internal routers in each AS.

- Perform a **traceroute** on some of the routes that go across the autonomous systems to verify that the shortest path is being used for routing. Make sure that traces and extended pings are performed on networks where redundant routes exist.

- If you encounter routing problems, use **traceroute** and **debug** commands to observe the routing update traffic on the ASBRs and internal routers.

Redistribution Example

This section presents a case study that addresses the issues associated with integrating RIP with OSPF. Complex internetworks typically include UNIX hosts and legacy routers, neither of which is likely to support OSPF. Because of this, most OSPF internetworks must also use RIP in select areas. This case study provides examples of how to complete the following phases of redistributing information between RIP and OSPF networks:

Phase 1: Configuring a RIP network

Phase 2: Adding OSPF to the core of a RIP network

Phase 3: Adding OSPF areas

Phase 1: Configuring a RIP Network

Figure 8-14 illustrates the RIP network. Three sites are connected with serial lines.

This RIP network uses a Class B address, 172.16.0.0, and a 24-bit subnet mask. All three routers are connected to the same major network, so each is configured with the **network 172.16.0.0** command.

Phase 2: Adding OSPF to the Core of a RIP Network

A common first step in migrating a RIP network to an OSPF network is to configure backbone routers that run both RIP and OSPF. This is while the remaining network devices run RIP. These backbone routers act as OSPF ASBRs. Each ASBR controls the flow of routing information between OSPF and RIP. In Figure 8-15, Router A, Router B, and Router C now act as ASBRs.

Figure 8-54 Typical RIP Network

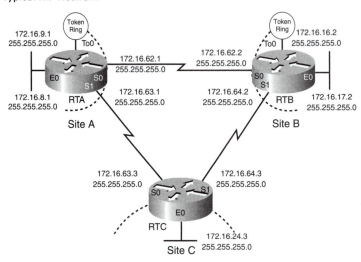

Figure 8-55 RIP with an OSPF Center

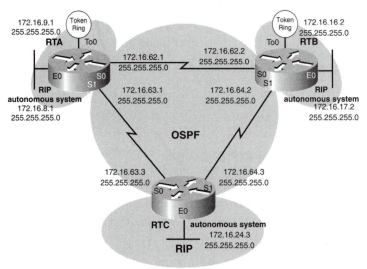

Because RIP does not need to run between the backbone routers, updates can be suppressed using the **passive-interface** command. Although Example 8-18 specifies RTA, the same commands can be entered on the other routers.

Example 8-18 passive-interface *Command*

```
Router A(config)#router rip
Router A(config-router)#passive-interface serial 0
Router A(config-router)#passive-interface serial 1
```

NOTE

The same configuration is used for all three routers except for the network numbers.

Instead of RIP updates, OSPF updates carry the redistributed information across the WAN links. The necessary OSPF routing and redistribution commands are shown in Example 8-19.

Example 8-19 *OSPF Routing and Redistribution Commands*

```
Router A(config)#router ospf 109
Router A(config-router)#redistribute rip subnets
Router A(config-router)#network 172.16.62.0 0.0.0.255 area 0
Router A(config-router)#network 173.16.63.0 0.0.0.255 area 0
```

The **subnets** keyword tells OSPF to redistribute all subnet routes. Without the **subnets** keyword, OSPF redistributes only networks that are not subnetted.

The redistributed RIP routes appear as external Type 2 (E2) routes in OSPF, as discussed in Chapter 6, "OSPF."

Mutual redistribution must be configured for other routers in the RIP domain (those not shown in Figure 8-15) to receive information from OSPF. Example 8-20 lists the necessary commands, which again are the same for Routers A, B, and C.

Example 8-20 *Mutual Redistribution*

```
Router A(config)#router rip
Router A(config-router)#redistribute ospf 109 match internal external 1 external 2
Router A(config-router)#default-metric 10
```

Note that the **redistribute** command includes the OSPF process ID, 109. The other keywords, **match internal external 1** and **external 2**, instruct RIP to redistribute internal OSPF routes, as well as external Type 1 and Type 2 routes. This is the default for OSPF redistribution. These keywords are required only if its behavior is to be modified.

As illustrated in Figure 8-15, no paths directly connect the RIP domains outside the core. In real-world networks, this is not always the case. If one RIP domain can communicate directly with another, there is a chance that they will exchange routes, resulting in a routing feedback loop. Route filters can be used to prevent these potentially disastrous loops.

The configuration shown in Example 8-21 allows the OSPF process on RTA to redistribute RIP information, only for networks 172.16.8.0 through 172.16.15.0.

Example 8-21 *Redistributing RIP Information*

```
Router A(config)#router ospf 109
Router A(config-router)#redistribute rip subnets
Router A(config-router)#distribute-list 11 in rip
Router A(config)#access-list 11 permit 172.16.8.0 0.0.7.255
Router A(config)#access-list 11 deny 0.0.0.0 255.255.255.255
```

These commands prevent RTA from advertising networks in other RIP domains onto the OSPF backbone. This prevents other boundary routers from using false information and forming a loop. When an OSPF backbone area is in place, the RIP domains can easily be converted into OSPF areas.

Phase 3: Adding OSPF Areas

Each RIP domain can be converted into an OSPF area independently of the other RIP domains. This allows the migration of one section of the internetwork at a time if desired.

When all three of the RIP domains have become OSPF areas, the three core routers serve as ABRs, as shown in Figure 8-16. Recall that ABRs control the exchange of routing information between OSPF areas and the OSPF backbone. Each ABR keeps a detailed record of the topology of its area and summarizes this information in its updates to other backbone routers.

Figure 8-56 Route Summarization Between OSPF Areas

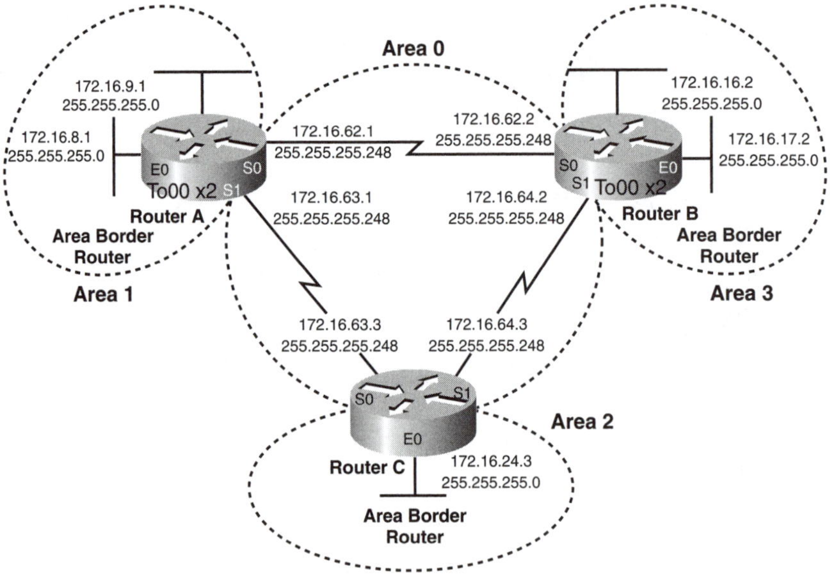

Notice that Figure 8-16 also presents a new addressing scheme in the core. A 29-bit mask, 255.255.255.248, is used to address WAN links and conserve address space. Meanwhile, a 24-bit mask remains on the LAN interfaces, resulting in variable-length subnet masks (VLSM). OSPF fully supports VLSM, but RIPv1 does not. With OSPF as the sole routing protocol, the network can now make the most of the advantages of VLSM. Example 8-22 shows the commands necessary to configure Router A for OSPF operation on all interfaces, with the appropriate masks.

Example 8-22 *Router A Configuration for OSPF Operation on All Interfaces*

```
Router A(config)#router ospf 109
Router A(config-router)#network 172.16.62.0 0.0.0.7 area 0
Router A(config-router)#network 172.16.63.0 0.0.0.7 area 0
Router A(config-router)#network 172.16.8.0 0.0.0.255 area 1
Router A(config-router)#network 172.16.9.0 0.0.0.255 area 1
```

Because OSPF is classless, each ABR can be configured to use route summarization. For example, Router A connects to eight networks, which occupy a contiguous address space. Therefore, this ABR can be configured as follows to send a single supernet route, which advertises all eight of the networks:

```
Router A(config)#router ospf 109
Router A(config-router)#area 1 range 172.16.8.0 255.255.248.0
```

Router A advertises one route, 172.16.8.0 255.255.248.0, which covers all subnets in Area 1 into Area 0. Without the **range** keyword in the **area** command, Router A would advertise each subnet individually, such as one route for 172.16.8.0 255.255.248.0, one route for 172.16.9.0 255.255.248.0, and so forth. The migration of the network from RIP to OSPF is now complete, and redistribution is no longer necessary.

Lab 8.6.1   Route Optimization Challenge Lab

In this challenge lab, you create and optimize a network using RIPv2 and OSPF.

Summary

This chapter demonstrated several ways to control routing update traffic, including passive interface, default routes, static routes, and route filtering. The chapter also clarified that route redistribution enables the exchange of routing information between dissimilar routing protocols and requires some care when configuring. Redistribution is when boundary routers connecting different autonomous systems exchange and advertise routing information received from one autonomous system to the other autonomous system.

In the next chapter, you will learn how to connect an enterprise network to an Internet service provider (ISP).

Key Terms

administrative distance   A rating of the trustworthiness of a routing information source. In Cisco routers, administrative distance is expressed as a numeric value between 0 and 255. The higher the value, the lower the trustworthiness rating.

autonomous system   A collection of networks under a common administration sharing a common routing strategy. Autonomous systems are subdivided by areas. An autonomous system must be assigned a unique 16-bit number by the IANA. Sometimes abbreviated as AS.

exterior gateway protocol (EGP)   Any internetwork protocol used to exchange routing information between autonomous systems. Not to be confused with Exterior Gateway Protocol (EGP), which is a particular instance of an exterior gateway protocol.

keepalive message   A message sent by one network device to inform another network device that the virtual circuit between the two is still active.

passive interface   A passive interface receives updates but does not send them. It is used to control routing updates. The **passive-interface** command can be used with all IP interior gateway protocols—RIP, IGRP, EIGRP, OSPF, and IS-IS.

policy routing   A routing scheme that forwards packets to interfaces based on user-configured policies. Such policies might specify that traffic sent from a particular network should be forwarded out one interface, while all other traffic should be forwarded out another interface.

route redistribution   Allowing routing information discovered through one routing protocol to be distributed in the update messages of another routing protocol.

Check Your Understanding

Complete all of the review questions to test your understanding of the topics and concepts in this chapter. The answers appear in Appendix B, "Answers to the Check Your Understanding Questions."

For additional, more in-depth questions, refer to the chapter-specific study guides on the companion CD-ROM.

1. What method is used to prevent a routing update from being sent out of a router interface?

   A. Redistribution

   B. Summarization

   C. Passive interface

   D. Gateway of last resort

2. What address does a router advertise for a default route?

   A. 255.255.255.255

   B. 0.0.0.0

   C. 255.255.0.0

   D. 1.1.1.1

3. What is the default administrative distance for the OSPF routing protocol?

   A. 1

   B. 90

   C. 110

   D. 120

4. What command imports static routes into routing protocol advertisements?

   A. **redistribute static**

   B. **distribute-list**

   C. **passive-interface**

   D. **route-map**

5. What command uses match statements to create a routing policy?

   A. **auto summary**

   B. **distribute-list**

   C. **access-list**

   D. **route-map**

6. What command establishes which route a router sends or receives in updates?

A. access-list

B. network

C. passive-interface

D. distribute-list

7. What command modifies the administrative distance for all OSPF routes?

A. distance 95

B. admin distance 110

C. distance 110

D. admin distance 95

8. Which of the following is a consideration when implementing redistribution?

A. Incompatible routing tables

B. Routing feedback (loops)

C. Overlap routing protocols

D. Two-way redistribution with multiple boundary routers

9. Which administrative distance represents the most reliable protocol?

A. 5

B. 90

C. 120

D. 200

10. Which IP interior gateway protocols support passive interface?

A. RIP, IGRP, EIGRP, and BGP

B. RIP, IGRP, EIGRP, IS-IS, and IPX

C. RIP, IGRP, EIGRP, OSPF, and IPX

D. RIP, IGRP, EIGRP, OSPF, and IS-IS

11. What does the router use to make a decision when it has learned two or more routes to the same destination from multiple routing protocols?

A. Hop count

B. Administrative distance

C. Metric

D. Route summarization

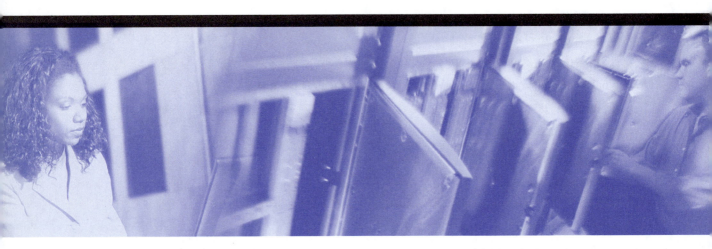

Objectives

Upon completing this chapter, you will be able to

- Describe autonomous systems
- Describe basic BGP operation
- Configure IBGP and EBGP
- Monitor BGP operation
- Understand the BGP routing process
- Identify and configure BGP attributes
- Describe the BGP decision process
- Apply BGP route filtering and policy routing
- Understand issues with redundancy, symmetry, and load balancing
- Understand BGP redistribution

You can reinforce your understanding of the objectives covered in this chapter by opening the interactive media activities on the CD accompanying this book and performing the lab activities collected in the *Cisco Networking Academy Program CCNP 1: Advanced Routing Lab Companion*. Throughout this chapter, you will see references to these activities by title and by icon. They look like this:

  Interactive Media Activity

  Lab Activity

Chapter 9

BGP

Routing protocols can be classified in many ways. It depends on where they are used in relationship to the enterprise. Protocols that run inside an enterprise are called *interior gateway protocols (IGPs)*. Examples of IGPs include RIP versions 1 and 2, IGRP, EIGRP, OSPF, and IS-IS. Protocols that run outside an enterprise, or between autonomous systems, are called *exterior gateway protocols (EGPs)*. Typically, EGPs are used to exchange routing information between Internet service providers (ISPs) or, in some cases, between a customer's autonomous system and the provider's network. *Border Gateway Protocol* version 4 (BGP4) is the most common EGP and is considered the Internet standard.

This chapter provides an overview of the different types of autonomous systems and then focuses on basic BGP operation, including BGP neighbor negotiation. This chapter also looks at how to use the Cisco IOS software to configure BGP and verify its operation. Finally, this chapter examines BGP peering and the BGP routing process.

Autonomous Systems

An internetwork is a group of smaller, independent networks. Each of these smaller networks may be owned and operated by a different organization. These organizations can include a company, a university, a government agency, or some other group. The Internet is one example of a single, although immense, internetwork.

Overview of Autonomous Systems

The operators of these individual networks desire independence or self-administration over their own systems. Because the routing and security policies of one organization might conflict with the policies of another, internetworks are divided into domains or autonomous systems. Each AS typically represents an independent organization and applies its own unique routing and security policies, as shown in Figure 9-1. EGPs facilitate the sharing of routing information between autonomous systems.

Figure 9-57 Autonomous Systems

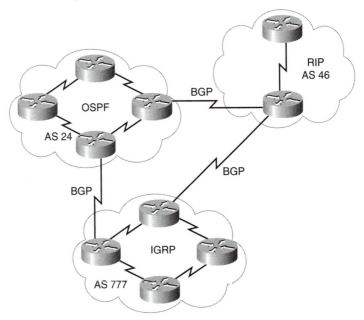

An AS is a group of routers that share similar routing policies and operate within a single administrative domain. An AS can be a collection of routers running a single IGP, or it can be a collection of routers running different protocols all belonging to one organization. In either case, the outside world views the entire AS as a single entity.

Each AS has an identifying number that is assigned by an Internet registry or a service provider. This number is between 1 and 65,535. AS numbers within the range of 64,512 to 65,535 are reserved for private use. These are similar to RFC 1918 IP addresses. Because of the finite number of available AS numbers, an organization must justify its need before it will be assigned an AS number.

Today, the Internet Assigned Numbers Authority (IANA) is enforcing a policy whereby organizations that connect to a single provider and that share the provider's routing policies use an AS number from the private pool, 64,512 to 65,535. These private AS numbers appear only within the provider's network and are replaced by the provider's registered number upon exiting the network. Therefore, to the outside world, several individual networks are advertised as part of one service provider's network. In principle, this process is similar to NAT. See Chapter 2, "Advanced IP Addressing Management."

During the early days of the Internet, an exterior gateway protocol, EGP version 3, was used to interconnect autonomous systems. EGP3 should not be confused with EGPs in general. Currently, BGP4 is the accepted standard for Internet routing and has essentially replaced the more limited EGP3.

The following sections detail the different types of autonomous systems, such as single-homed, multihomed nontransit, and multihomed transit. In addition to defining these three types of systems, the following sections examine BGP's role in connecting each type of AS to an ISP.

Single-Homed Autonomous Systems

If an AS has only one exit point to outside networks, it is considered a *single-homed system*. Single-homed autonomous systems are often called stub networks or stubs. Stubs can rely on a default route to handle all traffic destined for nonlocal networks. For the network shown in Figure 9-2, you would configure the routers in the customer AS to use a default route to an upstream service provider.

Figure 9-58 Single-Homed Autonomous Systems

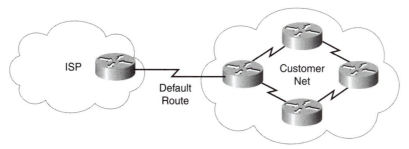

The following are three methods to advertise a customer's networks from the provider's perspective:

- **Use a static configuration**—The provider lists the customer's networks as static entries in its own router and advertises these routes upstream to the Internet core. This approach works well if the customer's networks can be summarized using a CIDR prefix, as discussed in Chapter 2. However, if the AS contains numerous discontiguous networks, route aggregation might not be a viable option.
- **Use an IGP**—Both the provider and the customers use an IGP to share information about the customer's networks, as shown in Figure 9-3. This provides the benefits associated with dynamic routing.
- **Use an EGP**—The third method by which the ISP can learn and advertise the customer's routes is to use an EGP such as BGP. In a single-homed autonomous system,

the customer's routing policies are an extension of the provider's policies. For this reason, the Internet number registries are unlikely to assign an AS number. Instead, the provider can give the customer an AS number from the private pool of AS numbers, 64,512 to 65,535, as shown in Figure 9-4. The provider strips these numbers when advertising the customer's routes toward the core of the Internet.

Figure 9-59 IGP with the ISP

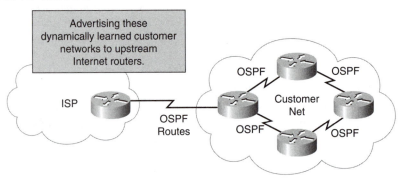

Figure 9-60 BGP with the ISP

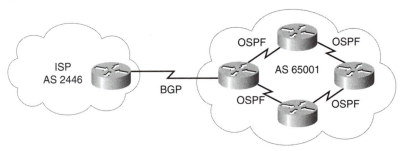

Notice that only the final solution requires the customers to enable BGP on their AS boundary router.

Multihomed Nontransit Autonomous Systems

An AS is a *multihomed system* if it has more than one exit point to outside networks. An AS connected to the Internet can be multihomed to a single provider or multiple providers. A nontransit AS does not allow transit traffic to pass through it. Transit traffic is any traffic that has a source and destination outside the AS. Figure 9-5 illustrates a multihomed and nontransit AS, shown as AS 24, which is connected to two providers, ISP1 and ISP2.

Figure 9-61 Multihomed Nontransit Autonomous Systems

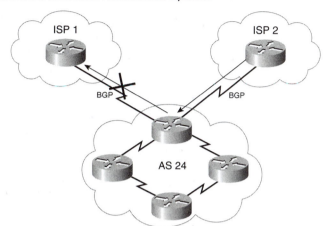

A nontransit AS advertises only its own routes to both providers to which it connects. It does not advertise routes it learned from one provider to another provider. This ensures that ISP 1 does not use AS 24 to reach destinations that belong to ISP 2 and that ISP 2 does not use AS 24 to reach destinations that belong to ISP 1. Of course, ISP 1 or ISP 2 can force traffic to be directed to AS 24 by way of default or static routing. As a precaution against this, the router at the border of AS 24 can filter incoming traffic to prevent transit traffic from passing through its border router.

Multihomed nontransit autonomous systems do not really need to run BGP4 with their providers; however, ISPs usually recommend it and often require it. As you will see later in this chapter, BGP4 offers numerous advantages, including increased control of route propagation and filtering.

Multihomed Transit Autonomous Systems

A multihomed transit system has more than one connection to the outside world and can be used for transit traffic by other autonomous systems. The multihomed AS views transit traffic as any traffic originating from outside sources bound for outside destinations, as shown in Figure 9-6.

A transit AS can route transit traffic by running BGP internally so that multiple border routers in the same AS can share BGP information. Additional routers may be used to forward BGP information from one border router to another. BGP can be run inside an AS to facilitate this exchange.

Figure 9-62 Multihomed Transit Autonomous Systems

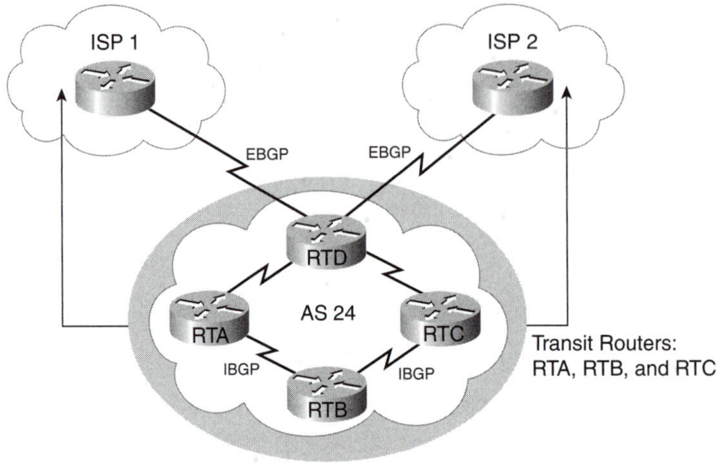

When BGP is running inside an AS, it is called Internal BGP (IBGP). When BGP runs between autonomous systems, it is called External BGP (EBGP). If the role of a BGP router is to route IBGP traffic, it is called a transit router, as with RTA, RTB, and RTC in Figure 9-6. Routers that sit on the boundary of an AS and that use EBGP to exchange information with the ISP are called border or edge routers.

When Not to Use BGP

In many cases, the routing policy that is implemented in an AS is consistent with the policy for the ISP. In these cases, it is not necessary, or even desirable, to use BGP to exchange routing information with the ISP. Instead, connectivity can be achieved through a combination of static routes and default routes.

Do not use BGP within the AS in the following situations:

- There is only a single connection to the Internet or the other AS.
- The Internet routing policy and route selection are not of concern to the AS.
- The BGP routers have insufficient RAM or processor power to handle constant updates.
- You have a limited understanding of route filtering and the BGP path-selection process.
- There is a low-bandwidth link between autonomous systems.

In Figure 9-7, Router A advertises a default network into the AS through a local IGP, such as RIP. A static route affords connectivity through Router B to the AS for the ISP. The ISP is running BGP and is recognized by other BGP routers on the Internet.

NOTE

In general, when there are different policy requirements than those of the ISP, it is necessary to use BGP to connect to an ISP.

Figure 9-63 When Not to Use BGP

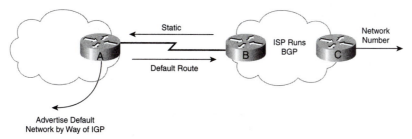

 Interactive Media Activity   Point and Click: When to Use BGP and When Not to Use BGP

After completing this activity, you will be able to decide when to use BGP and when not to use BGP.

Basic BGP Operation

BGP was most recently defined in RFC 1772. BGP's function is to exchange routing information between autonomous systems and guarantee the selection of a loop-free path. BGP4 is the first version of BGP that supports CIDR and route aggregation. Common IGPs such as RIP, OSPF, and EIGRP use technical metrics. BGP does not use technical metrics. Instead, it makes routing decisions based on network policies or rules.

This section offers a brief overview of how BGP works. It is followed by a more detailed examination of the various types of BGP packets and relationship states.

BGP Routing Updates

BGP updates are carried using TCP on port 179. In contrast, RIP updates use UDP port 520, whereas OSPF does not use a Layer 4 protocol. Because BGP requires TCP, IP connectivity must exist between BGP peers. TCP connections must also be negotiated between them before updates can be exchanged. Therefore, BGP inherits those reliable, connection-oriented properties from TCP.

To guarantee loop-free path selection, BGP constructs a graph of autonomous systems based on the information exchanged between BGP neighbors. BGP views the whole internetwork as a graph, or tree, of autonomous systems. The connection between any two systems forms a path. The collection of path information is expressed as a sequence of AS numbers called the AS Path, as shown in Figure 9-8. This sequence forms a route to reach a specific destination.

Figure 9-64 AS Path

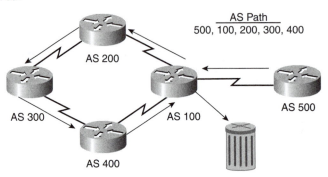

BGP Neighbors

When two routers establish a TCP-enabled BGP connection, they are called neighbors or peers. Each router running BGP is called a BGP speaker. Peer routers exchange multiple messages to open and confirm the connection parameters, such as the version of BGP to be used. If there are any disagreements between the peers, notification errors are sent, and the connection fails.

When BGP neighbors first establish a connection, they exchange all candidate BGP routes, as shown in Figure 9-9. After this initial exchange, incremental updates are sent as network information changes, as shown in Figure 9-10. As discussed in earlier chapters, incremental updates are more efficient than complete table updates. This is especially true with BGP routers, which might contain the complete Internet routing table.

Figure 9-65 How BGP Works

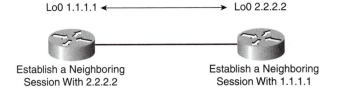

Figure 9-66 How BGP Works

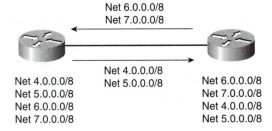

Peers advertise destinations that can be reached through them by using *update messages*. These messages contain route prefix, AS path, path attributes (such as the degree of preference for a particular route), and other properties.

The information for network reachability can change, such as when a route becomes unreachable or a better path becomes available. BGP informs its neighbors of this by withdrawing the invalid routes and injecting the new routing information, as shown in Figure 9-11. Withdrawn routes are part of the update message. BGP routers keep a table version number that tracks the version of the BGP routing table received from each peer. If the table changes, BGP increments the table version number. A rapidly incrementing table version usually indicates instabilities in the network or a misconfiguration.

Figure 9-67 How BGP Works

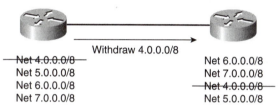

If there are no routing changes to transmit to a peer, a BGP speaker periodically sends keepalive messages to maintain the connection. These 19-byte keepalive packets are sent every 60 seconds by default. These packets present a negligible drain on bandwidth and the CPU time on a router.

BGP Message Types

Different message types play an essential role in BGP operation. Each message type includes the BGP message header.

The message header contains only three fields—a 16-byte Marker field, a 2-byte Length field, and a 1-byte Type field.

The Marker field is used either to authenticate incoming BGP messages or to detect loss of synchronization between two BGP peers.

The Length field indicates the total BGP message length, including the header. The smallest BGP message is 19 bytes, 16 + 2 + 1, and the largest possible message is 4096 bytes.

The Type field can have four values, 1 to 4. Each of these values corresponds to one of the four BGP message types:

- *Open message*—Establishes connections with peers. Includes fields for the BGP version number, the AS number, hold time, and Router ID.

- *Keepalive message*—This message type is sent periodically between peers to maintain connections and verify paths held by the router sending the keepalive. If the periodic timer is set to a value of 0, no keepalives are sent. The recommended keepalive interval is one-third of the hold time interval. The keepalive message is a 19-byte BGP message header with no data following it.

- *Notification message*—This message type is used to inform the receiving router of errors. This message includes a field for error codes, shown in Table 9-1, which can be used to troubleshoot BGP connections.

- **Update message**—The update message contains all of the information BGP uses to construct a loop-free picture of the internetwork. It has three basic components: Network Layer Reachability Information (NLRI), path attributes, and withdrawn routes. These three elements are described briefly in the following sections.

Table 9-9 Notification Message Error Codes

Error	Code
1 Message Header Error	1 Connection Not Synchronized 2 Bad Message Length 3 Bad Message Type
2 OPEN Message Error	1 Unsupported Version Number 2 Bad Peer AS 3 Bad BGP Identifier 4 Unsupported Optional Parameter 5 Authentication Failure 6 Unacceptable Hold Time
3 UPDATE Message Error	1 Malformed Attribute List 2 Unrecognized Well-Known Attribute 3 Missing Well-Known Attribute 4 Attribute Flags Error 5 Attribute Length Error 6 Invalid Origin Attribute 7 AS Routing Loop 8 Invalid NEXT_HOP Attribute 9 Optional Attribute Error 10 Invalid Network Field 11 Malformed AS_path
4 Hold Timer Expired	0 Unspecific
5 Finite State Machine Error (for errors detected by the FSM)	0 Unspecific
6 Cease (for fatal errors besides the ones already listed)	0 Unspecific

Interactive Media Activity   Drag and Drop: BGP Message Type

After completing this activity, you will be able to identify the properties of BGP message types.

BGP Neighbor Negotiation

The BGP neighbor negotiation process proceeds through various states, or stages, which can be described in terms of a finite-state machine (FSM).

The BGP FSM

Recall that FSM was defined in Chapter 5, "EIGRP." An FSM is a set of possible states that something can go through, what events cause those states, and what events result from those states. Figure 9-12 shows the BGP FSM, including these states and some of the message events that cause them.

Figure 9-68 BGP FSM

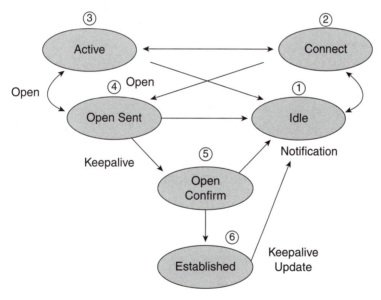

The six states of the BGP FSM are as follows:

- **Idle**—Idle is the first state of a BGP connection. BGP is waiting for a start event. It is normally initiated by an administrator or a network event. At the start event, BGP initializes its resources and resets a connect retry timer. Then it starts listening for a TCP notice that BGP can transition back to Idle from any other state in case of errors. The router starts its own transport connection to other BGP peers and listens for the peer's connection.

- **Connect**—In the Connect state, BGP waits for the TCP connection to be completed. If the TCP connection is successful, the state transitions to OpenSent. If the TCP connection fails, the state transitions to the Active state, and the router tries to connect again. If the connect retry timer expires, the state remains in the Connect state, the timer is reset, and a TCP connection is initiated. In case of any other event, initiated by the system or the administrator, the state returns to Idle.

- **Active**—In the Active state, BGP tries to acquire a peer by initiating a TCP connection. If it is successful, it transitions to OpenSent. If the connect retry timer expires, BGP restarts the connect timer and returns to the Connect state. While active, BGP still listens for a connection that may be initiated from another peer. The state might go back to Idle in case of other events, such as a stop event initiated by the system or the operator. When the ConnectRetry time expires, the router initiates a transport connection to the other peer.

  In general, a neighbor state that switches between Connect and Active indicates that something is wrong and that there are problems with the TCP connection. It could be because of many TCP retransmissions or the incapability of a neighbor to reach its peer's IP address.

- **OpenSent**—In the OpenSent state, BGP waits for an open message from its peer. The open message is checked for correctness. In case of errors, such as an incompatible version number or an unacceptable AS, the system sends an error notification message and goes back to idle. If there are no errors, BGP starts sending keepalive messages and resets the keepalive timer. At this stage, the hold time is negotiated, and the smaller value is taken. If the negotiated hold time is 0, the hold timer and the keepalive timer are not restarted.

  At the OpenSent state, BGP recognizes whether the peer belongs to the same AS or to a different AS. BGP does this by comparing its AS number to its peer's AS number. A same AS is an IBGP peer, and a different AS is an EBGP peer.

  When a TCP disconnect is detected, the state falls back to Active. For any other errors, such as an expiration of the hold timer, BGP sends a notification message with the corresponding error code. Then it returns to the Idle state.

- **OpenConfirm**—While in OpenConfirm state, BGP waits for a keepalive or notification message. If a keepalive message is received, the state goes to the Established state, and the neighbor negotiation is complete. If the system receives an update or keepalive message, it restarts the hold time, assuming that the negotiated hold time is not 0. If a notification message is received, the state falls back to Idle. The system sends periodic keepalive messages at the rate set by the keepalive timer. In the case of any TCP disconnect or in response to any stop event, initiated by the system or the administrator, the state returns to Idle. In response to any other event, the system sends a notification message with an FSM error code and returns to the Idle state.

- **Established**—Established is the final state in the neighbor negotiation. BGP starts exchanging update packets with its peers. If it is nonzero, the hold timer is restarted at the receipt of an update or keepalive message.

  Each update message is checked for errors, such as missing or duplicate attributes. If errors are found, a notification is sent to the peer. Any notification received while in the Established state causes the BGP process to drop the receiving peer back to Idle. If the hold timer expires, a disconnect notification is received from TCP. If a stop event is received, the system returns to Idle.

Interactive Media Activity   Drag and Drop: BGP Neighbor Negotiation

After completing this activity, you will be able to understand the BGP process for establishing neighbor relationships.

Network Layer Reachability Information

Rather than advertise reachable destinations as a network and subnet mask, BGP advertises them using *Network Layer Reachability Information (NLRI)*, which consists of prefixes and prefix lengths. The prefix represents the reachable destination, and the prefix length represents the number of bits set in the subnet mask. For example, 10.1.1.0 255.255.255.0 has a prefix of 10.1.1.0 and a prefix length of 24.

The NLRI consists of multiple instances of the two-tuple *length, prefix*. A tuple is a mathematical term for a set of elements. In this case, *two* refers to the fact that the set has only two elements. Therefore, the NLRI 19, 192.24.160.0 represents the prefix of 192.24.160.0, and the length is a 19-bit mask. In decimal terms, this NLRI refers to the supernet 192.24.160.0 255.255.224.0.

Withdrawn Routes

Withdrawn routes provide a list of routing updates that are no longer reachable and that need to be withdrawn or removed from the BGP routing table. Withdrawn routes have the same format as NLRI.

An update message that has no NLRI or path attribute information is used to advertise only routes to be withdrawn from service, as shown in Figure 9-11.

NOTE

24 bits are set in the subnet mask. Therefore, BGP would advertise it as 10.1.1.0/24.

Path Attributes

Much of the work in configuring BGP focuses on path attributes. Each route has its own set of defined attributes that can include path information, route preference, next hop, and aggregation information. Administrators use these values to enforce routing policy. Based on attribute values, BGP can be configured to filter routing information, prefer certain paths, or otherwise customize its behavior. Many of these attributes and policy configurations are explored later in this chapter, in the section The BGP Routing Process.

Every update message has a variable-length sequence of path attributes in the form of attribute type, attribute length, attribute value.

Because path attributes are used extensively when configuring routing policy, note that not all vendor implementations of BGP recognize the same attributes. The following are the four different attribute types:

- **Well-known mandatory**—An attribute that must exist in the BGP update packet. It must be recognized by all BGP implementations. If a well-known attribute is missing, a notification error is generated. This ensures that all BGP implementations agree on a standard set of attributes. An example of a well-known mandatory attribute is the AS_Path attribute.

- **Well-known discretionary**—An attribute that is recognized by all BGP implementations but that might or might not be sent in the BGP update message. An example of a well-known discretionary attribute is the LOCAL_PREF attribute.

- **Optional transitive**—An attribute that might or might not be recognized by all BGP implementations and, therefore, is optional. Because the attribute is transitive, BGP should accept and advertise the attribute even if it is not recognized.

- **Optional nontransitive**—An attribute that might or might not be recognized by all BGP implementations. Whether or not the receiving BGP router recognizes the attribute, it is nontransitive and is not passed along to other BGP peers.

Each attribute is identified by its type and attribute code. These codes and new attribute type codes that are used in the Internet are registered with the IANA. Table 9-2 lists the attribute codes that are currently defined.

Table 9-10 BGP Attribute Codes and Their Respective Types

Value	Attribute Code	Type
1	ORIGIN	Well-known mandatory
2	AS_PATH	Well-known mandatory
3	NEXT_HOP	Well-known mandatory
4	MULTI_EXIT_DISC	Optional nontransitive
5	LOCAL_PREF	Well-known discretionary

Table 9-10 BGP Attribute Codes and Their Respective Types (Continued)

Value	Attribute Code	Type
6	ATOMIC_AGGREGATE	Well-known discretionary
7	AGGREGATOR	Optional transitive (Cisco)
8	COMMUNITY	Optional transitive (Cisco)
9	ORIGINATOR_ID	Optional nontransitive (Cisco)
10	CLUSTER_LIST	Optional nontransitive (Cisco)
11	DPA	Destination preference (MCI)
12	ADVERTISER	(Baynet)
13	RCID_PATH/CLUSTER_ID	(Baynet)
255	Reserved for development	—

Several of these attributes are discussed later in this chapter. Cisco does not implement attributes 11, 12, and 13 because they do not add functionality. Therefore, they are not covered here.

 Interactive Media Activity   Point and Click: Classify the Attribute

After completing this activity, you will be able to identify the different BGP attribute types.

Configuring BGP

BGP configuration commands appear on the surface to mirror the syntax of familiar IGP commands. Examples of familiar IGP commands are RIP and OSPF. Although the syntax is similar, the function of these commands is significantly different.

Basic BGP Configuration

To begin configuring a BGP process, issue the following familiar command:

```
router(config)#router bgp AS-number
```

Notice that the Cisco IOS software permits only one BGP process to run at a time. Therefore, a router cannot belong to more than one BGP AS.

The **network** command is used with IGPs, such as RIP, to determine the interfaces on which to send and receive updates. This command also indicates which directly connected networks to advertise. However, when configuring BGP, the **network** command does not affect what interfaces BGP runs on. Therefore, configuring just a **network** statement does not establish a

BGP neighbor relationship. This is a major difference between BGP and IGPs. The **network** statement follows this syntax:

```
Router(config-router)#network network-number [mask network-mask]
```

In BGP, the **network** command tells the BGP process which locally learned networks to advertise. The networks can be connected routes, static routes, or routes learned by way of a dynamic routing protocol, such as RIP. These networks must also exist in the routing table of the local router, or they will not be sent out in updates. You can use the **mask** keyword with the **network** command to specify individual subnets. Routes learned by the BGP process are propagated by default but are often filtered by a routing policy.

For a BGP router to establish a neighbor relationship with another BGP router, issue the following configuration command:

```
Router(config-router)#neighbor ip-address remote-as AS-number
```

This command identifies a peer router with which the local router will establish a session. The *ip-address* argument is the IP address of the neighbor interface. The *AS-number* argument determines whether the neighbor router is an EBGP or IBGP neighbor. Figure 9-13 shows a sample BGP configuration. The configuration commands of both routers are shown in Example 9-1.

Figure 9-69 Sample BGP Configuration Scenario

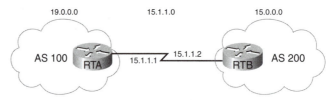

Example 9-1 *BGP Configuration*

```
routerA(config)#router bgp 100
routerA(config-router)#network 19.0.0.0
routerA(config-router)#neighbor 15.1.1.2 remote-as 200

routerB(config)#router bgp 200
routerB(config-router)#network 15.0.0.0
routerB(config-router)#neighbor 15.1.1.1 remote-as 100
```

 Lab 9.11.1 Configuring BGP with Default Routing

In this lab, you configure BGP to exchange routing information with two ISPs.

EBGP and IBGP

When configuring BGP, remember that it supports the following two types of sessions, each with slightly different configuration requirements:

- *EBGP session* —Occurs between routers in two different autonomous systems. These routers are usually adjacent to one another, sharing the same medium and a subnet. See RTA in Figure 9-14.

- *IBGP session* —Occurs between routers in the same AS and is used to coordinate and synchronize routing policy within the AS. Neighbors may be located anywhere in the AS, even several hops away from one another. An IBGP session typically occurs between routers in the same AS in an ISP.

Figure 9-70 EBGP and IBGP

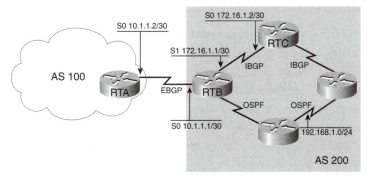

If the *AS-number* configured in the **router bgp** command is identical to the *AS-number* configured in the **neighbor** statement, BGP initiates an internal session. If the field values are different, BGP builds an external session.

EBGP and IBGP Configuration Example

In Figure 9-14, RTB speaks EBGP to RTA, which is a different AS, and it speaks IBGP to RTC, which resides in the same AS.

To start the EBGP process with RTA, use the following commands:

```
RTB(config)#router bgp 200
RTB(config-router)#neighbor 10.1.1.2 remote-as 100
```

Notice that the **remote-as** value of 100 in the **neighbor** command is different from the AS number of 200 specified in the **router bgp** command. Because the two AS numbers are different, BGP starts an EBGP connection with RTA. Communication occurs between autonomous systems.

The commands to configure IBGP are essentially the same as those to configure EBGP, except for the possible addition of the **update-source** *interface* keyword:

```
RTB(config)#router bgp 200
RTB(config-router)#neighbor 172.16.1.2 remote-as 200
RTB(config-router)#neighbor 172.16.1.2 update-source loopback 0
```

The **remote-as** value, 200, is the same as the AS number for the BGP on RTB. Therefore, BGP recognizes that this connection will occur within AS 200. It attempts to establish an IBGP session. In reality, AS 200 is not a remote AS at all; it is the local AS with both routers residing there. For simplicity, the keyword **remote-as** is used when configuring both EBGP and IBGP sessions.

Also notice the second **neighbor** command. It is used to assign an optional parameter to be used when communicating with that neighbor. It is typical to use multiple **neighbor** commands for the same BGP neighbor, each specifying a particular BGP option.

In this example, the option specified is **update-source loopback 0**. If multiple pathways to the neighbor exist, the router can use any IP interface to speak BGP with that neighbor. The **update-source loopback 0** command is used to instruct the router to use interface loopback 0 for TCP connections. This command is typically used in all IBGP configurations. Without this command, BGP routers can use only the closest IP interface to the peer. The capability to use any operational interface provides BGP with robustness in case the link to the closet interface fails. Because EBGP sessions are typically point-to-point, there is no need to use this command with EBGP.

Returning to the sample configuration, assume that the following route appears in the table for RTB:

```
O 192.168.1.0/24 [110/74] via 10.2.2.1, 00:31:34, Serial2
```

RTB learns this route by way of an IGP by using OSPF. AS 200 uses OSPF internally to exchange route information. RTB can advertise this network by way of BGP. Redistributing OSPF into BGP works. However, using the following BGP **network** command does the same thing:

```
RTB(config-router)#network 172.16.1.0 mask 255.255.255.252
RTB(config-router)#network 10.1.1.0 mask 255.255.255.252
RTB(config-router)#network 192.168.1.0
```

The first two **network** commands include the **mask** keyword, so only a particular subnet is specified. The third **network** command causes BGP to advertise the OSPF route without redistribution. Remember that the BGP **network** command works differently than the IGP **network** command.

 Lab 9.11.2   Configuring BGP with NAT

In this lab, you configure both IBGP and EBGP. You configure NAT with the S0/0 link to the ISP using the public IP address range of 66.122.33.96/27. The public network range is then advertised via BGP.

EBGP Multihop

These sample configurations have shown you how to configure EBGP and IBGP. However, what is the difference between the configuration types? Figure 9-15 shows some of the important characteristics of these BGP session types.

Figure 9-71 EBGP Multihop

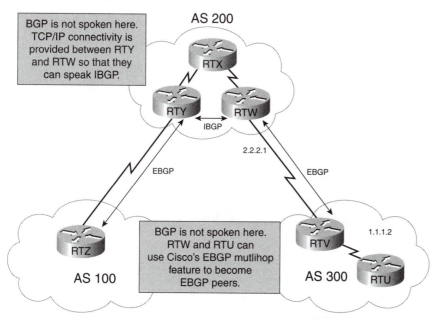

RTZ and RTY have established an EBGP session. EBGP peers are normally directly connected, but there are certain exceptions to this requirement. In contrast, IBGP peers merely require TCP/IP connectivity within the same AS. As long as RTY can communicate with RTW using TCP, both routers can establish an IBGP session. If needed, an IGP such as OSPF can provide IBGP peers with routes to each other.

In a typical configuration, an IBGP router maintains IBGP sessions with all other IBGP routers in the AS, forming a logical full mesh. This is necessary because IBGP routers do not advertise routes learned by way of IBGP to other IBGP peers to prevent routing loops. In other words, if the IBGP routers are to exchange BGP routes with each other, configure a full mesh. An alternative to this approach is to configure a route reflector. Lab 9.11.4b configures an IBGP router as a route reflector. You can find additional information on route reflectors on the Cisco.com.

As noted, EBGP neighbors must be directly connected to establish an EBGP session. However, look again at RTW and RTU in Figure 9-15. These routers can maintain an EBGP session even though a non-BGP router, RTV, separates them. In this situation, EBGP is running across a non-BGP router using a configurable option called EBGP multihop. EBGP multihop is a Cisco IOS software option that allows RTW and RTU to be logically connected in an EBGP session. This is despite the fact that RTV does not support BGP. You configure the EBGP multihop option on each peer with the following command:

```
Router(config-router)#neighbor ip-address ebgp-multihop [hops]
```

This command lets you specify how many hops, up to 255, separate the EBGP peers. The commands shown in Example 9-2 can be applied to the routers in this example.

Example 9-2 *EBGP Multihop Configuration*

```
RTW(config)#router bgp 200
RTW(config-router)#neighbor 1.1.1.2 remote-as 300
RTW(config-router)#neighbor 1.1.1.2 ebgp-multihop 2


RTU(config)#router bgp 300
RTU(config-router)#neighbor 2.2.2.1 remote-as 200
RTU(config-router)#neighbor 2.2.2.1 ebgp-multihop 2
```

In general, EBGP multihop is designed to allow the development of economical AS edge router solutions. A single router with sufficient RAM and CPU power to support BGP is used to handle the BGP routing needs. This router does not have to be an expensive modular, chassis-based system. EBGP multihop allows edge routers to provide sufficient WAN interfaces for the autonomous system's connectivity needs.

Clearing the BGP Table

When configuring BGP, changes made to an existing configuration might not appear immediately. To force BGP to clear its table and reset BGP sessions, use the **clear ip bgp** * command:

```
Router#clear ip bgp *
```

The asterisk (*) is a wildcard that matches all table entries. Therefore, all BGP routes are lost while the neighbor relationships are reset. This is expedient and very useful in a lab situation, but you should be careful when issuing this command on a production router. On an Internet backbone router, it might be more appropriate to use the following command with a specific IP address:

```
Router#clear ip bgp 10.0.0.0
```

The specific IP address must be the address of a BGP peer, not an address in the routing table. By specifying a particular network to clear, you prevent all BGP information from being temporarily lost.

Peering

Any two routers that have formed a TCP connection to exchange BGP routing information are called *peers* or *neighbors*.

Figure 9-16 shows the different types of BGP peering sessions you will encounter. An IBGP peering session is formed within AS 3, between RTA's loopback address and RTF's physical address. An EBGP session is also formed between AS 3 and AS 1 by using the two directly connected IP addresses of RTA and RTC. Another EBGP session is formed between RTF in AS 3 and RTD in AS 2, using IP addresses that are not on the same segment (multihop).

Figure 9-72 Building Peering Sessions

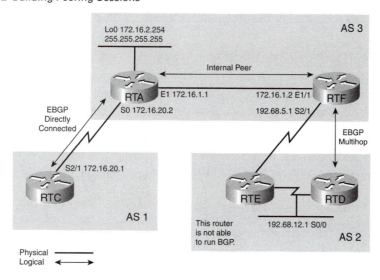

It is important to remember that the BGP peers never become established unless IP connectivity exists between them. In this example, OSPF is used to establish the required internal connectivity between RTD and RTE.

In the RTF configuration shown in Example 9-3, the **ebgp-multihop 2** command is used as part of the neighbor configuration. This indicates that the exterior BGP peer is not directly connected and can be reached at a maximum of two hops away. Remember that EBGP multihop is applicable only with EBGP, not with IBGP.

Example 9-3 *RTF Configuration*

```
ip subnet-zero
interface Ethernet1/1
ip address 172.16.1.2 255.255.255.0
interface Serila2/1
ip address 192.68.5.1
router ospf 10
network 172.16.0.0 0.0.255.255 area 0
network 192.68.0.0 0.0.255.255 area 0
router bgp 3
no synchronization
neighbor 172.16.2.254 remote-as 3
neighbor 192.68.12.1 remote-as 2
neighbor 192.68.12.1 ebgp-multihop 2
no auto-summary
ip classless
```

In Example 9-4, the **show ip bgp neighbor** command shows you how the peer connection looks after the neighbors are in an Established state. RTF sees neighbor 172.16.2.254 as an internal neighbor that belongs to AS3. The neighbor connection is running BGPv4 with a table version of 2. The table version changes every time the BGP table is updated.

The other RTF neighbor, 192.68.12.1, is also in an Established state. This is an external neighbor that belongs to AS2. Notice that the display indicates that this neighbor is two hops away because it was configured using the **ebgp-multihop** command.

Example 9-4 *RTF* **show ip bgp neighbor** *Output*

```
BGP neighbor is 172.16.2.254 remote AS 3, internal link
  BGP version 4, remote router ID 172.16.2.254
  BGP state = Established, up for 19:24:07
  Last read 00:00:06, hold time is 180, keepalive interval is 60 seconds
  Neighbor capabilities:
    Route refresh:advertised and received(new)
```

Example 9-4 *RTF* **show ip bgp neighbor** *Output (Continued)*

```
   Address family IPv4 Unicast:advertised and received
   Graceful Restart Capabilty:advertised and received
     Remote Restart timer is 120 seconds
     Address families preserved by peer:
       IPv4 Unicast
  Received 4231 messages, 0 notifications, 0 in queue
  Sent 4167 messages, 0 notifications, 0 in queue
  Default minimum time between advertisement runs is 5 seconds

 For address family:IPv4 Unicast
  BGP table version 159559, neighbor version 159559
  Index 90, Offset 11, Mask 0x4
  Route refresh request:received 0, sent 0
  10031 accepted prefixes consume 441364 bytes
  Prefix advertised 29403, suppressed 0, withdrawn 9801
  Number of NLRIs in the update sent:max 242, min 0

  Connections established 2; dropped 1
  Last reset 19:26:54, due to NSF peer closed the session
 Connection state is ESTAB, I/O status:1, unread input bytes:0
 Local host: 192.68.5.1, Local port: 11016
 Foreign host: 192.68.12.1, Foreign port: 179
```

Lab 9.11.4d   BGP Peer Groups

In this lab, you use BGP peer groups to simplify the configuration tasks.

BGP Continuity Inside an AS

BGP does not advertise routes learned by way of IBGP peers to other IBGP peers. If it did, BGP routing inside the AS would present a dangerous potential for routing loops. For IBGP routers to learn about all BGP routes inside the AS, they must connect to every other IBGP router in a full IBGP mesh. This full mesh needs to be only logical, not physical. In other words, as long as the IBGP peers can connect to each other using TCP/IP, a logical full mesh can be created even if the routers are not directly connected.

Figure 9-17 illustrates one of the common mistakes that administrators make when setting BGP routing within an AS. This ISP network has three points of presence (POPs)—San Jose,

San Francisco, and Los Angeles. Each POP has multiple non-BGP routers and a BGP border router running EBGP with other autonomous systems. The administrator has set up an IBGP connection between the San Jose border router and the San Francisco border router. Another IBGP connection has been set up between the San Francisco border router and the Los Angeles border router. In this configuration, EBGP routes learned by way of San Jose are given to San Francisco. EBGP routes learned by way of San Francisco are given to San Jose and Los Angeles. Last, EBGP routes learned by way of Los Angeles are given to San Francisco.

Figure 9-73 BGP Continuity Inside an AS

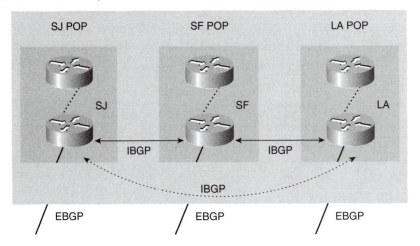

However, routing in this scenario is incomplete. EBGP routes learned by way of San Jose are not given to Los Angeles, and EBGP routes learned by way of Los Angeles are not given to San Jose. This is because the San Francisco router does not advertise IBGP routes between San Jose and Los Angeles. What is needed is an additional IBGP connection between San Jose and Los Angeles. This connection is shown as a dotted line in Figure 9-17.

Monitoring BGP Operation

This section covers some of the details of monitoring and verifying BGP operation.

Verifying BGP Operation

You verify BGP operation by using the key **show** commands listed in Table 9-3.

Table 9-11 Key BGP **show** Commands

Command	Description
show ip bgp	Displays entries in the BGP routing table. You can specify a network to get more detailed information about a particular prefix. Use the **subnets** keyword to get information about a particular prefix and all of its subnets.
show ip bgp summary	Displays a summary of all BGP connections.
show ip bgp neighbors	Displays detailed information for each BGP.
show ip bgp paths	Displays all of the BGP paths in the database.

If the router has not installed the BGP routes you expected, use the **show ip bgp** command, as shown in Example 9-5, to verify that BGP has learned these routes on RTB in Figure 9-18.

Figure 9-74 Sample Topology

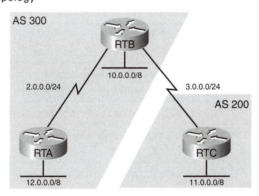

Example 9-5 **show ip bgp** *on Router-B*

```
BGP table version is 5, local router ID is 10.0.0.1
Status codes: s suppressed, d damped, h history, * valid, > best, i - internal
Origin codes: i - IGP, e - EGP, ? - incomplete

   Network          Next Hop          Metric LocPrf Weight Path
*> 10.0.0.0          0.0.0.0                0         32768  i
*  11.0.0.0          3.0.0.2                0             0  200 i
*  12.0.0.0          2.0.0.2                0             0  i
```

Notice that this command's output includes the BGP table version number, which increments each time the local router receives changed route information. The AS_Path, among other key attributes, is also included in this table. Routes that are considered the best are denoted by the > character and are installed in the router IP routing table.

An expected BGP route might not appear in the BGP table. If this happens, use the **show ip bgp neighbors** command to verify that the router has established a BGP connection with its neighbors. The most important information output of this command is the BGP state that exists between the neighbors. Anything other than "Established" indicates that the peers are not fully communicating.

The **show ip bgp neighbors** [*neighbor-address*] [*received-routes* | *routes* | *advertised-routes* | {*paths regexp*} | *dampened-routes*] [*received prefix-filter*] command supports a number of optional parameters and syntax, as shown in Table 9-4.

Table 9-12 show ip bgp neighbors Command Parameters

Parameter	Description
neighbor-address	Specifies the address of the neighbor whose routes have been learned. If this argument is omitted, all neighbors are displayed.
received-routes	Displays all received routes, including both accepted and rejected, from the specified neighbor.
routes	Displays all received and accepted routes. This is a subnet of the **received-routes** keyword output.
advertised-routes	Displays all the routes advertised to the neighbor.
paths regexp	Specifies a regular expression that is used to match the paths received.
dampened-routes	Displays the dampened routes to the neighbor at the IP address specified.
received prefix-filter	Displays the configured prefix list filter for the specified IP address.

The BGP Routing Process

This section describes the process that BGP uses to make routing decisions. Routes are exchanged between BGP peers by way of update messages. BGP routers receive the update messages, perform some policies or filters on the updates, and then pass the routes on to other BGP peers.

An Overview of the BGP Routing Process

The Cisco implementation of BGP keeps track of all BGP updates in a BGP table separate from the IP routing table. In case multiple routes to the same destination exist, BGP does not flood its peers with all of those routes. Instead, BGP picks only the best route and sends it to the peers. In addition to passing along routes from peers, a BGP router may originate routing updates to advertise networks that belong to its own AS. Valid local routes originated in the system and the best routes learned from BGP peers are then installed in the IP routing table. The IP routing table is used for the final routing decision.

The following sections detail the BGP routing process, implementing BGP routing policy, controlling BGP routing with attributes, and handling the BGP decision process.

The BGP Routing Process Model

To model the BGP process, imagine each BGP speaker having different pools of routes and different policy engines applied to the routes. This model is shown in Figure 9-19.

Figure 9-75 Route Exchange

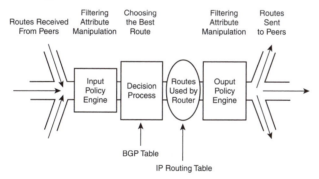

The model involves the following components:

- **Routes received from peers**—BGP receives routes from external or internal peers. Depending on what is configured in the input policy engines, some or all of these routes will make it into the router BGP table.
- **Input policy engine**—This engine handles route filtering and manipulation of attributes. Filtering is done based on parameters, such as the IP prefix, the AS path, and attribute information.

  The input policy engine manipulates the path attributes and influences BGP's decision process. This affects what routes it uses to reach a certain destination. For example, the policy chosen filters a certain network coming from a peer, it is an indication to BGP that it should not reach that network by way of that peer. A certain route can be given a better local preference than some other path to the same destination. This indicates that BGP should prefer this route instead of the other available routes.

■ **The decision process**—BGP goes through a decision process to decide which route or routes it wants to use to reach a certain destination. The decision process is based on the routes that made it into the router after the input policy engine was applied. This process is performed on the routes in the BGP routing table. The decision process looks at all of the available routes for the same destination, compares the different attributes associated with each route, and chooses one best route. This decision process is discussed in the section "The BGP Decision Process."

■ **Routes used by the router**—The best routes, as identified by the decision process, are candidates to be advertised to other peers. These routes are also presented to the routing engine to be placed in the IP routing table. Not all routes presented to the routing engine are placed in the routing table. This is because multiple protocols might present the same prefix for installation, and the router must choose from among them based on administrative distance. In addition to routes passed on from other peers, the router, if configured to do so, originates updates about the networks inside its own AS. This is how an AS injects its routes into the outside world.

■ **Output policy engine**—This is the same engine as the input policy engine, applied on the output side. Routes used by the router (the best routes), in addition to routes that the router generates locally, are given to this engine for processing. The engine might apply filters and might change some of the attributes, such as AS_Path or metric, before sending the update.

The output policy engine also differentiates between internal and external peers. For example, routes learned from internal peers cannot be passed on to external peers.

■ **Routes advertised to peers**—The routes advertised to peers are routes that made it through the output engine. They are advertised to the BGP peers, internal or external.

Implementing BGP Routing Policy

Input and output policies generally are defined using route maps. Route maps are used with BGP to control and modify routing information. Route maps define how the routes are redistributed between routing domains. Recall from Chapter 8, "Route Optimization," that the **route-map** command has the following syntax:

```
Router(config)#route-map map-tag [permit | deny] [sequence-number]
```

map-tag is a name that identifies the route map. *sequence-number* indicates the position that an instance of the route map is to have in relation to other instances of the same route map. Instances are ordered sequentially, starting with the number 10 by default.

For example, the **route-map** command might be used as follows to define a route map named MYMAP:

```
route-map MYMAP permit 10
! First set of conditions goes here.
route-map MYMAP permit 20
! Second set of conditions goes here.
```

When BGP applies MYMAP to routing updates, it applies the lowest instance first—in this case, instance 10. If the first set of conditions is not met, the second instance is applied, and so on, until either a set of conditions has been met or there are no more sets of conditions to apply. If the update does not match in any instance, the update is not redistributed or controlled.

You set the condition portion of a route map using the **match** and **set** commands. The **match** command specifies what criteria must be matched. The **set** command specifies an action that is to be taken if the routing update meets the conditions defined by the **match** command.

Example 9-6 shows the commands needed to create a simple route map. Access list 1 is used in the configuration as a way to specify routes.

Example 9-6 *Configuring a Simple Route Map*

```
RTA(config)#router-map MYMAP permit 10
RTA(config-route-map)#match ip address 1
RTA(config-route-map)#set metric 5
RTA(config-route-map)#exit
RTA(config)#access-list 1 permit 1.1.1.0 0.0.0.255
```

Recall that there are two types of access lists—standard and extended. The main difference is that a standard access list is applied to the source IP address, whereas an extended access list is normally applied to a packet's source and destination. However, when used to filter routes within BGP, the first address or wildcard bit set given in an extended access list applies to the prefix. The second address or wildcard bit set applies to the subnet mask of the advertised route.

Access list 1 identifies all routes of the form 1.1.1.*x*. A routing update of the form 1.1.1.*x* matches the access list and is propagated with a metric set to 5. This is because of the **permit** keyword in the access list.

A route map can be applied on the incoming BGP update using the keyword **in** or on the outgoing BGP update using the keyword **out**. Example 9-7 shows the commands needed to apply the route map MYMAP on the outgoing updates toward BGP neighbor 172.16.20.2.

Example 9-7 *Applying a Route Map to a BGP Neighbor*

```
RTA(config)#route bgp 100
RTA(config-route)#neighbor 172.16.20.2 remote-as 300
RTA(config-route)#neighbor 172.16.20.2 route-map MYMAP out
```

BGP Attributes

Traffic inside and outside an AS always flows according to the road map laid out by routes. If the routes are altered, the traffic behavior is affected. The following are some of the questions organizations and service providers ask about controlling routes:

- How can the private networks be prevented from being advertised?
- How can routing updates that come from a particular neighbor be filtered?
- How can I specify to use this link or this provider, rather than another one?

Controlling BGP Routing with Attributes

Through the use of attributes, BGP provides the answers to all of these questions and more. A BGP speaker can receive updates from multiple autonomous systems that describe different paths to the same destination. It must then choose the single best path for reaching that destination. After it is chosen, BGP propagates the best path to its neighbors. The decision is based on the value of attributes, such as Next Hop or Local Preference, that the update contains, as well as other configurable BGP factors. The following sections provide an overview of these key attributes that BGP uses in the decision-making process:

- Next Hop
- AS_Path
- Atomic Aggregate
- Aggregator
- Local Preference
- Weight
- Multiple Exit Discriminator (MED)
- Origin

The Next Hop Attribute

The Next Hop attribute is a well-known mandatory attribute, type code 3. In terms of an IGP, such as RIP, the next hop to reach a route is the IP address of the router that has announced the route. The next-hop concept with BGP is more complex and takes one of the following forms:

- For EBGP sessions, the next hop is the IP address of the neighbor that announced the route.

- For IBGP sessions, where routes originate inside the AS, the next hop is the IP address of the neighbor that announces the route. For routes injected into the AS by way of EBGP, the next hop learned from EBGP is carried unaltered into IBGP. The next hop is the IP address of the EBGP neighbor from which the route was learned.

- When the route is advertised on a multiaccess medium, such as Ethernet or Frame Relay, the next hop is usually the IP address of the router's interface. This is the interface connected to the medium that originated the route.

Figure 9-20 illustrates the BGP Next Hop attribute. RTC is running an EBGP session with router RTZ and an IBGP session with router RTA. RTC is learning route 128.213.1.0/24 from RTZ. In turn, RTC is injecting the local route 128.212.1.0/24 into BGP.

Figure 9-76 Next Hop Attribute

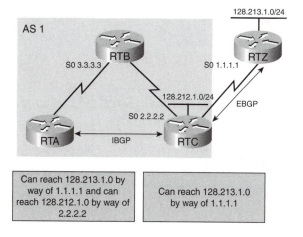

RTA learns about route 128.212.1.0/24 by way of 2.2.2.2, the IP address of the IBGP peer announcing the route. Therefore, according to the definition, 2.2.2.2 is the next hop for RTA to reach 128.212.1.0/24. Similarly, RTC sees 128.213.1.0/24 coming from RTZ by way of next hop 1.1.1.1. When it passes this route update to RTA by way of IBGP, RTC includes the next-hop information, unaltered. Therefore, RTA receives the BGP update about 128.213.1.0/24 with next hop 1.1.1.1. This is an example of the EBGP next hop's being carried into IBGP.

As you can see, the next hop cannot necessarily be reached by way of a direct connection. The next hop for RTA for 128.213.1.0/24 is 1.1.1.1, but reaching it requires a pathway through 3.3.3.3. Therefore, the next-hop behavior mandates a recursive IP routing table lookup for a router to know where to send the packet. To reach the next hop 1.1.1.1, RTA consults its IGP routing table to see if and how 1.1.1.1 can be reached. This recursive search continues until the router associates destination 1.1.1.1 with an outgoing interface. The same recursive behavior is performed to reach next hop 2.2.2.2. If a hop cannot be reached by way of an IGP, BGP considers the route inaccessible.

Next-Hop Behavior on Multiaccess Media

Recall that a network link is considered multiaccess if more than two hosts can potentially connect to it. Routers on a multiaccess link share the same IP subnet and can physically access all other connected routers in one hop. Ethernet, Frame Relay, and ATM are examples of multiaccess media.

BGP speakers should always advertise the route's actual source if the source is on the same multiaccess link as the speaker, as shown in Figure 9-21. In other words, RTC advertises a route learned from RTB, and RTC and RTB share a common multiaccess medium. Then when RTC advertises the route, it should specify RTB as the source of the route. If it doesn't, routers on the same medium would have to make an unnecessary hop by way of RTC to get to a router that is sitting in the same segment.

Figure 9-77 Next Hop on Multiaccess Medium

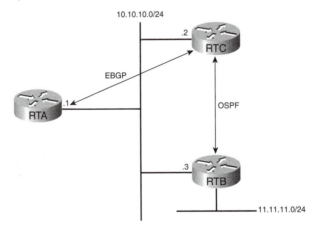

In Figure 9-21, RTA, RTB, and RTC share a common multiaccess medium. RTA and RTC are running EBGP, and RTC and RTB are running OSPF. RTC learns of network 11.11.11.0/24 from RTB by way of OSPF and advertises it to RTA by way of EBGP. Because RTA and RTB are running different routing protocols, it would seem logical that RTA would consider RTC (10.10.10.2) as its next hop to reach 11.11.11.0/24. However, this would not happen. The correct behavior is for RTA to consider RTB, 10.10.10.3, as the next hop because RTB shares the medium with RTC.

When the medium is broadcast, such as Ethernet and FDDI, physical connectivity is assumed, and the next-hop behavior is not an issue. However, when the medium is nonbroadcast, such as Frame Relay and ATM, special care should be taken, as described in the following section.

Next-Hop Behavior on NBMA Networks

On a nonbroadcast multiaccess (NBMA) network, the many-to-many direct interaction between routers is not guaranteed unless virtual circuits (VCs) are configured from each router to all other routers. The primary reason that most organizations implement a hub-and-spoke topology is because of cost considerations. In a hub-and-spoke topology, multiple remote sites have VC connected to one or more routers at a central site. Figure 9-22 shows next-hop behavior in an NBMA environment.

Figure 9-78 Next Hop Over NBMA

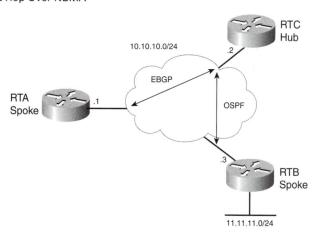

The only difference between the environments illustrated is that the medium in Figure 9-22 is an NBMA Frame Relay cloud. RTC is the hub router, and RTA and RTB are the spokes. Notice that the virtual circuits are laid out between RTC and RTA, and between RTC and RTB, but not between RTA and RTB. This is a partial-mesh topology.

RTA gets a BGP routing update about 11.11.11.0/24 from RTC and tries to use RTB, 10.10.10.3, as the next hop. This is the same behavior as on multiaccess media, as shown in Figure 9-21. Routing fails because no virtual circuit exists between RTA and RTB.

The Cisco IOS software supports a special-case parameter that remedies this situation. The **next-hop-self** keyword forces the router—in this case, RTC—to advertise 11.11.11.0/24 with itself as the next hop, 10.10.10.2. RTA then directs its traffic to RTC to reach destination 11.11.11.0/24. The syntax for this option is as follows:

```
Router(config-router)#neighbor ip-address next-hop-self
```

For RTC, issue the following command:

```
RTC(config-router)#neighbor 10.10.10.1 next-hop-self
```

The AS_Path Attribute

An AS_Path attribute is a well-known mandatory attribute, type code 2. It is the sequence of AS numbers that a route traverses to reach a destination. The AS that originates the route adds its own AS number when sending the route to its external BGP peers. Thereafter, each AS that receives the route and passes it on to other BGP peers prepends its own AS number to the list. Prepending is the act of adding the AS number to the beginning of the list. The final list has all of the AS numbers that a route has traversed. The AS number of the AS that originated the route is at the end of the list. This type of AS_Path list is called an AS_Sequence because all of the AS numbers are ordered sequentially.

BGP uses the AS_Path attribute as part of the routing updates (update packet) to ensure a loop-free topology on the Internet. Each route that gets passed between BGP peers carries a list of all AS numbers that the route has already been through. If the route is advertised to the AS that originated it, that AS sees itself as part of the AS_Path attribute list and does not accept the route. BGP speakers prepend their AS numbers when advertising routing updates to other autonomous systems (external peers). When the route is passed to a BGP speaker within the same AS, the AS_Path information is left intact.

Figure 9-23 illustrates the AS_Path attribute at each instance of the route 172.16.10.0/24, originating in AS 1 and passed to AS 2, AS 3, AS 4, and then back to AS 1. Notice how each AS that passes the route to other external peers adds its own AS number to the beginning of the list. When the route gets back to AS 1, the BGP border router realizes that this route has already been through its AS. The AS number 1 appears in the list, so AS 1 does not accept the route.

Figure 9-79 AS_Path Attribute

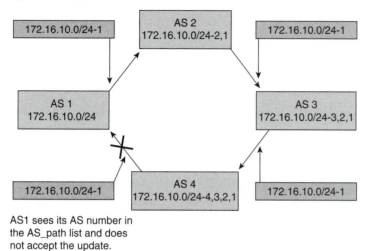

AS1 sees its AS number in
the AS_path list and does
not accept the update.

AS_Path information is one of the attributes that BGP looks at to determine the best route to reach a destination. In comparing two or more different routes, given that all other attributes are identical, a shorter path is always preferred. In case of a tie in AS_Path length, other attributes are used to make the decision.

Lab 9.11.3   Using the AS_PATH Attribute

In this lab, you use BGP commands to prevent private AS numbers from being advertised to the outside world. You also use the AS_PATH attribute to filter BGP routes based on their source AS numbers.

AS_Path and Private AS Numbers

In an effort to conserve AS numbers, customers whose routing policies are an extension of the policies of their provider generally are not assigned a legal or public AS number. Therefore, if a customer is single-homed or multihomed to the same provider, the provider generally requests that the customer use an AS number taken from the private pool: 64,512 to 65,535. As such, all BGP updates that the provider receives from its customer contain private AS numbers.

Private AS numbers cannot be advertised to the Internet because they are not unique. For this reason, Cisco has implemented a feature to strip private AS numbers from the AS_Path list before the routes get propagated to the Internet.

In Figure 9-24, AS1 provides Internet connectivity to its customer AS 65001. Because the customer connects to only this provider and has no plans to connect to an additional provider in the near future, the customer has been allocated a private AS number. Should the customer need connectivity to another provider, a legal AS number must be assigned.

Figure 9-80 AS_Path and Private AS Numbers

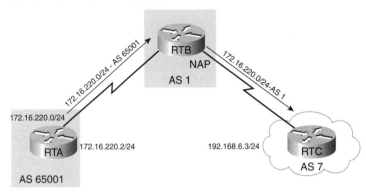

Prefixes originating from AS 65001 have an AS_Path of 65001. Notice the prefix 172.16.220.0/24 as it leaves AS65001. For AS1 to propagate the prefix to the Internet, it would have to strip the private AS number. When the prefix reaches the Internet, it would look like it originated from the provider's AS. Notice how prefix 172.16.220.0/24 reaches the network access point (NAP) with AS_Path 1.

BGP strips private AS numbers only when propagating updates to the external peers. This means that the AS stripping is configured on RTB as part of its neighbor connection to RTC.

Privately numbered autonomous systems should be used only when connected to a single provider. If the AS_Path contains a mixture of private and legal AS numbers, BGP views this as an illegal design. BGP does not strip the private AS numbers from the list, and the update is treated as usual. Only AS_Path lists that contain private AS numbers in the range 64,512 to 65,535 are stripped.

Example 9-8 demonstrates how BGP can be configured to prevent the leakage of private AS numbers into the Internet.

Example 9-8 **remove-private-as** *Keyword*

```
RTB(config)#router bgp 1
RTB(config-router)#neighbor 172.16.220.2 remote-as 65001
RTB(config-router)#neighbor 192.168.6.3 remote-as 7
RTB(config-router)#neighbor 192.168.6.3 remove-private-as
```

Notice how RTB uses the **remove-private-as** keyword in its neighbor connection to AS7.

The Atomic Aggregate Attribute

The Atomic Aggregate attribute is a well-known discretionary attribute, type code 6. It is set to either true or false. If it is true, this attribute alerts BGP routers that multiple destinations have been grouped into a single update. In other words, the BGP router that sent the update had a more specific route to the destination but did not send it. Because this can lead to routing problems, the Atomic Aggregate attribute warns receiving routers that the information they are receiving is not necessarily the most complete route information available. BGP can be manually configured to summarize routes by using the **aggregate-address** command.

Using the **aggregate-address** command with no arguments creates an aggregate entry, a supernet route, in the BGP routing table. This happens as long as the router knows at least one specific BGP route that belongs to that supernet. Therefore, if the router knows just one route, it can claim to know hundreds of others. This feature should be used with caution. The aggregate route is advertised as coming from the AS on the router and has the Atomic Aggregate attribute set to true. This shows that information might be missing. By default, the Atomic Aggregate attribute is set to true, unless the **as-set** keyword is specified.

Using the **as-set** keyword creates an aggregate entry. However, the path advertised for this route is an AS_Set consisting of all elements contained in all paths that are being summarized. Do not use this form of **aggregate-address** when aggregating many paths. This route must be continually withdrawn and updated as autonomous system path reachability information for the summarized route changes.

If the router is to propagate the supernet route only, not any more specific routes, use the **summary-only** keyword. When configured using this keyword, the router sends the supernet route and suppresses the more-specific routes known to BGP.

Example 9-9 shows the commands needed to configure a simple supernet advertisement, which is sent with the Atomic Aggregate attribute set to true.

Example 9-9 *Supernet Advertisement Configuration*

```
RTA(config)#router bgp 300
RTA(config-router)#neighbor 3.3.3.3 remote-as 200
RTA(config-router)#neighbor 2.2.2.2 remote-as 100
RTA(config-router)#network 160.10.0.0
RTA(config-router)#aggregate-address 160.0.0.0 255.0.0.0
```

If RTA is to suppress more-specific routes and update other BGP routers only about supernet 160.0.0.0 /8, issue this command:

```
RTA(config-router)#aggregate-address 160.0.0.0 255.0.0.0 summary-only
```

The Aggregator Attribute

Aggregator is a well-known discretionary attribute, type code 7. When you configure address aggregation, the router can also be configured to include its router ID and local AS number along with the supernet route. This attribute lets ISP administrators determine which BGP router is responsible for a particular instance of aggregation. Tracing a supernet to its original aggregator might be necessary for troubleshooting purposes.

The Local Preference Attribute

Local Preference is a well-known discretionary attribute, type code 5. The Local Preference attribute is a degree of preference given to a route for comparison with other routes to the same destination. Higher Local Preference values are preferred. Local Preference, as its name indicates, is local to the AS and is exchanged between IBGP peers only. Local Preference is not advertised to EBGP peers.

Routers within a multihomed AS may learn that they can reach the same destination network by way of neighbors in two or more different autonomous systems. In effect, there could be two or more exit points from the local AS to any given destination. Use the Local Preference attribute to force the BGP routers to prefer one exit point over another when routing to a particular destination network. Because this attribute is communicated within all BGP routers inside the AS, all BGP routers have a common view of how to exit the AS.

Consider the environment shown in Figure 9-25. Suppose that company ANET has purchased Internet connections from two service providers, XNET and YNET. ANET is connected to YNET by way of a primary T3 link and to XNET by way of a backup T1 link.

Figure 9-81 Local Preference Attribute

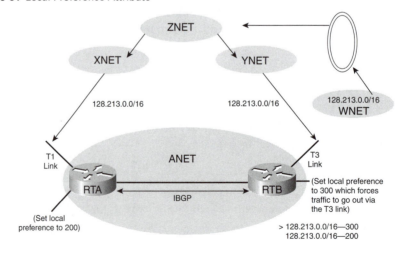

It is important for ANET to decide what path its outbound traffic will take. Of course, the network administrators for ANET prefer to use the T3 link by way of YNET in normal operation because it is a high-speed link. This is where Local Preference starts. RTB can give the routes coming from YNET a Local Preference of 300, and RTA can give the routes coming from XNET a lower value, such as 200. Because both RTA and RTB exchange routing updates by way of IBGP, they both agree that the autonomous system's exit point will be by way of YNET. This happens because of the higher local preference.

In Figure 9-25, ANET learns about route 128.213.0.0/16 by way of XNET and YNET. RTA and RTB agree on using YNET as the exit point for destination 128.213.0.0/16 because of the higher Local Preference value of 300. The Local Preference manipulation discussed in this case affects the traffic going out of the AS and not traffic coming into the AS. Inbound traffic can still come by way of the T1 link.

Manipulating Local Preference

In Figure 9-26, AS 256 receives route updates for network 170.10.0.0 from AS 100 and AS 300. The following are two ways to set the Local Preference attribute on the routers in AS 256:

- Use the **bgp default local-preference** command
- Use a route map to set local preference

Figure 9-82 Local Preference

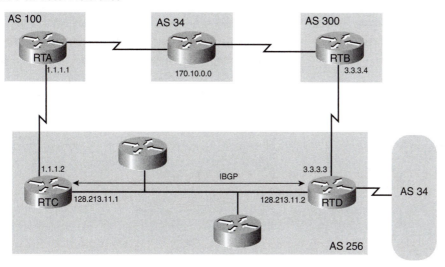

Using the **bgp default local-preference** command, set the Local Preference attribute on RTC and RTD, as shown in Example 9-10.

Example 9-10 bgp default local-preference *Command*

```
RTC(config)#router bgp 256
RTC(config-router)#neighbor 1.1.1.1 remote-as 100
RTC(config-router)#neighbor 128.213.11.2 remote-as 256
RTC(config-router)#bgp default local-preference 150


RTD(config)#router bgp 256
RTD(config-router)#neighbor 3.3.3.4 remote-as 300
RTD(config-router)#neighbor 128.213.11.1 remote-as 256
RTD(config-router)#bgp default local-preference 200
```

The configuration from RTC causes it to set the Local Preference of all updates from AS 100 to 150. The configuration from RTD causes it to set the local preference for all updates from AS 300 to 200. Because local preference is exchanged within the AS, both RTC and RTD determine that updates about network 170.10.0.0 have a higher local preference when they come from AS 300 than when they come from AS 100. As a result, all traffic in AS 256 destined for network 170.10.0.0 is sent to RTD.

As an alternative configuration, use a route map. Route maps provide more flexibility than the **bgp default local-preference** configuration command. When the **bgp default local-preference** command is used on RTD, the Local Preference attribute of all updates received by RTD is set to 200. This includes updates from AS 34. The configuration in Example 9-11 uses a route map to set the Local Preference attribute on RTD specifically for updates about AS 300.

Example 9-11 *Using a Route Map to Control Local Preference*

```
RTD(config)#router bgp 256
RTD(config-router)#neighbor 3.3.3.4 remote-as 300
RTD(config-router)#route-map SETLOCALIN in
RTD(config-router)#neighbor 128.213.11.1 remote-as 256
RTD(config-router)#exit
RTD(config)#ip as-path access-list 7 permit ^300$
RTD(config)#route-map SETLOCALIN permit 10
RTD(config-router-map)#match as-path 7
RTD(config-router-map)#set local-preference 200
```

Notice that this example uses the **ip as-path access-list** command, which matches the regular expression **^300$**. Essentially, this statement matches any routes that include AS 300 in their AS_Path attribute.

With the configuration, the Local Preference attribute of any update coming from AS 300 is set to 200 by instance 10 of the route map, SETLOCALIN. Instance 20 of the route map accepts all other routes.

The Weight Attribute

The Weight attribute is similar to the Local Preference attribute in that it gives higher preference to the route that has a greater weight, as shown in Figure 9-27. The difference is that the Weight attribute is local to the router and is not exchanged between routers. The Weight attribute influences routes coming from different providers to the same router—one router with multiple connections to two or more providers. The Weight attribute has a higher precedence than any other attribute. It is the most important attribute when determining route preference. The Weight attribute is Cisco-proprietary.

Figure 9-83 Weight Attribute

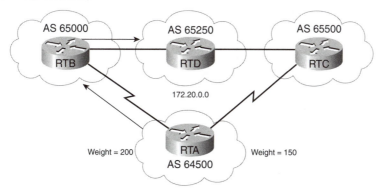

The path to 172.20.0.0 from Router A using AS 64500, 65000, 65250 is preferable because the weight is 200, as compared to the route via AS 64500, 65500, 65250, which has a weight of 150.

The Multiple Exit Discriminator Attribute

The MED attribute is an optional nontransitive attribute, type code 4. MED informs external neighbors about the preferred path into an AS that has multiple entry points. A lower MED is preferred over a higher MED.

Unlike Local Preference, the MED attribute is exchanged between autonomous systems, but a MED attribute that comes into an AS does not leave the AS. When an update enters the AS with a certain MED value, that value is used for decision-making within the AS. When BGP forwards the routing update to another AS, the MED is reset to 0. This is true unless the outgoing MED is set to a specific value.

When the route is originated by the AS itself, the MED value typically follows the route's internal IGP metric. This becomes useful when a customer has multiple connections to the same provider. The IGP metric reflects how close to or far from a certain exit point a network is. A network that is closer to exit point A than to exit point B has a lower IGP metric in the border router connected to A. When the IGP metric translates to MED, traffic coming into the AS can enter from the link that is closer to the destination. This is because a lower MED is preferred for the same destination. Both providers and customers can use this fact to balance the traffic over multiple links between two autonomous systems.

Unless otherwise specified, the router compares MED attributes for paths from external neighbors that are in the same AS. MEDs from different autonomous systems are not comparable because the MED associated with a route usually gives some indication of the AS internal topology. Comparing MEDs from different autonomous systems is like comparing apples and oranges. Still, if there is a reason to do so, the Cisco IOS software offers the **bgp always-compare-med** router command. An AS can use the MED to influence the outbound decision of another AS, as shown in Figure 9-28.

Figure 9-84 Multiple Exit Discriminator Attribute

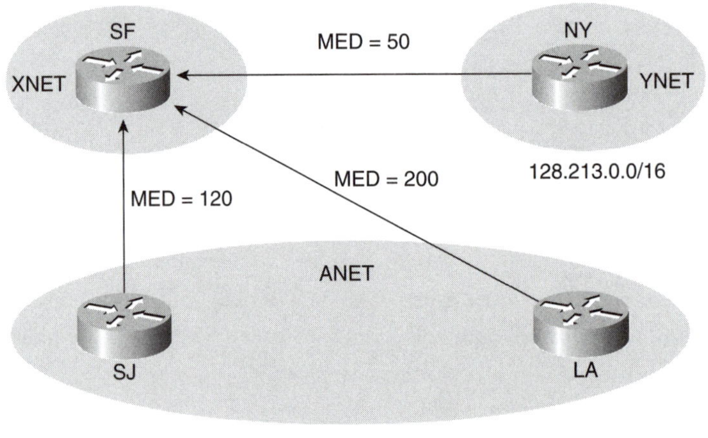

XNET receives routing updates about 128.213.0.0/16 from three different sources—San Jose as metric 120, Los Angeles as metric 200, and New York as metric 50. San Francisco compares the two metric values coming from ANET and prefers the San Jose router because it advertises a lower metric, 120. When the **bgp always-compare-med** command is used on the San Francisco router, it then compares metrics. It compares metric 120 to metric 50 coming from New York and prefers New York to reach 128.213.0.0/16. Notice that San Francisco can influence its decision by using local preference inside XNET to override the metrics coming from outside autonomous systems. Nevertheless, MED is still useful in case XNET prefers to base its BGP decisions on outside factors to simplify router configuration on its end. Customers who connect to the same provider in multiple locations can exchange metrics with their providers to influence the outbound traffic for each router. This leads to better load balancing.

MED Configuration Example

In Figure 9-29, AS 100 receives updates about network 180.10.0.0 from RTB, RTC, and RTD. RTC and RTD are in AS 300, and RTB is in AS 400.

Figure 9-85 MED Configuration Example

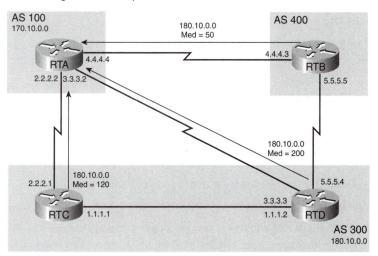

Use a route map to configure the MED attribute on a router, as shown in Example 9-12.

Example 9-12 *MED Attribute Configuration*

```
RTB(config)#route-map setmedout permit 10
RTB(config-route-map)#set metric 50
RTB(config)#router bgp 400
RTB(config-router)#neighbor 4.4.4.4 route-map setmedout out
```

By default, BGP compares only the MED attributes of routes coming from neighbors in the same external AS, such as AS 300 in the example. This means that RTA compares the MED attribute coming from RTC (120) only to the MED attribute coming from RTD (200). Even though the update coming from RTB has the lowest MED value, RTA chooses RTC as the best path for reaching network 180.10.0.0. To force RTA to include updates for network 180.10.0.0 from RTB in the comparison, use the **bgp always-compare-med** router configuration command.

RTA chooses RTB as the best next hop for reaching network 180.10.0.0, assuming that all other attributes are the same. The MED attribute can also be set when configuring the redistribution of routes into BGP. For example, on RTB the static route can be injected into BGP with a MED of 50. The preceding configuration causes RTB to send out updates for 180.10.0.0 with a MED attribute of 50.

Lab 9.11.4a   Configuring IBGP and EBGP Sessions, Local Preference, and MED

In this lab, you configure both IBGP and EBGP.

Lab 9.11.4c   The BGP COMMUNITIES Attribute

In this lab, you use the COMMUNITIES attribute to enforce a routing policy.

The Origin Attribute

The Origin attribute is a well-known mandatory attribute, type code 1, that indicates the routing update's origin. BGP allows the following three types of origins:

- **IGP**—The prefix is internal to the originating AS.
- **EGP**—The prefix was learned by way of some EGP, such as BGP.
- **Incomplete**—The prefix was learned by some other means—probably redistribution.

BGP considers the Origin attribute in its decision-making process to establish a preference ranking among multiple routes. Specifically, BGP prefers the path with the lowest origin type, where IGP is lower than EGP, and EGP is lower than Incomplete.

The BGP Decision Process

BGP bases its decision process on the attribute values. When faced with multiple routes to the same destination, BGP chooses the best route for routing traffic toward the destination. The following process summarizes how BGP chooses the best route:

1. If the next hop is inaccessible, the route is ignored. This is why it is important to have an IGP route to the next hop.

2. The BGP router prefers the path with the greatest weight. Weight is a Cisco-proprietary parameter.

3. If the weights are the same, the BGP router prefers the route with the largest local preference.

4. If the routes have the same local preference, the BGP router prefers the route that was locally originated by this router.

5. If the local preference is the same, the BGP router prefers the route with the shortest AS_Path.

6. If the AS_Path length is the same, the BGP router prefers the route with the lowest origin type. This is when IGP is lower than EGP and EGP is lower than Incomplete.

7. If the origin type is the same, the BGP router prefers the route with the lowest MED.

8. If the routes have the same MED, the BGP router prefers the route in the following manner. Paths containing AS_CONFED_SEQUENCE are local to the confederation and, therefore, are treated as internal paths. No distinction is made between Confederation External and Confederation Internal. BGP confederations are not covered in this book. For more information, consult Cisco's website at http://www.cisco.com/univercd/home/home.htm.

9. If all of the preceding scenarios are identical, the BGP router prefers the route that can be reached by way of the closest IGP neighbor. That means taking the shortest internal path inside the AS to reach the destination by following the shortest path to the BGP next hop. When both paths are external, the path that was received first is preferred.

10. If the internal path is the same, the BGP router ID is a tiebreaker. The BGP router prefers the route coming from the BGP router with the lowest router ID. The router ID is usually the highest IP address on the router or the loopback address.

BGP Route Filtering and Policy Routing

The following sections discuss some of the details of BGP route filtering and policy routing. These topics are covered:

- BGP route filtering
- Using filters to implement routing policy
- Using the **distribute-list** command to filter BGP routes
- The **ip prefix-list** command
- Sample **ip prefix-list** configuration

BGP Route Filtering

Route filtering empowers a BGP speaker to choose what routes to exchange with any of its BGP peers. Route filtering is the cornerstone of policy routing. For example, an AS can identify inbound traffic that it is willing to accept by filtering its outbound advertisements. Conversely, an AS can control what routes its outbound traffic uses by specifying the routes to accept from EBGP neighbors.

Policies that are even more precise can be defined by way of route filters. For example, BGP routes passing through a filter can have their attributes manipulated to affect the best-path decision process.

Both the inbound and outbound filtering concepts can be applied between peers and between routing protocols running on a single router, as shown in Figure 9-30. At the peer level, inbound filtering indicates that the BGP speaker is filtering routing updates coming from other peers. The outbound filtering limits the routing updates advertised from this BGP speaker toward other peers.

Figure 9-86 Inbound and Outbound Filtering

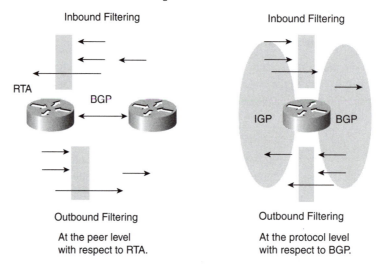

At the protocol level, inbound filtering limits the routing updates being redistributed into a protocol. Outbound filtering limits the routing updates being injected from this protocol. With respect to BGP, for example, inbound filtering limits the updates being redistributed from other protocols into BGP. Outbound filtering limits the updates being redistributed from BGP into an IGP.

The following sections examine the use of filters to implement routing policy and the use of distribute and prefix lists to filter routing updates.

Using Filters to Implement Routing Policy

Two distinct steps are involved in manipulating a route or a set of routes:

1. Identify the network number and subnet mask of the route to which the policies are to be applied. For BGP, this information is the NLRI. Recall that the NLRI consists of a prefix and prefix length pair. Throughout this section, the NLRI is called the prefix.

2. Implement the policies, which can be filtering out prefixes altogether or manipulating the attributes of a prefix to influence the routing decision.

The identification process typically relies on a route map. Prefixes can be selected by their destination network number, the AS from which the prefix originated, the AS_Path, or another specific attribute value. Prefixes are identified using the **match** statement from the route map. After a route map matches a given prefix, the actions specified by the route map are executed, and processing is considered complete. In other words, when a prefix matches, it is not passed through any remaining clauses in the route map.

What actions can the route map take after it has identified a match? The simplest actions are either to permit the route to pass through or to filter it out by denying it. Actions that are more complex adjust a prefix's attributes to influence the routing process in some way.

Notice that the route map can match a prefix based on several criteria, such as network number or AS_Path information. Also, notice that as soon as a route matches, no further comparisons occur. The order in which the matches are configured in the route map is important. If a route map clause that permits all routes is put at the beginning of the list, it overrides all the other policies configured.

Using the distribute-list Command to Filter BGP Routes

To restrict the routing information that the router learns or advertises, you filter routing updates. You apply route filters to or from a particular neighbor by using the **distribute-list** command. See Chapter 8 for more details about this command's syntax. In Figure 9-31, RTD in AS2 originates network 192.68.10.0/24 and sends it to RTF. RTF passes the update to RTA by way of IBGP, which in turn propagates it to AS1. By doing so, AS3 could become a transit AS advertising that it is a path to reach network 192.68.10.0/24.

Figure 9-87 Distribute Lists

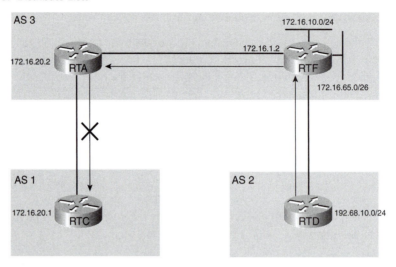

To prevent this situation from happening, configure RTA as shown in Example 9-13.

Example 9-13 *RTA Running Configuration Using the* **distribute-list** *Keyword*

```
RTA#show running-configuration
router bgp 3
no synchronization
neighbor 172.16.1.2 remote-as 3
neighbor 172.16.20.1 remote-as 1
neighbor 172.16.20.1 distribute-list 1 out
no auto-summary
access-list 1 deny 192.68.10.0 0.0.0.255
access-list 1 permit 0.0.0.0 255.255.255.255
```

The **distribute-list** keyword, used as part of a BGP **neighbor** statement, prevents RTA from advertising prefix 192.68.10.0/24 to RTC. The access list is used to identify the prefixes to be filtered, and the **distribute-list** and **out** keywords apply the filter to outgoing updates.

Notice that access list 1 concludes with a **permit 0.0.0.0 255.255.255.255** statement that is the same as a **permit any** statement. Remember that, when you use access lists for filtering, anything that does not match a **permit** statement is denied. Without the **permit 0.0.0.0 255.255.255.255** clause, all updates to RTC would be suppressed.

Configuring BGP **neighbor** statements to include the **distribute-list** keyword is effective for filtering specific routes, but controlling supernets can be more complicated.

Configuring a distribute list relies on creating an access list. If you use a standard access list, you have only limited functionality. RTA connects to multiple subnets in the 172.16.0.0/16 address space. The purpose is to advertise an aggregate address of 172.16.0.0/16, but not the individual subnets themselves. A standard access list would not work, because it permits more than you want. It filters based on the network address only. The following access list would permit not only the 172.16.0.0/16 summary, but also all of the components of that summary:

```
access-list 1 permit 172.16.0.0 0.0.255.255
```

To restrict the update to the 172.16.0.0/16 summary, use an extended access list. An extended access list is usually thought of as matching both source and destination addresses. In the case of a BGP route filter, an extended access list matches the network address first and then the prefix's subnet mask. Both network and mask are paired with their own wildcard bit mask using the following syntax:

```
router(config)#access-list number {permit | deny} network
    network-wildcard mask mask-wildcard
```

To permit the aggregate address, configure an extended access list to match the network address and also the 16-bit prefix mask, as shown in Example 9-14. Using this configuration, RTA does not send a subnet route, such as 172.16.0.0 /17 or 172.16.10.0 /24, in an update to AS1.

Example 9-14 *Access List Example*

```
RTA(config)#router bgp 3
RTA(config-router)#neighbor 172.16.1.2 remote-as 3
RTA(config-router)#neighbor 172.16.20.1 remote-as 1
RTA(config-router)#neighbor 172.16.20.1 distribute-list 101 out
RTA(config-router)#EXIT
RTA(config)#access-list 101 permit ip 172.16.0.0 0.0.0.0 255.255.0.0 0.0.0.0
RTA(config)#access-list 101 deny ip 172.16.0.0 0.0.255.255 255.255.0.0
0.0.255.255
RTA(config)#access-list 101 permit ip any any
```

If using an extended access list to accomplish this type of filtering seems confusing, that is not unusual. Improved user friendliness was one of the factors that motivated Cisco to include the **ip prefix-list** command in Cisco IOS Release 12.0. This command is described in the next section.

Lab 9.11.4b   BGP Route Reflectors and Route Filters

In this lab, you configure IBGP routers to use a router reflector and a simple router filter.

The ip prefix-list Command

You can use prefix lists as an alternative to access lists with many BGP route filtering commands. Using prefix lists rather than access lists has the following advantages:

- Significant performance improvement in loading and route lookup of large lists.
- Support for incremental updates. Filtering by way of extended access lists does not support incremental updates.
- A more user-friendly command-line interface.
- Greater flexibility.

You need to define a prefix list before applying it as a route filter. The Cisco IOS software allows a very flexible configuration procedure in which each statement can be assigned its own sequence numbers.

To define a prefix list, use the **ip prefix-list** *list-name* [**seq** *seq-value*] {**deny** *network/length* | **permit** *network/length*} [**ge** *ge-value*] [**le** *le-value*] command. Table 9-5 describes the parameters that are used with this command.

Table 9-13 ip prefix-list Command Parameters

Parameter	Description
list-name	Specifies the name of a prefix list.
seq	(Optional) Applies the sequence number to the prefix list entry being created or deleted.
seq-value	(Optional) Specifies the sequence for the prefix list entry.
deny	Denies access to matching conditions.
permit	Permits access for matching conditions.
network/length	Gives the network number and length, in bits, of the network mask.
ge	(Optional) Applies the greater-than-or-equal-to value (*ge-value*) to the range specified.
ge-value	(Optional) Specifies the lower limit of values in an allowable range of values—the from portion of the range description.
le	(Optional) Applies the lesser-than-or-equal-to value (*le-value*) to the range specified.
le-value	(Optional) Specifies the upper limit of values in an allowable range of values—the to portion of the range description.

Sample ip prefix-list Configuration

Example 9-15 shows the commands used to create a simple prefix list and apply it during BGP configuration. The commands define a prefix list called ELMO, which is applied to outgoing EBGP updates to 192.168.1.1 using a **neighbor** statement.

Example 9-15 *Sample IP Prefix List Configuration*

```
RTA(config)#ip prefix-list ELMO deny 0.0.0.0/0
RTA(config)#ip prefix-list ELMO permit 172.16.0.0/16
RTA(config)#router bgp 100
RTA(config-router)#neighbor 192.168.1.1 remote-as 200
RTA(config-router)#neighbor 192.168.1.1 prefix-list ELMO out
```

The real power of the **ip prefix-list** command is in its optional parameters. The keywords **ge** and **le** can be used to specify the range of the prefix length to be matched for prefixes that are more specific than the *network/length* value. The prefix length range is assumed to be from *ge-value* to 32 if only the **ge** attribute is specified. The prefix length range is assumed to be from **len** to *le-value* if only the **le** attribute is specified. Notice that a specified *ge-value* and *le-value* must satisfy the following condition:

len < *ge-value* <= *le-value* <= 32

For example, to accept a mask length of up to 24 bits in routes with the prefix 192.0.0.0/8, and to deny more-specific routes, use the following commands:

```
RTA(config)#ip prefix-list GROVER permit 192.0.0.0/8 le 24
RTA(config)#ip prefix-list GROVER deny 192.0.0.0/8 ge 25
```

These commands test to see if a given prefix begins with 192 in the first octet. After that, they are concerned with only how specific the route is by checking the mask's length. Therefore, both 192.168.32.0/19 and 192.168.1.0/24 match the **permit** statement, but 192.168.1.32/27 does not because its mask length is greater than the **ge** value, 25. Any routes with a mask equal to the **ge** value are also denied.

The **le** and **ge** keywords can be used together in the same statement:

```
RTA(config)#ip prefix-list OSCAR permit 10.0.0.0/8 ge 16 le 24
```

This command permits all prefixes in the 10.0.0.0/8 address space that have a mask length from 16 to 24 bits.

Each prefix list entry is assigned a sequence number, either by default or manually by an administrator. By numbering the **prefix-list** statements, new entries can be inserted at any point in the list. This is important because routers test for prefix list matches from lowest sequence number to highest. When a match occurs, the router does not continue through the rest of the prefix list. For efficiency, put the most common matches near the top of the list. The **show ip prefix-list** command always includes the sequence numbers in its output, as shown in Example 9-16.

Example 9-16 **show ip prefix-list** *Command*

```
RTA#show ip prefix-list
ip prefix-list ELMO: 3 entries
   seq 5 deny 0.0.0.0/0
   seq 10 permit 172.16.0.0/16
   seq 15 permit 192.168.0.0/16 le 24
```

Sequence numbers are automatically generated in increments of 5. The first sequence value generated in a prefix list is 5, then 10, then 15, and so on. If you manually specify a value for an entry and then don't specify values for subsequent entries, the assigned sequence values are incremented in units of 5. For example, the first entry in the prefix list has a specified sequence value of 3. Then no more sequence values are specified for the other entries, so the automatically generated numbers are 8, 13, 18, and so on. You manually specify prefix list sequence numbers like this:

```
RTA(config)#ip prefix-list ELMO seq 12 deny 192.168.1.0/24
```

You can manually specify sequence values for prefix list entries in any increment you want. However, if you unwisely specify the sequence values in increments of 1, additional entries cannot be inserted into the prefix list.

To display information about prefix tables, prefix table entries, the policy associated with a node, or specific information about an entry, use the **show ip prefix-list** command.

Finally, when using prefix lists, keep the following rules in mind:

- An empty prefix list permits all prefixes.
- An implicit deny is assumed if a given prefix does not match any entries of a prefix list.
- When multiple entries of a prefix list match a given prefix, the sequence number of a prefix list entry identifies the entry with the lowest sequence number. In this case, the entry with the smallest sequence number is considered the "real" match.

Redundancy, Symmetry, and Load Balancing

Redundancy, symmetry, and load balancing are crucial needs facing anyone in the process of implementing a high-throughput Internet connection. ISPs and their large customers require adequate control over how traffic enters and exits their respective autonomous systems.

Issues with Redundancy, Symmetry, and Load Balancing

Redundancy is achieved by providing multiple alternative paths for the traffic. This occurs by having multiple connections to one or more autonomous systems, as shown in Figure 9-32. Symmetry exists if traffic leaves the AS from a certain exit point and returns through the same point. Load balancing, as you have seen, results in the division of traffic optimally over multiple links. Together, these three requirements can be difficult to meet in a BGP environment, because any provider between a packet's source and destination can affect its path.

Figure 9-88 Redundancy, Symmetry, and Load Balancing

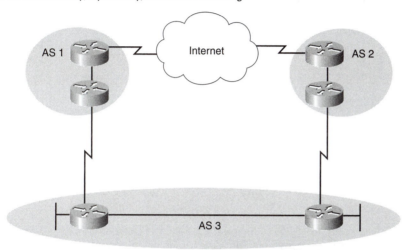

The general design problem of how best to implement redundancy, symmetry, and load balancing is common to every network. The specific solution, however, depends on the needs and unique configuration of an individual network. The following sections examine the general design issues of redundancy, symmetry, and load balancing, as well as configuration models for successful implementation.

Redundancy, Symmetry, and Load Balancing

Although corporations and ISPs prefer uninterrupted connectivity, disruptions still occur for a variety of reasons. Connectivity is not the responsibility of one entity. A connection to the Internet might involve a router, a CSU/DSU, premises wiring, the provider's physical layer, switching equipment, and numerous administrators. Each of these elements influences different parts of the connection. At any time, end-to-end connectivity can be jeopardized by human error, software errors, physical errors, or adverse unforeseen conditions, such as bad weather or power outages.

For these reasons, redundancy is generally desirable, but finding the optimal balance between redundancy and symmetry is crucial. Redundancy and symmetry can be conflicting design goals. The more redundant links a network has, the more unpredictable a packet's entrance and exit points become. For example, a customer might have multiple connections—one to a POP in San Francisco and another to a POP in New York—as shown in Figure 9-33. Therefore, traffic leaving San Francisco might come back through New York. Adding a third connection to a POP in Dallas makes connectivity even more reliable, but it also makes traffic symmetry more challenging. These are the trade-offs that network administrators must consider when implementing routing policies.

Figure 9-89 Redundancy, Symmetry, and Load Balancing

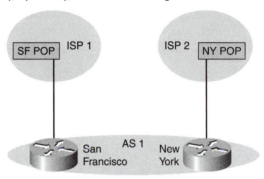

Companies might also feel geographic pressure to implement redundancy. Many contemporary companies are national, international, or multinational in nature, and their AS is a logical entity that spans different physical locations. A corporation with an AS that spans several geographic points can take service from a single provider or from different providers in different regions. In Figure 9-33, the San Francisco office of AS1 connects to the San Francisco POP of ISP1, and the New York office connects to the New York POP of ISP2. In this environment, traffic can take a shorter path to reach a destination by traveling by way of the geographically adjacent POP.

Because redundancy refers to the existence of alternative routes to and from a network, additional routing information needs to be kept in the routing tables. To avoid this extra routing overhead, default routing becomes an alternative practical tool that can be used to provide backup routes in case primary connections fail. The next section discusses the different aspects of default routing and how it can be applied to achieve simple routing scenarios.

Default Routing in BGP Networks

You have seen that default routes minimize the size of a routing table. They can also provide networks with redundancy in the event of failures and connectivity interruptions. BGP, like almost all IGPs, can distribute a default route. To provide redundancy, default information can be received from multiple BGP sources. In a BGP system, the Local Preference attribute can be manipulated on the various default routes. This is so that one default route is identified as primary (the highest Local Preference), and others are kept as backups. If the primary fails, a backup route with the next-highest preference can take its place.

In Figure 9-34, RTA is connected to RTB and is learning about two default routes—one by way of 1.1.1.1 and a second by way of 2.2.2.2. By using the Local Preference attribute, 1.1.1.1 can be given preference and made the primary default route. RTA uses 2.2.2.2 as a default only after 1.1.1.1 fails.

Figure 9-90 Default Routing in BGP Networks

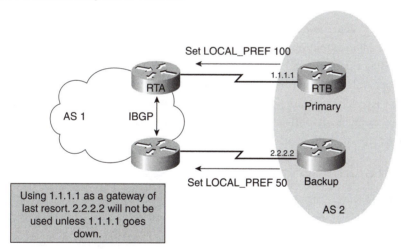

In Figure 9-35, the same behavior can be achieved as long as IBGP is running inside the AS. The Local Preference attribute, which is exchanged between IBGP peers, determines the primary and backup links.

Figure 9-91 Local Preference

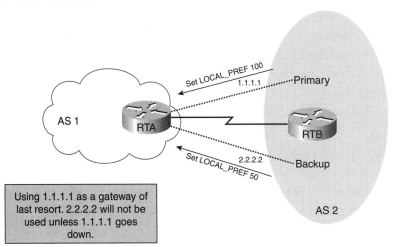

It is important to control default information in BGP because improper configuration can cause serious Internet routing problems. For example, a misconfigured BGP speaker could end up flooding a default route to all of its neighbors and quickly find itself consumed with default routed traffic from surrounding autonomous systems. To protect against misadvertisements, the Cisco IOS software provides a way to target default information at a specific neighbor by using the **default-originate** option with the **neighbor** command, as shown in Example 9-17.

Example 9-17 **default-originate** *Option with the* **neighbor** *Command*

```
RTC(config)#router bgp 3
RTC(config-router)#neighbor 172.16.20.1 remote-as 1
RTC(config-router)#neighbor 172.16.20.1 default-originate
```

NOTE

Both neighbors, 172.16.20.1 and 172.17.1.1, receive a default route from RTC. To propagate network 0.0.0.0, it would have to be a static route or a route learned by way of a dynamic routing protocol. It would also need to exist in the routing table.

If RTC is configured as shown in this configuration, it sends default information only to the specified neighbor. If a BGP router is to be configured to advertise a default to all of its peers, use the **network** command, as shown in Example 9-18.

Example 9-18 **network** *Command*

```
RTC(config)#router bgp 3
RTC(config-router)#neighbor 172.16.20.1 remote-as 1
RTC(config-router)#neighbor 172.17.1.1 remote-as 2
RTC(config-router)#network 0.0.0.0
```

Many network administrators choose to filter dynamically learned default routes to avoid situations in which traffic ends up where it is not supposed to be. Without dynamically learned default routes, a router must be statically configured with default information. Statically configured default routes typically provide more control over routing within an AS.

Symmetry

Symmetry is achieved when traffic leaving the AS from one exit point comes back through the same point. Symmetry always exists if an AS maintains a single connection to outside networks. However, the need for redundancy often results in multihoming an AS. If an AS has many different links to the outside world, traffic tends to flow asymmetrically. An asymmetric traffic flow can result in increased delay and other routing problems. In general, customers and providers want to see their traffic come back by way of the same point or close to the same point where it left the AS.

To promote symmetry, choose a primary path, and configure routing policies that force traffic to flow along this path. A default route with a low administrative distance or a high Local Preference might control the flow of outbound traffic, but inbound traffic can be more complex to manipulate. Through appropriate planning and use of BGP attributes and route filters, an AS can control which paths the outside world finds most desirable.

Load Balancing

Load balancing is the capability to divide data traffic over multiple connections. A BGP speaker might learn two identical EBGP paths for a prefix from a neighboring AS. If this happens, it chooses the path with the lowest route ID as the best path. This best path is installed in the IP routing table. If BGP multipath support is enabled and the EBGP paths are learned from the same neighboring AS, the best path might not be chosen. Instead, multiple paths are installed in the IP routing table. To enable BGP load balancing over equal-cost paths, use the **maximum-paths** command, which has the following syntax:

```
Router(config-router)#maximum-paths number
```

BGP supports a maximum of six paths per destination, but only if they are sourced from the same AS. If the **maximum-paths** option is not enabled, BGP installs only one path to the IP routing table.

Figure 9-36 illustrates how inbound and outbound traffic behaves. The path for outbound traffic to reach Net A depends on where Net A is learned. Because Net A is received from both San Francisco and New York, outbound traffic toward Net A can go by way of San Francisco or New York.

Figure 9-92 Load Balancing

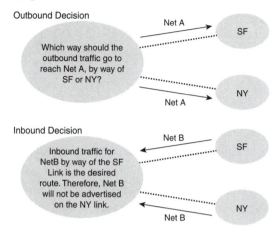

Multihomed Connections

Although running BGP when the AS is multihomed to the same ISP is not necessary, it is generally recommended. In Figure 9-37, the customer wants to configure only default routes toward the provider. The customer does not want any part of the Internet routing table. Although it might seem that a static configuration could work, BGP can offer a more powerful solution.

Figure 9-93 Multihomed Connections with a Single Provider

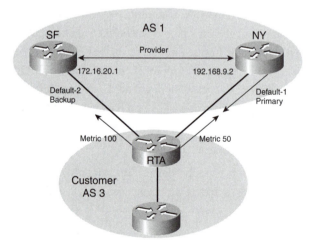

The customer wants to use one link as the primary traffic conduit and the other as a backup in case the primary link goes down. For outbound traffic, the customer could configure two static default routes with different administrative distances. This would create a primary route and a floating static route to be used as a backup. The default with the lower distance would be the primary.

However, the customer might want to learn the default route, or a few aggregate routes, dynamically from the provider using BGP. In this case, the ISP or the customer could filter the advertisements so that only minimum necessary routes are sent. The Local Preference attribute could then be used to prefer one default route over the other.

Assume that in Figure 9-37, the default route to New York is preferred over the default route to San Francisco. In normal operations, the customer would use the New York link as the primary link and the San Francisco link as a backup.

For outbound traffic, load balancing is not an option. This is because all traffic is sent over the primary path, and the secondary is kept as the backup. The absence of load balancing is offset by the fact that the customer's router requires less memory and processing power.

As for inbound traffic, the customer must carefully control updates to the provider. The customer can advertise its networks to the provider by way of BGP. This way, the provider has two paths to reach destinations within the customer's network. The customer can influence the routing decisions made by the ISP by manipulating the metrics advertised to the ISP. The provider directs its traffic toward the customer based on the metric value. In Figure 9-37, the customer advertises routes with a metric of 50 toward New York and a metric of 100 toward San Francisco. Therefore, traffic toward the customer takes the New York route. Example 9-19 shows a customer's boundary router configuration example.

Example 9-19 *Configuring BGP with a Multihomed Connection*

```
RTA(config)#router bgp 3
RTA(config-router)#no auto-summary
RTA(config-router)#neighbor 172.16.20.1 remote-as 1
RTA(config-router)#neighbor 172.16.20.1 route-map BLOCK in
RTA(config-router)#neighbor 172.16.20.1 route-map SETMETRIC1 out
RTA(config-router)#neighbor 192.168.9.2 remote-as 1
RTA(config-router)#neighbor 192.168.9.2 route-map BLOCK in
RTA(config-router)#neighbor 192.168.9.2 route-map SETMETRIC2 out
RTA(config-router)#exit
RTA(config)#route-map SETMETRIC1 permit 10
RTA(config-route-map)#set metric 100
RTA(config-route-map)#route-map SETMETRIC2 permit 10
RTA(config-route-map)#set metric 50
RTA(config-route-map)#route-map BLOCK deny 10
RTA(config-route-map)#exit
RTA(config)#ip route 0.0.0.0 0.0.0.0 172.16.20.1 50
RTA(config)#ip route 0.0.0.0 0.0.0.0 192.168.9.2 40
```

Notice in this configuration that default routing is handled by two static routes pointing toward the ISP routers. The default route by way of the New York link is set with a lower administrative distance and therefore is preferred. The SETMETRIC1 and SETMETRIC2 route maps influence the ISP to send incoming traffic by way of the primary path, New York. Meanwhile, the BLOCK route map prevents any BGP updates from AS 1 from entering AS 3.

What if this customer were multihomed to two different providers? The customer could control inbound traffic the same way—by manipulating advertised metrics using a route map. As for outbound traffic, the customer can either configure static default routes to the two providers or dynamically learn a default route from both providers. For static default routes, the administrative distance can be used to prefer one default route over the other, and one dynamically learned route can be preferred using the Local Preference attribute.

One good method of pointing defaults to both providers is to accept the same network from both providers and then statically configure a default route toward that network. The customer can manipulate this prefix's local preference as it is learned from both providers to choose one link over the other. If one default goes away because of a link failure toward one provider, the other default takes its place.

In Figure 9-38, the customer points its default routes toward the prefix 192.213.0.0/16, which it receives from both providers. The customer's routers apply a route map to incoming updates. The route map sets the Local Preference attribute so that the New York link is preferred. Therefore, the New York link is the primary link, and the San Francisco link is the backup.

Figure 9-94 Multihomed Scenario with Multiple Providers

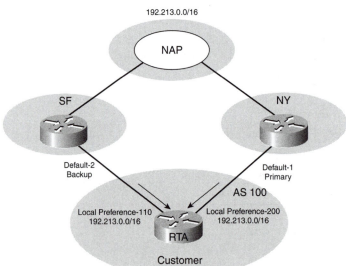

BGP Redistribution

The following sections discuss some of the details of BGP redistribution:

- BGP redistribution overview
- Injecting unwanted or faulty information
- Injecting information statically into BGP
- BGP redistribution configuration example

BGP Redistribution Overview

When dealing with BGP, route stability is an important issue. There is a close relationship between Internet route stability and the method used to inject routes into BGP. Information can be injected into BGP dynamically or statically. Dynamically injected routes come and go from the BGP routing table, depending on the status of the networks they identify. Statically injected routes are constantly maintained by the BGP routing tables, regardless of the status of the networks they identify. Therefore, although a dynamic advertisement ends if the network being advertised no longer exists, a static advertisement does not. Each method has pros and cons, as discussed in this section.

Dynamically injected information can be further divided into purely dynamic redistribution, in which all of the IGP routes are redistributed into BGP using the **redistribute** command. Dynamically injected information can be further divided into semidynamic redistribution, in which only certain IGP routes are to be injected into BGP using the BGP **network** command. This distinction reflects both the level of user intervention and the level of control in defining the routes to be advertised.

Information is injected dynamically into BGP by enabling all of the IGP routes of RIP, OSPF, EIGRP, and so on to be redistributed into BGP. Dynamic redistribution offers ease of configuration. All internal IGP routes dynamically flow into BGP, regardless of the protocols being used.

The semidynamic method of injecting information into BGP is to specify a subset of IGP networks. This is to be advertised by individually listing them for injection into BGP by using the **network** command. This method is more selective than a completely dynamic method. You can control which IGP-learned routes BGP advertises. Unfortunately, a **network** command is necessary for each route prefix, so when you're dealing with a large number of prefixes, maintaining semidynamic configurations is impractical. In fact, the Cisco IOS software sets the limit to 200 **network** statements. Ultimately, a semidynamic configuration provides greater administrative control but dramatically increases administrative overhead.

BGP assumes that prefixes specified by the **network** command exist in an IGP domain. This is verified by checking for them in the routing table. If an IGP has not learned about a local route, BGP does not advertise it. Of course, the **no synchronization** command can be used to disable this verification. However, in doing so, there is a risk that a router will advertise networks it cannot reach.

Injecting Unwanted or Faulty Information

Injecting routes into BGP by way of the **network** command might not always be practical or even possible. Injecting routes by way of redistribution can result in polluting other autonomous systems with unwelcome, incorrect, or otherwise undesirable information. Redistributing the entire IGP table into BGP could result in private addresses, or illegal addresses, being advertised outside the AS. In some cases, routes with inappropriate prefix lengths could make it upstream to the provider, where they are not needed. For example, host routes are generally greeted with disdain by annoyed systems administrators.

Mutual redistribution between IGP and BGP can also result in the propagation of flawed routing information. In this case, a BGP route that was injected from the outside could be sent back into BGP by way of the IGP. This happens as if the route originated within the AS. Figure 9-39 illustrates the danger of mutual redistribution between protocols.

Figure 9-95 Practical Design Example

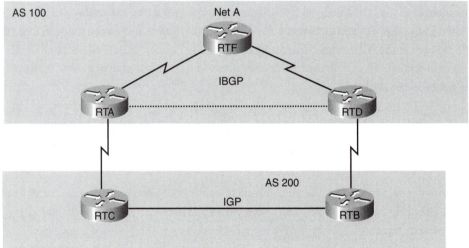

In Figure 9-39, AS 100 is the source of NetA and sends this information by way of BGP to AS 200. The border router RTC injects that information into the IGP, and RTB learns about it. RTB is configured to redistribute the IGP information into BGP. NetA ends up being advertised by way of BGP back to the Internet as if it originated from AS 200. This is very misleading to autonomous systems connected to the Internet, because NetA now has two sources rather than one source—AS 100 and AS 200.

To remedy these situations, special filtering should be put on the border routers to specify what particular networks should be injected from the IGP into BGP. For protocols that differentiate between internal and external routes, such as OSPF, configure the IGP to ensure that it will redistribute only internal routes into BGP. In the Cisco implementation, external OSPF routes are automatically blocked from being redistributed into BGP. You can override this behavior. Certain protocols might not distinguish between internal and external routes, such as RIP or IGRP. For these types of protocols, special route tagging should be performed to differentiate between external routes and internal routes.

Injecting Information Statically into BGP

Injecting information statically into BGP has proven to be the most effective means of ensuring route stability. Of course, this method also has drawbacks. To statically inject information into BGP, the IGP routes, or aggregates, that need to be advertised to other peers are manually defined as static routes. This ensures that these routes never disappear from the IP routing table and, hence, are always advertised. Administrators are often uncomfortable advertising routes to networks that might be down or unreachable. Whether it is appropriate to inject this information statically depends on the particular situation.

For example, if the route is advertised to the Internet from a single point, advertising a route that is actually down is debatable. Hosts trying to access that destination will fail, regardless of whether the route is advertised. On the other hand, if a route is advertised to the Internet from multiple points, advertising the route statically at all times might end up creating a black hole for traffic. If problems inside the AS do not allow the border router to reach the network it is advertising, traffic to that destination is dropped. This happens even though it could have been reached from some other entry point.

BGP Redistribution Configuration Example

As with IGP routes, all known static routes can be injected into BGP using the **redistribute** command. A subset of static routes can be injected using the BGP **network** command. The **network** command provides greater control while increasing the administrative burden. Figure 9-40 demonstrates how routing information can be injected dynamically into BGP. Issue the commands shown in Example 9-20 to configure RTB in Figure 9-40 to redistribute OSPF learned routes into BGP dynamically.

Figure 9-96 Injecting OSPF Routes Into BGP Dynamically

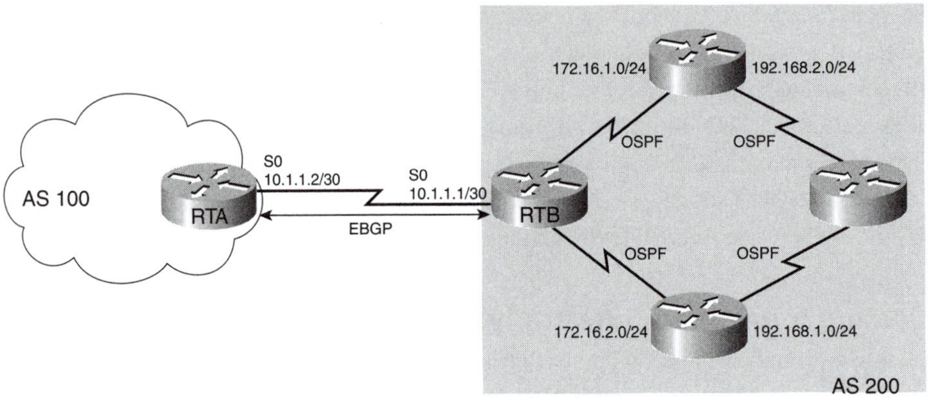

Example 9-20 *BGP Redistribution Configuration Example*

```
RTB(config)#router bgp 200
RTB(config-router)#neighbor 10.1.1.2 remote-as 100
RTB(config-router)#neighbor 10.1.1.2 route-map BLOCK-BAD-ADDRESSES out
RTB(config-router)#redistribute ospf 1 match internal metric 50
RTB(config-router)#redistribute static
```

For insurance, configure a route map that matches any private addresses that are not to be advertised outside the AS. This route map, appropriately called BLOCK-BAD-ADDRESSES, is applied to outbound BGP updates. Also, BGP has been configured to redistribute only internal OSPF routes and assign them a metric of 50. The **redistribute static** command dynamically populates BGP with any static routes RTB happens to be configured with. Alternatively, configure RTB to inject internal routes semidynamically by using the BGP **network** command, as shown in Example 9-21.

Example 9-21 *Injecting Internal Routes Semidynamically*

```
RTB(config)#router bgp 200
RTB(config-router)#neighbor 10.1.1.2 remote-as 100
RTB(config-router)#neighbor 10.1.1.2 route-map BLOCK-BAD-ADDRESSES out
RTB(config-router)#network 192.168.1.0
RTB(config-router)#network 192.168.2.0
```

If RTB is configured accordingly, it does not inject all of the internal routes into BGP. Only the two networks specified, 192.168.1.0 and 192.168.2.0, are injected, although all of them could have been configured the same way. In a sense, the BGP **network** command redistributes the specified IGP route into BGP, allowing for precise control.

Lab 9.12.1   BGP Challenge Lab

In this lab you configure EBGP between the company's core routers and the two ISP routers. You configure IBGP with peers to create a network that provides the International Travel Agency with a fully meshed, reliable, efficient core network.

Summary

BGP defines the basis of routing architectures in the Internet. Segregating networks into autonomous systems has logically defined the administrative and political borders between organizations. IGPs can now run independently of each other but still interconnect by way of BGP to provide global routing.

This chapter covered the details of the practical implementation of BGP as part of the overall design problem in building reliable Internet connectivity. This chapter examined specific BGP attributes and how they are applied individually and together to address this design problem. The terminology, attributes, and details of this chapter are specific to BGP. However, the general concepts and problems raised are pertinent to routing architecture design, regardless of the specific protocols being used.

Key Terms

Border Gateway Protocol (BGP)   An interdomain routing protocol that replaced EGP. BGP exchanges reachability information with other BGP systems. It is defined by RFC 1163.

EBGP session   Occurs between routers in two different autonomous systems. These routers are usually adjacent to one another, sharing the same medium and a subnet.

Exterior Gateway Protocol (EGP)   An Internet protocol for exchanging routing information between autonomous systems. Documented in RFC 904. Not to be confused with the general term *exterior gateway protocol*. EGP is an obsolete protocol that has been replaced by BGP.

IBGP session   Occurs between routers in the same AS. Used to coordinate and synchronize routing policy within the AS.

interior gateway protocol (IGP)   An Internet protocol used to exchange routing information within an autonomous system. Examples of common Internet IGPs are IGRP, OSPF, and RIP.

keepalive message   Sent periodically between peers to maintain connections and verify paths held by the router sending the keepalive.

multihomed system   An autonomous system that has more than one exit point to outside networks.

Network Layer Reachability Information (NLRI)   BGP sends routing update messages containing NLRI to describe a route and how to get there. In this context, an NLRI is a prefix. A BGP update message carries one or more NLRI prefixes and the attributes of a route for the NLRI prefixes. The route attributes include a BGP next-hop gateway address, community values, and other information.

notification message   Informs the receiving router of errors.

open message   Establishes connections with peers. Includes fields for the BGP version number, AS number, hold time, and Router ID.

single-homed system   An autonomous system that has only one exit point to outside networks.

update message   Contains all the information BGP uses to construct a loop-free picture of the internetwork.

Check Your Understanding

Complete all of the review questions to test your understanding of the topics and concepts in this chapter. The answers appear in Appendix B, "Answers to the Check Your Understanding Questions."

For additional, more in-depth questions, refer to the chapter-specific study guides on the companion CD-ROM.

1. What kind of AS features more than one exit point to outside networks but does not allow traffic to pass from one outside connection to another?

   A. Stub

   B. Multihomed nontransit

   C. Multihomed transit

   D. Totally stubby

2. In what situation is it inadvisable to run BGP?

   A. Stub AS

   B. Multihomed nontransit AS

   C. Multihomed transit AS

   D. When your AS policies differ from the ISP policies

3. What happens when a route is advertised to the AS that originated it?

   A. The AS sees itself as part of the AS_Path attribute list and does not accept the route.

   B. The border router prepends the AS number and advertises the router to other autonomous systems.

   C. The route is passed to other routers within the AS as an external route.

   D. The border router removes its AS number from the AS_Path list and redistributes the route.

4. What is one way to set local preference in BGP?

   A. Use the AS_Path attribute

   B. Use the global **prepend** command

   C. Use the **bgp default local-preference** command

   D. Use the **set as_path** command

5. What command identifies the state of BGP neighbors?

   A. **show ip route**

   B. **show ip bgp peer**

   C. **show ip bgp paths**

   D. **show ip bgp neighbors**

6. In which situation is it OK to turn off BGP synchronization on a border router?

   A. In a simple AS

   B. In a non-fully meshed transit AS

   C. When the AS is not a transit AS

   D. When internal reachability is not guaranteed

7. In a BGP system, which attribute can be manipulated on the various default routes so that at least one default route is identified as primary, with other default routes being kept as backups?

   A. Default-originate

   B. Local Preference

   C. Default Preference

   D. Maximum-paths

8. What condition causes a BGP router to install multiple paths to the same destination in its IP routing table?

   A. It learns two identical EBGP paths for a prefix from a neighboring AS, and both have the same route ID.

   B. It learns two IBGP paths for a prefix from a neighboring AS, and both have the same route ID.

   C. BGP multipath support is enabled, and the EBGP paths are learned from the same neighboring AS.

   D. Multipath support is enabled, and the EBGP paths are learned from different neighboring autonomous systems.

9. Which of the following can be used to filter routing updates based on NLRI?

    A. Passive interfaces

    B. Distribute list

    C. Static routes

    D. Default routes

10. What method injects all known static routes into BGP?

    A. Configuring default routes in the BGP border router

    B. Using the **redistribute static** command

    C. Configuring an IP prefix list with the static routes

    D. BGP supports only dynamically injected routes

11. How is transit traffic best defined when using BGP?

    A. Any traffic that has a source and destination inside the AS

    B. Any traffic that has a destination outside the AS

    C. Any traffic that has a source and destination outside the AS

    D. Any traffic that has a source outside a multihomed system

Glossary of Key Terms

access layer   Supplies traffic to the network and performs network entry control.

access list   A list kept by Cisco routers to control access to or from the router for a number of services (for example, to prevent packets with a certain IP address from leaving a particular interface on the router).

acknowledgment packet   An EIGRP router that uses acknowledgment packets to indicate receipt of any EIGRP packet during a reliable exchange.

administrative distance   A rating of the trustworthiness of a routing information source. In Cisco routers, administrative distance is expressed as a numeric value between 0 and 255. The higher the value, the lower the trustworthiness rating.

anycast   An identifier for a set of interfaces that typically belong to different nodes. A packet sent to an anycast address is delivered to the nearest, or first, interface in the anycast group.

area   A logical set of network segments (either CLNS-, DECnet-, or OSPF-based) and their attached devices. Areas are usually connected to other areas via routers, making up a single autonomous system or domain.

area ID   Multiple areas can be defined within an OSPF network to reduce and summarize route information.

authentication type and authentication data   OSPF supports different methods of authentication so that OSPF routers do not believe just anyone sending Hellos to 224.0.0.5.

Authority and Format ID (AFI)   1 byte, actually a binary value between 0 and 99, used to specify the IDI format and DSP syntax of the address and the authority that assigned the address.

autonomous system   A collection of networks under a common administration sharing a common routing strategy. Autonomous systems are subdivided by areas. An autonomous system must be assigned a unique 16-bit number by the IANA. Sometimes abbreviated as AS.

backbone   The part of a network that acts as the primary path for traffic that is most often sourced from, and destined for, other networks.

backup designated router (BDR)   The DR could represent a single point of failure, so a second router is elected as the BDR to provide fault tolerance.

Border Gateway Protocol (BGP)   An interdomain routing protocol that replaced EGP. BGP exchanges reachability information with other BGP systems. It is defined by RFC 1163.

checksum   This 2-byte field is used to check the message for errors.

classless interdomain routing (CIDR)   An IP addressing scheme that replaces the older system based on Classes A, B, and C. With CIDR, a single IP address can be used to designate many unique IP addresses.

Complete Sequence Number PDU (CSNP)   Used to distribute a complete link-state database on the router. CSNPs are used to inform other routers of LSPs that might be outdated or missing from their own database. This ensures that all routers have the same information and are synchronized. The packets are similar to an OSPF database description packet.

convergence   The speed and ability of a group of internetworking devices running a specific routing protocol to agree on an internetwork's topology after a change in that topology.

core layer   Provides an optimized and reliable transport structure by forwarding traffic at very high speeds.

core router   In a packet-switched star topology, a router that is part of the backbone and that serves as the single pipe through which all traffic from peripheral networks must pass on its way to other peripheral networks.

dead interval   How many seconds a router waits before it declares a neighbor down. The dead interval is four times the Hello interval by default, or 40 seconds.

designated router (DR)   For every multiaccess IP network, one router is elected the DR. The DR has two main functions—to become adjacent to all other routers on the network, and to act as a spokesperson for the network.

Dijkstra's algorithm   Also known as the shortest path first algorithm. A routing algorithm that iterates on path length to determine a shortest-path spanning tree. Commonly used in link-state routing algorithms.

distance vector routing   A class of routing algorithms that iterate on the number of hops in a route to find a shortest-path spanning tree. Distance vector routing algorithms call for each router to send its entire routing table in each update but only to its neighbors. Distance vector routing algorithms can be prone to routing loops but are computationally simpler than link-state routing algorithms.

distribution layer   Located between the access and core layers. Helps differentiate the core from the rest of the network.

domain   In IS-IS, this refers to a logical set of networks or any portion of an OSI network that is under a common administrative authority.

Domain-Specific Part (DSP)   Composed of the HODSP, the system ID, and the NSEL in binary format.

Down state   In the Down state, the OSPF process has not exchanged information with any neighbor.

dynamic routing   Routers follow rules defined by routing protocols to exchange routing information and independently select the best path.

EBGP session   Occurs between routers in two different autonomous systems. These routers are usually adjacent to one another, sharing the same medium and a subnet.

end system (ES)   Any nonrouting host or node.

End System-to-Intermediate System (ES-IS)   ES-IS discovery protocols are used for routing between end systems and intermediate systems.

Exchange state   In the Exchange state, neighbor routers use Type 2 DBD packets to send each other their link-state information. In other words, the routers describe their link-state databases to each other. The routers compare what they learn with their existing link-state databases.

ExStart state   Technically, when a router and its neighbor enter the ExStart state, their conversation is characterized as an adjacency, but they have not become fully adjacent.

Exterior Gateway Protocol (EGP)   An Internet protocol used to exchange routing information between autonomous systems. Documented in RFC 904. Not to be confused with the general term *exterior gateway protocol*. EGP is an obsolete protocol that has been replaced by BGP.

exterior gateway protocol (EGP)   Any internetwork protocol used to exchange routing information between autonomous systems. Not to be confused with Exterior Gateway Protocol (EGP), which is a particular instance of an exterior gateway protocol.

feasible distance (FD)   The lowest calculated metric to each destination.

feasible successor   A backup route. These routes are selected at the same time the successors are identified, but they are kept in the topology table. Multiple feasible successors for a destination can be retained in the topology table.

floating static route   A static route that is configured with an administrative distance value that is greater than that of the primary route or routes. Used for fallback routes or backup routes; they do not appear in the routing table until another route to the same destination fails.

Format Prefix (FP) field   The 3-bit FP identifies the type of address—unicast, multicast, and so on. The bits 001 identify aggregatable global unicasts.

full adjacency   With the Loading state complete, the routers are fully adjacent. Each router keeps a list of adjacent neighbors, called the adjacencies database.

Hello interval   How many seconds an OSPF router waits to send the next Hello packet.

hello packet   EIGRP relies on hello packets to discover, verify, and rediscover neighbor routers.

Hello PDU   Used to establish and maintain adjacencies. ESHs are sent from ESs to ISs. ISHs are sent from ISs to ESs. IIHs are sent between ISs. Note that ESH and ISH PDUs are ES-IS PDUs, not IS-IS PDUs.

High-Order Domain-Specific Part (HODSP)   Used for subdividing the domain into areas. This is roughly equivalent to a subnet in IP.

hold time (hold uptime)   How long to wait without receiving anything from a neighbor before considering the link unavailable. Originally, the expected packet was a hello packet. However, in current Cisco IOS software releases, any EIGRP packets received after the first hello reset the timer.

IBGP session   Occurs between routers in the same AS. Used to coordinate and synchronize routing policy within the AS.

Init state   OSPF routers send Type 1 packets, or Hello packets, at regular intervals to establish a relationship with neighbor routers.

initial domain identifier (IDI)   Identifies the domain.

Integrated IS-IS   An implementation of the IS-IS protocol for routing multiple network protocols. Integrated IS-IS tags CLNP routes, upon which IS-IS bases its link-state database, with information about IP networks and subnets.

Interdomain Part (IDP)   Consists of the AFI and IDI together. This is roughly equivalent to a classful IP network in decimal format.

Interface ID field   The 64-bit Interface ID field identifies individual interfaces on a link. This field is analogous to the host portion of an IPv4 address, but it is derived using the IEEE EUI-64 format. When this field is on LAN interfaces, the Interface ID adds a 16-bit field to the interface MAC address.

interface identifier   The level specific to a node's individual interface.

interior gateway protocol (IGP)   An Internet protocol used to exchange routing information within an autonomous system. Examples of common Internet IGPs are IGRP, OSPF, and RIP.

intermediate system (IS)   Another name for a router in an IS-IS system.

Intermediate System-to-Intermediate System (IS-IS)   The IS-IS routing protocols are used for hierarchical routing between intermediate systems.

keepalive message   A message sent by one network device to another network device to verify that the virtual circuit between the two is still active.

legacy technology   A technology that is supported because of a significant past investment or deployment.

link-state PDU (LSP)   Used by IS-IS to distribute link-state information. There are independent pseudonode and nonpseudonode LSPs for both Level 1 and Level 2.

link-state routing   A routing algorithm in which each router broadcasts or multicasts information on the cost of reaching each of its neighbors to all nodes in the internetwork. Link-state algorithms create a consistent view of the network and, therefore, are not prone to routing loops. However, they achieve this at the cost of relatively greater computational difficulty and more widespread traffic (compared with distance vector routing algorithms).

Loading state   After the databases have been described to each router, they may request information that is more complete by using Type 3 packets, link-state requests (LSRs).

metric   A method by which a routing algorithm determines that one route is better than another. This information is stored in routing tables. Metrics include bandwidth, communication cost, delay, hop count, load, path cost, and reliability.

multicast   An identifier for a set of interfaces that typically belong to different nodes. A packet sent to a multicast address is delivered to all interfaces in the multicast group.

multicasting   A technique for simultaneously advertising routing information to multiple RIPv2 devices.

multihomed system   An autonomous system that has more than one exit point to outside networks.

neighbor address   The network layer address of the neighbor router. This is Address in the EIGRP neighbor table.

neighbor table   Each EIGRP router maintains a neighbor table that lists adjacent routers. This table is comparable to the adjacency database used by OSPF. A neighbor table exists for each protocol EIGRP supports.

network entity title (NET)   An NSAP whose last byte is 0. The NET is used to identify a device.

Network Layer Reachability Information (NLRI)   BGP sends routing update messages containing NLRI to describe a route and how to get there. In this context, an NLRI is a prefix. A BGP update message carries one or more NLRI prefixes and the attributes of a route for the NLRI prefixes. The route attributes include a BGP next-hop gateway address, community values, and other information.

network mask   This 32-bit field carries subnet mask information for the network.

network service access point (NSAP)   A conceptual point on the boundary between the network and transport layers. The NSAP is the location where OSI network services are provided to the transport layer. Similar to an IP address.

Next-Level Aggregation Identifier (NLA ID) field   The 24-bit NLA ID field is used to identify ISPs. The field itself can be organized to reflect a hierarchy or a multitiered relationship among providers.

notification message   Informs the receiving router of errors.

NSAP selector (NSEL)   Identifies a process on the device. It is roughly equivalent to a port or socket in TCP/IP. The NSEL is not used in routing decisions.

open message   Establishes connections with peers. Includes fields for the BGP version number, AS number, hold time, and Router ID.

OSI protocols   The product of an international program formed to develop data networking protocols and other standards that facilitate multivendor equipment interoperability.

Partial Sequence Number PDU (PSNP)   Used to acknowledge and request link-state information.

passive interface   Receives updates but does not send them. Used to control routing updates. The **passive-interface** command can be used with all IP interior gateway protocols—RIP, IGRP, EIGRP, OSPF, and IS-IS.

policy routing   A routing scheme that forwards packets to interfaces based on user-configured policies. Such policies might specify that traffic sent from a particular network should be forwarded out one interface, while all other traffic should be forwarded out another interface.

priority queuing   A method of queuing that is used to guarantee bandwidth for traffic by assigning queue space to each protocol according to the defined rules.

public topology   The collection of providers that offer Internet connectivity.

query packet   An EIGRP router uses a query packet whenever it needs specific information from one or all of its neighbors.

queue count (Q Cnt)   The number of packets waiting in queue to be sent. If this value is constantly higher than 0, a congestion problem might exist at the router. A 0 means that no EIGRP packets are in the queue.

reported distance (RD)   A path's RD is the distance reported by an adjacent neighbor to a specific destination.

Reserved (Res) field   The IPv6 architecture defines the 8-bit Res field so that the TLA or NLA IDs can be expanded as future growth warrants. Currently, this field must be set to 0.

route redistribution   Allows routing information discovered through one routing protocol to be distributed in the update messages of another routing protocol.

route source   The identification number of the router that originally advertised that route. This field is populated only for routes learned externally from the EIGRP network.

route summarization   The consolidation of advertised addresses in OSPF and IS-IS. In OSPF, this causes a single summary route to be advertised to other areas by an area border router.

router ID   The function of the Hello packet is to establish and maintain adjacencies. So the sending router signs the fourth field with its router ID, which is a 32-bit number used to identify the router to the OSPF protocol.

router priority   This field contains a value that indicates this router's priority when selecting a DR and BDR.

Routing Information Protocol (RIP)   An IGP supplied with the FreeBSD version of UNIX. The most common IGP in the Internet. RIP uses hop count as a routing metric.

Routing Information Protocol version 2 (RIPv2)   Defined in RFC 1723 and supported in Cisco IOS Release 11.1 and later. RIPv2 is not a new protocol; it is just RIPv1 with some extensions to bring it up-to-date with modern routing environments. RIPv2 has been updated to support VLSM, authentication, and multicast updates.

routing metric   A method by which a routing algorithm determines that one route is better than another. This information is stored in routing tables. Metrics include bandwidth, communication cost, delay, hop count, load, path cost, and reliability. Sometimes simply called a *metric*.

routing table   EIGRP chooses the best routes to a destination from the topology table and places them in the routing table. Each EIGRP router maintains a routing table for each network protocol.

routing update   A message sent from a router to indicate network reachability and associated cost information. Routing updates are typically sent at regular intervals and after a change in network topology.

single-homed system   An autonomous system that has only one exit point to outside networks.

Site-Level Aggregation Identifier (SLA ID) field   The 16-bit SLA ID is used by an individual organization to create its own local addressing hierarchy and to identify subnets.

site topology   The level local to an organization that does not provide connectivity to nodes outside itself.

Smooth Round-Trip Timer (SRTT)   The average amount of time it takes to send and receive packets to and from a neighbor. This timer is used to determine the retransmit interval or retransmission timeout (RTO).

static routing   An administrator manually defines routes to one or more destination networks.

subnetwork point of attachment (SNPA)   The point at which subnetwork services are provided. This is the equivalent of the Layer 2 address corresponding to the Layer 3 (NET or NSAP) address.

successor   A route selected as the primary route to use to reach a destination. Successors are the entries kept in the routing table. Multiple successors for a destination can be retained in the routing table.

system ID   Identifies an individual OSI device. In OSI, a device has an address, just as it does in DECnet, whereas in IP an interface has an address.

Top-Level Aggregation Identifier (TLA ID) field   The 13-bit TLA ID field is used to identify the authority responsible for the address at the highest level of the routing hierarchy. Internet routers necessarily maintain routes to all TLA IDs. With 13 bits set aside, this field can represent up to 8192 TLAs.

topology table   Every EIGRP router maintains a topology table for each configured network protocol. This table includes route entries for all destinations the router has learned. All learned routes to a destination are maintained in the topology table.

two-way state   Using Hello packets, every OSPF router tries to establish a two-way state, or bidirectional communication, with every neighbor router on the same IP network.

Type 1: Hello packet   Establishes and maintains adjacency information with neighbors.

Type 2: database description packet (DBD)   Describes the contents of the link-state database on an OSPF router.

Type 3: link-state request (LSR)   Requests specific pieces of a link-state database.

Type 4: link-state update (LSU)   Transports LSAs to neighbor routers.

Type 5: link-state acknowledgment (LSAck)   Acknowledgment receipt of a neighbor's LSA.

unicast   An identifier for a single interface. A packet sent to a unicast address is delivered to the interface identified by that address.

update message   Contains all of the information BGP uses to construct a loop-free picture of the internetwork.

update packet   Used to update a router when the router discovers a new neighbor.

variable-length subnet masking (VLSM)   The ability to specify a different subnet mask for the same network number on different subnets. VLSM can help optimize available address space.

version, type, and packet length   The first three fields of the OSPF packet let the recipients know the version of OSPF that is being used by the sender, the OSPF packet type, and length.

Answers to the Check Your Understanding Questions

Chapter 1

1. The core and access layers are two of the three layers in the hierarchical design model. What is the third layer?

   A. Internetwork layer

   B. Distribution layer

   C. Workgroup layer

   D. Backbone layer

   Answer: B

2. What is a recommended practice for the core layer?

   A. Data compression for efficient link usage

   B. Avoiding redundant links

   C. Direct access by end users

   D. Avoiding access lists because of latency

   Answer: D

3. What is an important function of the access layer?

   A. It connects the campus backbone network devices

   B. It provides direct connections to the Internet

   C. It provides workgroup access to corporate resources

   D. It performs high-speed LAN switching

   Answer: C

4. What method should be used to prevent regular routing updates from constantly activating a dialup WAN link?

A. Dialer access list

B. Distance vector

C. Incremental updates

D. Snapshot routing

Answer: D

5. What feature characterizes a network that is reliable and available?

A. Load balancing

B. Securable

C. Queuing

D. Protocol integration

Answer: A

6. What is the primary purpose of dial backup?

A. Tunneling

B. Load balancing

C. Fault tolerance

D. Traffic prioritization

Answer: C

7. Which Cisco IOS software feature supports responsiveness on slow WAN links?

A. DDR

B. Tunnels

C. Queuing

D. Route summarization

Answer: C

8. Which three features are offered in the Cisco IOS software to optimize the efficiency of a WAN connection?

   A. Access lists

   B. Protocol tunnels

   C. Snapshot routing

   D. Compression

   E. Dynamic data aggregation

   Answer: A, C, D

9. What is a characteristic of a scalable routing protocol?

   A. Fast convergence

   B. Slow convergence

   C. Reachability limitations

   D. Simple configuration

   Answer: A

10. What is a characteristic of nonroutable protocols?

   A. No frame header

   B. No network layer addressing

   C. Appropriate for WAN links

   D. Best-route determination by broadcast

   Answer: B

Chapter 2

1. What feature lets a Cisco router act as a DHCP client?

   A. NAT

   B. DHCP

   C. DNS

   D. Easy IP

   Answer: D

2. What is a summarization address for the networks 172.21.136.0/24 and 172.21.143.0/24?

    A. 172.21.136.0/21

    B. 172.21.136.0/20

    C. 172.21.136.0/22

    D. 172.21.128.0/21

Answer: A

3. The subnet 172.6.32.0/20 is again subnetted to 172.6.32.0/26. What is the result?

    A. 1024 subnets

    B. 64 hosts per subnet

    C. 62 hosts per subnet

    D. 2044 subnets

Answer: C

4. What routing protocol does not contain subnet mask information in its routing updates?

    A. EIGRP

    B. OSPF

    C. RIP

    D. RIPv2

Answer: C

5. What method is used to represent a collection of IP network addresses with a single IP network address?

    A. Classful routing

    B. Subnetting

    C. Address translation

    D. Route summarization

Answer: D

6. According to RFC 1918, which of the following is a private Internet address?

    A. 10.215.34.124

    B. 192.32.146.23

    C. 172.34.221.18

    D. 119.12.73.215

Answer: A

7. Which of the following is a characteristic of IP unnumbered?

    A. Avoids wasted addresses on multiaccess links

    B. Efficient addressing on Ethernet links

    C. Uses another router interface address

    D. May be used with classful and classless routing protocols

    Answer: C

8. How many bits make up an IPv6 address?

    A. 32

    B. 48

    C. 64

    D. 128

    Answer: D

9. What is the purpose of IP helper addresses?

    A. To relay key UDP broadcast requests to hosts on the same subnet

    B. To relay key UDP broadcast requests to hosts on the other subnets

    C. To relay key TCP broadcast requests to hosts on other subnets

    D. To relay key TCP broadcast requests to hosts on the same subnet

    Answer: B

10. What are the three general types of IPv6 addresses?

    A. Class 1, Class 2, Class 3

    B. Class A, Class B, Class C

    C. Unicast, anycast, multicast

    D. Public, site, interface

    Answer: C

Chapter 3

1. What is an advantage of static routing compared to dynamic routing?

    A. Static routing sometimes yields unexpected results, even in small networks

    B. Routers that don't accept updates are less vulnerable to attack

C. The routing table contains only directly connected routes to router interfaces

D. Static routes remain in routing tables regardless of the mapped router interface status

Answer: B

2. What routing protocol would be used in a mixed-vender or legacy routing environment within an autonomous system?

A. RIPv1

B. RIPv2

C. IGRP

D. EIGRP

E. IS-IS

Answer: A

3. Which of the following commands would statically configure IGRP to use and propagate a default route?

A. **ip route 0.0.0.0 255.255.255.255**

B. **ip default-network**

C. **ip route default-network**

D. **ip default network 0.0.0.0**

Answer: B

4. What command must you use to automatically propagate a candidate default route to IGRP neighbors?

A. **ip default-network** *ip-address*

B. **ip default-gateway** *ip-address*

C. **default-information originate**

D. **redistribute static neighbors**

Answer: A

5. What is a disadvantage of static routing?

A. It can cause unpredictable routing behavior

B. There is no mechanism to recover from a failed link

C. All route information is transmitted in each update

D. It produces high-processor overhead

Answer: B

6. What is the primary purpose of configuring floating static routes?

    A. To provide unlimited adaptability to network topology changes

    B. To create a semiadaptable static routing scheme to activate backup routes

    C. To create static routes with an administrative distance of 1

    D. To create a static route that is more desirable than a dynamic route with equal administrative distance

Answer: B

7. What would be a logical routing protocol configuration approach to significantly reduce the convergence time in a large internetwork?

    A. Configure static default routes for stub networks

    B. Increase the router processor and memory capacity

    C. Configure static routes between all routers in the network

    D. Decrease the number of hops between all routes in the network

Answer: A

8. How are stub networks defined?

    A. Networks with only one router

    B. Networks with multiple ways into and out of a network

    C. Networks with only one ingress and egress point

    D. Networks with routing policies that are controlled by a single organization

Answer: C

9. What mechanism ensures that a router configured with an event-driven routing protocol regularly communicates with its neighbors?

    A. Hello timer

    B. MaxAge timer

    C. Triggered update

    D. Update timer

Answer: A

10. What routing protocol measures route desirability based on bandwidth and delay and maintains a topological database?

    A. RIPv2

    B. RTMP

    C. EIGRP

    D. OSPF

    E. IS-IS

    F. NLSP

    Answer: C

Chapter 4

1. What command disables the default network summarization in RIPv2?

    A. no ip rip-summary

    B. no rip auto-summarization

    C. no auto-summary

    D. no route-summarization

    Answer: C

2. What command displays summary address entries in the RIP database?

    A. show ip protocols

    B. show ip route database

    C. show ip rip database

    D. show ip route

    E. show ip rip

    Answer: C

3. What command allows the use of the first subnet of any network?

    A. ip subnet-zero

    B. no ip subnet-zero

    C. all-zero network

    D. ip network-zero

    Answer: A

4. What multicast address does RIPv2 use?

    A. 224.0.0.4

    B. 224.0.0.5

    C. 224.0.0.8

    D. 224.0.0.9

Answer: D

5. What is an advantage of multicasting RIPv2 updates instead of broadcasting them?

    A. Ethernet interfaces ignore the multicast messages

    B. It makes RIPv2 compatible with EIGRP and OSPF

    C. Hosts and non-RIPv2 routers ignore the multicast messages

    D. It enables faster convergence than RIPv1

Answer: C

6. Which statement describes the characteristics of RIPv1 and RIPv2?

    A. RIPv1 imposes a maximum hop count of 16, and RIPv2 allows for a maximum of 32 hops

    B. RIPv1 is classful, and RIPv2 is classless

    C. RIPv1 uses only hop count, and RIPv2 uses hop count and bandwidth

    D. RIPv1 sends periodical updates, and RIPv2 sends updates only as changes occur

Answer: B

7. Which three fields are now populated in the RIPv2 message format?

    A. Route Tag

    B. Subnet Mask

    C. Autonomous System

    D. Next Hop

    E. Protocol

Answer: A, B, D

Chapter 5

1. How do you configure automatic redistribution between IGRP and EIGRP?

    A. Configure the two protocols with different AS numbers

    B. Configure the two protocols with different DS numbers

    C. Configure the two protocols with the same AS number

    D. Configure the two protocols with the same DS number

Answer: C

2. What protocol combines the advantages of link-state and distance vector routing protocols?

A. RIP

B. OSPF

C. IGRP

D. EIGRP

Answer: D

3. What command shows the neighbors that EIGRP has discovered?

A. show eigrp neighbors

B. show ip eigrp neighbors

C. show router eigrp process-id

D. show ip eigrp networks

Answer: B

4. What multicast IP address does EIGRP use?

A. 224.0.0.110

B. 224.0.0.100

C. 224.0.0.11

D. 224.0.0.10

Answer: D

5. What table includes route entries for all destinations that the router has learned and is maintained for each configured routing protocol?

A. Topology table

B. Routing table

C. Neighbor table

D. Successor table

Answer: A

6. What establishes adjacencies in EIGRP?

A. DUAL finite-state machine

B. Hello packets

C. Topology table

D. Reliable Transport Protocol

Answer: B

7. What guarantees ordered delivery of EIGRP packets to all neighbors?

A. DUAL finite-state machine

B. Hello packets

C. Topology table

D. Reliable Transport Protocol

Answer: D

8. What does DUAL do after it tracks all routes, compares them, and guarantees that they are loop-free?

A. Inserts lowest-cost paths into the routing table

B. Determines the optimal path and advertises it to the neighbor routers using hello packets

C. Supports other routed protocols through PDMs

D. Sends a unicast query to the neighboring routers

Answer: A

9. How does EIGRP prevent routing loops from occurring with external routes?

A. By rejecting external routes tagged with a router ID identical to their own

B. By storing the identities of neighbors that are feasible successors

C. By rejecting all neighboring routers that have an advertised composite metric that is less than a router's best current metric

D. By storing in a special table all neighboring routes that have loops identified

Answer: B

10. On higher-bandwidth connections such as point-to point serial links or multipoint circuits, how long is the hello interval used by EIGRP?

A. 5 seconds

B. 10 seconds

C. 60 seconds

D. 120 seconds

Answer: A

Chapter 6

1. Which state are the routers in an OSPF network in after the DR and BDR are elected?

   A. ExStart

   B. Full

   C. Loading

   D. Exchange

   Answer: A

2. What is the default cost metric for OSPF based on?

   A. Delay

   B. Media bandwidth

   C. Efficiency

   D. Network traffic

   Answer: B

3. What command can you use to change the OSPF priority on an interface?

   A. **ip priority number ospf**

   B. **ip ospf priority number**

   C. **ospf priority number**

   D. **set priority ospf number**

   Answer: B

4. What IP address is used to send a multicast to only OSPF DRs and BDRs?

   A. 224.0.0.6

   B. 224.0.0.1

   C. 224.0.0.4

   D. 224.0.0.5

   Answer: A

5. Which of the following is a common feature associated with NBMA networks?

   A. Support for only two routers

   B. Support for more than two routers

   C. No election of DRs

   D. Full support for broadcast and multicast packets

   Answer: B

6. While troubleshooting a communication problem between two OSPF routers, you find that mismatched hello interval timers on the interfaces have caused the problem. Which command allows you to set the hello interval on the interfaces?

   A. **hello-interval**

   B. **ospf hello-interval**

   C. **ip hello-interval**

   D. **ip ospf hello-interval**

   Answer: D

7. What type of OSPF router generates routing information about each area to which it is connected and floods that information through the backbone?

   A. BR

   B. BDR

   C. Backbone

   D. ABR

   Answer: D

8. What type of OSPF router has at least one interface connected to an external autonomous system?

   A. ABR

   B. ASBR

   C. Backbone

   D. Internal

   Answer: B

9. What command configures a virtual link?

   A. Router#**area** *area-id router-id* **virtual-link**

   B. Router(config)#**ip-area** *area-id* **virtual-link** *router-id*

   C. Router(config-router)#**ip area virtual-link** *router-id area-id*

   D. Router(config-router)#**area** *area-id* **virtual-link** *router-id*

   Answer: D

10. What type of summarization occurs on ABRs and applies to routes from within each area?

    A. Internal summarization

    B. Interarea route summarization

    C. External router summarization

    D. Backbone summarization

    Answer: B

11. What command configures an area as an NSSA?

    A. Router(config)#**area** *area-id* **nssa**

    B. Router(config-router)#**area** *area-id* **nssa**

    C. Router(config-router)#*area-id* **nssa**

    D. Router(config)#**area nssa** *area-id*

    Answer: B

12. What command displays information about each area to which a router is connected and indicates whether the router is an ABR, ASBR, or both?

    A. **show ip ospf border-routers**

    B. **show ip ospf virtual-links**

    C. **show ip ospf** *process-id*

    D. **show ip ospf database**

    Answer: C

Chapter 7

1. Which type of location is most likely to use the IS-IS protocol?

   A. Branch office

   B. SOHO

   C. Service provider

   D. PSTN

   Answer: C

2. Which of the following are features of the IS-IS protocol? (Choose three.)

   A. Classful behavior

   B. Slow convergence

   C. Fast convergence

   D. Scalable

   E. Distance vector

   F. IGP

   Answer: C, D, F

3. OSI networking design and proper implementation provide which of the following? (Choose two.)

   A. Quality of service

   B. Proprietary architectures

   C. Transparency

   D. Four-layer model

   Answer: A, C

4. CLNS is located at which layer of the OSI model?

   A. Data-link layer

   B. Transport layer

   C. Application layer

   D. Network layer

   Answer: D

5. IS-IS was originally designed to route which protocol?

   A. IPX

   B. AppleTalk

   C. IP

   D. DECnet Phase V

   E. SNA

   Answer: D

6. How many routers can exist in a single IS-IS area?

A. 15

B. 50

C. 100

D. 500

E. 1000

Answer: C

7. What is identified by the information contained in the CLNS system ID field?

A. A process on a device

B. The domain

C. A single OSI device

D. Port or socket information

Answer: C

8. How many addresses does an NSAP have?

A. A single address for the entire router

B. An address for each configured interface

C. Multiple addresses for each configured interface

D. The number of addresses depends on the routing protocol chosen

Answer: A

9. Which of the following is the equivalent of using more than one NET with the IS-IS protocol?

A. Using CIDR

B. Using secondary addresses with IP

C. Using VLSM

D. Implementing dynamic routing

Answer: B

10. What command displays the least-cost paths to a destination NET?

A. **which-route**

B. **show isis topology**

    C. show clns route

    D. show isis routes

Answer: B

Chapter 8

1. What method is used to prevent a routing update from being sent out a router interface?

    A. Redistribution

    B. Summarization

    C. Passive interface

    D. Gateway of last resort

Answer: C

2. What address does a router advertise for a default route?

    A. 255.255.255.255

    B. 0.0.0.0

    C. 255.255.0.0

    D. 1.1.1.1

Answer: B

3. What is the default administrative distance for the OSPF routing protocol?

    A. 1

    B. 90

    C. 110

    D. 120

Answer: C

4. What command imports static routes into routing protocol advertisements?

    A. redistribute static

    B. distribute-list

    C. passive-interface

    D. route-map

Answer: A

5. What command uses match statements to create a routing policy?

   A. auto summary

   B. distribute-list

   C. access-list

   D. route-map

   Answer: D

6. What command establishes which route a router sends or receives in updates?

   A. access-list

   B. network

   C. passive-interface

   D. distribute-list

   Answer: D

7. What command modifies the administrative distance for all OSPF routes?

   A. distance 95

   B. admin distance 110

   C. distance 110

   D. admin distance 95

   Answer: A

8. Which of the following is a consideration when implementing redistribution?

   A. Incompatible routing tables

   B. Routing feedback (loops)

   C. Overlap routing protocols

   D. Two-way redistribution with multiple boundary routers

   Answer: B

9. Which administrative distance represents the most reliable protocol?

   A. 5

   B. 90

   C. 120

   D. 200

   Answer: A

10. Which IP interior gateway protocols support passive interface?

   A. RIP, IGRP, EIGRP, and BGP

   B. RIP, IGRP, EIGRP, IS-IS, and IPX

   C. RIP, IGRP, EIGRP, OSPF, and IPX

   D. RIP, IGRP, EIGRP, OSPF, and IS-IS

   Answer: D

11. What does the router use to make a decision when it has learned two or more routes to the same destination from multiple routing protocols?

   A. Hop count

   B. Administrative distance

   C. Metric

   D. Route summarization

   Answer: B

Chapter 9

1. What kind of AS features more than one exit point to outside networks but does not allow traffic to pass from one outside connection to another?

   A. Stub

   B. Multihomed nontransit

   C. Multihomed transit

   D. Totally stubby

   Answer: B

2. In what situation is it inadvisable to run BGP?

   A. Stub AS

   B. Multihomed nontransit AS

   C. Multihomed transit AS

   D. When your AS policies differ from the ISP policies

   Answer: A

3. What happens when a route is advertised to the AS that originated it?

   A. The AS sees itself as part of the AS_Path attribute list and does not accept the route.

   B. The border router prepends the AS number and advertises the router to other autonomous systems.

   C. The route is passed to other routers within the AS as an external route.

   D. The border router removes its AS number from the AS_Path list and redistributes the route.

Answer: A

4. What is one way to set local preference in BGP?

   A. Use the AS_Path attribute

   B. Use the global **prepend** command

   C. Use the **bgp default local-preference** command

   D. Use the **set as_path** command

Answer: C

5. What command identifies the state of BGP neighbors?

   A. **show ip route**

   B. **show ip bgp peer**

   C. **show ip bgp paths**

   D. **show ip bgp neighbors**

Answer: D

6. In which situation is it OK to turn off BGP synchronization on a border router?

   A. In a simple AS

   B. In a nonfully meshed transit AS

   C. When the AS is not a transit AS

   D. When internal reachability is not guaranteed

Answer: C

7. In a BGP system, which attribute can be manipulated on the various default routes so that at least one default route is identified as primary, with other default routes being kept as backups?

   A. Default-originate

   B. Local Preference

C. Default Preference

D. Maximum-paths

Answer: B

8. What condition causes a BGP router to install multiple paths to the same destination in its IP routing table?

   A. It learns two identical EBGP paths for a prefix from a neighboring AS, and both have the same route ID.

   B. It learns two IBGP paths for a prefix from a neighboring AS, and both have the same route ID.

   C. BGP multipath support is enabled, and the EBGP paths are learned from the same neighboring AS.

   D. Multipath support is enabled, and the EBGP paths are learned from different neighboring autonomous systems.

   Answer: C

9. Which of the following can be used to filter routing updates based on NLRI?

   A. Passive interfaces

   B. Distribute list

   C. Static routes

   D. Default routes

   Answer: B

10. What method injects all known static routes into BGP?

   A. Configuring default routes in the BGP border router

   B. Using the redistribute static command

   C. Configuring an IP prefix list with the static routes

   D. BGP supports only dynamically injected routes

   Answer: B

11. How is transit traffic best defined when using BGP?

   A. Any traffic that has a source and destination inside the AS

   B. Any traffic that has a destination outside the AS

   C. Any traffic that has a source and destination outside the AS

   D. Any traffic that has a source outside a multihomed system

   Answer: C

Case Studies

For CCNP 1 Advanced Routing, you will configure different types of networks for each case study. In the first case study, you will configure an EIGRP network. In the second network, you will configure an OSPF network. Finally, you will configure a BPP/OSPF network. Use the concepts and configuration methods you have learned throughout this book to complete these case studies.

Case Study 1: EIGRP

Plan, design, and implement the complex International Travel Agency EIGRP network that is shown in Figure C-1 and that is described as follows. Verify that all configurations are operational and functioning according to the guidelines.

Figure C-1 International Travel Agency EIGRP Network

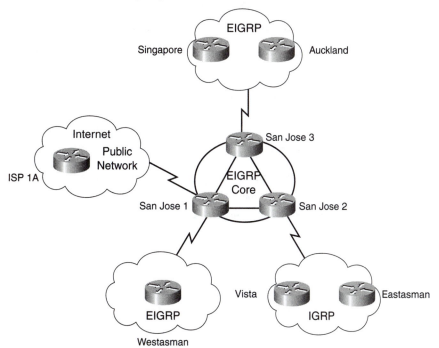

Scenario

The responsibilities of the network engineer with International Travel Agency include creating and maintaining the San Jose campus network, connectivity to all regional headquarters, and Internet access via one or more service providers. The San Jose campus network must maintain 99.9% availability while supporting 99% availability to regional headquarters.

The network will be based on and must meet the following requirements:

1. The San Jose core routers must run EIGRP.

2. The network has been allocated one Class B license.

3. Use VLSM on all serial interfaces as appropriate.

4. This network will have three branches. The regional headquarters in Singapore and Auckland will run EIGRP. The Westasman branch office will run EIGRP. The Vista and Eastasman branch offices will run IGRP.

5. Summarize all routes from each area into the core. Plan for approximately 30 networks in each area, with the exception of the core, which is exactly as shown in Figure C-1.

6. Redistribute routing information between EIGRP and the IGRP network.

7. In Westasman, implement EZ IP on the router for users.

8. In the IGRP cloud of Vista and Eastasman, configure a DHCP server for a LAN segment. Use an IP helper address so that a workstation on another segment in that area can obtain an IP address from the DHCP server.

9. Configure Internet connectivity through a static route.

10. Document the configuration and any difficulties that were encountered.

11. What were the implementation issues or limitations?

12. List two suggestions for improving this network configuration and design.

Case Study 2: OSPF

Plan, design, and implement the complex International Travel Agency OSPF network that is shown in Figure C-2 and that is described as follows. Verify that all configurations are operational and functioning according to the guidelines.

Figure C-2 International Travel Agency OSPF Network

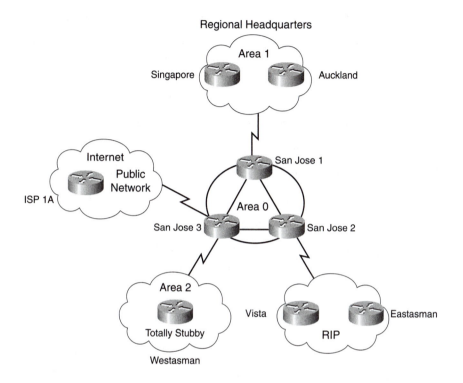

Scenario

The International Travel Agency has decided to change the network routing protocol. The responsibilities of the network engineer include creating, maintaining, and implementing changes to the network.

The network will be based on and must meet the following requirements:

1. The San Jose core routers must run OSPF and be configured in Area 0.

2. The network has been allocated one Class A license.

3. Use VLSM on all serial interfaces as appropriate.

4. This network will have three outer areas. The regional headquarters in Singapore and Auckland in Area 1 will run OSPF normally. The Westasman branch office in Area 2 will be a totally stubby network. The Vista and Eastasman branch offices will be RIP networks.

5. Summarize all routes from each area into the core. Plan for approximately 30 networks in each area in the figure, with the exception of the core, which is exactly as shown in Area 0 in Figure C-2.

6. Redistribute routing information between OSPF and the RIP network.

7. In the Westasman branch office in Area 2, implement EZ IP on the router for users.

8. In the Vista and Eastasman branch offices RIP cloud, configure a DHCP server on a LAN segment. Use an IP helper address so that a workstation on another subnet in that area can obtain an IP address from the DHCP server.

9. Configure Internet connectivity through a static route.

10. Document the configuration and any difficulties that were encountered.

11. What were the implementation issues or limitations?

12. List two suggestions for improving this network configuration and design.

Case Study 3: BGP/OSPF Routing

Plan, design, and implement the complex International Travel Agency BGP/OSPF network that is shown in Figure C-3 and that is described as follows. Verify that all configurations are operational and functioning according to the guidelines.

Figure C-3 International Travel Agency BGP/OSPF Network

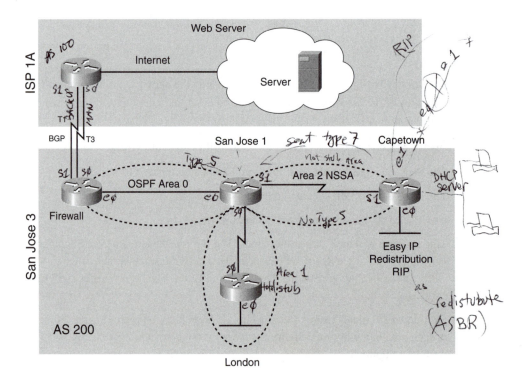

Scenario

The International Travel Agency relies heavily on the Internet for its advertising and sales. Therefore, it has been decided to establish a primary and a backup route to the Internet. Additionally, other network changes have been planned, as shown in Figure C-3 and described as follows. The responsibilities of the network engineer include creating, maintaining, and implementing changes to the network.

The network will be based on and must meet the following requirements:

1. The San Jose core routers must run OSPF and be configured in Area 0.

2. The network has been allocated one Class B license.

3. Use VLSM on all serial interfaces as appropriate.

4. This network will have three outer areas. The London branch office in Area 1 will be a totally stubby network. The Capetown branch office in Area 2 will be an NSSA. The third area will be a RIP network.

5. Summarize all routes from each area into the core. Plan for approximately 30 networks in each area in the figure, with the exception of the core, known as Area 0.

6. Redistribute routing information from RIP into OSPF. The RIP network should use default routing to access the rest of the network and the Internet.

7. In the RIP area, implement EZ IP for users.

8. This International Travel Agency network will be multihomed to ISP1A. The primary link will be a T3 connection. A backup T1 link will also be configured. All outbound and inbound traffic are to use the T3 link. The T1 link should be used only if the T3 link goes down.

9. (Optional) A firewall must be configured on the SanJose3 ASBR. This firewall should allow all traffic originating inside AS 200 to pass freely. No traffic originating from outside AS 200 should be permitted into the network.

10. Document the configuration and any difficulties that were encountered.

11. What were the implementation issues or limitations?

12. List two suggestions for improving this network configuration and design.

A

W